Abortion and Reproductive Justice

REPRODUCTIVE JUSTICE: A NEW VISION FOR
THE TWENTY-FIRST CENTURY

*Edited by Rickie Solinger (senior editor), Khiara
M. Bridges, Laura Briggs, Krystale E. Littlejohn,
Ruby Tapia, and Carly Thomsen*

Abortion and Reproductive Justice

An Essential Guide for Resistance

Marlene Gerber Fried and Loretta J. Ross

UNIVERSITY OF CALIFORNIA PRESS

University of California Press
Oakland, California

© 2025 by Marlene Gerber Fried and Loretta J. Ross

Library of Congress Cataloging-in-Publication Data

Names: Fried, Marlene Gerber, author. | Ross, Loretta J.,
    author.
Title: Abortion and reproductive justice : an essential
    guide for resistance / Marlene Gerber Fried and
    Loretta J. Ross.
Other titles: Reproductive justice ; 15.
Description: Oakland, California : University of
    California Press, [2025] | Series: Reproductive justice:
    a new vision for the 21st century ; 15 | Includes
    bibliographical references and index.
Identifiers: LCCN 2025005659 | ISBN 9780520421134 (cloth) |
    ISBN 9780520421141 (paperback) | ISBN 9780520421158
    (ebook)
Subjects: LCSH: Reproductive rights—United States. |
    Pro-choice movement—United States. | Abortion—
    Political aspects—United States.
Classification: LCC HQ767.5.U5 F75 2025 | DDC 362.1988/80973—
    dc23/eng/20250512
LC record available at https://lccn.loc.gov/2025005659

Manufactured in the United States of America

GPSR Authorized Representative: Easy Access System
Europe, Mustamäe tee 50, 10621 Tallinn, Estonia, gpsr.
requests@easproject.com

34 33 32 31 30 29 28 27 26 25
10 9 8 7 6 5 4 3 2 1

For all those who struggle daily to make their own reproductive decisions, and for the activists who commit themselves to that fight for justice.

CONTENTS

PREFACE

We completed this book shortly after the 2024 presidential election in the United States, but we undertook it in 2018. Just two years into Trump's first presidency, the opposition to reproductive health, rights, and justice was already emboldened, and while political alarm bells had been ringing for a long time, our urgency quotient went through the roof. The forces on the right that he unleashed were terrifying then, even more so now. Since then, our fears have been validated.

Groups such as the Abortion Abolitionists, previously considered extremists, are gaining power and influence at the grassroots level and within the Republican Party. They advocate capital punishment for anyone involved in an abortion, including those providing and accessing abortion care. Legislators in almost twenty states have introduced abortion abolitionist bills, and abolition is already a plank in the Republican Party platform in Texas.[1]

In his first term, Trump stacked the Supreme Court with staunch opponents of abortion. His appointees provided the votes for the 2022 decision in *Dobbs v. Jackson Women's Health Organization*, which overturned *Roe v. Wade* and removed all federal constitutional protections for abortion. Republican-controlled state legislatures quickly took up the legislative baton. As of November 2024, twenty-one states ban or restrict abortion earlier in pregnancy than under *Roe*. You will see that these laws disproportionately impact vulnerable populations who face compound barriers from multiple oppressions.[2] Nearly half of all states also ban gender-affirming care. As with abortion, these bans force people to travel for care or forgo it altogether.

We have documentation of devastating consequences since *Dobbs*. Four women have died—Josseli Barnica, Nevaeh Crain, Amber Nicole Thurman, and Candi Miller—three of them women of color. They were denied timely and necessary lifesaving care by hospitals and doctors who felt constrained by their state's laws. All four deaths were preventable. And in many other situations, pregnancy care was delayed until the fetus died in utero or after birth. In its 2023 report Human Rights Watch wrote, "Women and girls in need of reproductive healthcare are being met with systematic refusals, onerous financial burdens, stigma, fear of violence, and criminalization. Thousands are being forced to remain pregnant against their will."[3]

Abortion bans also hamper the effort to have children through IVF procedures. The Supreme Court of Alabama ruled that embryos had the same rights as children, opening the door to the possibility of physician prosecutions for destroying embryos in the IVF process. The three largest clinics in the state suspended operations; only one reopened, despite quick legislative action to exempt IVF providers from the law. Infant mortality has increased, and contraceptive services have declined in states with bans. Those monitoring the impact of *Dobbs* warn of more and worse to come.

But there has also been an outpouring of support for abortion rights and widespread resistance to the bans, certainly in reliably blue states but also in those that are more conservative, such as Kansas. Indeed, in the 2022 midterm elections advocates mobilized voters to reject bans, to expand state constitutional protections for abortion, and stave off a predicted electoral "red wave."

Even with sweeping Republican electoral victories in 2024, support for abortion rights remained strong. Seven of ten state referenda expanding and/or protecting abortion rights passed in Arizona, Colorado, Maryland, New York, Missouri, Montana, and Nevada. Although similar efforts in Nebraska and South Dakota failed, and the vote in Florida just missed the 60 percent needed to win, the fact remains that in the majority of cases, when the issue is put directly to the voters, their support for abortion rights prevails.

Yet it appears that many of the people who voted against bans also voted for candidates who support restricting abortion. How do we make sense of this dramatic disconnect? This book provides our answer. We use the reproductive justice (RJ) lens to disrupt old strategies and understandings, to analyze abortion politics of the past, and to make sense of the present. Through that lens we see that abortion is part of a wider landscape, one deeply rooted in the systems of oppression that define power and structure the lives of people in this country. Deciding whose reproduction is valuable has been a consistent theme in U.S. history. The book shows how racism, white supremacy, patriarchy, xenophobia, population control, and eugenics have been integral to these decisions.[4]

Still, the history we tell is not simply a tale of oppression. Throughout the book we turn to the stories of individual and collective resistance to illuminate reproductive justice thinking and practice. We are deeply committed to abortion rights, but we are also convinced that this pivot to a reproductive justice approach is the only way to secure reproductive freedom and bodily autonomy for all people. As we will discuss, the breadth of the analysis holds the possibility of transcending political divisions to build a more expansive movement.

However, neither reproductive justice itself, nor this approach to abortion, is widely known and accepted, even among many reproductive rights advocates. Those outside the movement are even less familiar with it. We want our book to bring greater visibility to this way of thinking and acting.

This project is also personal for us. Reproductive justice demands that we locate ourselves in the wider societal narrative. As you read this book, we ask you to consider how your life experiences and the identities you hold shape your understanding of—and stake in—reproductive justice. Here are our stories.

(Marlene) For me, the personal drove the political. I came to abortion rights advocacy through my experiences of pregnancy loss. Over a period of three years, I suffered two miscarriages of much-wanted pregnancies. I was devastated. Even now, two grown sons and four grandchildren later, the pain is close when I think back on that time. Until I had a miscarriage, I had no idea that 10 to 20 percent of pregnancies end that way, nor was I aware that anyone I knew had experienced one. Having spent my life until that point trying *not* to be pregnant, it had never occurred to me that I would have difficulty conceiving and carrying a pregnancy to term.

Miscarriage was not part of reproductive conversations, nor was pregnancy loss part of the public reality—there were no chat rooms, support groups, or books on the topic. It was a decade after a consciousness-raising group stirred my feminism and led me through my twenties, but no such community was available for pregnancy loss until I made the connection to abortion rights. My miscarriage experiences brought me to the abortion rights movement in 1976, when I was able to carry a pregnancy to term. I had an embodied sense of the connection between not being able to hold onto a wanted pregnancy and not being able to stop an unwanted one. Only later, when the feelings were less raw, was I able to use the notions of bodily autonomy and reproductive self-determination to put a conceptual logic to that intuitive understanding.

My journey to reproductive politics also came out of my participation in the social movements of the early 1970s—civil rights, anti–Vietnam War, gay rights, and second-wave feminism—which gave me an intersectional understanding of abortion rights. But the ideas of reproductive justice came later. In 1986 I attended a Sisters and Allies workshop, organized by the National Black Women's Health Project (NBWHP), where I met Loretta Ross, who introduced me to the RJ way of thinking about reproduction.

And there is, of course, a personal dimension here, too. Throughout my activist life I have been fighting the paralyzing guilt that results from my identities that locate me as both the oppressor and oppressed. I am a white middle-class Jewish person, an only child, and a first-generation college student (neither of my parents attended high school). At that workshop Loretta challenged me to park my white guilt or get out of the way. Although the internal tension remains, I am still heeding that lesson today. I feel especially impelled to repudiate the genocide against the Palestinians perpetrated by the Israeli government in the name of Jewish identity, not because it is worse than what is happening in the Congo, or Haiti, Sudan, Ukraine, and elsewhere, but because, as a Jewish person, it is especially my responsibility.

The NBWHP meeting was the beginning of a nearly forty-year relationship with Loretta, as allies, co-authors, co-conspirators, and friends. For me, this book is the culmination of many collaborations.

(Loretta) My reproductive justice story is like one of those jacks I played with as a girl. So many points sticking out I had to pick them up fast to avoid injury and losing. After a teen pregnancy due to incest, I rejected adoption and raised my son, co-parenting with my rapist cousin. This was a very complicated parenting experience for my son, me, and my entire family. In a seemingly quick seven years after his birth, I had an abortion, a miscarriage, and a sterilization, so the son I almost gave up for adoption became my singular claim to biological motherhood.

I did not enter the reproductive rights movement fighting for abortion. Personally, abortion was not a viable option for me when I was pregnant in Texas in 1968. By 1970 I was in college in Washington, DC, which had providentially legalized abortion three months before I needed one. I was part of that first generation of women who could take access to abortion for granted. My abortion struggle was not economic but familial. As a sixteen-year-old, I needed my mother's permission to obtain birth control. I sought her support even before I left home because I was, for the first time, asserting my sexuality on my own terms. Her Christian values made her refuse, although my parents were already helping raise my son. She was uncomfortable discussing sex and sexuality with her children; her daughters were the paranoid focus of her sexual fears. Every conversation about sex ended in her calling her daughters "sluts," and I couldn't bridge the gulf of mutual hurt feelings and her respectability politics.

Mom told me twenty years later that she was an incest survivor herself from age eight to sixteen. She got married to escape home, declining a chance to go to a local college because that would have required living at home with her abuser uncle. She had never had the opportunity to process her experiences of the 1930s. When I was a teenager, my mother, in her triggered state, also refused to consent to my abortion, so my older sister forged her signature on the form.

I developed my "reproductive consciousness" through a sterilization at age twenty-three due to a poorly designed and nearly toxic Dalkon Shield intrauterine device (IUD). After my fallopian tubes exploded due to acute pelvic inflammatory disease (PID) and I fell into coma, only an emergency hysterectomy saved my life. When I finally woke up in post-op, I was surrounded by medical students discussing their surgical techniques. I felt the implicit racism of their indifference that a twenty-three-year-old Black woman was no longer fertile and would start menopause in two years. My doctor assumed he had done me a favor and didn't need to apologize, and instead he congratulated himself for the excellent hysterectomy he had performed. The fact that he had misdiagnosed my acute PID for six months was just an "oops." Their blithe dismissal of my reproductive future angered me because I felt like my untreated PID due to using the Dalkon Shield was on the continuum of medical apartheid, a bizarre modern version of the Tuskegee Study. I successfully sued A. H. Robins, the manufacturer of the Dalkon Shield, and bought my first house with the proceeds.

Before the sterilization I was a personal feminist more than a political one. I believed that women deserved equality but I didn't work on women's issues. I was fortunate to be in DC at the time of the nascent anti-rape movement in Washington in the 1970s, which helped me attach words to my experiences, and I began to see my life as a template for other Black female survivors of childhood sexual abuse. I became a feminist when I reinterpreted my experiences and turned my rage into outrage as an activist.[5] My sexual life intersected rape, race, and reproduction.

My entry point into the reproductive rights movement was through fighting sterilization and sexual abuse in the 1970s and having lived as a single teenage mother. From that experience I understood that not all teenage girls consent to their sexual encounters, and in fact, many Black girls have little control over if and under what conditions they will have sex because of childhood sexual abuse.[6] My pregnancy, abortion, and sterilization all stemmed from the same source: a lack of sexual autonomy in a punitive misogynist context that failed to protect all girls while keeping us vulnerable and ill prepared to be sexually self-determining.

Our very different life histories and experiences shaped our undertaking of this project, as we hope your own will illuminate your reading of it. While we have a good deal of agreement about how we see the world, our differences of race, age, class, employment, and reproductive history are relevant. Our distinct vantage and entry points were provocative, in a good way. They stimulated our thinking and pushed us to clarify and reexamine our own underlying assumptions, and to hold each other accountable. The ways our experiences overlap and diverge shed light on the many forms that white supremacy and reproductive oppression can take, as well as the underlying similarities.

Our hope is that this book will be a contribution to academic scholarship, to education both within and outside formal academic settings, and to the ongoing fight for abortion rights, reproductive justice, and human rights.

ACKNOWLEDGMENTS

Our life's work of activism, teaching, and writing led us to this project. Gratitude and love to the colleagues, allies, students, and friends who paved the road to reproductive justice and are constant sources of inspiration. Byllye Avery holds the place of honor. Her early clinical practice embodied the understanding that for women of color, abortion was part of the totality of their lives and health, and she has never stopped leading the way. Toni Bond and Loretta Ross, two of the founding mothers of reproductive justice and movement leaders, have been in the forefront of developing and propagating the theory. Alice Skenandore, Oneida and Green Bay community member, traditional midwife, and foremother of SisterSong, insisted that the organization welcome reproductive justice advocates with pro-life views. Betsy Hartmann's pathbreaking scholarship alerted advocates to the need to confront racist population control and neoliberalism in reproductive theory and politics.

This book would also not exist without the vision and commitment of the series editor, widely respected historian Rickie Solinger, who saw the need for a radical history of abortion politics. She entrusted us, two non-historians to write it, shared her deep knowledge, provided unwavering support, and was a meticulous editor. Namrata Jacob was our close collaborator. Her probing intelligence, insights, and critical eye were pivotal in shaping and sharpening our analysis.

Our appreciation for the folks at UC Press for their hard work: Naomi Schneider, editor; Aline Dolinh, assistant editor; Jessica Moll, production editor; Chloe Wong, marketing manager; and freelancers Sharron Wood, Judith Loeven, and Victoria Baker, for copyediting, proofreading, and indexing. We are also indebted to friends and colleagues who generously contributed their time and insights. Deep appreciation to Andrew Byler, Shoshanna Ehrlich, Rusti Eisenberg, Anne Hendrixson, Stephanie Poggi, and Banu Subramaniam. Their comments were invaluable. Freelance developmental editor Carolyn Bond provided excellent guidance. Friends Abby, Barbara, Judith, Melinda, and Monica were there throughout, with steady and loving support.

Loretta's late son Howard Michael Ross brought light to her life and animated her understanding of reproductive justice. Marlene's sons Daniel and Michael, their partners, Kate and Ashley, and grandchildren—Landon, Lucas, Eloise, and Owen—anchor her in love and hope for the future. Marlene's husband, Bill Fried was a tireless editor, sounding board, and devoted champion, whose consistent love and legendary sense of humor are emotionally and intellectually sustaining.

Finally, we acknowledge our co-conspirators in the organizations that have been our political and professional homes: Collective Power for Reproductive Justice (formerly CLPP—Civil Liberties and Public Policy Program); the Committee on Women, Population and the Environment; the National Network of Abortion Funds; the School of Critical Social Inquiry at Hampshire College; SisterSong Women of Color Reproductive Justice Collective; Carrie Baker, Sylvia Dlugasch Bauman Professor of American Studies at Smith College; the Women's Global Network for Reproductive Rights; and Women Help Women. As incubators of activism and generative thinking, they foster our enduring commitment to collective resistance.

CHAPTER I

Telling Different Abortion Stories

Reproductive justice (RJ) is a new framework that Black feminist theorists developed for thinking about and analyzing the history and politics of reproductive experiences.[1] In this book we explain the framework and show how to apply RJ to abortion specifically. For shorthand, we sometimes refer to that process as RJ-ing abortion, that is, bringing the reproductive justice perspective—what we call *the RJ lens*—to our analysis. This primer provides the reader with the tools for a new understanding of abortion and opens new paths for advocacy. We do not assume readers have knowledge of the field. At the same time, we hope the book will be useful and interesting even to those who are already engaged in reproductive justice activism and scholarship.

ABORTION ACCESS TODAY

Our reproductive justice analysis of abortion is wide and deep; it goes far beyond the current state of abortion access. Nevertheless, we begin here with a discussion of the impacts of the 2022 Supreme Court decision overturning *Roe v. Wade*, a nearly fifty-year-old ruling that nationalized legal abortion in 1973. In the *Roe* ruling, seven of the nine justices on the Supreme Court decided that the Fourteenth Amendment of the U.S. Constitution provided an implicit, constitutionally protected right to abortion under that amendment's liberty guarantee, long interpreted as establishing the right to privacy. The Supreme Court justices who decided *Roe* said that the right to abortion should be understood as one of several personal rights, including the right to marry and the right to use contraceptives, which are also privacy rights.

On June 22, 2022, the court handed down its decision, *Dobbs v. Jackson Women's Health Organization,* cancelling *Roe* and its concept of the right to privacy and reestablishing each state's pre-*Roe* right to make its own laws governing abortion. However, a substantial group of congressional Republicans wanted legislation to ban abortion nationally, which would strip states of the right to make abortion laws. They did not accept the proposition that each state should legislate its own rules; soon after *Dobbs,* Senator Lindsey Graham (R-SC) introduced national legislation that would override state laws such as the 2023 measure Ohioans voted for in order to enshrine abortion rights in their state constitution. Many Republican politicians made their position clear: they wanted to ban abortion everywhere.

As of this writing, regulations governing abortion have been returned to the states. This means that thousands of pregnant people must navigate constantly changing state laws. Individuals must figure out, for example, where they can travel to get a surgical abortion or how they can obtain a medication abortion if they live in a state that has outlawed reproductive control after *Dobbs.* This is a significant obstacle for people who have no means of transportation or not much money, or who can't easily take time away from their job, or face any of the many other barriers to care. In fact, many people seeking an abortion are forced to figure out how the law in their state reads today and will read tomorrow, as state court decisions and legislatures are constantly changing the rules and responding to legal challenges.

Not all states are narrowing abortion rights and access after *Dobbs.* Some states have passed constitutional and/or statutory protections for abortion. In a few states, such as Massachusetts and Oregon, new legislation broadens access beyond *Roe*-era accessibility by allocating state funding for abortion, thus defining a pathway to reproductive freedom. But on the other side, in anticipation of *Dobbs,* thirteen states with Republican governors and majorities in their legislatures passed "trigger laws" that automatically banned abortion after the court's decision.[2] More such efforts followed *Dobbs.* Some of the bans went into effect immediately after *Dobbs*, while proponents of abortion rights in some states continue to mount court challenges.[3] It is likely that after this period of legal challenges and instability, about half of all states will have strict or nearly absolute bans on abortion.

The *Dobbs* decision set off shock waves among white middle- and upper-class women across the political spectrum who had believed that the "choice" guarantees of *Roe* would endure forever. But while *Dobbs* has reduced options for everyone who needs an abortion, activists from communities of color, people with disabilities, LGBTQIA+ organizations, low-income and poor communities, and many young people have an especially sharp understanding of the new terrain. Indeed, many people in the United States have been acutely aware that since 1973, *Roe* had not guaranteed safe and legal abortions for all who wanted or needed this procedure. *Roe* had made abortion *legal*, but *Roe* had not made abortion accessible or *available* to everyone.[4]

The limitations of *Roe*'s failure to address access were highlighted in 1976, decades before *Dobbs*, when Congress passed the Hyde Amendment banning federal Medicaid funding for abortion, effectively denying abortion rights and access to low-income pregnant people, who were then and are now disproportionately women of color. The death of Rosie Jiménez from an illegal abortion after Hyde is a painful illustration of its consequences, and of the inadequacies of *Roe*. Rosie Jiménez was a twenty-seven-year-old single mother with a five-year-old daughter. She was a college student in rural Texas, working to get her teaching credentials and struggling to make ends meet on her factory wages. She was also pregnant. Rosie felt that she could not have another child at that time. She did not have the money for a legal abortion, and the Hyde Amendment made her ineligible for any government assistance to help her pay for the procedure.[5] As we will see in the next chapter, the Hyde Amendment foreclosed decision-making about pregnancy options for millions of individuals like Rosie, and it also opened the door for other legislation that further eroded abortion access, all permissible under *Roe*.[6]

Rosie Jiménez took what she saw as her only option—she had an illegal abortion. She died a week later from septic shock caused by the unsterilized instruments used in the procedure. In her purse was a scholarship check for seven hundred dollars, which she could have used to pay for a safe and legal abortion, but she was saving the money to pay for the final six months of her education. According to *Roe v. Wade*, Rosie had the right to have an abortion; in reality, she did not. The right granted in *Roe* was meaningless to her.

Rosie Jiménez's story is not just about one person's inability to have a safe, legal, and funded abortion. Her death illustrates how abortion restrictions disproportionately harm the health and lives of all poor people capable of pregnancy who are, again, disproportionately people of color.[7] While the list of abortion restrictions—and their consequences—is familiar to abortion rights advocates, the fact that these restrictions harm people unevenly, according to their race and class, has never been the focus of mainstream abortion-rights advocacy organizations, although it is central to the intersectional RJ lens. Even when advocates adopt mainstream slogans such as "abortion is health care," they often pay little attention to how care is available to people—or not—depending on their race. One key reason for this racially disparate access is that people of color are twice as likely as white people to lack health insurance.[8]

A reproductive justice lens de-individualizes abortion. The RJ lens focuses on the structural, racial, social, and economic conditions that individuals have to consider when facing an unanticipated pregnancy. In the aftermath of the *Dobbs* decision, we are thinking a lot about Rosie Jiménez and the meaning of choice. When the Supreme Court overturned *Roe v. Wade*, many people believed that for the first time since 1973, abortion access was over. This belief shows us that Rosie is still invisible. Many people simply do not understand that *Roe* was never enough, that *Roe* had never guaranteed adequate reproductive health care for millions of Americans.

As we will show, mourning *Roe* and forgetting about the life and death of people like Rosie Jiménez tells us that individual "choice" is an inadequate way to think about abortion. Here we want to underscore that before the *Dobbs* decision, the Turnaway Study, a longitudinal study that compared the life consequences for people who received the abortions they sought with people who were unable to secure the abortion they wanted, revealed that women who were denied abortions face harsher poverty compared to those women who received the abortions they wanted.[9] Only when the Hyde Amendment is overturned and the needs and rights of people who have been most harmed by Hyde are prioritized, and other restrictions on abortion are lifted, will we achieve reproductive dignity, safety, and justice for all.

Today, reproductive justice activists and their allies are leading the fight for abortion access. In Texas, a coalition of Texas abortion funds and hundreds of other groups around the country invoke Rosie Jiménez's memory and honor it as they work to pass the law named for her. "Rosie's Law" was originally introduced in the Texas legislature in 2017.[10] At that time, Representative Sheryl Cole, a Democrat from Austin, Texas, who co-sponsored the bill, explained her support: "Rosie's Law will bring equitable, affordable health care to the communities that are often forgotten in our state. Our state's anti-abortion restrictions have hard hit low-income people, women of color, rural Texans, immigrants and young people."[11]

Sheryl Cole's proposed legislation reflects the work that needs to be done after *Dobbs* imposed new and even greater obstacles to care. Abortion seekers, people with pregnancy complications, and caregivers now face new, unknown, and constantly changing legal risks. Sometimes, accessing an abortion procedure becomes simply impossible. Supreme Court Justice Elena Kagan forecasted the disproportionate impact of *Dobbs* in her dissenting opinion: "Above all others, women lacking financial resources will suffer from today's decision."[12] In fact, 75 percent of people who have abortions live at or below the poverty line, and poverty is closely associated with race. Close to 25 percent of all American Indian or Alaskan Native peoples, and 20 percent of all Black and Hispanic women, live in poverty, compared to only 9 percent of their white counterparts.[13] Fifty-six percent of Black women and 55 percent of Native American women live in states that already have pre-viability bans restricting abortion access, even before the fetus can live outside the womb.[14]

Both before and after *Dobbs*, a disproportionately high percentage of abortions have occurred within the Black community for a number of reasons all shaped by wealth inequity. People who are racialized as non-white have been systematically excluded from quality reproductive health care and information, not only about abortion, but also about contraceptive access and effective evidence-based sex education. Medical racism and neglect are routine in medically underserved and otherwise vulnerable communities, where individual people must make their reproductive decisions in a hostile context without the ability to control the circumstances.

According to researcher Liza Fuentes, "Communities subject to health care discrimination, that lack high-quality health care and are denied the resources to raise children in safety and dignity, have the fewest resources to navigate the burdens of restrictive abortion laws, and for the same reasons are more likely to need abortion care."[15] In the period before *Dobbs*, the 14 percent of women between the ages of fifteen and forty-four who are Black accounted for 28 percent of abortions; Latinas are 21 percent of the same demographic but accounted for 25 percent of all abortions; and white women, who are 54 percent of the population, had 39 percent of all abortions.

Dobbs has also exacerbated dangers associated with pregnancy for Black women. As journalist Matt Gonzales observed after *Dobbs*, "Make no mistake. Black women are at greater risk of carrying potentially dangerous pregnancies to term, and increasing their risk of developing serious complications or dying as a result."[16] A Black woman is more than three times more likely than a white woman to die from pregnancy-related complications, and twice as likely to lose an infant to premature death.[17] The health and lives of many Black people are threatened now that they can be forced under *Dobbs* to stay pregnant, even under medically or economically unfavorable conditions. The reproductive justice lens shows us that a range of issues must be factored into our understanding of racial disparities in abortion rates in communities of color, including high rates of evictions and homelessness, food insecurity, poor transportation options, high rates of violence, violent deaths within their families, and the trauma of living in neighborhoods where neighbors also experience the threat of food scarcity, eviction, and homelessness.

The legal consequences of *Dobbs* will also be unevenly experienced. A study of more than 413 prosecutions of pregnant people who had been criminalized found that nearly 60 percent of the targets were women of color, and more than 70 percent of these people could not afford a lawyer.[18] Between 1973 and 2005, 71 percent of the cases involved low-income women; 59 percent were women of color; and 52 percent identified as Black. Even without convictions, those prosecuted were subjected to invasive investigations causing embarrassment, financial burden, trauma, and other negative consequences. *Dobbs* will not improve these statistics. Broad social and economic inequalities—the results of centuries of racism and white supremacy—drive these numbers. Unequal wages, poor housing conditions, segregated schooling, and targeted immigration surveillance make pregnancy, abortion, and childbearing hard to manage, or impossible. And this is not a comprehensive list of challenges.

In 1990, Arline Geronimus called the compounded health effects from the stress of living in a racist society "weathering."[19] Although her research was originally dismissed, today the intersection of racism and health is widely accepted. For example, we now understand that the higher risk of strokes, heart attacks, diabetes, obesity, and other comorbidities that were most frequently attributed to personal behavioral choices are, in fact, systemic issues.[20]

Dobbs is another tool of oppression. This 2022 Supreme Court decision subjects thousands of people who are or can become pregnant to the prejudices and medical ignorance of state legislators. Based on what analysts know about the past, they predict a likely increase in unwanted births among the same groups of people who already have high maternal mortality rates and devastating rates of infant mortality compared to their white counterparts.

BIRTHING REPRODUCTIVE JUSTICE

In 1994, twelve Black feminist activists coined the term *reproductive justice*. They were participating in a pro-choice conference in Chicago focused on President Bill Clinton's proposed health care reform plan.[21] The founding RJ activists raised objections to the Clinton plan, which mirrored the weaknesses that they, along with other women of color and white allies, had already identified in the "choice" framework: that the Clinton plan claimed each individual had the right to make their own reproductive decision while ignoring the fact that many individuals lacked the resources to access that right or to even make autonomous reproductive decisions. Loretta Ross explained, "We objected to the ways their proposals isolated reproductive rights issues from other social justice issues for vulnerable people. The proposals on the table did not make connections between the decision to become a mother— or not—and extremely relevant issues such as economics, immigration, and incarceration."[22] For example, the president's proposal did not include insurance coverage for abortion and contraception. Without government funding, low-income women, disproportionately of color, would not be able to access or afford those critical reproductive health services. The founders of the reproductive justice framework were leaders of organizations in the forefront of a growing movement of feminists of color committed to moving beyond the "choice" paradigm and developing more expansive and holistic agendas for health care and reproductive and sexual rights.[23]

As Black feminists, the creators of the reproductive justice framework began their analysis by centering their own lives.[24] Due to poor access to resources and services in many communities, the notion of choice simply did not describe their experiences. But the more expansive term, *reproductive justice*, did capture their reality and what they needed. Their radical shift in perspective created a powerful alternative to the old terms of the abortion debate that pitted the *right to choose* against *the right to life*.

Reproductive justice became the basis for creating a more flexible and encompassing foundation for reproductive freedom that was, as we explain later, grounded in human rights. Putting the most vulnerable people in the foreground—Black, Indigenous, Latinx, and LGBTQIA+ people, immigrants, and those with disabilities, among others—brought attention to the profound social, racial, and class inequalities that characterize reproductive experiences. It also highlighted the fact many people's lives were structured by several overlapping forms of oppression. The leaders in Chicago affirmed that access to abortion is a necessity, but it is only part of what people and communities marginalized by oppressive systems need in order to support parenthood, health, and general well-being. As we will see, the struggles of people of color to have children and to build families on their own terms, and to be pregnant only when they choose, reveal the entire interlocking system of domination contained in white supremacy.[25] Insisting that vulnerable people have the right to give birth and nurture their children is an act of radical resistance.[26]

A decade later, Asian Communities for Reproductive Justice (now Forward Together) expanded on the original idea of RJ, capturing its breadth and pointing out the need to change who controls underlying power structures: "We believe reproductive justice is the complete physical, mental, spiritual, political, economic, and social well-being of women and girls, and will be achieved when women and girls have the economic, social and political power and resources to make healthy decisions about our bodies, sexuality and reproduction for ourselves, our families and our communities in all areas of our lives."[27] In 1997, three years after the Chicago conference, a new organization, Sister-

Song Women of Color Reproductive Justice Collective, articulated the core tenets of the RJ agenda, that all persons have: (1) the human right not to have a child; (2) the human right to have a child; and (3) the human right to parent children in safe and healthy environments.

From the beginning, reproductive justice was not conceived of as a static or closed framework. In their primer, *Reproductive Justice: An Introduction*, Ross and Solinger describe reproductive justice "as an open source code that people have used to pursue fresh critical thinking regarding power and powerlessness."[28] Today, RJ is a robust theory that continues to evolve. It is also a dynamic political movement. When new constituencies adapt the theory to their experiences, they expand its boundaries. For example, the growing movement for transgender and gender-expansive rights and awareness led to the addition of a fourth RJ tenet, one that makes explicit the reproductive justice commitment to encompassing sexual and gender freedom and the human right to maintain personal bodily autonomy.

When we focus on justice rather than on equal rights or choice, we emphasize the importance of fighting oppression, addressing multiple and interconnected spheres of domination and power, and achieving accountability from those responsible for the hydra-like sites of reproductive oppression. This insight has enabled the reproductive justice movement to appeal to activists from abortion rights and other movements who have also been inspired to reframe their struggles.[29] For example, disability rights advocates, activists for the rights of pregnant and birthing people, and some environmentalists now cast their work in terms of *justice* and link their cause and their activism to reproductive justice.

Although the language of reproductive justice was new in 1994, the fight for it was not. Black women, for example, had a long tradition of activism at the intersection of gender and racial oppression. Reproductive justice draws on that history and on Black feminism, the activism and theorizing that developed from the late 1960s onward.[30] Indeed, in all communities of color where people had direct experience of overlapping systems of oppression and a long history of resistance, the new name, reproductive justice, provided new tools for analyzing power, grounded in important insights from Black feminism. In this chapter we orient readers to the reproductive justice way of thinking about abortion politics and set out the core components of the reproductive justice framework necessary for thinking about all reproductive issues in this holistic and interconnected way.

First we will illustrate why we need to apply the reproductive justice lens, and we also provide the tools of reproductive justice. Using the RJ lens, we tell an expansive story of reproduction, a story that acknowledges—and does not block out—the existence of reproductive oppression, its harms, and its perpetrators. Throughout the book we use legal scholar Dorothy Roberts's term *reproductive oppression* to connect abortion to the lesser-known history of laws and policies aimed at destroying the physical and social conditions necessary for an individual to make their own decisions about pregnancy.[31]

We are indebted to feminist activists and scholars of color for shining the light on reproductive oppression. Just being able to see it, let alone resist it, requires radically recalibrating the lens. Our analysis of RJ-ing abortion in theory and practice rests on their work.[32] In order to have a full picture of abortion, we need to include a complex range of experiences in our analysis. Applying the reproductive justice lens to abortion challenges stereotypes about who has abortions as well as who does not. It also exposes obstacles to reproductive health care even where abortion is legal, and it explains how an individual's experience of abortion reflects the intersectional history of the community they live in and the resources that community can or cannot offer.

To illustrate these points we use excerpts from three contemporary narratives collected by the storytelling project We Testify.[33] These moving, honest, but rarely heard abortion stories contain the principles we use to guide the process of RJ-ing abortion, taking our understanding of reproductive justice from theory to practice. Which of your assumptions do the stories call into question? For example, after reading them you might consider whether you had assumed that abortion was experienced only by cisgender women (people who are comfortable with the identity of female assigned at birth). Does including transgender men in the story of abortion change how you think about bodily autonomy? Do the differences among people's abortion needs and experiences open new space for empathy and solidarity, or do they foreclose it? Do the stories change your ideas about the way abortion care is delivered? How do you link your own reproductive experiences to the people, the institutions, and the resources of your own community?

We follow these narratives with a discussion of core principles that these voices clarify about the project of RJ-ing-abortion. We then go on to define key foundational concepts that will be at the center of this book.

Jack Qu'emi Gutiérrez

I had a medical abortion when I was 20.[34] I was a poor undergraduate student in a crumbling relationship with poor mental health. Making the decision to have an abortion wasn't difficult, but accessing it was. I'm an AfroLatinx person with no health insurance. The medical route was a smooth $500 out of pocket and the whole time I was paying I was kissing my rent, textbooks, and groceries goodbye.

It wasn't just the physical and logistical aspects of having a medical procedure, but the emotional labor of navigating a space where I was constantly misgendered; to be repeatedly called by the wrong pronouns was almost as draining as the procedure itself. Around that same time, Florida passed legislation that required an individual to have a trans-vaginal ultrasound before undergoing their abortion. Experiencing that only set off far too many feelings of dysphoria, violation, and shame.

Stephanie

I grew up in a home plagued by domestic violence. Fear ruled our family. Fear ruled my life. When I found out at 17 that I was pregnant. I couldn't tell my parents. They would have forced me to continue the pregnancy against my will. I searched the internet to see what my options were to get an abortion without my parents' permission. My state had a parental notification law, requiring that a parent physically be present with me, as well as an original birth certificate with both of our names listed proving they were indeed my parents, and ID's proving our identities. It was impossible for me.

I learned about the judicial bypass process, and began calling a hotline. I called for 2 days. Until I received an answer I considered throwing myself down the stairs. I even considered ending my life knowing a pregnancy would be the end of my future. That is how desperate I was. I finally got connected with an attorney who agreed to take my case pro-bono and finally felt some relief. I had an ultrasound, and I was forced to see it even though I didn't want to. I had to gather police records from the times my father was charged with child abuse after beating me and leaving me with bruises. I turned in all those papers to a judge who, thankfully, approved my judicial bypass and I had the abortion I needed. Not everyone is so lucky.[35] Parental notification laws do nothing but put those of us who are already in danger in more harm's way. I now work as a social worker focused on advocacy in the Latino community.

Alejandra Pablos

I tell my story because I do not want to stay in the dark any longer. There is an incredible amount of stigma, lies, myths out there about abortions, and I see no justice in that. Immigrant women are not just here to have a lot of babies and live off of public services.[36] I chose an abortion because comprehensive sex education wasn't a thing. I made this choice because I did not want to be a parent.

The decisions we make are supported by our very own lived experiences. Trust us. I know that when a mom is separated from her daughter, whether it is a country that separates them or an immigration prison, you might as well rip her heart out. I know this because my mother had to suffer through our separation once. I was detained in an immigration prison for two years, and my mom and my family visited every weekend. We do not deserve that punishment. At the moment, in this society, you can say my choice of creating a family was made for me anyway. It is not fit for a child to come into a world that locks people away for decades and profits off of their bodies, or a world that lets brown people die of preventable diseases simply because they are poor. I want people to know that there are other dreams I have. I have dreams of legalizing all of my people, the 11 million, especially the criminalized. I have dreams of abolishing police and prisons so that I won't be afraid for my people and my loved ones. I have dreams of eliminating borders so that all my people can migrate freely and live the healthy, full lives they are destined to live.

APPLYING THE RJ LENS TO ABORTION, OR
RJ-ING ABORTION

We draw six principles from these narratives as the core components of RJ-ing abortion. Together they teach us how to apply a reproductive justice lens to abortion, but not as an analytic recipe or prescription. Rather, as Ross and Solinger explain, they are guides to seeing the world through the lens of people who have been most affected by reproductive oppression.[37]

(1) Our identities, and therefore our reproductive lives, are inevitably intersectional, involving multiple and overlapping systems of oppression. Jack, Stephanie, and Alejandra, like all of us, live intersectionality through their multiple identities.[38] Even though they were able to obtain their abortions, poverty, youth, parental consent laws, abstinence-only sexuality education, gender identity, and anti-immigration policies are all part of their abortion stories that pose significant obstacles to exercising their human right to abortion.

(2) Center the lived experiences of those with the least societal power. Twentieth-century pro-choice politics has focused primarily on the experiences and needs of white middle- and upper-class cisgender women, reflecting the identities of movement leaders and participants. RJ-ing abortion tells us to look instead at the experiences of people like Jack, Stephanie, and Alejandra, whose stories have been missing from the dominant abortion narrative. This shift in perspective shows that racism, transphobia, immigration, Christian nationalism, and nativism are all significant parts of many people's abortion experiences.

(3) Understand that the legal right to abortion is not enough to ensure that everyone can exercise that right. Jack, Stephanie, and Alejandra are not legal scholars, but they have firsthand knowledge of this truth. All three of their accounts are about the barriers they had to overcome to obtain an abortion despite its legal status. Their stories illustrate that for abortion to be accessible to all people who need one, there will have to be profound structural changes in society. Seeing abortion as both a human rights and social justice issue emphasizes this principle.

(4) Connect an individual's experience to the history and experiences of their communities.[39] An individual's access to abortion is determined in part by the resources and services that are available in their community. People make choices based on the limited options they have and the context in which they live. Jack did not have the option to be served by a gender-inclusive health care facility; there simply wasn't one where they lived. Jack, Stephanie, and Alejandra all had abortions in states with multiple barriers, all seriously limiting the ability of people with the least amount of power to obtain abortions.[40]

RJ-ing abortion offers an alternative to the highly individualistic concepts of personal oppression, personal rights, and personal autonomy that drive the framework of individual choice. Alejandra's entire community faces the same barriers to care.[41] That is why her big dreams are not just for herself. She is dedicated to removing borders and eliminating practices that criminalize her people. Reproductive justice is the only theory and movement that intertwines the individual and the community and asserts entitlements for both based on human rights.[42]

(5) Agency and oppression coexist in the same frame. Jack, Stephanie, and Alejandra were victimized by unjust systems, but they are not merely victims. They were determined to exercise reproductive self-determination, even though it meant having to overcome nearly impossible obstacles. Theirs are stories of oppression, survival, and resistance.

(6) Appreciate the importance of community-based and community-supported strategies in providing access to abortion and contraception. To overcome the barriers to access, Jack, Stephanie, and Alejandra needed help from personal and community support networks. For example, finding a pro bono lawyer was the turning point in Stephanie's story.[43] Grassroots activists who provide information, abortions, accompaniment, referrals, and funding are all a crucial part of the reality of abortion access throughout the world.

These six principles for analyzing abortion are visible through the RJ lens. They are not revealed if we think of abortion only as an individual choice. Grounding our analysis in this way shows that abortion is not isolated from other human rights and social justice issues; it is part of a larger sphere of reproductive politics. What emerges is a more complex picture of the many threads that come together within an individual abortion experience. The concept of reproductive justice is broad enough to capture all these interconnections.

RJ-ing abortion brings into focus histories of discrimination and reproductive coercion enacted through the interlocking systems of race, class, and gender domination. To increase and protect their own wealth, status, and property, people in power (referred to as "elites")—enslavers, employers, doctors, legislators, judges—use these systems to control reproductive capacity and sexuality.[44] We will see that elites have consistently imposed repressive reproductive policies unequally by race and class, with the most brutal and coercive measures directed at people of color. In that regard, abortion is aligned not just with policies that directly regulate fertility but also with seemingly unrelated strategies, including policies governing immigration, violence, education, welfare, taxes, and mass incarceration. Along with the coercive "encouragement" of childbearing by young white women, all of these areas shape the size and composition of the population. A reproductive justice analysis contends that all overarching economic and social policies are, in effect, population policies that seek to manage human capital.

The RJ lens shows that anxieties about maintaining white racial domination (white supremacy) underlie reproductive politics,[45] and that our racially stratified system of reproduction yields an arena in which childbearing and families are differentially valued and empowered. This system determines who is a "legitimate" reproducer, defines the conditions imposed on reproduction, and allocates the resources available to support or impede an individual's reproductive decisions.

KEY CONCEPTS

Reproductive justice uses a group of foundational concepts as tools to analyze abortion with the reproductive justice lens, the process we call

RJ-ing abortion. We develop these concepts over subsequent chapters; here, we introduce them so we can move forward with a common language and set of ideas. The concepts we define here describe *how to look through the RJ lens* and suggest *what we will find* when we do.

White supremacy is an all-encompassing political, economic, and social system of domination. It is the ideology that some white people use—consciously and sometimes unconsciously—to justify their power, privilege, and control over people defined as not-white. White supremacy is both a biological fiction and an ideological commitment to dominate the world. DNA science has proven that the idea that there are separate races of people is a fictitious product of racialized science that primarily serves to support an ideology of racial supremacy—a body of ideas—used to justify the abuse of power and exploitation of people and the planet as a wealth-building strategy.

White supremacy is the ideological connective tissue among forces involved in maintaining racial hierarchy in the United States, and it refers to the resulting system of oppression. As philosopher Charles Mills wrote in *The Racial Contract*, "Whiteness is not really a color at all, but a set of power relations."[46] Obviously, not all white people believe in white supremacy, and not all who believe in ideological white supremacy are white.

Until recently, white supremacy has largely been invisible to many white people who experience their privileges simply as "reality." This was possible in part because white supremacy animates other forms of oppression that aim to define a person's identity and social position, such as racism, sexism, homophobia, transphobia, anti-Semitism, Islamophobia, nativism, Christian nationalism, and ableism.[47] Each of these forms of oppression is also treated as "merely natural," not as a system that people have constructed and that people can change.[48]

The intersections among these systems of oppression profoundly affect both an individual's and a group's access to power and status. In essence, white supremacy is the belief in biological determinism—that one's perceived race predicts one's destiny and place in the racial hierarchy of belonging and ownership. Thus, a reproductive justice analysis explains how these systems of oppression constrain an individual's ability to make reproductive decisions. The relationship between ideological whiteness, white identities, and white privilege can be explained in a metaphor coined by writer Walter Rhein: No white person is alive who robbed the bank, but all white people get to spend the proceeds.[49]

In recent years anti-racist social justice activists have called out and confronted white supremacy, determined to expose the ideology to public scrutiny, as, for example, after a white policeman brutally murdered George Floyd in 2020. The reproductive justice movement along with the movements for Black Lives Matter, Defund the Police, immigrant rights, environmental justice, and labor rights, among others, have pressed us to see white supremacy as a totalizing force that knits many movements together in resistance.

We also see white supremacy at work in the dramatic racial disparity in death rates from the COVID-19 pandemic and in the largely white, violent crowd that followed President Trump's invitation to invade the United States Capitol Building on January 6, 2021, for the purpose of overturning the 2020 election. They rioted not because white votes weren't counted, but because Black votes were.

Intersectionality explains that oppressions are interconnected. It teaches us to think holistically about our own lives and experiences, and instructs us to notice that we move through our lives conditioned by a number of factors: our race, our age, our class, and our geographical location, for starters.[50] We can look at each factor individually, but intersectionality helps us to see how those factors overlap to create our *lived experience*—a term that refers to people's day-to-day lives. In essence, intersectionality requires analyzing which parts of one's identities make one vulnerable to the discriminatory treatments that others without those identities don't face. People who experience systematic oppression have long understood this intersectional principle because it described and explained their lives even before they had the language to express it.[51]

In 1989, five years before the concept of RJ was introduced, legal scholar and activist Kimberlé Crenshaw coined the term *intersectionality* to capture the reality of a client who was denied a job because of both racial and gender bias.[52] At that time, the law did not allow her to express her client's experience of discrimination based on *both* her identities as a Black person and as a woman. Crenshaw had to create a new concept—intersectionality—so the court could begin to understand her client's reality. This concept and process are at the center of RJ-ing abortion: Individuals who encounter obstacles to reproductive health care, including abortion, are typically encountering the consequences of oppression due to their gender status, their economic status, their status as noncitizens, their racial status, and other biases. Recognizing and analyzing the relevance of intersectionality to abortion access is key.

Patriarchy is a system of social organization and control in which people defined as men have power over other people in all areas of life because, the ideology claims, men are naturally superior to others, especially when patriarchy intersects with white supremacy.[53] Traditionally, the ideology of patriarchy recognizes only two genders—male and female—and defines heterosexuality as the only legitimate form of sexual expression and marital arrangements.[54] Proponents claim that biology and genetics justify male superiority and men's unique relationship to social power and authority. Patriarchy views people who reject this system—for example, feminists and bisexual, transgender, and queer people—as threats to a society properly ordered by traditional male power. Those who reject patriarchy, such as people who support the right to reproductive autonomy, may be targeted by restrictive laws, policies, and public opinion. Many people who believe in patriarchy rely on the authority of various religious teachings, even though the U.S. Constitution specifically provides for the separation of church and state.

Stratified reproduction refers to the ways that the white supremacist hierarchy is reproduced and maintained through childbearing. Within the hierarchy, children who are considered white, identified within the gender binary, in the middle and upper classes, born in the United States, and without disabilities are accorded value. Within the white supremacist hierarchy, other children—especially children of color—have historically been defined as lacking value. Some people who possess power in various arenas—legislators, judges, physicians, bankers, and others—promote various racist and ableist theories and strategies to support the birth of the "right" sorts of babies. Eugenics and population control policies (defined below) provide valuable tools for this project.[55] In this book, we group several practices under those ideologies, encompassing policies that restrict access to the full range of reproductive health care, including abortion services, coercive sterilization, and forced pregnancy.

Eugenics is a pseudoscientific theory that emerged in Great Britain in the nineteenth century. Social theorists and scientists embraced eugenics as a useful tool for justifying British colonialism and suppressing labor protests in England. It was based on a belief that racial superiority and inferiority are biologically based and eternally fixed: The elites and all colonizers were racially superior whites; the subjugated "natives" of other countries were biologically inferior "coloreds," requiring behavioral restraints and a regime of tough work discipline imposed by their "betters." Poor and working-class whites were seen as "non-white" when they protested their harsh labor conditions in England. British eugenicists claimed that society was in decline and could only be resuscitated if reproduction by "superior people" was encouraged and rewarded, while reproduction by "inferiors" was strictly discouraged, even punished. "Inferiors" were only meant to reproduce sufficient numbers of workers to sustain and enrich Great Britain's colonial empire. The rationale for eugenics meant that strategies to improve the lives of people of color and poor and working-class whites were futile as these people were genetically incapable of benefiting from such efforts. Thus, elites and colonizers relieved themselves of responsibility for addressing the miserable conditions created by their wealth-producing endeavors.

By the late nineteenth century eugenicist ideas were taken up by intellectuals, policymakers, jurists, physicians, and other influential groups in the United States and deployed to justify Jim Crow laws in the South after the Civil War, Native genocide, and anti-immigration policies, among other repressive social goals. In the 1930s and 1940s, the Nazi regime in Germany explicitly drew on the U.S. uses of eugenics and its genocidal policies against Native Americans to justify their annihilation of "inferiors" across Europe—Jewish people, Romani (often referred to using the offensive term *Gypsies*), homosexuals, and disabled populations, among others. Explicit eugenicist practices fell out of favor in the United States after World War II, but its core ideas and goals continued to influence public policies governing reproduction, as nineteenth-century eugenics morphed into twentieth-century "population control."

Population control emerged as a key goal of demographers, politicians, and other authorities in the mid-twentieth century, when population experts warned that both globally and in the United States, too many people were being born and that "overpopulation" was a ticking bomb that could destroy the planet. These futurists incorporated the central idea of eugenics: that controlling and *refining* reproduction is necessary for global economic growth and stability. Population control thinkers identified "overpopulation"—chiefly "excess reproduction" by Black and brown women—both in the United States and worldwide, as the cause of poverty, communism, and environmental degradation. They also saw political unrest as a societal threat.

Academic and policy analysts used "scientific" calculations to "prove" there were more people on the planet than could be supported by the available natural resources, including food, water, air, and land. U.S. theorists championed the idea that social disorder driven by overpopulation in poor countries with "non-white" populations was an invitation to communist regimes in Russia and China to step in, restore order, establish new spheres of influence, and reduce the influence of the United States around the world. The proposed solution was to curtail the rate of reproduction of people in poor countries and in poor neighborhoods.

U.S.-based population controllers incorporated their theories into national and international development policies, spearheaded by powerful elites representing private organizations and governmental agencies in the United States. For example, the U.S. Agency for International Development (USAID) would provide aid only to countries agreeing to aggressive family planning campaigns designed to depress the fertility of poor people in the developing world, while family planning programs in the United States were supported by Republicans and Democrats if they targeted people of color at home.[56]

Using the reproductive justice lens, we will show that ideas fueling population control are flawed, gendered, and racist. Feminist critics argue that corporate and military degradation of the environment are far more powerful drivers of planetary endangerment than reproduction. These analysts call for an approach to achieving environmental sustainability that respects human rights, including those based on reproductive justice and social justice.[57] In chapter 3, we explore the critique in greater detail.

Neoliberalism is an economic and political philosophy that is robust in the United States and other Western countries. Neoliberalism promotes free trade, corporate deregulation, globalization, and reduced government spending on social welfare. The neoliberal model focuses on an *individualist* rather than on a *systemic* approach for understanding and solving society's problems. Even if individuals have constitutional rights, the government is not obligated to guarantee the ability of individuals to take any actions to enable people to exercise these rights.

In this book you will encounter several examples of the problems neoliberalism presents in the realms of reproductive politics and policy. For example, "choice" is a neoliberal framing of abortion and other aspects of reproductive health care that does not pay attention to whether and which individuals have access to the resources or conditions necessary to make reproductive choices. Critics of neoliberalism ask what does *choice* mean to a person if they cannot afford the cost of an abortion? If they have to travel hundreds of miles each way to access an abortion and have no childcare? Or if they have no transportation to any health care facility, or they lack internet access, which would enable them to obtain abortion pills outside the formal medical system? What does choice mean if there is a crowd of protestors outside the clinic, blocking the door? Or if there is no practitioner available to perform the procedure for a trans or nonbinary client? What meaning does choice have to a person in a prison, jail, detention center, or mental hospital when all their decisions are constrained by institutional policies and authorities? And do people who live in communities that are overpoliced and oversurveilled really have a choice to use abortion pills unless our movements take care to mitigate their risks?[58]

RJ-ing abortion rejects basing access to reproductive health care on the flimsy individualist concept of "choice," when so many people do not live under conditions where real choice is possible. RJ-ing abortion demands government actions grounded in social justice and human rights. In many cases the difference between relying on choice or relying on human rights to structure lived experience is not merely an abstract distinction but a matter of life and death.[59]

Human rights is a global legal framework based on the belief that every person possesses an inalienable group of basic rights simply because they are a human being. This idea contrasts sharply with the idea that rights are based on membership in a particular group such as a tribe or a family, or because of a person's status as a citizen in a country, or because they refrain from certain behaviors, like participating in gay relationships. Here we argue that human rights are universal, indivisible, and interconnected.[60]

Our modern concept of human rights comes from the 1948 United Nations Universal Declaration of Human Rights (UDHR), a document intended to supersede the laws of any particular country.[61] The UDHR, therefore, expresses a human-centered doctrine based on global norms, standards, conventions, and treaties that can protect individuals and groups from abuses by their own governments. As eloquently stated in its preamble, "Recognition of the inherent dignity and of the equal and inalienable rights of all members of the human family is the foundation of freedom, justice, and peace in the world."[62]

The founders of reproductive justice based their theory on the foundation of *human rights*, a concept they deemed a more valid and complete expression of their needs than *legal rights*. By aligning their project with human rights, the RJ movement allied itself with oppressed people throughout the world, from those resisting dictatorships in Latin America to those who continue to resist the legacy of racist settler colonialism in South Africa despite the formal end of apartheid in 1990, to Indigenous groups in Alaska who use human rights arguments in their struggle for recognition, self-determination, freedom, and liberation.

In 1994, three months after the June meeting in Chicago where twelve Black women cocreated reproductive justice, the UN held the Conference for Population and Development in Cairo, Egypt, where attendees formally recognized reproductive rights as human rights. Loretta Ross, a well-known RJ founder, attended the Cairo meeting as part of a women of color delegation from the United States. Their mission was to bring the experiences of the members' communities to global policy discussions that had, up until then, been dominated by white middle-class voices. The delegation produced a policy report in advance of the Cairo meeting that highlighted the reproductive oppression of U.S. women of color. This was the first time a sizable number of U.S. women of color were able to bring *their* histories of systematic and institutionalized denials of reproductive freedom to the global stage.

At the Cairo meeting Ross was inspired by the participants' rejection of population control, by their emphasis on the systematic underdevelopment of Global South countries by structural adjustment policies imposed by Global North financial institutions, and by the elevation of human rights as the basis for abortion rights and for reproductive rights generally.[63] She brought human rights ideas back home and incorporated them into the newly minted concept of "reproductive justice" at a time when the concepts of human rights and reproductive justice were both unfamiliar to most people in the United States.[64]

Placing reproduction within the human rights arena added important dimensions to reproductive justice analysis and activism. This development used global language and standards for expressing and building broad-based transnational solidarity and resistance to reproductive oppression. U.S. activists working internationally saw that when they linked reproduction, gender issues, and sexuality to human rights, the moral force of their efforts to influence policymakers and the general public grew stronger.

As we have noted, even though rights are defined in the U.S. Constitution, the government has no obligation to ensure that individuals can access and exercise their rights. Constitutional law, as it has been historically interpreted, chiefly confers only negative rights, and it prioritizes freedom from government interference and coercion. However, as we have seen, constitutional law does not affirm positive human rights that guarantee that individuals are the beneficiaries of constitutional laws. Of course, this purported freedom from coercion is markedly absent when it comes to protecting reproductive autonomy in decisions about abortion and birth control.

In contrast, under a human rights regime the government has the obligation to provide "enabling conditions" ensuring that people have access to their constitutionally established rights and that they can exercise those rights. For example, in countries where abortion is considered a human right, a government must guarantee not just that abortions are legal; it must also guarantee that abortion services are accessible to all people living in the country.

In teaching the applicability of the concepts of reproductive justice, advocates often compare it to the decision to fly in a commercial airplane. The government does not have the power to tell a person if they must fly, where they must fly, when they must fly, or even which airline to use. Those are *negative* rights that protect individual choices. However, the government does have *positive* rights obligations that protect the ability to exercise those choices. It must ensure that the planes are safe to fly, that anti-monopoly competition keeps airfares affordable, and that access to airports is reasonably distributed throughout the country. Safety, affordability, and access are key human rights standards applied to many personal decisions like buying cars or using public transportation. Why can't the individual decision to obtain an abortion receive the same constitutional consideration as the regulation of airlines or cars? It would not be logical to let people who have religious objections to flying regulate the airline industry.

Yet around the world, the people who do not accept the fact that abortion is routine medical care have the power to determine whether this human right is accessible, affordable, and safe. Even worse, they go in the opposite direction and pass laws that make abortion less safe, more expensive, and extremely difficult to obtain, along with mandating criminal sanctions against providers and patients. Making abortion exceptional violates the ethics of reproductive justice and basic human rights standards. RJ-ing abortion means that people should not have fewer human rights just because they are pregnant.

The concepts that we sketched out here illustrate why we need to apply the reproductive justice lens to abortion, and they also point to the tools for RJ-ing abortion. Throughout this book we argue that the intersections of eugenics, population control, and stratified reproduction within white supremacy connect abortion to a complex story of reproductive politics, a story that does not obscure, but acknowledges, the existence of reproductive oppression and the harms it has caused millions of people. RJ-ing abortion allows us to see how an individual's experience of abortion is connected to the rights and resources available in their community and in the nation.

BEYOND CHOICE VERSUS LIFE: KEEPING IT REAL

Applying the reproductive justice lens to abortion gives us a way to get beyond the dominant framing of the debate, most often understood as an unbridgeable divide between two competing worldviews, "pro-choice" and "pro-life." In this view, pro-choice affirms the individual's reproductive autonomy and their right to end a pregnancy. Throughout this book we use the term *mainstream* to refer to the dominant understanding of abortion rights, and also to the movement itself. By selecting the expression *pro-choice* soon after the Supreme Court's *Roe v. Wade* decision in 1973, the mainstream abortion rights advocacy movement hoped to secure a wide base of support, including from neoliberals, libertarians, and economic conservatives, groups that center the individual's personal freedom and speak about rejecting expansive government power. To mainstream advocates in 1973, *choice* seemed like a politically neutral slogan and less threatening than abortion-rights and women's-rights language. It left open the possibility that someone could support choice *and* oppose abortion.

The pro-life side has focused on denying pregnant individuals the "right to choose" by devaluing their life choices and prioritizing the fetus's (or, as pro-lifers put it, the "unborn child's") right to live. They do not define the moral universe of abortion as a matter of balancing the rights of a pregnant person with those of a fetus. Instead, they reduce all moral issues to one: the protection of fetal life, arguing that "it's a child, not a choice."

In 1990, the Council of Catholic Bishops hired one of the world's largest public relations firms to help pro-life forces seize the moral high ground. This firm was charged with creating "a broad-based public education and information campaign" to lift up and broadcast the voices of the bishops on abortion.[65] Images of babies were at the center of all campaign materials. In many ways, that campaign was a success, capturing the high ground of "life" and "babies" for the antiabortion campaign, rendering pregnant people invisible and irrelevant—or, worse, portraying them as murderers. The truth that the pregnant person is unquestionably a person who has a human right to make life decisions is obscured.

Indeed, any person who can become pregnant may face an abortion decision. This includes people who support abortion and those who oppose it; people who intend never to become pregnant and people who are willingly pregnant; people who are pregnant but do not want to be; and people who wanted to be pregnant but whose life situation has changed. Perhaps they face a catastrophic health situation while pregnant.

These categories of pregnancy experiences are neither static nor mutually exclusive. For example, after a natural disaster such as a hurricane or wildfire, some people with previously desired pregnancies seek abortions after losing their partners, homes, or family.[66] Even without such a dramatic event, many kinds of changes in life circumstances, such as job loss; relationship changes; health issues experienced by the pregnant person, the fetus, or a family member; educational opportunities; or housing matters, may press a person to change their path. Sometimes it goes the other way; people who become pregnant by "accident," even if having a child was the last thing they intended, may decide that they want to have a baby and to carry the pregnancy to term.

To reiterate, the "choice versus life" paradigm leaves no room for these layered, ambiguous, complex, and everyday situations. Opponents of abortion appeal to religion, philosophy, and morality in an effort to focus the public debate away from women's lives and toward questions about the status and moral value of a fetus.

On the other side, supporters of choice hold up the value of women's lives and their moral agency, that is, their capacity for making moral decisions for themselves. Reproductive justice moves us beyond "choice" versus "life" and directs us to think about the life circumstances and feelings of pregnant people. We can then begin to understand the extent to which abortion is not a single issue and that it involves all aspects of a person's life.

Abortion is not an uncommon experience; worldwide, one in four pregnancies ends in abortion.[67] People in all countries, and of all religious, ethical, and political beliefs, have abortions. Some experience difficult feelings afterward; others do not. Consider the devout Catholic mother who called Marlene for a referral to an abortion provider. She said, "I think I will burn in hell for this, but my daughter's life comes first."[68]

While it may seem surprising, a person's view on the human life question does not necessarily determine whether or not they will have an abortion, or even whether they think it should be legal and available.[69] According to testimonies from people who have had abortions and clinic workers, some people who have abortions believe that they are taking a human life and still decide it is the best decision they can make given their circumstances.[70] Nor, as we will see, is the legal status of abortion a determining factor. In fact, the number of abortions tends to be even higher when it is illegal.[71] We will, therefore, not engage with these questions of morality and the status of fetal life.

Both the pro-choice and the pro-life sides of the debate focus on the meaning of ending a pregnancy, but they both leave out a crucial issue: a person's right to *have* children. This right is, of course, a primary concern for people and communities existing in a culture that has consistently devalued or condemned their fertility, and has even punished various targeted groups for reproducing.

Indeed, many critics have pointed out that the choice/life divide does not respond to the circumstances of people whose lives are primarily structured by oppression, people who do not see themselves as having choices in any sphere.[72] RJ activists hope that by bringing together seemingly disconnected issues such as racial and class differences in maternal and infant mortality, deaths from COVID-19, and rates of incarceration, to name a few circumstances, a wider reproductive justice framework for abortion can not only accomplish a change in our thinking but can also create opportunities for building new political alliances.

STRUCTURE OF THIS BOOK

In this chapter we explained what we mean by looking at abortion through a reproductive justice lens (RJ-ing abortion). We defined reproductive justice and the other basic concepts we use throughout the book, orienting the reader to the lens through which we view abortion. We included the origin of the term and its relationship to the more widely known framework of choice. RJ-ing abortion reveals the complicated dimensions of abortion and shows how the basic structures of reproductive oppression intersect. This chapter highlights the experiences of those who bear the brunt of reproductive oppression.

In chapter 2 we apply the RJ lens to abortion policy in three pivotal eras in the history of abortion in the United States: nineteenth-century criminalization, twentieth-century legalization, and the subsequent and ongoing backlash period. We see that eugenics and population control consistently show up in battles over the criminalization and legalization of abortion. We pay special attention to the pivotal role of abortion in perpetuating white supremacy, a critical yet often overlooked dimension. We weave together the white population's fears of being replaced by immigrants and men's fears about losing control over "their" women's reproduction and lives. The race and class divisions that persist in society are also present in reproductive advocacy movements. In particular, we see how activists of color and their allies prioritized resistance to sterilization abuse as a necessary part of abortion rights, while the white mainstream choice movement did not.

In chapter 3 we look more deeply into the policies justified by eugenics and population control, and in particular at the history of forced sterilization and the resistance to it. We highlight the endurance of underlying eugenic goals with three examples: C.R.A.C.K. (now Project Prevention), an organization that pays pregnant people who use illegal drugs or alcohol to be sterilized or to use long-acting reversible contraceptives (LARCs); coerced sterilizations in the California prison system; and coerced sterilizations in detention facilities run by U.S. Immigration and Customs and Enforcement (ICE). All three are recent examples in which eugenic aims are hidden behind the stated intention of expanding choices for low-income women, protecting their health, and protecting the environment from dangerous overpopulation.

In chapter 4 we turn to RJ-ing abortion in practice. We describe the different waves of RJ activism and their impact on abortion politics. We also hear from individuals working in the field who describe how they bring the RJ lens to their abortion advocacy, research, clinical, and legal practice. Since *Dobbs*, reproductive health clinics and other organizations working on the ground have stepped up their activities to meet as much of the need for abortions as they can. Some clinics relocated, and new ones have been built in states without bans. National and international organizations, including the National Network of Abortion Funds and its grassroots member funds, the Brigid Alliance, Women on Web, Women Help Women, and less formal groups like the Mexican feminist organization Las Libres, all report surges in activity to provide people with information and access to abortion pills. In chapter 4 we look at these efforts in greater detail. All give us hope for achieving a more expansive and liberatory vision of reproductive justice.

In chapter 5 we look at abortion internationally, focusing on examples of activists taking a reproductive justice approach, in some cases explicitly. We see how reproductive justice intersects with powerful game-changing strategies including self-managed abortion with pills.

RJ-ING ABORTION NECESSITATES CHANGING OUR LANGUAGE

The language surrounding abortion and reproduction used in legislation, court cases, policy statements, and popular culture has always reflected a patriarchal understanding of gender. It presumes that pregnancy, childbirth, abortion, and breast cancer are experienced only by cisgender women. This misunderstanding leads to denials of care and treatment that can be harmful, as Jack describes above. The reproductive justice analysis provides us with a more expansive understanding that sexual oppression is experienced by vulnerable people of all genders, all of whom need the full range of reproductive health services. Acknowledging this reality means adopting language that more adequately reflects it. Accordingly, many organizations no longer use "women" or the pronoun "she" in the context of reproductive health and rights. There are several alternatives, including "people with the capacity for pregnancy," "pregnant and birthing people," and elaborating the category of women more inclusively by adding other designators, such as "women, both cisgender and trans" or "*all* women."

The question of appropriate language remains unresolved, is sometimes contentious, and is in flux. Some people who fall outside the traditional binary framing object to language that they feel makes them invisible, while some feminists argue that dropping "women" erases their struggles for rights and against discrimination. In this book we try to be as inclusive as possible. Following the lead of transgender and nonbinary activists as much as we can, we use gender-neutral language and pronouns and avoid language that implies that gender and sexual oppression are grounded in biology. However, when referring to laws and policies we use the same language found in those laws for clarity.

Keep in mind that gender is not a biological given any more than race is. Both are socially constructed as ways to enforce power relations determined by white supremacy. In this way language is a system of power. At the core of this book is the observation that power of all kinds—institutional, interpersonal, political—is present in our bodies and in our lives. The interactions between those with power and those without together create policy and reality in every era.

Abortion and Reproductive Justice is neither a linear nor a complete account of abortion politics through the ages. Rather, in the book we look at key moments in the story of abortion in order to identify the through lines that shape abortion politics, reproductive oppression, and reproductive justice over time.

CHAPTER 2

Racializing Reproduction

In this chapter we begin by reviewing the historical contexts within which Africans, African Americans, Indigenous people, and immigrants made their reproductive lives in North America and then in the United States. Soon after they arrived on the North American continent, white elites began to shape and control these contexts. Their central purpose was to populate the continent for the benefit of white people. To accomplish this goal, they developed laws and policies to achieve racially stratified consequences of reproduction. At the outset, we will look at how their actions shaped the reproductive lives of people in targeted communities. As always, we place the principles of reproductive justice at the heart of this discussion.

In the next part of the chapter, we look at three key periods in the history of U.S. abortion policy: first, the era of abortion criminalization in the nineteenth century; second, the nearly three decades, from 1945 to 1973, when the movement to legalize abortion gathered momentum and force; and third, the decades after the Supreme Court's *Roe v. Wade* decision in 1973, when the backlash movement against legalization defined, organized, and pursued its mission.

HISTORY AND THE REPRODUCTIVE JUSTICE LENS

To begin with, when we lead with the experiences of enslaved Black people, of Indigenous people, and of immigrants, we are clarifying once again that to understand reproductive politics, we must move to the center those whom whites have consistently forced to the margins. We cannot understand the complexities of fertility management or reproductive experience if we merely pay attention to the elites and their communities. For centuries on the North American continent, white people considered themselves to be elites in relation to Indigenous, enslaved, and Asian immigrant communities. Whites living in North America and then in the United States for several generations defined some newer immigrants as "white" while still treating them with a milder yet comprehensive form of reproductive oppression, a topic we will also address. Crucially, we also specifically focus attention on the lived reproductive experiences of people of color. We are committed to interrupting the racism we are explaining. Our intent is to enact reproductive justice on the page.

Here we want to underscore again that the creation and maintenance of white supremacy in the United States has depended on passing and implementing laws and policies governing labor, property, sex, and other matters. These government actions have targeted people whom the power elites have defined and redefined over time as "nonwhite" in order to justify control over their reproductive lives. Elites have targeted others as "inferior" reproducers for reasons in addition to race, such as having some kind of a physical or mental disability, their gender expression, or other prejudicial reasons. The first section of this chapter will provide short histories of the ways that law and policy, the military, and everyday norms have targeted racialized others by placing reproductive barriers and other coercions in their path to ensure that whites would prosper. Indeed, from the beginning of white settlement, the processes of burdening and stigmatizing the reproductive capacities of specific groups have been essential to creating white supremacy, both ideologically and reproductively.

In this first section we will also focus on some of the ways that enslaved people, Indigenous people, and immigrants, resisting white supremacy and asserting their own interests, managed their fertility under the slave regime, on the Trail of Tears, in city tenements, and elsewhere. Since the law forbade enslaved people to learn to read or write, they could not leave a written record of their own stories. Indigenous women and many immigrant women told their stories in languages inaccessible to white people, who had the resources to write and publish what became the official histories of these matters.

Because documentation is so fragmentary, and the scant evidence we have is tricky to interpret, historians, including some who focused on abortion, largely ignored how enslaved Black women and other women of color in the past acted to control to their own fertility. Thus, for years, stories of defiance remained hidden in most historical accounts. Today we need further evaluation of the scraps of evidence that do exist, from the records of doctors, plantation owners, religious leaders, and enslaved, Indigenous, and immigrant midwives in order to reveal the agency of women of color, whether they lived within the system of chattel slavery or another system of oppression.

For centuries, white people, the compilers, editors, and authors of the historical record, and often proponents themselves of white supremacy, whether consciously or not, omitted the perspectives of these women and assumed that a whitewashed story of reproduction was adequately comprehensive. By centering the reproductive lives of the most vulnerable people, the RJ perspective helps us understand that these—often secret—acts were crucial to the lives of many people, their families, and communities. Of course, evidence of secret acts exists only in bits and pieces, the "shards and bones, parts of conversations, and laconic responses to frightening questions."[1]

We emphasize that the RJ framework does not merely add information about people who were previously omitted from the historical record. It asks us to challenge widely accepted but false narratives about race and reproduction. Take, for example, claims about the birth rates of enslaved women. Standard racist histories of the slavery regime typically refer to the robust "natural increase" of enslaved women. In the same way, racist accounts have made enduring claims that Native women are immune from labor pains and lack the ability to be nurturing mothers. These white-generated fictions, offered without legitimate historical evidence, also include claims that poor immigrant women typically reproduced wantonly and lovelessly.

Such racist stereotypes, which prevailed for centuries and to some extent still have life, create thoroughly inaccurate distinctions between white women and others. On one hand, we have the stereotype that makes white pregnant women into ideal containers for future white citizens and *naturally* ideal mothers, especially if they belong to the "right" social and economic class. In contrast, despite the fact that Black "mammies" were forced to mother white children, the stereotypes of women of color who birth and mother their own children are profoundly degrading, branding them as low, worthless, maternally inept, breeding children of low value who lack the qualities to be American citizens. These two characterizations depend on each other for meaning. The reproductive justice framework dismantles both.

Going back to the problem of how to explain the abnormally high birth rates of enslaved women: In the past, historians and others have used data showing the fecundity of enslaved women as evidence that they were well fed and not overworked. Today we know these birth rates should really be ascribed to the sexual violence of forced breeding and rape. "Natural increase" is merely a term that has been used to obscure the inhumane behavior of white people toward enslaved and other women of color. An RJ analysis provides a far more accurate explanation for disparate birth rates, one that details rather than denies the ruthless actions of white supremacy and its role in building and sustaining slavery, and the pervasive system of racialized reproduction in the United States more generally.

To underscore a central point: We can see today that an inaccurate analysis of the high birth rates among enslaved women has served white supremacy in several ways. It has painted the slavery system as benign or, worse, as nurturing the health of enslaved women. When enslavers and their apologists have boasted about high birth rates, they have strategically buried the truth that the system depended on horrific acts against enslaved women's bodies to sustain itself. That false narrative draws an invidious distinction between the tender, chaste bodies of white women and the gross, overly sexualized, reproductive bodies of others, an enduring difference that has been a key engine of all forms of white supremacy on the North American continent since white settlers arrived and soon after began "importing" enslaved people and stealing Indigenous land.

REGULATING REPRODUCTION THROUGH BRUTALITY

Let us begin with the various ways that women, whose only resources may have been their own determination to protect themselves and be nurtured by their families and communities, attempted to manage their fertility as best they could under cruel regimes of reproductive and other forms of terror fueled by white supremacy. Recent historians studying white, European settlement on the North American continent in the seventeenth and eighteenth centuries have argued that the settlers' military and legal drive for white supremacy was neither inevitable nor "natural."[2] In the seventeenth century, white settlers defined their own people as racially superior and imposed white supremacy on Native people as a strategy for serving the economic, social, territorial, and political needs of elite white people.[3] Early white settlers and, later, American citizens used direct violence, laws, policies, and customs to assign differential value to individuals and communities and, most critically, to their fertility. These valuations were based on the settlers' understanding of racial identities and on racist ideas about intellectual and physical abilities, social worth, and the settlers' economic interests.[4]

Creating and maintaining white supremacy is an ongoing project that requires persistence and flexibility. Over time, power elites have faced continuing challenges to this system of domination. Typically, they have responded by implementing new forms of oppression and sharpening racial distinctions. This has occurred repeatedly in the form of enacting laws and policies defining some women's reproductive capacity as a valuable source of white citizens, and other women's reproductive capacity as merely economically valuable, a resource for replenishing a cheap labor force. Once these distinctions were institutionalized by laws and policies, different groups of reproducing women faced entirely different lives according to their assessed reproductive value.

From the Naturalization Act of 1790, which limited citizenship to "free white persons ... of good character," until the passage of the Fourteenth Amendment to the U.S. Constitution (1868), which included a provision establishing "birthright citizenship," every law stipulating the terms of citizenship extended that status only to people who were designated as white. The government did not grant Native Americans status as citizens until 1924. Throughout periods of massive immigration in the late nineteenth and early twentieth centuries, law and policy defined certain immigrants—for example, Italians, and Jews from eastern European countries—as "non-white," which had negative consequences, even though the law did not deny these groups citizenship.[5]

Instead of democratizing the power of the legal system, the white supremacist laws in the nation's founding era and going forward generated profound disputes over questions of power, inequality, and rights. These laws reveal a number of the crises that white people faced in their efforts to create the United States as a "white nation": the instability of race as a category; the weaknesses of white supremacy as a stable, ruling regime; and the challenges of creating gender and reproduction as sites of domination.

During much of the period under discussion, neither Black nor white women were granted full citizenship, and neither group could expect the law to protect their bodies. Under the slavery regime, Black women were property owned by enslavers, and white women, whose offspring were heirs to the white family's wealth, amounted to containers of their fathers' or husbands' property interests. White women could not own property themselves, enter into contracts, or seek relief in courts through lawsuits. Plus, they were forced to breed in ways that, while different from those of enslaved women, were also coercive and necessary to the project of building white wealth.

NATIVE AMERICANS: TARGETS FOR GENOCIDE

During the period of settler colonialism in the seventeenth and eighteenth centuries, when European whites occupied and colonized what they called the "New World," they defined Indigenous people as threats to white control of the vast, resource-rich continent.[6] Using the reproductive justice lens, we see the deadly assaults on Indigenous people—the intentions and impacts of settler colonialism—as "reproductive disappearing," an effect that caused "massive trauma, unresolved grief, and a legacy of genocide."[7]

White soldiers and colonists used war and forced migrations to displace and eliminate Native peoples and to steal their lands and its wealth. Whites compelled Native Americans to leave their millennia-old ancestral homes on the eastern edges of North America and move farther and farther west, opening new territory for the U.S. military to claim while also fomenting war against Western tribes and stealing their lands.[8] During the most infamous forced migration, the Trail of Tears from 1830 to 1850, white soldiers drove sixty thousand Native peoples out of the southeastern states. The Native peoples, whose numbers were already decimated by European diseases and violence, continued to perish as the U.S. military pushed them westward. Many thousands died from a combination of exhaustion, lack of food, the physical brutality of white drivers, and the violent interruption of Native community life and health practices and rituals, including those associated with birthing and raising healthy children.

During these decades of the mid-nineteenth century, while the slavery system was still intact, the federal government directed white soldiers to destroy Native women's reproduction in order to prevent the birth of future generations of Native peoples. This brutal policy was meant to facilitate white settler access to Native-held lands, as well as to extend white nationalism from the East Coast of the continent to the West.[9] In his heartbreaking account of the genocide perpetrated against

Native Americans, David Stannard writes, "The European habit of indiscriminately killing women and children when engaged in hostilities with the natives of the Americas was more than an atrocity. It was flatly and intentionally genocidal. For no population can survive if its women and children are destroyed."[10]

Beginning about 1870, in post–Civil War America, just when the Fourteenth Amendment granted emancipated Black people U.S. citizenship and, implicitly, the right to parent their own children, the U.S. government imposed policies on Indigenous people that aimed to destroy their parental rights. During this period, state and local government officials and the military, making determinations about who was not fit to mother their own children, forcibly removed Native children from their families and tribes on reservations. They sent the children to government- and church-run boarding schools and to the households of white families, often hundreds of miles away.

At these sites the children were forced to speak English, dress and wear their hair like American children, deny their parents' teachings, and undergo other forms of cultural and physical assault. Children who were caught speaking in their native languages or practicing Indigenous religions and other belief systems were severely punished. Eventually there were more than 350 such "boarding schools" across the United States, supported by the government for over a hundred years.[11]

Today, more than seventy-five years after the Universal Declaration of Human Rights was adopted by the United Nations General Assembly, enshrining the rights and freedoms of all human beings, the practices of forced assimilation aimed at destroying Indigenous culture and practices, family formation, and the transmission of traditional beliefs is increasingly acknowledged as cultural genocide. Of course, Indigenous people always understood that they were in a fight for literal and cultural survival where families and children fiercely resisted these practices.[12]

BRUTAL REPRODUCTIVE CONTROL DURING THE SLAVERY REGIME AND JIM CROW

The same generations of U.S. politicians, policymakers, military men, and white settlers who, across the nineteenth century, aimed to decimate Indigenous people were also in charge of the slavery regime, wringing profits from the bodies of African-born people and African Americans. In order to maintain the system of chattel slavery, local, state, and federal officials, enslavers, and other managers of white power wrote laws giving themselves control over Black people's reproductive bodies. This was even more important after Congress passed the Act to Prohibit the Importation of Slaves in 1807, which outlawed the international slave trade and made it impossible to import new slaves. Childbearing by enslaved women was the only way enslavers could increase their human property and their profits. They forbade enslaved women to use contraception to avoid pregnancy or abortion to end pregnancy, severely punishing those they discovered trying to manage their own reproductive bodies.

Further, enslavers intensified the sexual and reproductive torments they imposed on enslaved women. In addition to the violence of enslavement itself—including physical bondage, children sold to faraway slavers, inhumane work schedules, food deprivation, and physical torture—enslavers routinely raped enslaved women and imposed forced mating as a breeding strategy.[13] The laws and courts in all Southern states permitted sexual violations of enslaved bodies and did not punish enslavers for sexual and reproductive violence. Enslaved women in Northern states were also deeply vulnerable to sexual aggression by their enslavers.

On the plantation and on smaller farm units, enslaved women had neither sexual legal rights nor any rights at all regarding motherhood. Still, enslavers' brutality never fully achieved its goals. Black women refused slave breeding when they could by using whatever strategies and techniques they could draw on, in some cases relying on Black midwives who would clandestinely provide or assist with contraceptives, abortions, and infanticide. Through these secret acts, Black women expressed their own reproductive intentions and resisted enslavers' intentions.[14]

In many cases where Black women did not give birth to enough children to satisfy their captors, enslavers called in white doctors to conduct investigations. Physicians typically, and not altogether unreasonably, concluded that the women surely possessed secret strategies for "destroying the foetus." According to an 1860 essay by Dr. John Morgan, a physician in Tennessee, Black women hoarded special knowledge that facilitated their refusal to birth children into slavery.[15] Incredibly, though, the doctor ignored the more obvious cause for infertility and low birth rates: the brutality of enslavement.[16]

In fact, infant mortality rates were unnaturally high due to poor nutrition and to the terrible work demands imposed on pregnant women. Many enslaved women's pregnancies ended with stillborn babies, and a very high percentages of infants died soon after birth. Best estimates indicate that 50 percent of enslaved infants were stillborn or died within the first year of life. These high infant death rates occurred in the context of high birth rates, which strongly indicates that most enslaved women experienced dangerously frequent and debilitating serial pregnancies.[17]

After the South lost the Civil War and enslavement was outlawed by the Thirteenth Amendment to the U.S. Constitution (1865), formerly enslaved people asserted their independence and economic autonomy. White people perceived their actions as potentially lethal challenges to their power, and they were specifically fearful of the specter of Black-led rebellions by four million formerly enslaved people. Whites also worried about economic competition from Black agriculturalists and other entrepreneurs, and they used their fears to justify intensified violence against Black bodies.

White employers and other authorities developed new strategies to protect white supremacy, which was still essential to the country's economic, cultural, and political power as well as to its social logic and identity. To this end, by 1867 nearly every Southern state had enacted convict leasing laws, Black codes, and other statutes that compensated *enslavers* for the end of the slavery regime. In addition to instituting "reparations," payments enslavers received from tax-funded sources for each freed enslaved person, the laws restricted Black people's labor, their right to travel, access to education, right to vote, physical safety, and status as citizens.[18]

Another powerful engine protecting white supremacy was the climate of fear that white mobs and racist individuals and organizations like the Ku Klux Klan maintained. White men perpetrated thousands of violent acts against freed Blacks, including lynching, massacres, and horrific sexual violence, such as public gang rapes and bodily mutilation before and after lynching. This reign of terror continued to shape the lives of formerly enslaved people. It enabled ordinary white people as well as white elites to protect a socially and economically stratified and racially segregated "national body," with white men, and only white men, as power holders.

The childbearing of Black women, once possessively pursued as a wealth-producing strategy for enslavers, was degraded after emancipation. Former enslavers now treated many Black children as near slaves, using them as low-cost or no-cost agricultural laborers who worked in the fields next to their sharecropping parents. Even after enslavement officially ended, some white employers managed to hold on to children as both household and field laborers, separated from their mothers and other family members in a continued degradation of Black motherhood, family, and community. This was at the same time that white officials were introducing child removal in Indigenous communities.

After emancipation, although many people were still living under near-slavery-era conditions, many others decided to move North to escape labor exploitation, family separation, and violence. They initiated what came to be called the Great Migration. Between 1910 and 1970, approximately six million Black people moved from the South to the North.[19] Many women were catalyzed by a vision of living conditions that would, for one thing, allow them authority over their own bodies. They imagined the North as a place without racialized rape and other forms of sexual assault, where they could live in cities that offered economic, educational, social, and medical opportunities, including access to abortion and contraceptive services.

IMMIGRATION

Using the RJ lens, we see that elites also considered the fertility of immigrant women a threat to maintaining the United States as a white nation. To this end, in the late nineteenth century the government restricted immigration of females from certain countries, such as China. At the same time, the United States willingly admitted Chinese men, chiefly because rigidly racist wage scales enabled employers to pay them much lower wages than they had to pay white male workers. The number of massive infrastructure projects in that era, such as building the first transcontinental railroad, made these cheap immigrant laborers valuable to American capitalists, but Chinese workers soon became targets of white resentment and nativism; they were the first immigrant group accused of "stealing" American jobs.[20] White working-class laborers pressured the government for policies to protect their economic interests against the new immigrants, which, together with concerns about compromising white racial purity, led to the passage of the nation's first anti-immigration laws. The Page Act of 1875 and the Chinese Exclusion Act of 1882 became the templates for subsequent restrictive and race-based immigration policies.

After the Fourteenth Amendment to the Constitution passed in 1868, with a "birthright" provision granting U.S. citizenship to all persons born on United States soil, politicians had a particularly strong reason to construct new immigration restrictions. They passed laws that blocked the ability of Chinese and others considered non-white to have children in the United States while continuing to allow the exploitation of immigrant labor. The Page Act explicitly refused Chinese women entry to the United States on "moral" grounds, defining them as a threat "to the sanctity of white families, imperiling the nation."[21] Policymakers characterized Chinese women as prostitutes or sexually promiscuous. American eugenicists who promoted these ideas claimed that the alleged promiscuity of Chinese women was a biologically inherited trait that, if passed on to future generations, would debase the "blood" of the nation.

By the time of the Chinese Exclusion Act of 1882, which banned all Chinese people from immigrating, the data showed the "success" of restrictive policies: For every one thousand Chinese men living in the United States, there were forty-eight Chinese women. This skewed gender ratio was compounded by anti-miscegenation laws that remained on the books in various states until the 1967 Supreme Court decision in *Loving v. Virginia*.[22] Although law enforcement did not often bring charges against interracial couples, these laws, which forbade "non-white" men from having sexual relationships with white women, remained enforceable, creating fatal obstacles for most Chinese immigrants who wished to create families in the near-total absence of Chinese women on U.S. soil.[23]

At the same time that new immigration laws excluded female Asian immigrants, the existing immigration policies permitted the entry of over fourteen million men *and* women from Anglo-Saxon and Nordic countries, who were given preferential treatment because, according to U.S. officials and others, they were white.[24] We can see that whiteness itself was a malleable concept, dictating the differential treatment of groups of people who all looked "white" by federal, state, and local governments and private entities.[25] Public and private institutions, drawing on prejudices and exclusionary traditions, used both formal and informal practices to refuse the status of "white" to both Irish and Jewish people, among others, reducing the immigration opportunities of people in these groups without denying them citizenship. Consistently, those in power aimed to shape reproductive outcomes—and the complexion of the population—to secure the United States as a "white" country.[26]

In the late nineteenth century, politicians (including U.S. president Theodore Roosevelt), scientists, academics, physicians, and business elites, among others, framed their fear of immigration and its impacts as a concern about "race suicide," sounding the alarm that unregulated immigration and childbearing of "non-whites," who allegedly had higher fertility rates than whites, threatened the country's white identity and the dominance of its white citizenry.[27] In the second half of the nineteenth century, charges of race suicide fueled both anti-immigrant and antiabortion campaigns.

ABORTION POLICY BEFORE AND DURING CRIMINALIZATION

We will focus now on three key periods in United States history when politicians tailored reproductive policy—and specifically abortion policy—according to their perception of national interests. To reiterate, the three periods we will look at here are, first, the era of abortion criminalization in the nineteenth century; second, the nearly three decades, from 1945 to 1973, when the movement to legalize abortion gathered momentum and force; and third, the decades after the Supreme Court's *Roe v. Wade* decision in 1973, when the backlash movement against abortion legalization defined, organized, and pursued its mission.

Studying each of these periods, separately and together, we can see how the mechanisms locking in white supremacy worked. In each period, important groups of elites—politicians, economists, physicians, lawyers, legislators, journalists, and others—pursued abortion laws and policies and developed professional practices that favored white reproduction in order to ensure that the United States would thrive as a country for the benefit of white people. An RJ analysis recognizes and problematizes this history and highlights the abortion-related strategies that various elites developed to position people of color as inferior to white people.

Abortion was legal in most U.S. states for nearly a hundred years after the country's founding in 1776. In 1821 the Connecticut legislature passed the first law that criminalized abortion, restricting the use of dangerous drugs to carry out an abortion. This law was not strictly an antiabortion measure. Instead, it was a poison-control measure, meant to protect (white) women from the effects of commonly used toxic methods of ending pregnancy. Between 1821 and 1841, ten states and one federal territory passed similar laws.[28] These new laws provide us with solid evidence that many thousands of white women had been using these drugs to induce abortions; otherwise, legal restrictions would not have been necessary.

Until the mid-nineteenth century, the United States followed English common law regarding abortion, allowing a pregnant white woman to decide whether to have an abortion up to the time she experienced "quickening," the point in pregnancy when a woman feels the physical sensation of fetal movement, which is commonly between the fourth and sixth months of pregnancy. From trials and published proof, we know that even in the face of new state statutes, many white women continued to make their own decisions and have abortions. Women who were protected by husbands and fathers were much less likely to be publicly exposed and punished than relatively resourceless, unprotected white women who violated these laws.

Although there is scant official documentation, we know that enslaved women had abortions and used contraception, assisted in these acts by enslaved midwives and nurses who provided the only health care that was available to enslaved people on plantations. These actions were extremely perilous, both because the only available methods might well have been dangerous and because if an enslaver found out, the consequences for destroying potential "property" would likely be extremely harsh.

As we have seen, whiteness was a form of property, a "rare, inalienable commodity" that could only be passed on through white mothers.[29] Historian Rickie Solinger explains that in the nineteenth century, various white cultural authorities invested white motherhood with a "new glory."[30] They defined white women's reproductive bodies as "the nation's most precious resource" because white reproduction produced white citizens.[31] Even in a context where abortion was more broadly illegal, purchasing contraceptive materials was a difficult, secretive, and increasingly illegal act. What's more, nineteenth-century contraceptives were hardly reliable. Still, many white women followed their own preferences and found ways to prevent pregnancy and birth, causing the white birth rate to drop continually for most of the nineteenth century, which was also the result of surging illegal abortions.[32]

In the post–Civil War era the new commercialization of abortion made the practice visible to the public and revealed that it was widespread. Newspaper advertisements for medicines to bring on "suppressed menses" and for clinics to treat "menstrual irregularities" were common, even in religious publications. A huge and intensely competitive market in commercially available abortifacients flourished, including medicines distributed through the mail and by pharmacists.

When the *Boston Medical and Surgical Journal* issued its first major statement on abortion in 1844, the publication described abortion as a thriving and profitable business.[33] We cannot know for certain the total number of abortions during this period, which women got them, or the precise number of deaths, but historian James Mohr's extensive review of physicians' records and writings show that more than 25 percent of pregnancies ended in abortion during the same years that state legislatures were outlawing the practice.[34] These were probably mostly procedures performed on white women who had access to the kinds of physicians tracked in this study. In the 1870s, the *New York Times* estimated that there were over two hundred full-time abortionists in New York City in addition to other doctors who performed abortions, despite the fact that New York State had criminalized abortion in 1827.[35]

We know that women in all regions of the country, in both cities and rural areas, demanded abortions.[36] Mohr noted that medical societies and medical writers agreed that abortion became an open and pervasive practice after 1840.[37] "By the 1860s the vast majority of writers on abortion, even those who estimated the total incidence of abortion rather conservatively, reinforced the belief that the practice was common to 'every village, hamlet, and neighborhood in the United States' and that it seemed to thrive as well on the prairies as in large urban centers."[38] In 1873, a doctor in Michigan observed that it was rare to find a married (white) woman who had not had at least one abortion.[39] Acknowledging the everyday importance of abortion to their lives despite criminalization, many women, white and Black, shared their knowledge with each other. One observer remarked, "It was axiomatic to a judge on the Colorado frontier in 1870 that a girl's 'mother or any other old lady' would be both willing and able to offer her information on restoring menstrual flow after a missed period."[40]

RJ-ing abortion tells us to pay attention to how race and class structured the practice of abortion during the era in which it was criminalized. Evidence shows dramatic variations in both standards of care and cost, depending on the clientele. As we would expect, when experienced people, not necessarily physicians, performed abortions, the procedures were almost always safer than when a pregnant woman tried to perform an abortion on herself. Prior to the Civil War, female midwives performed all manner of reproductive health care. At the turn of the century, they delivered half of the babies born in the United States. Midwifery was interracial; half of the women who provided reproductive health care were Black women; other midwives were Indigenous and white.

Native midwives attended almost all births on reservations.[41] In the rural South during and after enslavement, Black "granny midwives" were the primary source of birth care among enslaved individuals and others. After emancipation, they continued their work in rural and remote parts of the South. Black women had home births to avoid discrimination and the cost of having their babies at hospitals. Granny midwives would accept food or even chickens as payment for births and abortions.[42]

White women had different options depending on their economic status. In the mid-nineteenth century, some "regular" doctors (those with some formal training in Britain or the United States or who had apprenticed under a doctor) charged wealthy clients from one hundred to five hundred dollars (four thousand to twenty thousand dollars today), prices that put their services out of reach for Black and other women with few resources.

In the mid-nineteenth century, nonphysician providers (homeopaths and midwives) charged much less. Their advertised fees were less than five dollars (about two hundred dollars today), which was still a lot of money for wives or daughters of farmers and laborers. For example, Mrs. Fenno, who performed abortions in Somerville, Massachusetts, charged ten dollars (about 360 dollars today) and added an additional five-dollar charge for a return visit or checkup. Madame Restell, the most highly publicized and outspoken of the people doing abortions in New York City, dispensed abortifacients and all but openly performed surgical abortions. She catered to wealthy, probably exclusively white, clients, charging them the highest prices, but she also accepted less from poorer clients.[43]

Abortions, even in the criminal era, were at least as safe as childbirth for white women.[44] Indeed, the United States had one of the highest rates of maternal mortality in the world at that time, with both pregnancy and childbirth—then, as now—deadlier for Black women.[45] In the mid-nineteenth century in the South, the rate of infant mortality for enslaved Black babies was 1.6 times higher than that for white infants.[46] Due to malnourishment, inhumane work schedules, and generally poor living conditions, slave mothers had high rates of spontaneous abortions, stillbirths, and deaths shortly after birth. Still, even self-abortions were safer than childbirth.[47]

According to historian Judith Leavitt, it is almost impossible to overstate the extent to which the fear of death—the "shadow of maternity," as she calls it—framed women's lives, regardless of race and class. Most women knew someone who had died in childbirth. One woman, for example, wrote that her friend "died as she had expected to" as a result of childbirth, as had six other childhood friends.[48]

> Most married women, and some unmarried women had to face the fact that the physical and psychological effects of recurring pregnancies, confinements and postpartum recoveries, which all took their toll on their time, their energy, their dreams and their bodies ... nine months of gestation could mean nine months to prepare for death. A possible death sentence came with every pregnancy.[49]

In this reality, Leavitt emphasized that women took care of each other and created support networks to provide whatever aid they could to birthing women.[50]

As birth rates declined and rates of abortion rose among white, married, middle-class women, religious and secular authorities were desperate to find ways to increase childbearing among these women. White educators, clergy, and social theorists such as the prominent abolitionist and champion of women's education Catharine Beecher, wrote many articles and lectured widely to white audiences, insisting that the most important job of white middle- and upper-class women was to channel their energies into creating and caring for their households, children, and husbands. Beecher was joined by many experts who insisted that for white women, sexual intercourse should occur exclusively for procreation, not pleasure, a dictum they popularized through women's magazines, novels, and other expressions of the emergent culture industry.[51]

Beecher's positions underscore the enormous difference in value that she and other white authorities granted to Black and white reproducers. She wrote many of her treatises on reproduction and motherhood during the slavery era, when, as we have seen, Black women were denied the status of "mother" and were entirely excluded from the "glory" associated with white motherhood. Even voluntary motherhood, the feminist ideal that women should have the power to decide how much sex and how many children to have, was itself class based and racialized. Its white feminist champions included Susan B. Anthony, who vociferously opposed the widespread availability of abortion and contraception. Anthony described female chastity, purity, and moral virtue as key markers of superior, asexual female whiteness.[52] White feminists promoted abstinence as a key strategy for white women, rich, middling, and working-class, to define themselves as superior to poor Black and immigrant women, who were criticized for having too much sex and too many children. Outspoken white proponents of "chastity" and "purity" did not highlight the reality that white women who possessed these characteristics were less likely to die from pregnancy or childbirth.

This confluence of disparate, intersecting, and sometimes conflicting interests was the backdrop for the nineteenth-century campaign to criminalize abortion. Framing this history within the RJ lens, we shine a light in the next section on the white supremacist ideas and eugenicist strategies at the core of the antiabortion campaign. The campaign was a significant part of the ongoing effort to increase the right kind of white reproduction and maintain government control over the bodies of all women.

THE DOCTORS' CAMPAIGN TO CRIMINALIZE ABORTION

In 1867, just after the end of American slavery, doctors in the American Medical Association (AMA), a white-only organization in the process of gathering legitimacy and power, initiated an intensive campaign to criminalize abortion. For its physician-leaders, this was an "impassioned crusade" launched to end white women's thousands of secret visits to physicians and irregular medical practitioners who performed abortions in cities, towns, and villages all over the United States. They were determined to establish themselves as the singular, rightful gatekeepers of white reproduction. Notably, the first front on which physicians fought for professionalization was abortion.[53]

The key mark of their success was that by 1890, every state had passed a criminal abortion law solidifying and extending doctors' professional standing and social status, as well as their political power. Most of these state criminal laws remained in effect until the 1973 Supreme Court decision *Roe v. Wade*, although enforcement was uneven and inconsistent throughout the criminal era. From the late nineteenth century until *Roe*, when law enforcement conducted investigations of criminal abortion, the cases almost always involved practitioners serving white women.[54]

The new nineteenth-century laws responded to the fact that for much of that century, "regular" doctors competed for patients with nonphysician abortion practitioners, including midwives and others who did not possess AMA-approved medical credentials. This was important because many physicians serving white women expected their highest earnings to come from their gynecological and obstetric work; the criminalization campaign was a battle to keep this work for themselves and away from the competition.

After the end of slavery, skilled granny midwives who assisted with both births and abortions represented both real competition for white men and a threat to how obstetricians viewed themselves. Campaign leaders exploited racial and class prejudices when they openly and viciously denigrated midwives, associating the profession generally with old Black women and Indigenous and immigrant women. Male gynecologists claimed midwifery was a degrading means of obstetrical care. Dr. Joseph DeLee, a prominent opponent of midwifery, said, "The midwife is a relic of barbarism.... The midwife has been a drag on the progress of science and the art of obstetrics."[55] Yet early research found that midwives had better maternal outcomes than hospital births.[56] Still, drawing on racist tropes, doctors described midwives as "ignorant, unskillful, and dirty," and they blamed midwives for the high rates of abortion and for infant and maternal mortality.

Physicians saw themselves as elite members of a trained profession with access to tools such as forceps and other modern technologies, as well as to up-to-date hospitals. White doctors excluded Black and Indigenous women from practicing within their institutions and denied them access to medical instruments.[57] To protect its white members, the AMA successfully promoted physicians as the only legitimate expert practitioners for "women's diseases," pregnancy, and childbirth, and it asserted physicians' professional superiority over all others.[58] We know now, thanks to the work of dedicated women of color feminists and bioethicists, that doctors developed the fields of obstetrics and gynecology by experimentally treating enslaved Black women without their understanding or consent, and often to their painful and debilitating detriment. Dr. Marion Sims, known as the father of gynecology, was a pioneer, experimenting on the bodies of a number of enslaved women, including Anarcha, Lucy, and Betsey, without administering anesthetic or obtaining consent.[59] Sims's work was one episode in a shameful history that includes many examples of medical exploitation of Black bodies, including the morally corrupt Tuskegee experiments, in which physicians denied treatment to Black men with syphilis, again without the subjects' knowledge or consent; and Johns Hopkins University physicians' use of genetic material—and their monetary gain from this material—taken from the body of a relatively resourceless Black woman, Henrietta Lacks, who was not informed and did not consent to the myriad uses of material from her body.[60]

The doctors' campaign also incorporated racist nativism, the idea that the interests of native-born white people should be protected against the incursion of immigrants onto American soil. Preying on fears that will be familiar to today's readers, activist doctors warned that when white women aborted their fetuses, they were allowing "hyper-fertile" immigrants to replace white Anglo-Saxon Protestant Americans. In the words of one physician, "The annual destruction of foetuses" among native-born American women had become so "truly appalling" that "the Puritanic blood of '76 will be but sparingly represented in the approaching [1876] centenary [of the United States]."[61]

Antiabortion physicians pressured white women to adhere to the contours and content of the traditional female role in order to preserve and underscore their whiteness. At that time, in the post–Civil War era, women's roles were undergoing significant changes. For example, in the 1860s and 1870s some state legislatures passed laws allowing married women to own property, liberalized divorce laws, forced some state universities to admit women, and debated women's right to vote. Who would women be—what would "woman" even mean?—if white women were granted all these privileges and could have command over their bodies, just like men? Could women even be granted the latitude to pursue sexual relations freely, like men, and, putatively, like Black women?

The doctors were determined to thwart these transformations of white female roles, and especially to curtail new freedoms that could blur the differences between white and Black women—a horrifying consequence in their eyes. Predictably, the doctors in the campaign largely ignored the medical needs and cultural identities of women defined as non-white, women who, in the post-emancipation period, were also fighting for new freedoms, some of which would, of course, have previously been associated entirely with white women, another unacceptable result.[62]

Speeches and published statements show that in general the white physicians leading the campaign in the nineteenth century were not concerned with the overall increase in abortions but only with their increased frequency among white Anglo-Saxon middle- and upper-middle-class women. Dr. Horatio Storer, the leader of the campaign, explained that his opposition to abortion was connected to his opposition to immigration. He identified the widespread use of abortion among native-born white women as a crisis for the survival of the Anglo-Saxon race.[63] Commenting on population expansion in the United States to the west and south, Storer expressed his hope that the expansion would be comprised of white people fit to populate the states that would join the Union as a result of this migration. Storer called on white women to accept their reproductive duty: "Shall these regions be filled by our own children or by those of aliens? This is a question our women must answer; upon their loins depends the future destiny of the nation."[64] The campaign, as a strategy to increase the birth rate among the "right" people, gave the AMA an important role in establishing and maintaining the racial, class, and gendered status quo.[65]

Toward the end of the nineteenth century Dr. Storer drew on English geographer and statistician Francis Galton's new pseudoscientific, racist theory of eugenics to support the criminalization of abortion as a strategy for increasing white births.[66] Galton's theory of eugenics advocated for financial rewards to promote marriages among the most "fit" members of society to improve the quality of the population. Eugenicists such as Galton and Dr. Storer argued that racial superiority and inferiority were biologically based and genetically inherited. They prescribed laws and policies designed to restrain the reproduction of "lower-quality" Americans, who would inevitably pollute the quality of the population. Only if reproduction was guided by "scientific" eugenicist principles would the United States remain a powerful nation that preserved white people's entitlement to racial supremacy, power, and wealth.[67]

The white doctors' campaign against abortion and support for eugenic "science" were separate but mutually reenforcing efforts. In the late nineteenth and early twentieth centuries, doctors were able to mobilize receptive audiences among scientists, biologists, social scientists, cultural authorities, and the general public by linking the two campaigns, which shared the belief that selective breeding would improve the nation's "racial health."[68] Leaders of both efforts claimed to be acting in the best interests of *all* individuals and of society as a whole when, in fact, they were serving and preserving the interests of native-born white people and actively justifying the denigration of immigrants and people of color.

ABORTION ACCESS DURING CRIMINALIZATION: RACISM AND CLASSISM PREVAIL

RJ-ing abortion draws our attention to the different reproductive opportunities and experiences women have had depending on their race and class. Black granny midwives continued to provide abortion and contraception to Black women. Immigrant midwives primarily served immigrant women. And, since the criminalization of abortion largely targeted white women, it is unlikely that enforcement of the new antiabortion laws extended to Native women on reservations. Most likely, Indigenous women continued to protect and transmit traditional information and methods for managing fertility, including by abortion, from one generation to the next.[69]

Throughout the criminal era, white women with economic resources had access to private doctors who could perform abortions in secret for any reason a woman might have for wanting an abortion, or, according to the law, to preserve the pregnant person's health or life. In fact, though, state laws rarely if ever spelled out conditions that would permit a physician to perform a legal abortion.[70] Doctors themselves had a good deal of discretion about when a woman's medical situation would permit a legal, lifesaving abortion. However, physicians would also frequently perform secret abortions for entirely nonmedical reasons if the girl or woman asking was a friend or relative or if her story stimulated the physician's sympathy.

The fact that physicians had so much control over abortion further solidified their power over reproduction and deepened the powerlessness of unwillingly pregnant white people. Over time, however, doctors began to disagree with each other about when an abortion was justified, especially since advancements in obstetric science and methods of care reduced the incidence of medically necessary abortions. By the 1930s, most legal abortions were performed in hospitals. Doctors set up "abortion committees" to decide who had the right to a therapeutic abortion. This process ensured that all abortion decisions were made by a group, so no individual doctor would be acting without the approval of his colleagues.[71]

When a woman seeking an abortion appeared before one of these committees, which were created primarily in the 1940s and 1950s, she faced a panel that included a gynecologist, a psychiatrist, and other medical professionals—usually all males—and asked for permission to get an abortion. The physicians demanded that the supplicant "prove" herself "worthy" of the privilege. Only a small number of women even got the chance to plead their case, since few could meet the requirements of providing two letters of diagnosis, one from a private ob-gyn who had examined her and another from a psychiatrist verifying a legitimate reason for the procedure.[72] Sometimes a woman was granted a therapeutic abortion on the condition that she would agree to be sterilized at the same time, but overall very few permissions were granted.[73]

Looking at these rules through an RJ lens makes clear how they functioned to virtually guarantee that women with access to the committees and who might get permission from them were overwhelmingly white, middle- or upper-class, private-paying patients.[74] Low-income women and women of color were shut out by a combination of their race and poverty; plus, even in the mid-twentieth century, many hospitals were segregated, so women of color had no chance even to walk in the door.

During the 1964 outbreak of German measles (also known as rubella), a viral infection that can seriously damage fetuses, 10 to 20 percent of all therapeutic abortions were performed on women who had contracted the virus.[75] Access to therapeutic abortion was difficult, and often impossible, for low-income women of color around the country who had German measles while pregnant.[76] Of the sixty-four women whom the abortion committee at Atlanta's Grady Hospital granted therapeutic abortions, only two were Black, yet African American children were at much greater risk for rubella than white youngsters and comprised almost half the cases.[77]

Abortion rates in this era were three to four times higher for Black women than for white. Plus, between 1951 and 1962 the number of abortion-related deaths of women of color more than doubled, accounting for half of the maternal deaths of Black women, compared to 25 percent for white women. Black women who relied on midwives and other nonphysician practitioners were often harmed by having their abortions in nonsterile, out-of-hospital environments, often performed by individuals who lacked proper medical equipment. People who obtained abortions under these conditions were not likely to get prescriptions for one of the new antibiotics so effective against infections associated with aseptic operations. And, of course, if an abortion under poor conditions went badly, the patient likely lacked the resources to seek medical care; was unlikely to gain entry to many segregated hospitals; and would be unable to pay for legal representation if she were dragged into court to testify against a "criminal" practitioner.[78]

Activist and theorist Frances Beal, cofounder of the Third World Women's Alliance in 1970, called attention to the disproportionate racial harms.[79] But police, public health officials, and politicians generally overlooked the dangers Black women and people of color experienced from illegal abortion. Sensational media coverage of illegal abortions almost always focused on white women as "victims" and ignored all others.[80]

Reproduction was a core site of political struggle during the criminal era, with individuals and communities secretly resisting state efforts to control their sexuality and childbearing. During the Great Depression of the 1930s and in subsequent decades, when these secrets were suspected, police frequently turned a blind eye to skilled illegal practitioners. The authorities believed that these experts were public health assets in the community, people who provided an everyday and necessary, if criminal, service. Declining birth rates among women of all races, classes, and religions suggests that women were using contraception and abortion to prevent fertility throughout the criminal era.[81]

This prompts us to ask why legislators, both then and now, continue to pass restrictive legislation if laws against abortion do not stop people from seeking and obtaining the procedure? The RJ framework suggests an answer: The laws are central to the racialization of reproductive management. We assume that surely various authorities knew women would continue managing their own bodies, so for some antiabortion leaders, the intended purpose of such laws was not to eliminate the practice of abortion. Rather, criminalizing abortion reinforced and normalized the idea that pregnancy and childbearing were legitimate arenas for the police and others to exercise power over women and their bodies, raising the chances that white women's sexuality would be inextricably tied to childbearing.

At the same time, from the 1960s on, the government whittled away at and outright denied social provision for low-income women of color with children. Passing punitive welfare legislation was one significant way that the government deployed racialized reproductive politics to reinforce stratified reproduction.[82] The federal program Aid to Families with Dependent Children (AFDC), though wholly inadequate to sustain poor families, was a vehicle for the government to exert social control over women. Johnnie Tillmon, welfare rights and feminist activist and one of the founders of the National Welfare Rights Organization (1966), captured that aspect of welfare: "The man [the government] runs everything. In ordinary marriage, sex is supposed to be for your husband. On A.F.D.C., you're not supposed to have any sex at all. You give up control of your own body. It's a condition of aid. You may even have to agree to get your tubes tied so you can never have more children just to avoid being off welfare."[83]

Welfare policy stimulated African American women's organizing in that period. Hundreds of local groups coalesced in 1966 to form the National Welfare Rights Organization (NWRO), a movement that was composed mostly of Black women.[84] Here is Tillmon again: "For a lot of middle-class women in this country, Women's Liberation is a matter of concern. For women on welfare, it's a matter of survival." She and other welfare rights activists were not merely seeking financial benefits; they were demanding recognition of their right to parent their children with respect and dignity.

Looking back, we can see that NWRO practiced intersectional reproductive justice politics when they included support for women to control their own reproduction in their agenda. In 1971, NWRO's national convention included a panel on abortion, with Tillmon's important caution: "We know how easily the lobby for birth control can be perverted into a weapon against poor women. The word is choice.

Birth control is a right, not an obligation. A personal decision, not a condition of a welfare check."

Despite the clarity of welfare rights advocates, the mainstream feminist and choice movements did not incorporate childbearing rights into their agendas. As we will see, this was another significant race and class fault line.

THE FIGHT FOR ABORTION LEGALIZATION IN THE 1960S AND 1970S

Experts in various fields have estimated that there were as many as 1.2 million abortions annually before legalization, a number that reveals the ineffectiveness of antiabortion laws in the face of women's determination to control their fertility and their lives.[85] Partly in response to this record of massive lawbreaking, several states liberalized their abortion laws before *Roe*, as polls showed increasing support among the general public for the reform of existing laws and for more comprehensive legalization. At that time abortion was not the defining and divisive political party–driven issue it is today.[86] Many Democrats and Republicans favored legalization. In fact, a Gallup poll measuring attitudes toward abortion during the 1972 presidential campaign showed that more Republicans than Democrats were in favor of leaving the abortion decision to a woman and her doctor.[87] No published polls from that time appeared to have identified respondents according to race. We can, however, surmise that the Gallup organization targeted white voters.

Doctors, public health workers, and other health professionals involved in caring for people who had suffered the effects of illegal abortions, often self-abortion, initiated the first efforts to reform abortion laws in the mid-1950s. Lawyers soon joined the effort. These early advocates did not promote legal reform as a women's- or sexual-rights issue but as *harm reduction*: Legal reform was a way to prevent avoidable deaths. Ironically, that rationale echoed the concerns of the 1821 Connecticut lawmakers who ushered in the first era of abortion criminalization. Two supporters of harm-reduction reform in the 1960s, a lawyer and a former prosecutor, put it this way: "'We are confronted with a sea of heartache and confusion and the tragic wastage. . . . How many women must be sacrificed to needless suffering and death,' they asked, before the laws were reformed?"[88]

In the ten years before *Roe*, a growing consensus among medical and legal professionals emerged in support of reforming the law, with some physicians and lawyers advocating for outright repeal of antiabortion laws. A number of lawmakers and jurists at that time signaled their unease about the impacts of criminalization, pointing out that millions of otherwise law-abiding women were boldly defying the law by having criminal abortions. They feared that if a society tolerated this kind of lawbreaking, day in and day out, across the country, that tolerance would constitute a sharp blow against the rule of law itself. For that reason, many concluded that antiabortion laws should be overturned.

The high-profile 1962 case of Sherri Finkbine, a middle-class, married, white woman, the mother of four children and host of the popular children's television show *Romper Room*, drew widespread attention to the burdens of criminalization, even for a white woman with financial resources. Early in her fifth pregnancy Finkbine took the tranquilizer thalidomide to help her sleep. When she found out that the drug had caused fetal anomalies, she tried to get a therapeutic abortion in Phoenix, Arizona, where she lived. After no hospital would agree to her request, Finkbine flew to Sweden for a legal abortion, which was clearly not an option for people without her economic resources.

Finkbine drew the public's sympathy, a response stimulated, at least in part, by her race and class, as well as by eugenic fears that that she would give birth to an "imperfect" child with severe disabilities. Her widely publicized situation prompted the American Law Institute (ALI) in 1962 to propose a model for abortion law reform that allowed doctors to perform abortions in a range of circumstances, including disability of the fetus, and that protected them from liability.[89] The model influenced the liberalization of the laws in several states before *Roe*.[90]

The AMA, which had led the nineteenth-century campaign for criminalizing abortion, reversed its position in the 1960s and played an important role in the fight for legalization, naming illegal abortion as an urgent public health crisis.[91] Almost every public hospital at that time had a ward devoted to treating people with "botched" abortions, a disproportionate number of whom were women of color suffering from the effects of dangerous self-abortions due to a lack of access to safe procedures. The presence of so many women in hospitals because of unsafe abortions became emblematic for many disparate causes: anti-abortion groups, pro-legalization groups, and people who promoted the idea that all abortionists were butchers, a stereotype with long-term impacts on the lives of physician providers up to the present day.

Some physicians who had directly encountered women in hospital wards suffering from infections and other abortion-related harms were moved to provide abortions themselves and to engage in political action regarding legalization. During the criminal era, some doctors risked imprisonment and loss of their medical licenses when they defied the law and provided safe, albeit illegal, abortions. Sociologist Carole Joffe has called these individuals "doctors of conscience," practitioners who were medically competent, did not exploit their patients, and were primarily motivated not by money but by compassion for the women.[92] Many other practitioners were similarly driven. For example, naturopath Ruth Barnett in Portland, Oregon, performed forty thousand abortions and never lost a patient.[93]

But within the AMA, among its almost entirely white membership, support for abortion-law reform was not universal. Some members who objected to even minimal changes in existing laws exerted pressure within the organization that tempered its support for overhauling state laws.[94] At first, the AMA distanced itself from demands for total legalization and called only for the modest reform of expanding hospital-based therapeutic abortion. Even after the AMA changed its position in 1970 and supported full legalization, it did so cautiously, framing abortion as "good medical practice." It appealed to "the standards of sound clinical judgment" and, like most other reformers at that time, never mentioned women's rights.

In the 1950s, "overpopulation" became a powerful argument for the decriminalization of abortion.[95] Population controllers argued that it was the chief cause of both global and domestic problems, including poverty, hunger, economic stagnation, and environmental destruction. They also claimed that overpopulation caused political instability and led to the rise of communism in "underdeveloped" countries, and that it contributed to political disorder, including the civil rights demonstrations in the United States. Proponents of overpopulation theory were emphatic when they argued that the problem was urgent and the solution required aggressive family planning programs involving both voluntary and coercive sterilization. In the mid-twentieth century, this fear affected abortion law and policy. As we will see, the forerunners of reproductive justice took the lead in opposing this analysis.

Population control groups had initially opposed abortion, which they saw as an ineffective solution to the exploding "population bomb."[96] However, these groups changed their position on abortion after the environmental group the Sierra Club published Paul and Anne Howland Ehrlich's influential 1968 book, *The Population Bomb*, which explicitly promoted legal abortion as a population control strategy. That same year the Ehrlichs founded the organization Zero Population Growth (ZPG) to advocate for abortion legalization; ZPG's name became its slogan and a popular rallying cry for emergent environmental activism.[97]

According to the Ehrlichs and their neo-Malthusian followers, rapid population growth spelled doom for the United States and for the world, especially in "underdeveloped" countries with majority Black and brown populations. Worldwide, both nongovernmental organizations and official government programs pushed contraception.[98] Even though predictions regarding population growth were not, as it turned out, accurate, policymakers and the general public accepted the Ehrlichs' calculations and their racially fraught apocalyptic vision.

With reproductive justice sensitivities, we can see that the populationists had simply updated nineteenth-century eugenicist ideas to make calculations about who should become a mother and who should not, about which children were of value to the nation—and the world—and which were not. The preoccupation with excessive reproduction in the so-called Third World easily bled into a condemnation of the reproductive patterns of people of color in the United States. In 1965, the U.S. Senate Subcommittee on Foreign Aid Expenditures held hearings on the global population problem during which J. Edgar Hoover, director of the FBI, linked overpopulation to the crime rate in inner cities.[99] U.S. Secretary of the Interior Stuart Udall also testified at the hearings, saying, "I think really for the United States to try and lecture or prod other countries around the world on this problem before we have set our own house in order is not proper."[100]

In 1970 the idea of overpopulation continued to gain traction in the U.S. Congress when Senator Robert Packwood (R-OR) explicitly raised the need for legislation to address the "population explosion" and its alleged devastations. He introduced a bill in the Senate in 1970 to allow any doctor to perform an abortion if a woman requested it.[101] Even though the bill did not draw enough support in Congress, organizations opposing population growth such as the Sierra Club used it to help them gain a power base in policy arenas. In 1972, the U.S. government created the Commission on Population Growth and the American Future and charged it with formulating a population policy for the nation. The group's final report recommended liberalization of abortion laws nationwide and support for government-funded abortions.[102]

In the next section we will see that participation by populationist organizations tainted the movement for abortion rights. Population control politics cemented long-standing racial divisions among feminists within the abortion rights struggle.

FEMINISTS AND ABORTION LEGALIZATION

The fight to legalize abortion in the late 1960s became part of a tsunami of activism by communities that faced systemic oppression and who organized powerful social movements for human rights and social justice. Millions of people, many of whom had never been politically active before, were mobilized by these social justice winds.[103] The movements were not politically monolithic; the movement advocating for abortion legalization was no exception. Here, as elsewhere, we pay particular attention to racial and political divisions among abortion rights activists.

The abortion rights movement was rooted in Black feminism, an intellectual and political action project whose perspectives laid the foundation for what became the reproductive justice framework. But another sector of the abortion rights movement, which included people who identified with white, liberal feminism, was rooted in population control and eugenics. These two sources of ideas and values were, inevitably, in conflict and exacerbated divisions of race and class that persist to this day.

In the 1960s and 1970s Black feminists developed a holistic, intersectional, and radical politics of abortion and reproductive rights that challenged the status quo and all of its structured inequalities associated with gender, race, and class. Black feminist analysis was based on centuries of Black women's experiences as targets of coercive reproductive policies that had been imposed to ensure stratified reproduction; policies were sometimes pronatalist, as they were during enslavement, but they were mostly antinatalist.

Carrying that history, Black feminists participated in the movement for abortion rights before and after *Roe*, but not in a single-issue, choice-defined way. The Black feminist reproductive freedom agenda centered the right of all women, regardless of race or class, to *have* children, which was, as they argued, as important to a person's autonomy, safety, and human dignity as abortion rights. According to that view, having children is never *only* an individual decision for a woman of color. It is also an act of political resistance and an affirmation of the rights to reproductive and sexual autonomy and the fundamental right to sustain family and community. In that way, fifty years ago Black feminists were essentially RJ-ing abortion. The approach continues to be relevant precisely because the list of resources necessary for reproductive autonomy is dynamic and evolving.

The mainstream second-wave women's liberation and abortion rights movements did not share this expansive understanding of reproductive freedom. Instead, these movements, comprised largely of white middle-class women, focused on establishing their members' individual right not to have children while ignoring Black activists who were fighting for the right *to have* children and families. We remain grateful to the scholars and activists of color and their allies who retrieved that history.[104]

Here we underscore that combatting population control in general, and fighting for sterilization guidelines designed to protect against abuse in particular, were absolute priorities for women of color in the movement for reproductive freedom. Even though Black feminists' efforts to incorporate those concerns into the mainstream movement were not successful, overall, their persistent focus laid down crucial principles that endured and inspired the next generation.

In those years, the Black feminist perspective that foreshadowed RJ was also mostly absent in the broad movements for racial equality and justice. Although Black women were dedicated participants in the civil rights and Black nationalist movements, the male leadership followed sexist practices and ideas and often did not acknowledge feminists' contributions. Male leaders consistently told women activists to step back and accept a subordinate role. Feminists of color refused, insisting that activists had to address the coercive sterilization of women of color and the lack of access to abortion and contraception as direct attacks on individual bodily autonomy and on the health and survival of their communities. To illustrate the work of these Black feminists, we profile here a few of the activists and organizations in the forefront of this struggle.

Frances Beal, leader of the Black Women's Leadership Caucus in the Student Nonviolent Coordinating Committee (SNCC), a key civil rights organization, was also a founder of the Third World Women's Alliance (TWWA), the Alliance Against Women's Oppression (AAWO), and the Coalition to Fight Infant Mortality. Beal introduced the idea that Black women had to fight against the "double jeopardy" that their gender and race presented, a concept she also linked to social class. Beal championed a broad intersectional politics that placed legal abortion in the larger struggle for liberation. As she explained:

> The lack of the availability of safe birth control methods, the forced sterilization practices and the inability to obtain legal abortions are all symptoms of a decadent society that jeopardizes the health of black women (and thereby the entire black race) in its attempts to control the very life processes of human beings. This repressive control of black women is symptomatic of a society that believes it has the right to bring political factors into the privacy of the bedchamber. The elimination of these horrendous conditions will free black women for full participation in the revolution, and thereafter, in the building of the new society.[105]

The Third World Women's Alliance was active from 1970 to 1980. It was one of the first feminist of color organizations to connect class, race, and gender and to bring this form of feminism to the larger women's liberation, anti-racist, and anti-imperialist movements.[106] The group took stands against economic exploitation and racism and called for an end to all oppression and exploitation. Their specific demands defined education, health care, jobs, and reproductive rights as constituent elements of basic human rights. In her history of TWWA, *We Were There*, activist/scholar Patricia Romney lifted up Beal's leadership as well as the crucial roles she and other women in TWWA played in the second-wave feminist movement. She notes, "Women in the Alliance were third world feminists before the concept of third world feminism had been developed."[107]

In 1973 several Black feminists, including Florynce Kennedy, part of the legal team that successfully sued to liberalize New York State's abortion law before *Roe*, created the National Black Feminist Organization (NBFO). NBFO's purpose, as articulated in the founding statement, was to challenge the assumption that women's liberation movement was the exclusive property of white middle-class women, and that any Black women involved "were 'selling out,' 'dividing the race.'" Kennedy and the other founders were committed to creating a feminism that "address[es] ourselves to the particular and specific needs of the larger, but almost cast-aside half of the Black race in Amerikkka, the Black woman." The statement continued, "We will continue to remind the Black Liberation Movement that there can't be liberation for half the race."[108]

Although NBFO officially ended two years later (1975) over political differences, the organization opened the political space for new groups to emerge. Black feminist, lesbian, socialist activists who had left NBFO founded the Combahee River Collective in 1974. The collective's theory and practice, like those of the TWWA, were based on an intersectional understanding of oppression. Activist, writer, and scholar Keeanga-Yamahtta Taylor explains that the group's ideology was grounded in "the historical reality of Afro-American women's continuous life-and-death struggle for survival and liberation." The collective made clear in its inaugural statement that freedom and liberation for Black women and for all women requires that all systems of oppression—heterosexism, sexism, economic exploitation, and racism—be dismantled.

Combahee Collective members were known as lesbians who were not separatists—feminists who were committed to living apart from men and heterosexual women. The group's members included heterosexism (the system that privileges heterosexuality) as a pillar of Black people's oppression, which distinguished it from other feminist organizations of that time. Their founding statement articulates the group's history and its mission:

Black, other Third World, and working women have been involved in the feminist movement from its start, but both outside reactionary forces and racism and elitism within the movement itself have served to obscure our participation.... Black feminist politics also have an obvious connection to movements for Black liberation, particularly those of the 1960s and 1970s. Many of us were active in those movements (Civil Rights, Black nationalism, the Black Panthers).... It was our experience and disillusionment within these liberation movements, as well as experience on the periphery of the white male left, that led to the need to develop a politics that was anti-racist, unlike those of white women, and anti-sexist, unlike those of Black and white men.[109]

In the 1970s, feminists of color were adamant that making the right to have children a priority was distinct from the position of the male-led Black nationalist groups that opposed contraception and abortion. The Nation of Islam, the Black Panther Party, and initially the Puerto Rican activist group the Young Lords Party (YLP) preached that the duty of women in their communities was to reproduce as often as possible in order to swell the number of Black and brown people fighting against white supremacy and racism.[110] Feminists within these groups and in their own organizations did not dispute the importance of the racial struggle, but they rejected the proposed solution and chastised the men in these organizations for not supporting women's autonomy and power. As Pat Parker, a Black lesbian activist and poet, wrote,

The male left has duped too many women with cries of genocide into believing it is revolutionary to be bound to babies. As to the question of abortion, I am appalled at the presumptions of men. The question is whether we have control of our bodies which in turn means control of our community and its growth.... [W]e know when to have babies or not. And I want no man regardless of color to tell me when and where to bear children.[111]

When Latina feminists in the YLP faced the same male pressures to increase their production of babies, they pushed back hard. YLP women were strong supporters of reproductive rights and created a radical politics, unique at that time, that encompassed both feminism and nationalism, a politics and ideology that emphasized racial identity, pride, and self-determination. The feminists had an important impact: YLP was the first nationalist group of color to incorporate the elements of reproductive rights into its agenda, including access to voluntary birth control, safe and legal abortion, a quality health care system, free day care, and an end to poverty among Puerto Ricans and other people of color. These provisions foreshadowed the program that founders of reproductive justice called for a generation later.[112]

Prioritizing the right to have children, Black, Native American, and Latina women resisted sterilization abuse, consistently pointing out that the fight against it could not be separated from the fight to legalize abortion. Just a year after *Roe*, in 1974 in New York City, Dr. Helen Rodriguez Trías, along with Dr. Raymond Rakow and Maritza Arrastía, founded the Committee to End Sterilization Abuse (CESA), the first activist group in the United States dedicated to publicizing and fighting against coercive sterilizations at public hospitals.[113] CESA demanded that the Department of Health, Education, and Welfare (now the Department of Health and Human Services) issue regulations to prevent coercion. They saw that requiring a waiting period between an initial visit to a doctor to schedule a sterilization and the date of the procedure itself was especially essential. Among other violations, this provision was meant to end the all-too-common "delivery table" sterilizations, during which women were sterilized immediately following labor and delivery. In 1977 the New York Health and Hospitals Corporation met CESA's demands and unanimously approved the new guidelines. CESA became the inspiration for activists who worked in existing organizations and created new ones.

ORGANIZING FOR ABORTION RIGHTS WITHIN THE WOMEN'S HEALTH MOVEMENT

Many women of color who founded and worked in women's reproductive health clinics were part of the women's health movement that developed in the 1960s to address the discrimination and disempowerment women faced in medical settings because of their gender, race, and class.[114] That movement was focused on the lack of affordable and women-centered care for women from marginalized populations, which was particularly absent. Central to this approach was the belief that giving women the ability to get the care they need and deserve was about empowerment. Women's health activists were committed to providing women with the knowledge about their bodies that could empower them in health care settings. The movement challenged the top-down model of service provision and demanded acknowledgment and respect for women's expertise. Activists also challenged the patriarchal medical establishment and created alternative institutions that provided affordable women-centered care. For example, the Federation of Feminist Women's Health Centers taught self-examinations and menstrual extraction before and after *Roe*.

At that time activists also created the Boston Women's Health Book Collective to provide trustworthy information from a feminist perspective and to monitor and advocate for changes in health policy. The Boston group's policy successes included adding better information on medical packaging about the risks of contraceptive pills and other related products. The collective also raised awareness about the potential dangers of estrogen replacement therapy as well as the risk of toxic shock from tampons. Its impact on activism has been enormous. The collective is best known globally for publishing in 1971 the hugely influential book *Our Bodies, Ourselves*. Millions of people globally relied on it for a wealth of updated evidence-based information. In 2011 it was recognized as one of the best nonfiction books since *Time* magazine's founding, and as of 2024, advocates in thirty-four countries have created translations and adaptations.

Beginning in the 1980s, women of color in the women's health and reproductive rights movements formed organizations and engaged in coalitions to advocate specifically for the reproductive rights and health needs of women in their communities. The National Black Women's Health Project (NBWHP), founded in 1984 and now called the Black

Women's Health Imperative, was the catalyst for other groups that emerged at the grassroots and national levels.[115]

Byllye Avery, the visionary founder of NBWHP, began her career in the women's health movement. Before *Roe* in 1973, she referred low-income Black women to an abortion provider in New York, which had already liberalized its abortion laws. After legalization, Avery cofounded the Gainesville Women's Health Clinic to provide pregnancy and abortion services. Through that work she became connected with other Black abortion providers and activists in the Federation of Feminist Women's Health Centers. Avery joined the board of the National Women's Health Network, where she forged close ties with the founders of the Boston Women's Health Book Collective, a largely white organization.[116] Avery credits these groups for supporting her work and the efforts of other women of color.[117]

Some women of color were part of the Jane Collective in Chicago, a group of mostly white women dedicated to putting abortion care and control in women's own hands. With that goal, Jane prefigured the current movement for self-managed abortion. The "Janes" worked in direct violation of the law, initially offering abortion counseling and referrals to abortion services. In a relatively short period the group evolved into an abortion-provision service. Between 1969 and 1973 the volunteers in Jane performed over eleven thousand safe, illegal abortions. Jane charged a relatively small fee and never turned away anyone who did not have funds.[118] After New York State liberalized its laws, Jane referred people with resources to clinics in New York City; Jane's local clients were increasingly low-income women of color who could not travel for an abortion.

WHITE ALLIES IN THE ABORTION RIGHTS MOVEMENT

As we look at this history, we recognize the political diversity within the white-led second-wave feminist movements of the 1960s and 1970s.

Its radical wing was mostly comprised of women who came to reproductive activism after participating in the civil rights and anti–
Vietnam War movements in male-dominated leftist groups, and in
groups of lesbians who were committed to gender freedom but who did
not insist on gender separatism. The predominantly white liberal wing
of the movement dominated the choice movement and did not generally adopt the priorities articulated by women of color, but many white
allies within it did. Here we'll look at two white-led organizations,
inspired by the Committee to End Sterilization Abuse (CESA), which
linked coercive sterilization to the Hyde Amendment and to embed-
ding abortion rights within a larger agenda.

After CESA's success in securing sterilization guidelines for New
York State residents in 1977, the organization's founder, Dr. Helen Rod-
ríguez Trías, and several white feminist activists in New York created
the Committee for Abortion Rights and Against Sterilization Abuse
(CARASA), also in 1977. CARASA drew a direct link between the government's funding of sterilizations and its simultaneous refusal to fund
abortions. CARASA attributed the dramatic rise in coerced sterilizations to the Hyde Amendment's termination of abortion funding for
poor women, which CARASA activists saw as a "de facto governmental
population control policy."[119]

In 1978 activists from CARASA and CESA, along with feminists from
the socialist feminist organization the New American Movement (NAM),
founded the Reproductive Rights National Network (R2N2). In addition
to supporting abortion rights, R2N2 promoted the broad multi-issue
agenda developed by women of color. Its principles of unity included
opposition to sterilization abuse, support for racial and economic justice,
and opposition to homophobia. The organization became a national home
for activists with an expansive reproductive rights agenda.

R2N2 was an umbrella group whose membership included a wide
range of mostly white-led organizations and individual activists from
grassroots feminist groups, national left organizations, and independent
clinics. While its leadership committee was composed primarily of

white activists, members of the Alliance Against Women's Oppression and other Black feminists led a powerful women of color caucus.[120]

CARASA and R2N2 were outliers in the white-led pro-choice movement that dominated abortion advocacy in the late 1970s and beyond. Nonetheless, they played a critical role by creating a place for many white activists who had been alienated by the politics of mainstream organizations. Together, CARASA and R2N2 amplified the importance of responding to sterilization abuse and population control, provided a trenchant critique of the concept of choice, and supported the broad agenda espoused by feminists of color. They joined with CESA to press for sterilization guidelines and to support Puerto Rican and Native American activists' efforts to publicize their own medically coercive experiences and critiques of population control. Ultimately, however, R2N2 was not able to survive its internal racial tensions and could not sustain itself as a multiracial organization. In 1984, after the women of color caucus left the organization, the remaining white leadership disbanded the group.

MAINSTREAM ABORTION RIGHTS ACTIVISM

The mostly white mainstream movement leading the effort to legalize abortion never adopted the project of ending coercive sterilization or took up the other broad priorities and powerful analyses pioneered by women of color. Indeed, many advocates in the pro-choice mainstream accepted the validity of coercive public policies to reduce public expenditures for poor women and their children and to pursue the goals of population control. In retrospect, the inability of white mainstream organizations to comprehend and support Black women's experiences and perspectives was shocking, especially since many white reproductive rights activists had been part of the civil rights movement. But many white feminists in the mainstream movement appear to have been unable to find the connection between the simultaneous fights for the legalization of abortion and for the guidelines against sterilization abuse.

Additionally, at that time most white activists did not have an intersectional perspective that could have helped them understand the conditions required for reproductive freedom across race and class differences.[121] Many white women failed to see that all people who can reproduce need abortion rights *and* access to birth control *and* to the other supports that are necessary for making decisions about having healthy children and families. These ideas had not been the focus of mainstream, white-led reproductive politics, although some white feminists did come to embrace intersectionality in the 1990s following the leadership of women of color.

The mainstream view of reproduction and the activism it gave rise to did not consider the punitive policies that vulnerable people confronted when they wanted to have children or sought an abortion. The pro-choice movement was focused solely on legal abortion as a neoliberal, individual right to choose and did not confront its own limited race- and class-inflected vision, even though their feminism did have a radical thread.[122]

White liberal feminists transformed the fight for legal abortion by demanding that women, not doctors, have control over abortion decisions. This was a critical and radical shift that took the focus away from legislators' and doctors' arguments about criminal abortion as a danger to women's health and lives and stressed instead a woman's right to bodily autonomy. White feminists were clear that both the birth control pill, first available in the United States in 1960, and legal abortion held out the promise of greater sexual freedom for women, and that access to both could enable women to engage in heterosexual intercourse without fear of pregnancy or motherhood.[123]

But the vision of white mainstream feminists was limited. They imagined a better future for themselves and challenged the white male power that still controlled health care, including the fields of gynecology and obstetrics. At the same time, many white activists did not address the economic and racial hierarchies that fueled reproductive inequalities. For example, the 1968 debates about reproductive policies within the National Organization for Women (NOW) show that its white, middle-class members connected abortion rights with demands for equal access to educational and career opportunities, childcare, and other reforms that would enable women to combine motherhood and professional advancement. But that career agenda totally ignored the labor needs of working-class women and women of color, who called for safer work conditions, living-wage paychecks, access to unions, decent medical care and housing, and safe neighborhoods as key to their reproductive freedom.

Crucially, the largest mainstream, white-led, pro-choice advocacy groups failed to support the call for sterilization guidelines. The National Organization for Women did not take a position on the proposed national guidelines, but some local chapters, such as California NOW, strongly opposed the waiting period stipulations. These feminists were only thinking about "individual choice": Why should a woman who had made up her mind to terminate her fertility be forced to wait for the procedure? They saw this as a form of coercion.

The white women who opposed waiting periods overlooked the real coercions faced by so many women of color and poor women in the absence of mandatory waiting periods and consent. Groups that traditionally supported abortion rights, including the National Abortion Rights Action League (NARAL), Planned Parenthood Federation of America (PPFA), Zero Population Growth, and the Association for Voluntary Sterilization (AVS), all opposed the sterilization guidelines in the 1970s.

The leaders of these white-led pro-choice groups were determined to maintain sterilization as a matter of individual choice, just as they defined their right to abortion. Many white middle-class women could never imagine being coerced into sterilization. These women were focused on trying to convince doctors to permit their patients— desirable white reproducers—to terminate their fertility if they chose. They argued that doctors' permissions were unnecessary, paternalistic, and insufferable impediments to their right to choose.[124]

We cannot overemphasize the gap in experiences and perspectives that divided supporters and opponents of the guidelines, nor can we understate the damaging consequences of white activists' determination to define the reproductive rights movement according to their own experiences alone. Failure of the mainstream groups to support *any* guidelines governing sterilization was a powerful marker of the racial divide within the reproductive freedom movement.[125] The potential for cross-racial alliances was thwarted by the failure of the mainstream movement to stand with women of color in support of the guidelines. California sterilization abuse activist Evelyn Martinez remembers, "I think we were a little surprised that the support we just assumed would be there because we were all struggling for women's rights wasn't there. It was like somebody threw cold water in your face. We've all been struggling for certain issues like equal pay." Coalition member Gloria Molina adds:

> They [mainstream women's movement] got more caught up in the remedy we were proposing than in the dilemma of the problem.... They didn't want the thirty-day waiting period or the three-day waiting period.... I've got to tell you that it was a real tough situation, feeling that here we are, feminist women together working on these issues and here's a group of women ... who don't seem to understand our issues and aren't sympathetic.[126]

Activists of color also saw the problems inherent in the *Roe* decision and in other features of reproductive law, policy, and activism. They agreed that the national legalization of abortion was a significant victory, but they were justifiably concerned that *Roe* would not address their communities' needs. After all, *Roe*'s exclusive focus on pregnancy terminations ignored a person's companion right *to have* children and families. Nor did *Roe* acknowledge everyone's need to live in a community with all the resources required to support reproduction, reproductive autonomy, and family building.

Notably, the 1980 Supreme Court decision *Harris v. McRae*, which validated the Hyde Amendment's denial of federal funds to support the abortions of indigent women, relied on the principle that the government had no responsibility for causing or ameliorating the poverty of poor pregnant women. White pro-choice feminists and feminist organizations did not significantly object to this decision in 1980 or over time.

In the years after *Roe*, Black feminists feared that legalizing abortion would be another tool for devaluing and controlling their reproduction, and that it would privilege pregnancy termination and degrade their right to reproduce. After *Roe*, the National Council of Negro Women raised this issue forcefully and frankly, echoing an earlier statement by Johnnie Tillmon:

> The key words are "if she chooses." Bitter experience has taught the black woman that the administration of justice in this country is not color blind.... A young pregnant woman recently arrested for civil rights activities in North Carolina was convicted and told that her punishment would be to have a forced abortion. We must be ever vigilant that what appears on the surface to be a step forward, does not in fact become yet another fetter or method of enslavement.[127]

Roe did not extend abortion rights to all, although many white activists believed that the Supreme Court decision had settled the abortion issue. Activists moved on to other issues, such as championing legal responses to violence against women and supporting LGBTQIA+ rights.[128] Many years later, reflecting on the period after the *Roe* decision, a former member of Jane said, "At that point, we all sort of scattered, moved onto other things. I mean, we really thought, the fact that it was legal meant it wouldn't be as political anymore, that it would fade a lot as any kind of a social issue. But we were wrong. We were wrong."[129] Indeed, they were wrong, and it was a dangerous miscalculation.

POST-*ROE* BACKLASH MOVEMENT

As the broad coalition that had framed abortion rights in the context of women's liberation fragmented and began to devote its activist efforts to other causes, a backlash movement against legal abortion and the gains in civil rights was consolidating its power and initiating a profound swing to the political right.[130] It is particularly important here to understand the role of reproductive politics generally and of abortion specifically in this shift. We note from the outset that the antiabortion movement and the political right were not the same then as they are now. But as we will show, the underlying themes were the same.

The liberalization of state abortion laws that preceded *Roe* had already motivated the Catholic Church to accelerate its antiabortion activism, and it was poised to respond to *Roe*. As we argued in chapter 1, because *Roe* left a huge gap between the formal, constitutional right to abortion and the actual ability of people to obtain one, it opened the door to attacks on abortion access. Almost immediately after *Roe*, opponents began to reinforce that gap with legislative challenges at both the state and federal levels. We reiterate that the inequality of access *was* the essence of the post-*Roe* abortion story.

The first big victory after *Roe* for which the Catholic Church could take significant credit was the Hyde Amendment, the legislative initiative that went into effect in 1977 prohibiting the use of federal funds to pay for abortion except in cases of rape and incest. Hyde's burdens fell most harshly on people who carried intersecting vulnerabilities, those who were poor *and* lived outside of supportive communities *and* suffered various forms of institutionally based racial discrimination. For Henry Hyde, the law's author, the amendment was part of a larger strategy: "I certainly would like to prevent, if I could legally, anybody having an abortion, a rich woman, a middle-class woman, or a poor woman. Unfortunately, the only vehicle available is the ... Medicaid bill."[131] The Hyde Amendment opened the door to a broad array of restrictions on the abortion rights of all women.

Legislative victories boosted the growth of both the right and the antiabortion movements and brought them closer together. Before *Roe*, the Catholic Church and grassroots Catholics had led the opposition to abortion law reform. Many evangelical Christians had also been active in the state-level battles, but they did not join the Republican Party until the 1980 election. During that presidential campaign, Ronald Reagan promised to introduce a Human Life Amendment (HLA) to the Constitution in order to protect "life from the moment of conception." Even though the HLA did not succeed, Reagan's commitment and the stepped-up attacks on abortion by the Republican Party solidified the Christian right's allegiance to the party.[132]

The New Right gained power through the 1970s and '80s by bringing together a range of previously unconnected issues, which were shaped directly and indirectly by racist ideas and attitudes, especially those attacking poor and Black women's reproduction.[133] Opposition to abortion was a catalyst for its growing influence, but it wasn't the only one. New Right leaders tapped into decades-old grassroots movements that opposed a wide range of liberal initiatives, including the Equal Rights Amendment (ERA), bans on school prayer, school integration, the termination of the tax-exempt status of segregated schools, and the liberalization of attitudes about gender and sexuality. These issues were all instrumental in moving Southern evangelicals and Northern white Catholics from the Democratic Party to the Republican Party.[134]

With the inclusion of each of these issues, the right expanded its base. Historians Gillian Frank and Neil Young identify the underlying glue: "racial dog whistles and outright racist ideas, such as linking social safety nets to so-called 'welfare queens,' opposing busing and school integration, or invoking the specter of black crime."[135] Conservative anti-welfare initiatives dovetailed with the antiabortion movements' attacks on tax-funded programs that helped women of color access reproductive health care. In that context, conservatives would certainly have understood Reagan's promise about the HLA (1983) as another dog whistle, a commitment to protect white lives, not all lives. And in case there was any doubt, antiabortion literature and campaigns prominently featured white babies and white pregnant women.

The evangelical leaders in the forefront of this effort included founders of the core institutions on the right: Jerry Falwell of the Moral

Majority; Pat Robertson of the Christian Broadcasting Network; Jim Bakker of the Praise the Lord Club, which had the largest viewing audience of any daily program in the world; and Paul Weyrich of the Heritage Foundation. These organizations were activist and fundraising powerhouses that provided the names and addresses for a massive database that fueled the New Right's emergence as a political force in the late 1970s. Its name signaled a rejection of traditional conservatism and was meant to parallel and provide a dramatic contrast to the unruly, progressive New Left.

By the 1980s the New Right was the most influential wing of the Republican Party, successfully mobilizing its broad constituency to support patriarchy and white supremacy *and* to oppose legalized abortion and LGBTQIA+ rights. Within that constellation of issues, leaders on the right had identified the energizing power of calls to restrict abortion and to control women's sexuality. They took the state-level antiabortion efforts to a new level, creating a national multi-issue movement and attacking LGBTQIA+ rights in their effort to split the Democratic Party, much of which was still Catholic at the time.[136]

In the 1980s, Loretta Ross, who was working at the Center for Democratic Renewal (formerly the National Anti-Klan Network), and Jean Hardisty, researcher and founder of Political Research Associates, were among the first to call attention to the synergies between extremists on the right and in the antiabortion movement.[137] Hardisty emphasized that the New Right was especially effective in bringing together secular and religious conservatives, using the themes of white supremacism, scapegoating Jews and other immigrants, "rabid anti-communism," patriarchy, and anti-unionism.[138] Hardisty saw that the right was successfully mobilizing the discontent and anger of large parts of the population, which she saw as a frightening warning about the potential threat coming from connecting millions of disparate individuals into a political movement.

Hardisty and Ross also called attention to the connections between the pro-violence sectors of the two movements. In the late 1980s and

1990s, a militant wing of the antiabortion movement allied itself with prominent white supremacists and neo-Nazis, including the founder of the White Aryan Resistance (WAR), who condoned the murders of an abortion provider and his escort in Pensacola, Florida.[139] White supremacist leaders made opposition to abortion a rallying point for a white Christian revolution.[140] Some white religious leaders, politicians, and others began supporting small but high-profile antiabortion groups that used right-wing antiabortion language to justify violence against abortion clinics, their staff, and providers.

Joe Scheidler, head of the Pro-Life Action League (PLAL), was the godfather of direct action and violent opposition to abortion. He was in the forefront of organizing a 1984 bombing campaign that targeted twenty-five abortion and reproductive health clinics. Michael Bray, a leading member of the group the Army of God, cited biblical justifications for violence against clinics and advocated maiming and murdering abortion providers.[141] Ultimately, he went to prison for bombing clinics.

In the 1990s, Tim Bishop, leader of the Aryan Nations, bragged about joining the antiabortion movement: "Lots of our people join in. It's part of our Holy War for the pure Aryan race."[142] The group drew on stereotypes of Jewish doctors and cast them as enemies of the white race, claiming that Jewish people were not white and that their abortion practices killed "real" white people.[143] While not all people in the antiabortion movement supported anti-Semitism and other forms of racism, the extremists who championed violence did. Paul Hill, the person who murdered abortion provider Dr. David Gunn and clinic escort James Barrett, wore a Nazi uniform when he demonstrated outside abortion clinics.

Since 1973, opponents of abortion have murdered eleven people in the United States and subjected many others to regular harassment, including constant death threats and attacks on their places of work.[144] Even though the people murdered for their association with abortion have thus far been white, we think that antiabortion vigilante violence sends an especially frightening message to people of color. Can it not help but invoke historical and contemporary cases of brutality and hatred often sanctioned by the police and other authorities? In the months since the *Dobbs* decision, armed demonstrators and extremist groups such as the Ku Klux Klan and the Proud Boys have made themselves highly visible in antiabortion protests.[145] We believe that the overlap between the violent wings of both movements must be perceived by many Black people as a serious racist threat.

Today there are various factions on the right and within the antiabortion movement with overlapping interests and shifting boundaries and who share core tactics and ideology. Throughout its evolution, the right has steadily focused on white electoral and white supremacist ideological power in preparation for the time in the near future when white people will no longer constitute the majority of the U.S. population.[146] Many people who identify with the political right are terrified about this impending demographic racial shift. They combine it with hostility to abortion to justify their racialized focus on women's reproduction as providing the possibility of demographic repair.[147] For example, in Iowa in 2018 a school board candidate posted support for a new antiabortion law: "We need more children of Caucasian descent.... [W]e [whites] are being outnumbered."[148] Indeed, today Iowa has one of the nation's strictest antiabortion laws, presumably considered by some to be an aid to bolstering white reproduction in the state.

The antiabortion movement, and the right in general, continue to expand their power with its most forceful threat, Donald Trump's centrality in American politics. The organizations that comprise the right are on a continuum of extremism and violence. Here we name a few of the dominant segments. Most people and commentators ignore the nuances articulated below, referring to any and all as the right.

The religious right, often used interchangeably with the Christian right, is a broad coalition that came together in the late 1970s, rallying people around promoting traditional values and morality, opposition to the secular state, and opposing efforts to keep religion out of the public arena. Its initial strength came from bringing evangelical Christians and

Roman Catholics together in the Republican Party. Jerry Falwell's Moral Majority was the organizational embodiment of its strength and politics.

The hard right and far right subscribe to particularly virulent forms of racism, ethnic exclusion, religious exclusivity, and a desire for authoritarian rule. Some far-right groups see civil war as inevitable, while others pursue the strategy of capturing control over status quo institutions. White supremacy is central to its project, as is a desire to maintain a patriarchal society.[149] This wing of the right has now taken power in the Republican Party.

The alternative right (alt-right), a term coined in 2008 by Richard Bertrand Spencer, head of a white nationalist think tank, describes a coalition of groups that value "white identity" and the preservation of white "Western civilization." During the first Trump presidency the alt-right grew in numbers and visibility; its highest-profile event was the Unite the Right rally in 2017. While the visible presence of alt-right groups has diminished, their racist and anti-Semitic views endure in the mainstream of the right, and they were in force at the January 6, 2020, insurrection at the Capitol.

CONCLUSION

Where are we in the present, post-*Dobbs* moment? While it is still too soon to fully assess the impact of state bans and restrictions enacted after *Dobbs*, we do know that the abortion access landscape today has radically changed and is still in flux. As of this writing, twenty-four states have banned abortion, and the uneven racial and class impacts of the bans on maternal health and mortality are already clear.[150] A December 2022 report by the Commonwealth Fund, in the first six months after *Dobbs*, showed more limited access to affordable health insurance coverage, worse health outcomes, and lower access to maternity care providers.

In the short term, there has been an increase in births in states with bans, especially those that are also bordered by other states with bans, and the rate of births is higher among young women and women of color. For example, about ten thousand more babies were born in Texas in the year after it introduced its abortion ban. But, for various reasons, some observers predict that the increased births due to lack of abortion access is not a long-term trend. For example, abortion services are being relocated to states without bans. Until *Dobbs*, many people who bore the brunt of abortion restrictions found a way to obtain their abortions even when it meant forgoing other basic needs.[151]

Since *Dobbs* we have seen a significant surge in requests for abortion pills, and access to medication abortion through telehealth is increasing. According to new research, self-managed abortions rose by more than twenty-six thousand in the two years after the Supreme Court overturned *Roe v. Wade*.[152] While a case threatening access to abortion via telemedicine was not successful in 2024, there will be other attacks, with the justices giving opponents of abortion a road map to follow.[153]

Still, the RJ lens leads us to question why opponents of abortion have been so focused on passing laws that restrict abortion access, a strategy that seems to undermine or contradict the population control goals of white supremacy. In contrast to other policies that politicians and policymakers crafted to reduce childbearing by devalued populations, restrictive abortion policies post-*Roe* and post-*Dobbs* seem to force those same people to have children despite their intentions.

The reproductive justice lens helps us clarify this apparent policy contradiction in which elites use strategies that at once appear to be compelling motherhood for some people and compelling restricted reproduction for others.[154] As we have seen across this wide swath of history, politicians, policymakers, and other elites are so focused on increasing white births that they are not concerned with differential burdens across race and class; it is collateral damage they can live with. However, the right did not anticipate the fierce resistance that *Dobbs* unleashed.

Going forward, we will see how the women of color leaders and their allies, including those we introduced in this chapter, continue to lead the resistance to white supremacy. They built a radical movement for reproductive health, rights, and justice outside the mainstream pro-choice movement and laid the foundation for today's movement.[155] The agenda at the center of this movement included opposition to sterilization abuse and population control, as well as resistance to the patriarchal, racist, and for-profit capitalist health care system. Several new organizations were founded by and for women of color, and they developed expansive definitions of reproductive rights and health. They were spurred to action by the attacks on abortion and by the absence of voices within the choice movement prioritizing the perspectives of communities of color. In the next chapter we follow the threads that link past and present sterilization abuse, which is still the most widespread basis for enduring eugenically driven, antinatalist policies in the United States. This form of oppression, and stories of resistance against it, are the focus of chapter 3.

CHAPTER 3

Reprocide

Eugenics and Sterilization Abuse

In RJ-ing abortion, we have shown how white supremacists summoned government officials, physicians, lawyers, academics, and religious authorities to regulate reproduction. In addition, using the reproductive justice lens, we made visible how feminists of color and their allies linked their analyses and their activism to critiques of both abortion restrictions and forced sterilization. They explored the inextricable connection between abortion and sterilization and revealed how these procedures, each and together, are implicated in white supremacy.

In this chapter we again put the spotlight on coercive sterilization in order to provide a vivid account of how coercive reproductive management has been the most enduring method of implementing eugenic and population control policies. This is not a departure from RJ-ing abortion. Indeed, we think of abortion and sterilization as two sides of the same coin. Abortion restrictions aim to compel pregnancy for people who are considered desirable reproducers. Sterilization laws and policies aim to compel childlessness for those deemed undesirable reproducers. Coerced abortion has also been used to accomplish both outcomes. In her reflection on the *Dobbs* decision, legal theorist and activist Michele Goodwin connects *Dobbs* to *Buck v. Bell* (1927), the Supreme Court decision that determined that forced sterilization of certain populations was constitutional and permissible: "On one hand, there is a law that says that certain categories of people shall be prevented from determining their own reproductive destiny, such as to be able to have a child.... On the other hand are lawmakers enacting reproductive laws saying, 'We will force you to have children even when you don't want to,' and there's a lot in common in that."[1] Goodwin is especially concerned with the ways that race, gender, and class considerations have shaped the laws and the definitions of fitness to reproduce. She calls attention to the fact that the denial of bodily integrity and autonomy is the same whether forcing pregnancy or forcing sterility.

The capacity to give birth may be a source of individual, family, and community fulfillment and honor. An individual may feel relief and empowerment after an abortion or sterilization, or they may feel humiliation and rage, depending on whether the procedures are coerced or chosen. And, as Goodwin notes, these outcomes are not experienced randomly. A reproductive justice analysis shows us that the side of the coin that comes up for an individual is very likely determined by their relation to the systems of oppression within white supremacy.

The eugenicist ideas that physicians invoked in their nineteenth-century campaign to criminalize abortion were also useful in justifying the compulsory sterilization laws that state legislatures enacted in the early decades of the twentieth century and beyond. Initially, eugenicists pursued policies that emphasized "positive eugenics" encouraging and incentivizing "desirable reproducers"—healthy, high-achieving white people—to have as many children as they could.[2] When so-called positive eugenics did not yield "enough" "high-quality" babies, eugenicists and their medical and political allies turned to "negative eugenics," policies that targeted "low-quality" reproducers and replaced persuasion and incentives with tactics that aimed to coercively limit the reproduction of these people. State legislators crafted laws mandating sterilization to achieve this goal.[3]

In 1907, Indiana was the first state to enact a law providing for the involuntary sterilization of "confirmed criminals, idiots, rapists, and imbeciles."[4] By the 1920s, more than thirty states had passed such laws The majority of sterilizations were carried out in prisons, hospitals, and homes for the "feebleminded," a term popularized by prominent psychologist and eugenicist Henry Goddard in his 1912 book, *The Kallikaks: A Study in the Heredity of Feeble-Mindedness.* Goddard coined the term to explain what he described as an inherited condition accounting for a "range of mental deficiencies and socially deviant behavior,"[5] such as alcoholism, prostitution, sexual promiscuity, and general criminality. Goddard believed that the condition would be eradicated only by preventing the feebleminded from reproducing.[6] Today, this term is considered obsolete and offensive.

Eugenicists relied on criminal convictions and more informal methods to justify sterilization. They developed what we now know were merely pseudoscientific instruments, such as IQ tests, to certify and separate "imbeciles" from various grades of "superior" white, middle- and upper-class people. Eugenicists and others claiming expertise in the arena of "population quality," including educators and medical professionals, freely marked for sterilization various groups and individuals, typically people of color, poor people, individuals diagnosed with physical and mental disabilities, and women diagnosed as possessing an "excessive interest in sex."[7]

From the 1920s through the 1960s, physicians sterilized between sixty thousand and seventy thousand people under state eugenic sterilization laws.[8] In California, legal and medical authorities classified twenty thousand people, disproportionately Black and Mexican, as mentally ill and oversaw their institutionalization and sterilization.[9] Crucially, the Supreme Court ruled that state eugenic laws were constitutional with its 1927 decision *Buck v. Bell*. Carrie Buck was a young white woman living in foster care in Virginia. Her foster family had found her performance in school and her work as their housekeeper satisfactory. However, when Carrie told her caretakers that she had been raped by a member of her foster family, her foster parents blamed her for the incident and sent Carrie to an institution for the "feebleminded," where she was sterilized "for the health of the patient and the welfare of society." Authorities justified Carrie's fate in part by pointing to her genetic history: Carrie's mother, whom authorities had earlier designated as a prostitute, had been incarcerated and sterilized in the same institution and was also tagged as sexually abnormal and "feebleminded." The same authorities branded Carrie's daughter with the identical diagnosis and reproductive fate.

The case was contrived from the beginning.[10] At the time of Carrie's ordeal, eugenicists in Virginia were looking for a case to test the constitutionality of the Virginia state law mandating eugenic sterilization. Carrie Buck's case fit the bill; it presented what the experts believed was an airtight justification for state-sanctioned eugenic sterilization.[11] Not taking any chances, the Court heard a defense of Carrie Buck that was paid for by the institution where she was held, the very institution that already defined her as feebleminded and tagged her for sterilization. Not surprisingly, the U.S. Supreme Court upheld the law and approved mandated sterilization by an 8–0 vote. In an opinion that was popular in 1927 but today reveals the brutal biases of the time, Justice Oliver Wendell Holmes wrote, "It is better for all the world, if instead of waiting to execute degenerate offspring for crime, or to let them starve for their imbecility, society can prevent those who are manifestly unfit from continuing their kind. Three generations of imbeciles are enough."[12] The *Buck v. Bell* decision legally empowered doctors to claim that by performing a sterilization, even without the patient's knowledge or consent, they were acting in the best interest of both the person and the public good.

Eugenic science clearly embodied racial and gendered stereotypes of the early twentieth century, and in Buck's case it specifically reflected contempt for poor white people. Eugenics reflected mainstream white beliefs.[13] Nationally respected biologists, physicians, journalists, and professors who uncritically accepted its tenets as scientifically sound were among the most powerful and successful promoters of eugenics.[14] Many reform minded progressives, such as birth control advocate Margaret Sanger, supported eugenics and believed that such laws were necessary for "improving society, socially and biologically."[15] Eugenicist ideas embedded in law, policy, and public attitudes had the greatest impact on the lives of individuals who lacked the resources to defend themselves against a charge of so-called biological inferiority.

In the United States, where racism and white supremacy were entrenched in the fabric of the nation's history and culture, eugenics quickly gained currency. Professors taught eugenics in courses at over three hundred colleges and universities, including elite institutions such as Harvard and Stanford. The subject was woven into secondary school curricula in high school textbooks that integrated discussions of social relations, family formation, biology, and national population goals.[16] Eugenics was also lifted up and spread through popular culture. For example, in the 1917 film *The Black Stork*, promoted as a eugenic love story, a doctor persuades a couple to let their child born with vaguely defined "severe" disabilities die for the good of all.[17] Eugenics also became the subject of church sermons, "Fitter Family" exhibits at state fairs, and thousands of articles published in popular magazines and newspapers that touted the benefits of "responsible" reproduction.

EUGENICS: FROM THE UNITED STATES TO NAZI GERMANY

Not long after eugenics became a cultural and political touchstone in the United States, officials in Nazi Germany drew inspiration from its theories and practices. Throughout the 1930s and early 1940s, the Nazi regime adopted eugenics as the justification for forcibly sterilizing 360,000 "undesirable" German citizens, people the Nazis defined as possessing a range of physical and mental disabilities and genetic characteristics that rendered them eugenic failures. The Nazi regime, explicitly pointing to the practices, policies, and laws in the United States, described both the sterilization and outright murder of whole populations as necessary for eradicating biological threats to the purity of the Aryan race.[18]

After World War II, at the Nuremberg trials in 1946–47, during which the United States, France, Great Britain, and the U.S.S.R. together put the Nazi leadership on trial for crimes against peace, war crimes, and crimes against humanity, many Nazis defended themselves and the regime by citing *Buck v. Bell* and arguing that the United States was a leader in efforts to subordinate individual rights to the "common good." The Nazi defense cited widespread willingness in the United States to define certain individuals and groups as "inferior," rationalizing Germany's own use of sterilization and death as tactics for protecting and reshaping the population. While the term *feeblemindedness* is no longer used, legal scholar Jasmine E. Harris notes that *Buck v. Bell* had devastating long-term impacts in the United States and around the world. Harris notes that the decision "remains relevant, not because it embraced involuntary sterilization but, rather, because it used the highest court in the nation and the power of its laws to broadcast a lasting message to those with disfavored bodies and minds that their societal value lies not in their lives, but in their deaths."[19]

Despite the popularity of eugenics in the United States, there were prominent biologists and social scientists at the time who argued that the so-called science of eugenics rested on a collection of naive assumptions and flawed methodologies.[20] Among the critics were Thomas Hunt Morgan, Nobel Prize–winning geneticist at Columbia University, and Princeton embryologist Edwin Grant Conklin. These scientists published papers discrediting eugenicists' claims of scientific validity and exposing the racist and xenophobic prejudices at the core of this work. But before the *Buck v. Bell* decision, their critiques primarily appeared in academic papers and private correspondence. After the decision, and in the face of increasingly nativist debates over immigration, the critics became more vocal and public.

Still, many cultural and politics leaders—and their followers—in the United States continued to accept the basic claims of eugenics. And over succeeding decades, the Supreme Court never completely rejected sterilization as a legitimate state goal. The court's 1942 decision *Skinner v. Oklahoma* asserted that a white man who was incarcerated for stealing a chicken could not be subjected to punishment by sterilization, but this narrow decision did not constitute a denial of government-funded sterilizations in principle. The justices did issue a warning in *Skinner*, no doubt reflecting knowledge of what was happening in Nazi Germany in 1942: "In evil or reckless hands [the government's power to sterilize] can cause races or types which are inimical to the dominant group to wither and disappear."[21]

After World War II, as Americans learned about the Nazis' reliance on eugenics to justify murdering millions of Jews, itinerant Romani (also known as Roma), people with disabilities, and others, eugenics appeared to lose its grip on American society.[22] Most states repealed their compulsory sterilization laws by the 1970s, but we shall see that eugenicist ideas remained deeply entrenched among medical providers, policymakers, and the public at large.[23] State legislators targeted African Americans, Latinos, Native Americans, welfare recipients, people with disabilities, and people who were incarcerated, cutting funding for programs supporting prenatal care, capping welfare benefits based on family size, subjecting other maternal and child welfare programs to severe budget cuts or elimination, revoking food assistance, and allowing sterilization as a tactic to curtail the reproduction of certain populations.[24] All of these policy initiatives aimed to tailor the composition of the population in the United States by race and class.

Outcries against eugenics and sterilization abuse in the past are a critical part of the historical record. They are also cautionary tales that should alert us to be vigilant about contemporary efforts to "improve" society through manipulating reproduction. We pay close attention to Goodwin's warning that after *Dobbs*, coercive abortion and sterilization are not only possible but likely in coming years.

Many people have raised ongoing concerns about the newer frontiers of reproductive engineering, asking what prejudices are involved when prenatal genetic testing and laboratory fertilization programs name certain characteristics as undesirable, and typically offer abortion as the solution? And who decides if certain IQ scores, criminality, manic depression, unpopular sexual orientations, and other characteristics that some physicians and others may label as disabilities should be eliminated?

In April 2023 the International Coalition to Stop Designer Babies called on the UN to oppose human genetic modification (HGM) because "designing children's genes runs counter to accepted basic visions of diversity and the inclusion and equality of all vulnerable individuals and minority groups. Rather than competitively genetically 'enhancing' children, we want to encourage a world that celebrates and accepts all individuals and groups of people and that does not rely on oppressive and biological determinist prejudices about what constitutes a 'better' human being. Allowing HGM would exacerbate existing social inequalities. It would be an act of scientific irresponsibility and, in a time of rising neo-fascism, of political irresponsibility as well."[25]

FROM EUGENICS TO POPULATION CONTROL

The idea at the heart of eugenics, that limiting reproduction within targeted communities would solve many of society's problems, fueled a mid-twentieth-century ideology and enabling policies, which together are known as *population control*. The proponents of population control made some efforts to distance themselves from the stain of American and Nazi eugenics, but the concept clearly drew on the same racist assumptions.[26] Although some demographers in the United States and Europe argued for reducing the population overall, the chief concern among most academics and experts working in the population domain was the *race and class* composition of the world's population. Typically, population-control demographers characterized white population growth in the developed countries of the Global North in positive terms. They defined this growth as a route to bolster the proportion of whites in these nations, a ratio that in the mid-twentieth century was forecast to decline relative to other groups. White population growth, they argued, was also the key to the increased geopolitical strength of "advanced" countries, as well as crucial for building a growing consumer base for capitalist economies. The same demographers perceived high fertility rates in Asia, Africa, and Latin America as threatening global disaster, both environmentally and politically.[27]

This vision of the looming global catastrophes caused by "overpopulation" was featured in a popular and influential book by Paul and Anne

Howland Ehrlich, *The Population Bomb*, published in 1968 at the height of the public fixation on the "population explosion." Its authors wrote, "In the 1970's the world will undergo famines—hundreds of millions of people will starve to death."[28] Such scenarios were typical of the apocalyptic predictions that demographers, biologists, and politicians offered to the American public. They were modern applications of the visions of nineteenth-century British economist Thomas Malthus, who had issued the dire warning that unless curbed, the human population would double every twenty-five years. Malthus's prediction turned out to be completely inaccurate. While world population did double approximately every twenty-three years in the first half of the nineteenth century, in the twenty-first century the pace slowed, doubling every sixty-one years. For the remainder of this century, the rate of growth is predicted to slow even further, peaking by 2100.[29]

In the Cold War era, from approximately 1947 to 1991, organizations such as the Population Council, the International Planned Parenthood Federation, and the United Nations Fund for Family Planning Activities argued that high birth rates among poor minority and ethnic populations throughout the world constituted urgent threats to the political stability of white-led, non-communist societies. "Population experts" in these organizations predicted that, without effective population control, the United States and other countries would experience a surge of anti-capitalist fervor and burgeoning global communist influence. U.S. policymakers were persuaded by these urgent warnings to tie foreign aid in the developing world to the acceptance of aggressive family planning programs. Aiming to achieve population declines among poor people around the globe as the only way to reduce poverty and save the planet, U.S. organizations relied on economic incentives and direct coercion. Sterilization was the preferred method in most cases. But in China, for example, coercing abortion was a key tactic of the country's one-child policy.

As we saw in chapter 2, population policy and practices in the United States mirrored the country's strategies in the international arena. At home, population control tactics involved extensive use of sterilization and other methods that took personal bodily and reproductive control away from targeted groups of people, such as girls and women of color. For example, in the 1990s, long-acting reversible contraceptives (LARCs) became an attractive option to medical personnel because this contraceptive method was inserted and removed—controlled—by medical personnel, not by the individual user. Populationists also promoted programs in which medical staff had the right to force sterilization, LARCs, and abortions on vulnerable people.[30]

FEMINISTS OF COLOR LEAD THE RESISTANCE TO STERILIZATION ABUSE

In chapter 5 we will see that the global women's health movement, especially in the Global South, focused its opposition to population control on the rejection of sterilization abuse and other coercive contraception methods, including Norplant and forced abortion. Here we discuss the U.S. context in the 1960s and 1970s, when activists engaged in individual and collective actions against sterilization abuse. Through grassroots community organizing, lobbying, and several high-profile lawsuits, advocates publicly exposed the widespread and routine use of reproductive coercion against African Americans, Native Americans, and Latinas.[31] With these efforts, activists successfully stopped some of the most egregious violations against targeted populations.

During the 1960s and 1970s, many doctors regularly performed medically unnecessary hysterectomies without informing the patients that the operation would effectively sterilize them.[32] Some nurses and social workers routinely ignored requirements to obtain patients' consent when they sought fertility services. Sometimes medical professionals told people they would lose public assistance, such as Aid to Families with Dependent Children, if they did not agree to sterilization while undergoing childbirth or another medical event.[33] In the South, physicians who were paid by the state disproportionately sterilized Black women living in prisons and mental hospitals.[34] Between 1970 and 1980, doctors performed between 100,000 and 150,000 such sterilizations using public funds. More than half of the women sterilized were Black.[35] These operations were so common that Black women referred to medically unnecessary sterilizations (via hysterectomy) as the "Mississippi appendectomy," highlighting both the operation's prevalence in a region that was very dangerous for Black women and the fact that most of the operations were performed deceptively.[36]

Authorities did not hide their punitive and racist intentions.[37] In her pathbreaking 1981 book *Women, Race, and Class*, Black activist and intellectual Angela Davis names Dr. Clovis Pierce in South Carolina, who, in the 1970s, was unabashed in his determination to sterilize mothers on Medicaid with two or more children: "According to a nurse in his office, Dr. Pierce insisted that pregnant welfare women 'will have to submit [*sic*] to voluntary sterilization' if they wanted him to deliver their babies.... He said that he was '... tired of people running around and having babies and paying for them with my taxes.'"[38] Pierce warned one woman, "Listen here, young lady.... If you don't want this sterilization, find another doctor."[39] Dr. Pierce received some $60,000 in taxpayers' money—over $400,000 today—for the sterilizations he performed. A group of citizens called the Silent Majority supported his position. They circulated a petition that read, "We believe it is unfair to the taxpayers and the children of the welfare recipients for their parents to continue having children. We feel the children of welfare families would be better cared for if the number of the family were limited.... [I]n such cases, sterilization should take place."[40]

These practices and the racist attitudes supporting them were not confined to the South. In a 1972 national survey, 94 percent of ob-gyn respondents said they favored withholding welfare benefits from poor women who had more than three children and refused sterilization.[41] Many physicians were particularly willing to sterilize women of color. This was true all over the country. Here are several particularly striking examples: Ninety-five percent of women sterilized in New York

City in 1995 were Puerto Rican, and physicians employed by the federally funded Indian Health Service sterilized 25 percent of Native
American women living on reservations, mostly via medically unnecessary hysterectomies. Evidence exists showing that doctors lied to the
women, telling them that the operations were necessary due to their
individual health conditions. On some reservations, the rate of sterilization was as high as 40 percent.[42]

In addition, pursuing population control goals, the federal Department of Health, Education, and Welfare funded sterilizations in Puerto
Rico; by the end of the 1960s, 35 percent of women, two-thirds in their
twenties, had been sterilized.[43] While most of the sterilizations were not
overtly coercive, activists caution that the procedures were absolutely
not expressions of reproductive choices. Sometimes women opted for
sterilization because they were given incorrect information, such as that
the effects of the operation—infertility—would not be permanent.
Also, the sterilized women of Puerto Rico were facing "choices" that
were constrained by poverty and lack of alternatives. Indeed, during the
peak years of sterilization in Puerto Rico, abortion was illegal.[44]

Beginning in the 1960s, many women of color activists and civil
rights organizations organized to stop coerced sterilizations, calling out
social welfare agencies, hospitals, and physicians who performed the
operations without consent. Fannie Lou Hamer, cofounder of the Mississippi Freedom Democratic Party, was the first civil rights leader to
speak publicly about the abuse. At a 1964 conference on racism, she
talked about her own hysterectomy performed by a white doctor: "The
wrongs and the sickness of this country have been swept under the rug,
but I've come [to] tell it like it is."[45] She connected her experience to
legislative threats:

> One of the other things that happened in Sunflower County, the North
> Sunflower County Hospital, I would say about six out of the ten Negro
> women that go to the hospital are sterilized with the tubes tied. They are
> getting up a law that said if a woman has an illegitimate baby and then a
> second one, they could draw time for six months or a five-hundred-dollar

fine. What they didn't tell is that they are already doing these things, not only to single women but to married women.[46]

Hamer was referring to the proposed state bill HB 180, which would charge an unmarried person receiving public assistance, also known as aid to dependent children or "welfare," with a felony if they gave birth to an additional child. The recommended penalty was a prison sentence of one to three years, or, instead of incarceration, the person could "choose" sterilization.[47] In 1964, the Student Nonviolent Coordinating Committee (SNCC) circulated a pamphlet entitled "Genocide in Mississippi," which spelled out the racism embedded in the proposed legislation:

> HB 180 is an attempt to reduce the number of Negroes in Mississippi either by destroying their capacity to reproduce, or by driving them from the state. That it is, in short, a program of officially supported and sanctioned genocide. On the surface the legislation (HB 180) is designed to discourage illegitimacy.... However, HB 180 is clearly something quite different.... [T]he arguments of the legislators who supported the bill indicate that the intent of the measure is to eliminate the population of Negroes from Mississippi.[48]

In 1965 alone, an estimated sixty Black women were sterilized immediately after giving birth at the same hospital in Sunflower County where Hamer had been violated.[49] Hamer continued her advocacy, denouncing involuntary sterilization and linking the practice to police brutality and other manifestations of state-sanctioned violence.

As we learned in chapter 2, women of color also led the fight against coercive sterilization in the 1970s, inside and outside the abortion rights movement. Three lawsuits elevated the visibility of these abuses and were especially instrumental in changing sterilization practices. In 1973, Women of All Red Nations (WARN) brought the first legal challenge, on behalf of Norma Jean Serena, a woman of Muscogee (Creek) and Shawnee ancestry, one of the thousands of Native women sterilized by Indian Health Service doctors.[50] Native American activists saw sterilization as a symptom of the fundamental harms of colonization:

Terminating a Native American woman's fertility diminished her personal and social power. Moreover, sterilization, like the forcible removal of Native children to white boarding schools in the nineteenth and twentieth centuries, was a path to destroying Native culture.

Serena's lawsuit charged both reproductive and cultural genocide. She had been sterilized without having given consent, and her two children were taken from her.[51] The outcome of her case was mixed. A federal district court in Pittsburgh, Pennsylvania, ruled that the social workers who took Serena's children had misrepresented the facts of the case and the purpose of their own actions. The court awarded Serena $17,000 in damages (about $110,000 today) and, after three years, it returned the children to her custody, but only when she threatened further legal action. Serena's sterilization claim was not successful. The court determined that she had consented to the operation, despite the fact that she testified to having no recollection of doing so, and the consent form was dated the day *after* her surgery.[52]

Nevertheless, advocates and Serena's lawyer believed the case was a fundamental victory for several reasons. It drew public attention to the epidemic number of Native American sterilizations and continuing instances of child removal from Native American families. It also exposed the history of cruelty and violence in Native American boarding schools and the ongoing effort to destroy Native families and culture. For the first time, social workers were held accountable for their part in these practices. The case also inspired Constance Redbird Pinkerton Uri, a Choctaw-Cherokee physician and law student, to compile information about sterilization abuse of Native women, which she used to pressure the Government Accounting Office (GAO) to conduct an investigation. The GAO reviewed the Indian Health Service records from 1973 to 1976, and the resulting report substantiated the claims of widespread coercion, leading to more activism and legal actions.[53]

In Alabama in 1973, the same year as the Supreme Court's *Roe v. Wade* decision, the Southern Poverty Law Center filed a lawsuit, *Relf v. Weinberger*, on behalf of two young sisters. While *Relf* received much less attention than *Roe*, the litigation made its way through several levels of courts and eventually exposed the full scope of sterilization abuse targeting African Americans and raised public awareness about the role of the government in coercive sterilization. As a result, the government was pressured to issue new federal guidelines regulating sterilization. The case involved Minnie Lee Relf, age twelve, and her sister, Mary Alice, age fourteen.[54] Public officials had declared both girls "mentally unfit" and marked them for sterilizations without their parents' understanding or substantive consent.[55] Health workers pressured the girls' mother, who could not read or write, to give her "consent" by putting an "X" on the medical permission form.

Gerhard Gesell, judge of the U.S. District Court for the District of Columbia, concluded in 1974 that federally assisted family planning sterilizations were only permitted with the "voluntary, knowing, and uncoerced consent of individuals competent to give their consent."[56] On the basis of his ruling in the Relf sisters' case, Gesell ordered the Department of Health, Education, and Welfare to draft new guidelines. The ruling also prohibited the practice of threatening women on welfare with the loss of benefits if they refused sterilization, and it established standards for informed consent.[57]

But there was no justice for the Relf sisters, who never received *any* compensation for the brutal termination of their fertility, a fundamental violation of the girls' human rights, or for their suffering.[58] In 2020 journalist Linda Villarosa interviewed the sisters and poignantly reported that each sister still slept with a brown doll, "shadows of the children stolen from them." Minnie Lee explained her loss: "Every time I see somebody like my cousin or my niece Debbie with their child, I think about it. Seeing these little pretty babies, I wish that was me."[59]

Grassroots activism generated significant support for these lawsuits and brought increased pressure for change. In chapter 2 we introduced CESA, the Committee to End Sterilization Abuse, the New York–based organization that succeeded in inspiring grassroots activism in other states. In California, the Chicano Rights Project of the Mexican

American Legal Defense Fund sued the Los Angeles County Medical Center in 1978 on behalf of ten Chicano women, demanding the end to involuntary sterilizations of undocumented Mexican women.[60] In support of this lawsuit, *Madrigal v. Quilligan*, a coalition of community-based women's groups and leftist organizations organized demonstrations to raise awareness and raised funds to pay for the lawsuit. Like the New York groups, California activists connected population control in the Third World to sterilization abuse in the United States and supported the fight for abortion rights.

Madrigal v. Quilligan accused a group of doctors of sterilizing women without their consent during procedures that were neither requested by the women nor medically necessary.[61] As the attorney representing the ten women put it, "Throughout the entire period the doctors were not using medical reasons to perform these sterilizations, but were using social reasons."[62] In other words, the doctors performed the procedures based on their own racist and classist judgments that poor women of color and society overall would be better off if their patients had fewer children.[63] The plaintiffs demanded financial compensation, and, going forward, counseling, as well as the adoption of consent forms translated into Spanish at all federally funded hospitals.

In court, the women recounted how they had been coerced. Some had been forced to sign consent forms during labor; others were never asked for consent nor informed in any way about what doctors were doing to them. Most of the women said that they had not understood that the tubal ligation operation would permanently end their child-bearing capacity. Despite their powerful testimonies and direct corroboration from a whistle-blower physician and other staff, the judge, Jesse W. Curtis, ruled against the women. He decided that the doctors were acting in "good faith" because they legitimately believed the women had understood the operation and had given their consent.

Judge Curtis expressed sympathy for the women's "severe physical and emotional stress" as a result of the sterilizations, but he did not think that the doctors were at fault. Instead, he saw a culture clash between the Mexican women's desire for large families and the pervasive belief in the United States and held by many hospital personnel that if the fertility of Mexican-origin women was not controlled, their excessive children would place a burden on society.[64] The judge revealed that his own thinking was rooted in population control ideology when he said, "I do not think it is surprising that you might find a doctor who believes that people who are inclined to have big families shouldn't."[65] Historian Elena Gutiérrez associated the judge's reasoning with widespread white fears about the number of Latino immigrants coming to the United States and the so-called "Latinization of California." We also see this as an earlier expression of white nationalists' Great Replacement conspiracy theory in the 2020s.[66]

Although the *Madrigal* plaintiffs did not receive justice, the case had important consequences. It raised awareness among Chicana women about their role in making change. As Georgina Torres-Rizk, a lawyer for the *Madrigal* plaintiffs, said, "It is minority women who must take it upon themselves to ensure that their right to determine whether or not to bear children be preserved in order to halt the genocidal practices which are occurring the name of 'family planning' in this country."[67]

Together these efforts led to the adoption in 1979 of new federal guidelines incorporating several of the activists' demands: a mandated thirty-day waiting period between a sterilization request and the operation; prohibition of common practices such as a threatened loss of government benefits if the person did not agree to be sterilized; available and accessible counseling; and the requirement that all services and information be provided in the patient's spoken language.

The new guidelines marked progress, but activists knew more was needed. The guidelines lacked provisions for oversight and accountability and did not address in any way the need to dismantle eugenicist and population-control ideologies that fueled sterilization abuse. Without effective attention to these matters, coercive sterilizations were likely to continue. Going forward, as we will see, activists were right to be concerned.

DISABILITY JUSTICE AND REPRODUCTIVE JUSTICE

In the early 2000s, leaders who were working on disability issues intentionally moved away from the disability rights framing and moved to a justice perspective, signaling their intersectional approach centering people with disabilities.[68] In 1990, activists in South Africa introduced the idea "nothing about us without us," which captured the fight for visibility and power. This motto and its claim became a central tenet of disability rights and now of the disability justice movement. According to Sins Invalid, a performance collective that has played a critical role in the U.S. movement's evolution, disability justice "marks a point of departure rather than a destination. It is an invitation to those of us working on disability issues, to continue to support one another to find a language as powerful and expansive as our movement's vision."[69]

The shift from disability rights to disability justice reflects the same change we have seen in the area of reproduction. Both movements use the human rights framework and are committed to making opposition to sterilization abuse a central concern. Still, forging alliances between the two movements has been a challenge. As we have seen, in the 1950s and '60s, white-led reproductive rights and choice organizations such as Planned Parenthood drew on widespread anti-disability eugenics and population control ideas to garner support for birth control and abortion rights.

Fears about giving birth to a child with severe disabilities were also stoked by two high-profile events in the abortion sphere that were used to garner support for legalizing pregnancy termination. In 1962 Arizona television personality Sherri Finkbine sought an abortion when she learned that thalidomide, which she had taken to control nausea and deal with insomnia during pregnancy, had caused birth defects. Even though her doctor recommended Finkbine have an abortion, the Phoenix hospital with which the doctor was affiliated refused to allow it. Ultimately, Finkbine went to Sweden, where she was able to have the procedure. Her case garnered enormous public attention for a number of reasons, including that a high percentage of Americans did not believe that this white, middle-class woman should be forced to have a less-than-perfect baby.

Also at that time, between 1962 and 1965, a global pandemic of rubella, or German measles, broke out, a dangerous event for pregnant women since a pregnant woman's exposure to this illness can cause serious birth defects.[70] In fact, during the pandemic thousands of children whose mothers were exposed to rubella during pregnancy were born with serious heart and vision problems. Several thousand of other rubella-affected pregnant women did not give birth, having had miscarriages during their pregnancies or having found someone to terminate their pregnancy, despite the illegality of abortion at that time.[71] Again, public opinion largely supported the abortion option for these women.

Although at the time the technology did not exist to screen pregnant people to detect the effects of thalidomide or German measles, knowledge of the possibilities of fetal damage intensified fears about giving birth to "damaged" children and led to increased support for prenatal testing for genetic anomalies such as Down syndrome.[72] Although a pregnant person could make their own decision after receiving a diagnosis, social and medical pressure favored the assumption that they would have an abortion. Abortion rights advocates countered claims about fetal rights by emphasizing the impacts of fetal deformity on the disabled person and their family. For example, Lawrence Lader, the founder of the National Association for the Repeal of Abortion Laws (NARAL), advised abortion rights advocates who were debating abortion before *Roe* to "keep hammering on … the deformed and unwanted infant, … the horror of bringing a deformed child into the world with half a head, no arms, etc."[73]

After *Roe* had established a constitutional right to abortion, pro-choice groups moved away from disability-based justifications for abortion, but opponents of abortion exploited the issue. In the late 1970s they made the fetus ("unborn child") the center of their concerns. Technology provided a window into the womb that antiabortion forces used to generate empathy for the fetus, stake out new moral high ground, and mount new legislative attacks on abortion.[74] Since the early 2000s the antiabortion movement has pursued state and federal selective abortion bans—laws banning abortion on the basis of race, gender, or disability. Supportive politicians claimed that the laws were meant to protect people with disabilities, but, their critics note, the laws do nothing to correct misinformation surrounding disability or to provide the resources and support necessary to parent a child with disabilities.

Many on the pro-choice side have also been vulnerable to criticism. In 2011 scholar-activists Sujatha Jesudason and Julia Epstein acknowledged that many abortion rights supporters "portray disability as a tragic state that justifies abortion—even for wanted pregnancies."[75] Echoing their concern, activist Erin Matson pointed to a tweet from Richard Dawkins, British evolutionary scientist, a high-profile proponent of atheism, and a self-described pro-choice advocate, "For what it's worth, my own choice would be to abort the Down fetus and, assuming you want a baby at all, try again. Given a free choice of having an early abortion or deliberately bringing a Down child into the world, I think the moral and sensible choice would be to abort." When he clarified the tweet in a subsequent 2014 blog post, he emphasized that it would certainly be the pregnant person's decision, but he doubled down on disability: "When you have the choice to abort it early in the pregnancy, the decision to give birth to a Down's baby might actually be immoral from the point of view of the child's own welfare."[76]

Disability rights activist Imani Barbarin is concerned that the same attitudes prevail today. In her 2023 reflection on the *Dobbs* decision, she wrote that advocating for abortion in order to avoid having a child with disabilities continues to be a barrier to joint action between abortion rights and disability rights advocates: "Abortion advocates need to stop saying that the main reason to want abortion is to not have a disabled child.... There's nothing like entering a space and the only reason they want access to this medical procedure is to not have somebody like you in their life. This is turning away tons of pro-abortion advocates who have disabilities."[77]

The antiabortion movement is hypocritical when it claims that only its adherents value *all* lives while the abortion rights side is rife with eugenicists.[78] Disability justice scholar Robyn Powell exposed the flaws in their claim. "Opponents of abortion focus only on the issue of fetal disability and ignore the rights and experiences of the pregnant person with a disability."[79] According to Powell, the restrictions abortion foes pursue cause the greatest harm to people with disabilities, who tend to have a harder time accessing reproductive health care, have higher rates of unplanned pregnancies, and are at greater risk of dying during pregnancy.

The expansive reproductive justice lens on abortion suggests strategies to bridge these divides. Abortion rights supporters must first learn about and take responsibility for past discrimination. Only then can they make a sincere commitment to centering disability justice based on clarity about the underlying interconnections between disability justice and reproductive justice, ideas and movements with common expansive goals.

Like other vulnerable people, those living with disabilities have borne and continue to experience the full force of coerced sterilization and other attacks on bodily autonomy. State eugenic laws enacted in the early twentieth century that mandated sterilization were, in fact, primarily aimed at people with disabilities. And those violations did not end when state legislatures, chastened by association with Nazi eugenics, nullified the laws after World War II. Instead, in the 1970s and 1980s legislators passed new laws that permitted the sterilization of people with disabilities without their consent.

A 2022 report by the National Women's Law Center (NWLC) found that as of 2019, laws in thirty-one states plus Washington, DC, allow this practice.[80] People in favor of laws permitting sterilization without consent deny that these laws are intended to prevent births of children with disabilities or to take away parenting options from people with disabilities. Rather, they claim that the laws are meant to help people with disabilities. Their plea appeals to many guardians or parents of people with a disability who genuinely believe that sterilization is the best way to protect a person incapable of protecting themself from pregnancy and parenthood. The laws allow for a judge to decide if a person is capable of giving consent to terminate their fertility. If the judge determines that the person in question is not capable, then that judge or a guardian has the power to make the decision for them.

Most disability justice advocates unconditionally reject these laws and argue that reproductive justice advocates should as well. According to the NWLC report, these laws promote "forced sterilization, even if the parents or the guardian think it is for the disabled person's own good."[81] The point is that the laws provide for overt denials of an individual's bodily autonomy. Activists also point to a lack of transparency: Judicial decisions are usually made in secret, and no records exist tracking the race or class characteristics of the disabled people who are sterilized under these laws. And court cases that are on the record show that many such decisions incorporate the same prejudices displayed in the earlier era, such as concerns about preventing "feeblemindedness," with the same differential gender, race, and class impacts.[82] Women with intellectual and developmental disabilities are sterilized more often than women without disabilities, and at much younger ages. Black women with disabilities are more likely to be sterilized than their white counterparts.[83] In 2022, U.S. Congress representative Ayanna Presley (D-MA) noted significant racial disparities involving disability and state violence, claiming, "Nearly half of the individuals murdered by police in the US have a disability, and Black girls with disabilities are criminalized in US schools at four times the rate of their white peers, beginning as early as preschool."[84]

While the NWLC report acknowledged that in some sterilization cases people are actually making their own decisions, it also raised important questions about the meaning of and conditions for "choice" in this context. The authors of the report note that some people lack the economic resources necessary to support having a child; are unable to access other forms of contraception or an abortion; do not have access to adequate sex education; and may face external pressures to "choose" sterilization. Those who have children may be in danger of losing custody simply because of the way that court-related and other authorities understand their disability. As we have seen, policies governing sterilization often depend on stereotypes that define and portray disabled people as incapable of making their own decisions regarding reproduction, parenting, and sexuality.[85]

Disability justice advocates worry that the *Dobbs* decision and abortion bans are likely to intensify discrimination against people with disabilities who have traditionally been blocked or significantly constrained from obtaining reproductive health care and achieving bodily autonomy. *Dobbs* precludes options for people who take medications for their disability. For example, the anti-seizure medicine Depakote may be harmful to a fetus. Under a six-week abortion ban, a person who takes the drug is unlikely to know they are pregnant.[86] Once a pregnancy is confirmed, options are already foreclosed: Abortion is no longer possible. At that point, it is too late to protect both the person and their pregnancy by slowly stopping the drug.[87]

Disability justice activists have offered prescriptions for bringing reproductive justice and disability justice advocates together. Scholar-activist Alison Kafer has made a strong case for what she calls a "crip, disability approach," an intersectional framework for understanding accessibility. Post-*Dobbs*, she crafted an accessibility statement for her classes that includes information about gender-affirming care, pregnancy and abortion, and immigration. She explains, "Trans and/or undocumented students cannot devote their full attention to their studies if they are concerned about being captured by the state or if their capacities are being challenged. The same is true for students grappling with an unwanted pregnancy, or unable to find reliable birth control, or in need of prenatal care."[88]

Ericka Ayodele Dixon, an African American disability and transgender justice advocate, has set out necessary conditions for future alliances between reproductive justice and disability justice: "First and foremost, we must listen to and follow the lead of our BIPOC [Black, Indigenous, and People of Color] disabled community, the members of which have been pushing back against eugenic policies since time immemorial."[89] Dixon calls on reproductive justice activists to see beyond abortion and recognize that the real issue is the right to self-determination. She urges us to ask what self-determination means today as the escalation of eugenic attacks against trans and disabled people festers and expands. Since *Dobbs*, pregnant people are opting for early screenings to make their decisions about whether to continue a pregnancy even though the tests are performed too early to actually detect much about the health of the fetus.[90]

Based on principles similar to Dixon's, Robyn Powell calls for a "disability reproductive justice" agenda to oppose the multiple threats that people with disabilities face to the right to parenthood, sexuality, and pregnancy.[91] Both Dixon and Powell are optimistic about the potential for solidarity between the disability and reproductive justice movements, in part because both are deeply committed to bodily autonomy and self-determination.

STERILIZATION ABUSE OF TRANSGENDER PEOPLE

An RJ analysis requires us to examine the reproductive oppression of trans people as part of abortion advocacy. Medical professionals and others have historically (and still today) targeted people who are LGBTQIA+, especially those who are transgender, for mandatory sterilization and other forms of reproductive oppression. In chapter 5 we will look at this form of oppression internationally. Here we focus on the United States, where attacks on trans rights and the rights of LGBTQIA+ people in general, along with opposition to abortion rights, have been at the center of the right's social and political agenda for decades, and have escalated since *Dobbs*.

As we saw in chapter 2, Black lesbian feminists and their allies had an intersectional understanding of feminist and pro-choice politics which put LGBTQIA+ issues into the forefront of oppression. While today the linkages are accepted in both movements, at that time they were not. In 2003, following the U.S. Supreme Court decision in *Lawrence v. Texas*, which recognized the right to privacy for people who identify as LGBTQIA+, activists at the LGBT Community Center in New York published "Causes in Common," a statement connecting LGBTQIA+ and reproductive justice issues: "Reproduction is a choice that evolves out of sexuality, not an unavoidable consequence of sexuality. Individual human autonomy in the conduct of our sexual lives is integral to our liberty. The pro-choice and LGBT liberation movements refer most fundamentally to the freedom to manage the affairs of our bodies without the interference of government."[92]

Even though opinion polls show that the *Dobbs* decision overturning *Roe* has been extremely unpopular among people across the country, opponents of abortion are stepping up their efforts to deny bodily autonomy to everyone. Since *Dobbs*, legislatures and governors in Republican-controlled states are ever more intent on pursuing anti-trans agendas, introducing 220 bills specifically targeting transgender people in the first half of 2023.[93] Many Republican candidates for political office fully support these efforts. The most frequently passed bills are those that ban gender-affirming care for transgender youth, require or allow misgendering of transgender students, refuse to allow transgender students to participate in sports according to their current gender, outlaw drag performances, censor school curriculum, and ban books.[94]

In analyzing *Dobbs*, several commentators have warned of additional harmfully tailored legislation in the future and an increase in violence and other hate acts against LGBTQIA+ people. Journalists Amy Littlefield and Heron Greenesmith draw attention to the frightening similarities between the five-decades-long legislative and judicial assault on abortion that culminated in *Dobbs* and today's coordinated efforts to pass anti-trans bills. They urge us to avoid the temptation to focus narrowly on medical debates and instead see a bigger picture relevant to justice: "Any public conversation about gender-affirming care must be situated in an understanding of the wider context—the aggressive and deadly assault on bodily autonomy that affects everyone—Black, brown, low-income, and disabled people most of all."[95]

Conservative politicians and policymakers are laser focused on anti-trans laws and policies. For example, in Texas the governor directed the state's child welfare agency to open child abuse investigations into parents who let their trans children access gender-affirming care.[96] In 2022 and 2023, Florida's Board of Education imposed new restrictions on gender-affirming treatments for minors, drag shows, bathroom usage, and which pronouns can be used in school. A new state law extends the existing ban on public schools from teaching about gender and sexuality through the twelfth grade. Educators who are found in violation could lose their teaching license. Governor Ron DeSantis, failed Republican candidate for the presidential nomination in 2024, proudly proclaimed, "We are going to remain a refuge of sanity and a citadel of normalcy, and kids should have an upbringing that reflects that."[97]

Littlefield and Greenesmith see a tight connection between these initiatives, hateful rhetoric, and physical violence. Tucker Carlson, formerly the most popular host on Fox News, and other leaders on the right repeatedly refer to gender-affirming care as murder.[98] Right-wing commentator and podcast host Matt Walsh said on the air, "Gender-affirming care should be legally considered a capital crime and it should earn the prescribed penalty for such crimes. But if we can't have that, then prison will have to suffice."[99] These statements are disturbingly in line with the language and tactics of abortion opponents whose inflammatory language has incited deadly action in the past.[100] Shortly before the 1993 murder of Dr. David Gunn, his assassin Paul Hill circulated what came to be known as the "justifiable homicide pledge." While some signers later withdrew their names, at that time it was the most complete list of activists willing to publicly support murdering doctors who perform abortions.[101] As we saw in chapter 2, abortion provider Dr. George Tiller was murdered in 2005 by an antiabortion zealot after years of being stalked, slandered, and attacked. In at least twenty-nine episodes of *The O'Reilly Factor*, Fox News anchor Bill O'Reilly, who hosted the show between 1996 and 2017, referred to him as "Tiller the baby killer."

Salon reporter Gabriel Winant wrote that "O'Reilly didn't tell anyone to do anything violent, but he did put Tiller in the public eye, and help make him the focus of a movement with a history of violence against exactly these kinds of targets."[102] The week before he died, Dr. Tiller received an anonymous letter that said, "Somebody should kill you, so you can't kill anymore." After Dr. Tiller's murder, Randall Terry, head of the antiabortion group Operation Rescue, said, "Tiller was a mass murderer.[103]

In the case of abortion, the intensification of hateful rhetoric was accompanied by increased violence, and we are seeing the same deadly connection directed against trans people. Shoshanna Goldberg, a lawyer with the LGBTQIA+ advocacy organization the Human Rights Campaign, warned of the dangers from reinforcing a culture of bias in the context of virulent racism, sexism, and homophobia. In 2022 at least thirty-two trans people were murdered, and the number of assaults against LGBTQIA+ people continues to rise.[104]

At the same time, these attacks have also catalyzed strong, coordinated resistance among LGBTQIA+ and reproductive health, rights, and justice organizations. The Positive Women's Network is one of several transgender organizations advocating for trans-centered reproductive justice: "We define trans-centered reproductive justice as an approach to reproductive justice that centers the experiences, needs, and power of those whose genders and sexualities are most marginalized."[105]

Transgender activist and blogger KC Clements explains their perspective on how reproductive justice can bring the two together: "In shifting the paradigm from the single-issue of (cis) women's access to abortion to a movement for bodily autonomy that includes and centers trans people (especially trans women and especially trans women of color) we can create an intersectional movement that is able to address the root socioeconomic issues that prevent all of us from true reproductive justice as opposed to just addressing those issues that impact people with the most privilege."[106]

In many communities grassroots activists have organized bold and creative actions to resist book banning and censorship of LGBTQIA+-sponsored activities, such as drag queen reading hours in libraries and schools, which are increasingly under attack. In 2022 a group of men wearing clothing and logos associated with the all-male, far-right, neo-fascist Proud Boys disrupted a reading hour at the San Lorenzo Library, about twenty-five miles from San Francisco.[107] According to police, they shouted homophobic and transphobic slurs. As in other places where such attacks have occurred, the library expressed its support for the story-time event: "Attempts to intimidate and silence others are not tolerated in libraries," it said. "We are grateful to [storyteller] Panda Dulce for showing bravery and resilience and finishing the storytime event. We will continue to celebrate Pride Month and offer programming that reflects the diverse voices and experiences of all our communities."[108]

In Oklahoma, 150 demonstrators occupied the capitol building to protest bills limiting hormone replacement therapy. Student Jack Petocz organized statewide walkouts in Florida to protest Governor DeSantis's "Don't Say Gay" bill, HB 1557, officially titled the "Parents Rights in Education Act." Petocz was indefinitely suspended from school, but after widespread pressure and support he was allowed back in school. Despite pledging that they would take no more disciplinary action, administrators placed a notice of severe violation in his record, preventing him from running for class president. Petocz, however, was not daunted. He became policy director for Gen-Z for Change, a non-profit organization that uses social media to organize youth.[109] Although more than a dozen legislatures have passed similar legislation, a growing number of legislatures in states controlled by Democrats continue to pass laws protecting and expanding transgender health care and LGBTQIA+ rights overall. Fourteen states and Washington, DC, have "shield" laws or policies that support access to gender-affirming care for youth. In eleven of these states, state legislatures have enacted statutes that protect access to care. In three states, governors have extended protections through executive orders. An estimated 146,700 transgender youth live in states with "shield" laws or policies. This is about half of transgender youth in the United States.[110]

As of June 2023, some federal judges, even in Republican-controlled Alabama, Indiana, and Florida, temporarily blocked anti-trans legislation pending further review, and in Arkansas a judge permanently barred the state from enforcing a law that prohibited minors from obtaining puberty blockers and cross-sex hormones, considered by many medical groups to be the best-practice treatments for gender dysphoria.[111] Thus far states have not been able to successfully argue for overriding the due process and equal protection rights of transgender youths, their parents, and their doctors.

Health care providers, too, are playing an important role in defending gender-affirming care. For example, after the Tennessee legislature banned care for minors in 2023, CHOICES, a reproductive health clinic in Memphis, Tennessee, boldly proclaimed on its website they would make care available to sixteen- and seventeen-year-olds until the state law went into effect, asserting that "CHOICES is proud to stand with transgender and nonbinary youth in our communities."[112] President and CEO of the clinic, Jennifer Pepper, said, "Bans on gender affirming care are based on discriminatory and harmful ideologies. They are driven by a combination of misinformation, prejudice and a disregard for the lived experiences and autonomy of marginalized communities." The clinic's branch in Illinois is continuing to offer abortion and gender-affirming care.

Groups dedicated to expanding abortion access and who were aligned with the reproductive justice framework led the way in defending gender-affirming care and prioritizing transgender issues in their organizing work. In 2013 the New York Abortion Access Fund (NYAAF) was among the first abortion funds to highlight gender inclusivity with its choice of language on their website underscoring the organization's respect for every person's reproductive autonomy. The National

Network of Abortion Funds (NNAF) explicitly affirms transgender rights. The organization We Testify (initiated by the NNAF and now an independent group) was created to raise the visibility and heighten public awareness of the full range of people who need abortions and reproductive health care, including people who are transgender. Doctors and advocates who prescribe abortion pills through telehealth to people who live under telehealth bans deliver reproductive health care and gender-affirming care.

Some choice organizations that were traditionally mainstream have recently come out as strong promoters of gender inclusivity. Rebecca Hart Holder, president and CEO of Reproductive Equity Now, formerly NARAL Pro Choice Massachusetts, is a champion for both reproductive justice and trans rights, clearly articulating the interconnected fight: "It's all a part of a misogynistic, homophobic and transphobic coordinated attack on bodily autonomy; all a part of a cynical campaign of control."[113] And in response to the tidal wave of anti-trans legislation, the Planned Parenthood Federation of America and many of its state affiliates have issued statements affirming that abortion rights and trans rights are inextricably linked, expressing support for both.[114]

RJ-ing abortion shows us that coercive sterilization of people whom politicians and others consider valueless as potential reproducers has historically been an essential aspect of reproductive policies, even if this reality has sometimes been eclipsed by a single focus on abortion. In this post-*Dobbs* period, with abortion so consistently in the spotlight, we worry that the injustice of sterilization abuse will again be overshadowed. Connecting abortion and sterilization and raising awareness of reproductive coercion is, as Michele Goodwin observed, especially important now. In both cases, those most harmed are people who lack the resources to protect themselves. In the next section we highlight three examples of coercive sterilization that underscore our concerns. We look at the so-called drug-abuse prevention practices of C.R.A.C.K. / Project Prevention, a California-based organization; the policies within California prisons that permit coerced sterilizations of incarcerated people; and the forced sterilizations of immigrant women in detention carried out under the aegis of U.S. Immigration and Customs Enforcement. By looking at the work of these organizations, we can see how controlling the pregnancies of low-income women and women of color through the "war on drugs," mass incarceration, and immigrant detention expresses the racist imperative to control all pregnancies in order to maintain white supremacy in the United States.

C.R.A.C.K. / PROJECT PREVENTION

In 1997 Barbara Harris, a social worker in California, founded Children Requiring a Caring Kommunity (C.R.A.C.K.), a privately funded nonprofit organization that offered three hundred dollars to people addicted to illegal drugs or alcohol if they agreed to be sterilized, or two hundred dollars if they accepted long-term contraceptives such as Norplant or an IUD.[115] Harris said that she wanted to prevent more children from going through the suffering of drug withdrawal, which she had witnessed with her adopted children, all born to mothers addicted to crack.

But Harris also expressed her contempt for women with addictions, whom she compared to dogs: "We don't allow dogs to breed. We spay them. We neuter them. We try to keep them from having unwanted puppies, and yet these women are literally having litters of children."[116] C.R.A.C.K.'s flyers and billboards advertised its cynical individual-blaming slogans such as "Don't let a pregnancy ruin your drug habit," a message that resonated with prominent conservatives. Radio talk show host Dr. Laura Schlessinger contributed ten thousand dollars to the group and gave Harris a national platform.[117] Jim Woodhill, a Houston venture capitalist and member of the right-wing organization Republican Rebel Alliance, donated $125,000 so C.R.A.C.K. / Project Prevention could hire Chris Brand, a British psychologist, to expand the group overseas. Journalist Barry Yeoman characterized Brand's intention: "Brand ... claims that blacks are intellectually inferior to whites, and

[he] advocates taking a 'eugenic' approach to 'wanton and criminal females.'"[118]

Some people who objected to coercion and the echoes of eugenics were nonetheless drawn to Harris's expressed goal of reducing unintended and unwanted pregnancy among people addicted to drugs. Dr. Peter Beilenson, former Baltimore city health commissioner, explained his support: "While it is rather coercive to pay people to do things, I don't have much problem with encouraging people to use reversible birth control at a time when they might not be in full possession of their faculties."[119]

But C.R.A.C.K. was never about providing assistance to "encourage" people to make a better choice. Instead, it targeted vulnerable people for coercion. Opponents of C.R.A.C.K. tied it to the state-mandated eugenic sterilizations at the beginning of the twentieth century, charges that Harris consistently denied. Rather bizarrely, she claimed that she was protecting children by making sure they were never conceived.[120] After a torrent of early criticism, Harris toned down her rhetoric and changed the organization's name to Project Prevention. Still, in a 2003 interview journalist Helen Ubiñas remained skeptical about Harris's claims: "And is it about the kids, really? Or is it about the 'haves' making decisions for the 'have nots' about who should be allowed to reproduce? There's something frightening and familiar about that. It stinks of eugenics, of the coerced sterilization of poor Southern blacks in the last century."[121]

Scholars Jacquelyn Monroe and Rudolph Alexander Jr. were also skeptical. They questioned whether an individual suffering from chemical dependency and poverty and possibly other issues such as homelessness and lack of access to food can really make a free "choice"? If you have nowhere to live, with not enough money to buy food for yourself and your family, and have an addiction, how can you make a free choice?[122]

The group's own statistics suggest that it did in fact engage in racial targeting. In its first three years of operation, C.R.A.C.K. / Project Prevention made 60 percent of its payments to Black and Latina women.

Medical ethicist George Annas observed, "If the state of California was doing this, then people would be beside themselves, but because a private nonprofit organization is doing this, then it doesn't seem quite as scary."[123] The fact that Project Prevention is a privately funded organization does not make its tactics—trading money for (in)fertility—less problematic. Further, journalist Jed Bickman found that Project Prevention blurred the line between "public" and "private" since most birth control procedures carried out under its auspices were paid for through Medicaid.[124]

ORGANIZING AGAINST C.R.A.C.K.

Women of color led the opposition against C.R.A.C.K. Grassroots activists organized protests in California, Chicago, Houston, Pittsburgh, Cleveland, Detroit, New Orleans, and Florida. In Seattle, Communities Against Rape and Abuse (CARA), outraged by the organization's tactics and goals, mobilized community members. They removed flyers from buses and other public places, held workshops and a teach-in, and produced a "Crack Pack organizing kit" to support future campaigns.[125]

CARA amplified its activities on a national level through alliances with INCITE! Women of Color Against Violence and the Committee on Women, Population and the Environment (CWPE), a national group that exposed and opposed population control.[126] CWPE led a national letter-writing campaign to mainstream newspapers and magazines to counter the positive publicity C.R.A.C.K. had received. CWPE called for grassroots actions to remove C.R.A.C.K. billboards and demanded that health professionals and public officials condemn sterilization as a solution to drug use.

Other national organizations joined the effort. The National Black Women's Health Project and the Center for Women Policy Studies both accused C.R.A.C.K. / Project Prevention of preying on vulnerable members of society, exploiting poor people, and spreading racist beliefs.[127] The founder of National Advocates for Pregnant Women (now Pregnancy Justice), Lynn Paltrow, an attorney and longtime advocate for abortion rights, played a significant role in the resistance to C.R.A.C.K.[128] She warned that the group was "a propaganda machine used against pregnant women to take away their civil and human rights … and to mark infants born to drug users as less valuable than those born to non-drug users."[129]

The American Public Health Association publicly announced their opposition to C.R.A.C.K./Project Prevention in several of their policy statements.[130] Government and transportation worker unions in Washington, DC, also passed resolutions: C.R.A.C.K. is a "program that is racist and it will alienate us (the bus drivers) from much of the community that we seek to serve…. [W]e would like to … work to put into place real provisions of a caring community, such as drug treatment, decent jobs, affordable healthcare."[131]

The mainstream choice organizations, however, were not involved in the opposition to either C.R.A.C.K./Project Prevention or the war on drugs. It is true that abortion rights organizations were preoccupied with responding to the deadly violence against abortion clinics and providers. Nonetheless, failing to oppose C.R.A.C.K. was another missed opportunity for building alliances across class and racial lines. In fact, when the largest high-profile pro-choice organizations did not step up and honor the priorities of communities of color, racial divisions in the movement were deepened.

In the early 2000s, scientists produced clear data showing that the descriptions of the damaging impacts of crack cocaine on fetuses and infants were incorrect. Dr. David Lewis summarized sixteen years of research when he wrote that "the fetal and infant health problems previously associated with crack cocaine use are better explained by malnutrition and a lack of pre-natal care. In fact, a comprehensive research review shows no consistent negative association between maternal cocaine exposure and children's physical growth, developmental test scores, or performance on receptive and expressive language tests."[132] Lewis's findings were consistent with the work of other top addiction scientists, thirty of whom signed a joint statement in 2004 declaring that the "crack baby" was a racist myth.[133] The leading studies showed that when pregnant or parenting substance abusers are subjected to criminal prosecution, the outcomes are poor for both mothers and children. The National Perinatal Association finally issued a statement in 2017 cautioning against punitive mechanisms to encourage treatment, noting that such policies can backfire, driving women away from prenatal visits or leading them to have their baby outside a hospital.[134]

Several other national organizations, including the March of Dimes, Amnesty International, the American College of Obstetricians and Gynecologists, and the National Organization on Fetal Alcohol Syndrome, have all similarly condemned legislation that may have a chilling effect on a pregnant person's willingness to seek out help. The American Medical Association has said that "non-punitive public health approaches to treatment result in better outcomes for both moms and babies."[135] Nonetheless, the crack baby myth continued to shape public policy. A number of states took the punitive approach favored by many in law enforcement and most conservative politicians, who stubbornly insisted that punishment is the best deterrent to drug use, a position not borne out by social science or medical research. The war on drugs drove mass incarceration and intensified efforts to control and punish, especially Black pregnant people, whom many Americans accused of undeservedly collecting welfare benefits, raising their taxes, and supporting children who were threatening and poisoning the country's population. These claims do not accurately reflect the facts, but rest instead on stereotypes of people who were vulnerable to the criminal justice system.

More recently, Project Prevention adapted the myth and expanded its focus to other drugs, including oxycodone, OxyContin, and methamphetamine, and it began paying for other contraceptive options besides sterilization and LARCs. In 2019 Project Prevention sponsored billboards in North Carolina that featured a photo of a white pregnant woman administering heroin to herself with the caption "Get birth control, get cash."[136] In that same year in West Virginia, Project Prevention targeted pregnant opioid users, pointing to "oxytots" (babies born to women addicted to oxycontin) as the new "crack babies," who had been iconically portrayed as a Black problem.[137] The symbolic white oxytots stood for the white majority of those charged and convicted of Oxy-Contin and methamphetamine abuse as well as those who die from overdoses.[138] Strikingly, the medical and public health communities rarely recommended punitive consequences for the white OxyContin users.[139]

Harris founded Project Prevention during the era of "welfare reform," the period when public policies were drastically reducing financial and other supports for poor women and their children, and the period of emergent mass incarceration. In that context, its supporters were able to tap into a huge well of racism, anti-welfare-ism, misogyny, and drug war hysteria. But the organization's significance was not simply an expression of the particular politics and culture of the late twentieth-century politics. Most damaging in the long run, it paved the way for subsequent efforts at surveillance of pregnant people, especially those who are poor and of color.[140]

Despite research debunking claims and fears about prenatal substance use, today we continue to see prosecutions of pregnant people, child removal, and various forms of coercion, extending the terrible legacy of punitive approaches to substance use during pregnancy. In 2017 a judge in Tennessee offered reduced sentences to people who agreed to be sterilized, and in 2018 an Oklahoma judge offered a reduced sentence to a woman convicted of cashing a counterfeit check if she agreed to be sterilized. As Paltrow warned, the pregnant women who were prosecuted in the name of the war on drugs were the proverbial canaries in the coal mines; first the states took away rights from vulnerable people, and then they took them from everyone else.

C.R.A.C.K./Project Prevention and Harris are particularly high-profile participants in a large-scale project that criminalizes pregnant women in order to build support for fetal rights and to limit reproductive autonomy more generally. This is the reality in our current post-

Dobbs world, where Republican legislators and judges criminalize and punish increasing numbers of people without regard for their dignity or freedom to make their own decisions about their sexuality, gender, and childbearing.

STERILIZATIONS IN CALIFORNIA PRISONS

A reproductive justice analysis explains that we must pay attention to and understand reproductive injustice wherever it occurs, including in the U.S. prison system. In the United States prisons are government institutions, but many carceral sites are increasingly run by private companies that turn them into sites of wealth production. Government-run prisons along with those that are privately run constitute a collectivity that critics of the prison system have called the "prison industrial complex." This term points to the fact that the system of punishment in the United States is comprised of a tangle of punitive institutions that serve interests other than the interests of the people held by these institutions.[141] The Central California Women's Facility in Chowchilla exemplifies the role of the prison industrial complex in reproductive oppression. In 2001 Justice Now, a prison abolition and reproductive rights and health advocacy group, brought attention to California's eugenic history. Justice Now publicized the fact that forced sterilizations continued in the state's prisons long after the state legislature banned them in 1979.[142] Prison administrators continued to take advantage of a legal loophole allowing payments to private doctors who performed the sterilizations.

The award-winning documentary film *Belly of the Beast*, released in 2020, featured Kelli Dillon, who, while incarcerated at Chowchilla, was forcibly sterilized by hysterectomy, the same method the Indian Health Service chose for sterilizing so many Native American women in the late twentieth century. Neither Dillon's doctor nor prison officials informed her about the sterilization. She only learned about it a year later, when she saw a doctor for another medical problem. Dillon describes her feelings when she found out: "I was angry, I was hurt, I was scared, I was sad, I felt despair. Basically, you drugged me, and you performed this heinous act against me. It's like a form of rape."[143]

The film recounts how Dillon and Justice Now led the fight for survivors' justice. They sued the Department of Corrections and Rehabilitation for damages in 2006. Like the women in the 1978 *Madrigal v. Quilligan* lawsuit, Dillon lost her case, but the publicity and investigations that resulted from the suit raised public awareness and outrage. The public learned that in the two decades after the repeal of the law permitting sterilizations in prison, prison doctors sterilized at least 148 pregnant women incarcerated at two California prisons shortly after giving birth.[144] The majority of those sterilized were Black and Latina women, reflecting the disproportionate racial composition of California's prison population.[145]

Prison officials denied they were coercing anyone to undergo sterilization. When ProPublica reporter Corey Johnson interviewed the top health manager of the Valley Women's Prison, one of two facilities where over 148 people had been sterilized, the manager characterized the surgeries as an empowerment issue, claiming the institution was simply providing those who were incarcerated the same options as people had on the outside.[146] The receiver for the California women's prison system (an official appointed by a federal court to oversee and directly manage the provision of medical services in the system because the state was found to be providing unconstitutional levels of care) said that the doctors may have genuinely believed that the sterilizations were a matter of reproductive justice.

Dr. James Heinrich and a nurse on his staff referred two-thirds of the 148 women who underwent sterilization. This physician was the subject of several complaints and an investigation. In defending the referrals, Heinrich insisted that the women were making their own decisions. He considers the questions raised about his medical care unfair and voiced his suspicions about the women's motives. Revealing his own motives, Heinrich told the Center for Investigative Reporting that the money expended on sterilizing people in prison was minimal "compared to what you save in welfare paying for these unwanted children—as they procreate more.... They all wanted it [the sterilization] done." Without apparent evidence, Heinrich added, "If they come a year or two later saying, 'Somebody forced me to have this done,' that's a lie. That's somebody looking for the state to give them a handout."[147]

In the California prison system, physicians sterilized hundreds of people via hysterectomies, ovary removal, and other procedures that included endometrial ablations, all under questionable circumstances and without obtaining lawful consent. Some of the people who were sterilized had signed consent forms, but an assessment of the forms concluded that the prisons were providing people with documents that used difficult, opaque language requiring a reading level higher than the average American adult possesses.[148] In 2022 the National Health Law Program offered California prison officials a set of recommendations for making the form accessible to people with disabilities, those with limited English proficiency, LGBTQIA+ people, and anyone with limited reading skills.[149]

As we saw earlier, people targeted by C.R.A.C.K. / Project Prevention have dubious access to reproductive choices. In the same way, incarcerated people do not have meaningful access to true consent and choice. The fact is that people under state control have negligible, if any, personal power regarding bodily autonomy and other matters in the face of totalizing prison authority.[150] Kimberly Jeffrey, a formerly incarcerated person, told a reporter in 2014 that she resisted pressure from a prison staff member to get a tubal ligation, even while she was under sedation and strapped to an operating table. "Being treated like I was less than human produced in me a despair." To her, the state prison officials were "the real repeat offenders."[151] So long as prisons remain closed institutions with little accountability (despite the federal court's appointment of a receiver), the reality "inside" remains hidden. The privatization of prisons, remaking institutions as for-profit entities, exacerbates the situation since these facilities have no responsibility to be open about their practices.[152]

In 2014, after eight years of advocacy led by Justice Now, California banned sterilization as a form of birth control in prisons.[153] After the ban, a coalition led by California Latinas for Reproductive Justice (CLRJ) and including the Disability Rights Education and Defense Fund (DREDF), California Coalition for Women Prisoners, and Back to Basics LA successfully advocated for a state law to compensate people who had been sterilized. This legislation established the Forced or Involuntary Sterilization Program, making California the first and only state to recognize its role in prison sterilizations.[154] In 2021 the California legislature allocated $7.5 million to compensate survivors, both those who were sterilized under earlier eugenic laws (1909–79) and those sterilized after 1979. However, some women's claims have been rejected because the statute does not clarify what, exactly, constitutes a sterilization and consent.[155] For example, endometrial ablations are not classified as a method of sterilization, but they do, in fact, greatly reduce the chances for a healthy pregnancy. The attorney who helped write the law said that refraining from a specific definition of sterilization had been deliberate in order to allow for it to encompass the realities of unethical medical practice.

Gabriella Solano, a survivor of sterilization abuse, forcefully reminds us that more than money is necessary to redress the harms: "They're trying to compensate everybody for what they did to us, but for me, no amount of money is going to fix what they've done. They need to do more than just that. None of the doctors there were reprimanded, it was like nothing happened, like what they did to us was ok."[156] Solano's statement reflects the anguish and anger of millions of people who are rendered choiceless and are deprived of the ability to make their own decisions about abortion, childbearing, pregnancy, and sexuality. She underscores a central insight of RJ-ing abortion: White supremacy connects abortion, eugenics, and coercive sterilization. All are instruments of population control.

STERILIZATIONS IN ICE DETENTION CENTERS

Tragically, the road to reproductive justice for immigrants has been rocky in the United States. One terrible example of the intersection of immigration, incarceration, and sterilization abuse was exposed in 2020, when Dawn Wooten, a nurse who worked at Immigration and Customs Enforcement, filed a whistle-blower complaint with the Department of Homeland Security. Wooten pointed to the high rate of medically unnecessary gynecological procedures, including hysterectomies, performed at the Irwin County Detention Center (ICDC) in Georgia. Wooten and other nurses had been particularly struck by the actions of one doctor: "We've questioned among ourselves, like, goodness he's taking everybody's stuff out.... That's his specialty, he's the uterus collector. I know that's ugly ... is he collecting these things or something.... Everybody he sees, he's taking all their uteruses out or he's taken their tubes out. What in the world?"[157] She charged that staff regularly ignored the informed consent requirement. "These immigrant women, I don't think they really, totally, all the way understand this is what's going to happen depending on who explains it to them."[158]

Doctors at the detention center exploited many of the women's lack of English proficiency and their lack of knowledge about reproductive health issues. Karina Cisneros Preciado, one of the witnesses at a hearing of the U.S. Senate Permanent Select Committee on Investigations on the sterilizations, told senators that a doctor at ICDC prescribed Depo Provera to her without letting her know that the medication was a contraceptive.[159] She testified that had she known this, she never would have taken it because she had heard complaints about various forms of contraception from other women in her family. "To this day, I am extremely scared to go to any doctor for myself and for my kids."[160]

Eventually, more than forty low-income immigrant women, all with minimal skills in English, joined a class action lawsuit.[161] Written testimonies, statements, interviews, and reviews of medical records gathered from over eighty women documented that they had undergone invasive and unnecessary medical procedures. According to the evidence and testimony, women began to object to their treatment in 2018, but staff did not address their complaints. Journalists writing about this case were struck by the similarity between the situation of those currently detained and the women who had been sterilized in Los Angeles in the 1970s.[162] We can also see the chilling resemblance between these recent detention sterilizations and sterilizations that doctors performed on Japanese women in the United States who were interned in remote sites in the American West during World War II as "enemy aliens.[163]

In the ICDC case, lawyers for the women who were incarcerated filed a temporary restraining order to prevent retaliation from prison staff, but the women still worried that they would be deported for speaking out about the abuses they had suffered. Their fears were substantiated when reports surfaced that six women who had signed complaints were deported, and holds on deportation were removed for seven others.[164]

The detention center in Georgia, like the California prisons where women were unlawfully sterilized, was run by several private companies. Elizabeth Methene, an attorney representing some of the women in the facility, and Pramila Jayapal, a U.S. congressional representative from Washington's Seventh Congressional District, saw private ownership as especially problematic because in these companies, profit making takes precedence over the quality of services. They also argued that existing standards for overseeing federal detention are ineffective: "[The guidelines] have no teeth; there is no oversight or accountability, nor transparency. Like prisons, jails and mental hospitals, detention centers are closed institutions. Most people go through detention without legal representation, leaving them with even fewer protections."[165]

Alejandra Pablos's experience recounted in chapter 1 shows that people in detention frequently face reproductive abuses in addition to sterilization and administration of unidentified medications, including denial of abortion services and forced separation from their children.[166] Medical professionals point to the general lack of medical care, proper sanitation, and other conditions that put pregnant people at risk. In the first two years of the first Trump administration's harsh immigration policies, the number of miscarriages of women in detention nearly doubled.[167]

The Georgia-based women-of-color-led nonprofit organization Project South took the lead in organizing the campaign to shut down the Irwin County Detention Center.[168] Originally founded in 1986 as the Institute to Eliminate Poverty and Genocide, Project South is rooted in the civil rights movement in the South. Today the organization remains dedicated to "cultivating strong social movements in the South powerful enough to contend with some of the most pressing and complicated social, economic, and political problems we face today."[169]

Other Georgia-based organizations also worked on the complaint against ICDC, including Georgia Detention Watch, the South Georgia Immigrant Support Network, and the Georgia Latino Alliance for Human Rights. The complaint listed many examples of inhumane and life-threatening treatment of detained people, including the denial of necessary medications, improper responses to serious medical situations, filthy living conditions, and inedible food, in addition to the range of reproductive abuses.[170] One person provided this description: "When I met all these women who had had surgeries, I thought this was like an experimental concentration camp. It was like they're experimenting with our bodies."[171] A woman who had been sterilized invoked the long history of coercive, eugenically driven activity, saying, "I now know that what happened to me at Irwin is not a one-off aberration—it's also a legacy of American slavery and white supremacist pseudo-science going back many decades."[172]

Congresswomen Jayapal, Annie Kuster (D-NH), Sheila Jackson Lee (D-TX), Sylvia Garcia (D-TX), and Lois Frankel (D-FL) sponsored H. Res. 1153, "condemning unwanted, unnecessary medical procedures on individuals without their full, informed consent." The resolution passed the full House on October 1, 2020, and mandated a full investigation by the Department of Homeland Security.[173] The congresswomen publicly expressed their outrage in a joint statement. Frankel put the sterilizations at ICDC into historical context: "Mass hysterectomies have a long and shameful history in the United States, and forced sterilization has been used to further white supremacy, ableism, and other forms of discrimination."[174] Jayapal expressed the need for the resolution: "We will not stand by and allow history to repeat itself—a shameful history of medical abuse targeting Black people, Indigenous people, people of color, immigrants, poor people and people with disabilities."[175]

Despite a directive from the secretary of Homeland Security, violations at immigrant detention centers have not ended.[176] In July 2022 Project South, along with the Southern Poverty Law Center, filed a new complaint alleging the sexual assault of immigrants at the Stewart Detention Center in Georgia, claiming that "the abuses are endemic to immigrant detention with little-to-no oversight."[177] The new complaint demanded the immediate closure of Stewart, the release of people still detained there, reparations, and a path to immigration relief in the United States for the brave survivors who came forward.[178]

Immigration rights advocates across the country call for the systemic approach of closing all immigrant detention centers.[179] Project South issued a comprehensive and intersectional statement, "Health, Healing and Liberation, from Medical Practitioners, Public Health Practitioners, Healers, and Birth Workers," which not only condemns the actions at ICDC but also underscores the need for a full transformation of health systems in order to terminate and repair these targeted harms.[180]

All of these examples and voices highlight the need for dedicated vigilance to eradicate eugenics in all areas of reproductive health services rather than treating each area—abortion, sterilization, and so forth—as individual, and disconnected, problems.[181] Further, they require us to acknowledge our own complicity. As Mark Largent writes, having a eugenics-free society is not simply about getting rid of a few bad apples. "We must rescue the American eugenics movement and the advocates of compulsory sterilization laws from the dustbin of history—not to celebrate their prejudices or apologize for their mistakes, but to confront our connection with them. We need to appreciate our relationship with the eugenicists' assumptions if we want to begin to challenge our own deeply problematic assumptions about other people's supposed social inadequacies."[182]

While the examples in this chapter focus on policies directly aimed at reproduction, other government actions also undermine the right to have children.[183] For example, child exclusions denying additional benefits for children conceived and born while the family is receiving welfare, unequal funding of public schools, mass incarceration, and racial disparities in health care access and service delivery are all examples of population control in action. RJ-ing abortion provides the tools to identify and respond to modern-day population control initiatives as their policy and on-the-ground manifestations evolve. We hope this analysis and the courageous examples of resistance will inspire future activism.

CHAPTER 4

Reproductive Justice in Action

Voices from the Front Lines

In previous chapters we saw how applying the reproductive justice lens to abortion vastly expands the meaning of reproductive rights and reproductive autonomy. Reproductive justice connects abortion with the complexities in the lived experiences of people across race, class, and other apparent boundaries. In this chapter we focus on how reproductive justice changes the ways we act. Today, RJ activists use intersectional analysis and advocacy across a range of strategies: devising national and grassroots activities; responding to and reinventing legal, medical, and research practices; and realigning organizational and movement practices so that they express RJ values.[1]

In the first part of the chapter, we look at crucial moments in RJ movement history and identify certain core strategies that continue to shape the movement. In the second part of the chapter, advocates directly engaged in the current battles for abortion access share how RJ-ing abortion shapes their advocacy, clinical, spiritual, legal, and research activities. Their work gives us insight and inspiration.

We pick up the story of RJ-ing abortion activism in the mid-1990s, after Women of African Descent for Reproductive Justice (the group that met in Chicago) named and claimed the term. For clarity, we follow the evolution of reproductive justice chronologically, although its development and emergence as a force has not been linear. Both oppression and resistance are dynamic processes.

THE REPRODUCTIVE JUSTICE MOVEMENT
FLEXES ITS MUSCLES

As we described in chapter 1, the founders of reproductive justice intended to reflect the reproductive experiences of Black people in their communities but never intended RJ to be a simple replacement for "choice." However, in some respects that is what happened. After RJ activists positioned abortion access within their broad intersectional framework, the RJ lens became more compelling than choice, even for many in the pro-choice movement.[2] Throughout the book we refer to the choice movement as "mainstream," the term that activists of color and their radical allies use to distinguish it from an intersectional approach.

An early test of the RJ movement's power and ideas came in 1995, after the National Organization for Women (NOW), the Feminist Majority, Planned Parenthood, and the National Abortion Rights Action League (NARAL) put out a call for the March for Choice. For decades these large groups, which drew in mostly white, middle- and upper-class women supporters, had defined the movement's center in terms of choice, establishing it as the prevailing frame.

SisterSong, along with other RJ organizations representing women of color and young people, firmly rejected the narrow framing of choice because it ignored so many issues of concern to their communities. Leaders of the RJ groups also objected to the lack of diversity in the leadership of the March for Choice and made clear that they would not mobilize their constituencies to participate unless the steering committee broadened the event's political agenda, diversified the leadership, and allocated funds so people from underresourced communities could come to Washington, DC.[3] These changes did not come without a struggle. La'Tasha Mayes, founder and executive director of New Voices Pittsburgh, was frank in her assessment of the problem:

> They [the March leadership] didn't know 'cause "freedom of choice" sounded perfect [to them]. Obviously, that doesn't resonate with women of color, and they [mainstream groups] ask the question "Why don't women of color participate?" I'm like "Well, obviously, it doesn't resonate with them or their experiences."[4]

At that time, in the early 2000s, reproductive justice was becoming a rallying cry for women of color and also for radical white allies who shared the critique of the choice movement.[5] The march leadership should have realized that building a huge national mobilization required participation from the communities that the RJ groups represented, but it was slow to understand and to meet the demands of RJ leaders. Finally persuaded, the march's steering committee made the changes signaling that they were serious about expanding the scope and the reach of the event. They renamed the demonstration the March for Women's Lives, expanded the steering committee to include the National Latina Institute for Reproductive Health, the Black Women's Health Imperative, and SisterSong, and appointed Loretta Ross as the march's codirector. NOW announced the changes in its newsletter:

> This March is about demanding political and social justice for women and girls regardless of their race, economic, religious, ethnic or cultural circumstances. This March is for young and older women, straight women and lesbians, sons and fathers, able and disabled, rich and poor to stand side by side in a show of unity and determination to "never go back" and in fact, move forward with full equality and reproductive justice for all. The excitement is building![6]

Still, inequalities and dissent prevailed. Some organizations ran on shoestring budgets while others had much more extensive resources, a situation that created obstacles to equal leadership and participation. Nevertheless, the original steering committee representing the most well-funded groups in the movement decided that leadership organizations, which now included women-of-color-led groups, had to contribute equal amounts to the costs of the march. Organizations led by women of color and youths did not have the funds to do this, and they found this "pay to play" approach fundamentally unacceptable. The RJ leaders insisted on eliminating the financial buy-in requirement and demanded transportation subsidies so young people and people from communities of color could go to Washington for the event. The steering committee agreed to these important concessions.[7] As a result, the march fulfilled its promise: Over one million people filled the National

Mall in the largest women's march in U.S. history to date. And while large numbers of people of color had not participated in past mobilizations for choice, this time a large contingent of people marched under a banner with a new slogan, "Women of Color for Reproductive Justice."[8] The rich diversity of speakers and performers was also unprecedented.

This history illustrates the way that reproductive justice leaders fought for the changes that were beginning to transform the pro-choice movement, fulfilling what activist/historian Zakiya Luna has called creating a "narrative of credit." The leadership of NOW and the other large mainstream choice organizations gave credit to SisterSong and to the crucial role this organization played in the march's success, but even more critical was that SisterSong members themselves witnessed the change. Over the following years, participants at organizational gatherings told and retold the story of the march as a dramatic illustration and proof of the group's mantra: "Doing collectively what we cannot do individually." For Luna, the story of the march "demonstrates why an organization like SisterSong exists and provides evidence that its reproductive justice analysis can be deployed successfully on a national scale."[9]

These victories required ongoing vigilance. In 2014 the question of "credit" reemerged in a public clash between the reproductive justice and choice movements after Planned Parenthood removed the term "choice" from its website. In a *New York Times* interview discussing the change, Cecile Richards, then president of the Planned Parenthood Federation of America, failed to acknowledge the work of women of color for driving this change. SisterSong and other RJ groups wrote an open letter to PPFA forcefully articulating their concerns, including this key matter, "This [omission] is not only disheartening but, intentionally or not, continues the cooptation and erasure of the tremendously hard work done by Indigenous women and women of color (WOC) for decades."[10]

At the same time, Monica Simpson, executive director of SisterSong, saw an opportunity for future collaboration. She tactfully framed

PPFA's misstep as an "oversight," which had the positive effect of forcing a dialogue about how that organization could work effectively with the RJ movement. In an important move, Simpson made space at a SisterSong national meeting for Richards to apologize publicly in person for withholding the movement-changing credit that was due to women-of-color organizations.

Calling in PPFA (that is, working with the organization) instead of writing them off was not a trivial gesture on the part of SisterSong. It was a critical strategic move that extended and accelerated movement transformation. Nia Martin-Robinson, then director of Black leadership and engagement at Planned Parenthood, described the SisterSong open letter as a learning opportunity: "The organization [PPFA] has since deepened its commitment to 'making sure that we're giving credit, space, visibility and power to the folks who have been leading this work around the reproductive justice movement.'"[11] Still, the media continued to give the biggest megaphone to the mainstream choice organizations—both during the 2004 march and afterward.

Given these obstacles, the fledgling reproductive justice movement achieved a major victory when it reoriented the 2004 march away from "choice" language toward using RJ terminology. But this was only a beginning. The movement still had to contend with the fact that leaders of the largest choice organizations had not yet understood that reproductive justice embodied a fundamentally new and different analysis and road map for action. Changing the "branding" did not mean those groups had embraced the reproductive justice agenda or moved away from an abortion-centric, pro-choice focus.[12] In fact, after the march, mainstream organizations reverted to characterizing abortion as a matter of individual, personal choice, even as they adopted the language of reproductive justice.

In response, the founders of the RJ movement expressed their concern about the "misappropriation and co-optation of RJ language by those who ignore the realities of institutionalized inequality that circumscribe the reproductive experiences of vulnerable people."[13] Indeed, the embodied realities of the women who created reproductive justice were the movement's heart, its integrity, and its authenticity. Ross's characterization of this new paradigm as an "open source code" suggested that it was meant to be elastic and inclusive.[14] At the same time, she understood that it was necessary to preserve the heart. While everyone is entitled to the same human rights, it is important to keep front and center the conditions of life of those who have been marginalized.[15]

"CHOICE" VERSUS JUSTICE

Throughout the 2000s the reproductive justice movement grew in numbers and influence. Activists created new groups and policy agendas, and some organizations changed their names to reflect the RJ understanding and agenda. In 2007 SisterSong became SisterSong Women of Color Reproductive Justice Collective, Law Students for Choice became Law Students for Reproductive Justice, Choice USA became United for Reproductive and Gender Equity (URGE), Nurses for Choice became Nursing Students for Reproductive and Sexual Health, and National Advocates for Pregnant Women is now Pregnancy Justice.

While initially attracting only women of color and radical white-led organizations and allies, reproductive justice increasingly spoke to new generations of activists, and it has had a transformational impact on the choice movement. For fifty years or so, the most visible proponents of reproductive rights have depended on "choice" for rhetoric, messaging, and policy agendas, but the reproductive justice activists have consistently argued that "choice" was misleading and inadequate.[16] Framing abortion as a "choice" drew on assumptions that were simply not relevant to their communities. What did "choice" mean to a pregnant person lacking adequate financial resources, who didn't have decent housing or access to steady employment? Or whose schooling opportunities in the community were very poorly funded? Or whose neighborhood was situated near a toxic dump or lacked grocery stores or medical facilities? Or who lived in a state where accessing contraception was very difficult and getting an abortion was a criminal act? A pregnant person who lived under these conditions could understandably assess their situation and conclude they had no reproductive choices.

While the pro-choice movement claimed to speak for all women, it generally did not. Its leadership and membership typically ignored the race and class constraints that prevented people from being equally positioned to make reproductive decisions. Critics of the "choice" framing identified additional strategic shortcomings. They argued, for example, that decades of the mainstream movement's singular focus on abortion rights had failed to stop the erosion of abortion access beginning with the Hyde Amendment in the late 1970s and continuing over time to harm the most vulnerable people. Moreover, "choice" had not fulfilled the promise of drawing in new constituencies to support abortion rights.

Some mainstream pro-choice activists agreed about the limitations of "choice." They saw the need for a more compelling approach, but there was no general agreement within that movement about what should replace the old language and ideas.[17] In 2008, the Opportunity Agenda, the Ford Foundation, and a group of reproductive justice organizations conducted communications research to determine which messages used by the media, politicians, activists, and citizens best conveyed their political ideas about reproductive rights.[18] The report showed that the public was not broadly familiar with either the term "reproductive justice" or the RJ movement. According to the study, many people, given the option, preferred to associate their stance toward abortion with the message that abortion should be "safe, legal, and rare." These findings fueled reluctance among mainstream groups about accepting a broadened RJ focus and changing their language. The report identified the challenges to change. "Arrayed against society's embrace of reproductive justice are deeply embedded attitudes and values about individualism and personal responsibility. The 'choice' framework influences public opinion to support abortion access, in line with the profound belief, shared even by people with the least power and fewest resources, in every individual's ability to 'get ahead in America if they just try hard enough.'"[19]

Tensions between the pro-choice and RJ movements continued into the 2010s. PPFA and NARAL, the largest national reproductive rights groups, straddled the line between framings. Both used reproductive justice language publicly at the same time as they continued to argue over language issues internally with their divided memberships. Many within their ranks wanted to fully endorse reproductive justice. However, the more powerful factions in each organization feared losing their core base of support. They also worried that the abortion cause would get lost in the broader reproductive justice framework.

Concerns about diffusing the battle for abortion rights even came from some groups that were allies of the reproductive justice movement. For example, Jon O'Brien, former head of Catholics for Choice (CFC), expressed the fears of many white activists when he publicly voiced a critique of adopting the RJ framework and language: "Seeking to have an impact on everything can lead to having no impact on anything.... There is a danger of turning allies into adversaries.... Abortion becomes something to talk about later—but not today."[20]

Ann Furedi, former CFC board member and head of Britain's largest abortion-providing organization, agreed with O'Brien and was even overtly hostile to reproductive justice.[21] Her book *The Moral Case for Abortion* is a staunch defense of "choice," where she argues that it is *the* container for the basic principles of autonomy, self-determination, and individual freedom, and she accuses RJ theorists of undermining these values.[22]

RJ leaders argued that O'Brien and Furedi misunderstood the thrust of reproductive justice. Marlene Fried, Loretta Ross, and Rickie Solinger wrote a response on behalf of a group of RJ leaders:

> O'Brien is concerned that reproductive justice does not allow for focused advocacy. We disagree. Having a broad, intersectional analysis does not

mean that every organization has to fight on all fronts all the time. Achieving reproductive justice does require countering an opposition that is itself broad and intersectional, as it pursues an anti-woman, pro-patriarchal, and racist agenda. No one organization can possibly do this alone. It is precisely because we do not and cannot all work on the same issues that we need the cross-cutting analysis and shared values encompassed in reproductive justice. Embracing that framework enables us to shape our particular piece of the advocacy in ways that support each other's work, without undermining our common long-term goals and values, and without sacrificing any group's human rights for the political expediency of achieving limited gains.

The shift from choice to justice does not, as O'Brien says, devalue the autonomy of women who face obstacles. Instead, locating women's autonomy and self-determination in human rights rather than in individual rights and privacy gives a more inclusive and realistic account of both autonomy and what is required to ensure that all women have it. Advocating for reproductive justice was not counter-posed against being "pro-choice" or supporting abortion rights. Rather, reproductive justice reframed and included both.[23]

These events and the debates they stimulated were a significant part of the journey from choice to justice. They surfaced enduring fears and frustrations about the challenges of taking on intersecting oppressions. We find lessons for the present in the political consequences of past events. Consider, for example, a 2011 political disagreement in Mississippi over two initiatives on the state ballot, one of which was a proposal requiring that a person produce a government-issued photo identification in order to vote, at an approximate cost of fourteen dollars. Opponents argued that this amounted to a poll tax and violated the Voting Rights Act (1965).[24] Still, the measure passed, 62 percent to 38 percent. The other measure defined a fertilized egg as a person with full human rights. If passed, it would have outlawed all forms of abortion and many forms of birth control, as well as many forms of fertility treatment, and would potentially have criminalized miscarriage. That measure was defeated 55 percent to 45 percent.

Reproductive justice activists saw the power in joining the two initiatives under the umbrella of human rights and opposing both, but white pro-choice leaders focused solely on the fetal rights amendment.[25] Loretta Ross saw this as another missed opportunity for coalition building, and as a cautionary tale with implications for future activist strategies. She said:

> We'll never know if the outcome would have changed had reproductive rights organizers stopped and listened to what Black organizers on the ground were telling them about the connection between reproductive oppression and voting rights. We'll never know if a blueprint for defeating laws that disenfranchise Black and brown voters might have been developed and modified for use in other gerrymandered and voter suppressed states.[26]

A decade later, after Donald Trump's efforts to overturn the 2020 presidential election, the connections between voter suppression and undermining abortion rights were again in the spotlight. Republicans introduced 360 bills at the state level to aggressively target and disenfranchise Black voters and, simultaneously, filed 536 bills to ban or severely restrict abortion rights. Interdisciplinary scholar Carol Mason describes the frightening connections: "The same violent brew of paramilitary warriors, white supremacists and Christian militants that we saw descending on the Capitol building merged to oppose abortion with lethal force decades ago."[27] Again, feminists of color led this intersectional fight. One powerful example is the Georgia-based organization Women Engaged, which is dedicated to protecting and expanding voting rights. Cofounded by Malika Redmond, formerly of SisterSong, this organization helped bring large numbers of Black women to the polls in 2020 and 2022 and was instrumental in turning the U.S. Senate blue.[28]

Thanks to the connections drawn by reproductive justice groups, most supporters of abortion rights today, including those in traditional pro-choice organizations, understand that voting rights are a necessity for achieving reproductive justice. But, as important as it is to protect

Black and other disenfranchised voters, voting is not the center of the RJ movements' theory of change. As we shall see, RJ-inflected abortion activism is more radical and ultimately more transformative.

REPRODUCTIVE JUSTICE ACTIVISM POST-TRUMP 2016 AND POST-*DOBBS*: PLAYING OFFENSE

In recent years the ideas at the heart of reproductive justice have had a broad and growing appeal, and the movement has continued to gain visibility and support. RJ's breadth and focus on intersectionality, and its foregrounding of racism, resonate with the politics of new social justice movements that have emerged in response to the explicit white supremacy and racist hate that Donald Trump and the far right have stoked and spread, especially since 2016.

Greater acceptance of RJ does not mean that the idea of choice has disappeared from abortion advocacy nor that all abortion rights supporters are on board with reproductive justice. In fact, the concept of choice continues to inspire action, and many advocates still use this term to declare the right to bodily autonomy. The slogans "My body, my choice" and the more graphic "Keep your rosaries off my ovaries" are mainstays at rallies. There is little doubt that over the decades the idea that only "I" should be able to make decisions about "my" body has ignited the fight for abortion rights.

Today, however, the concept of bodily autonomy has also been RJ-ed. It does not simply refer to the right *not* to have a child. Within the RJ framework, bodily autonomy also boldly and emphatically refers to the right to *have* a child. It includes disability and pregnancy justice, as well as LGBTQIA+ rights. It stands against forced sterilization and other medical abuses. Bodily autonomy encompasses the entire reproductive justice agenda.

The RJ movement is on the offensive, reimagining strategies, modifying old approaches, adding new ones, and making clear that only an expansive and robust understanding of "choice" will get us more than we had under *Roe.* This work predates the Supreme Court's 2022 *Dobbs* decision. Over the past decade reproductive justice leaders have reshaped abortion rights advocacy, centering obstacles to abortion access, especially for the most vulnerable people. Former NARAL affiliate and one of the organizations leading the abortion advocacy in Texas is Avow. The new name proclaims, "To avow means to declare openly, bluntly, and without shame. Now more than ever, our state needs bold and unapologetic advocacy for abortion rights."[29] While the contours of activism in the post-*Dobbs*, post-*Roe* era are still unfolding, Avow's name captures essential aspects of unabashed reproductive justice resistance.

At the same time, we do not want to overstate the unity within and between the choice and the reproductive justice movements. In the post-*Dobbs*, post-*Roe* period, extraordinary numbers of people are unable to access abortion and reproductive health care. We are concerned that when advocates reach for all-encompassing messages emphasizing the similar needs for reproductive health care that people have across race and class, these messages once again mask significantly different lived experiences and access to resources.

Below we preview the dominant strategies used by the reproductive justice movement: holistic advocacy, storytelling, rethinking activist history, creating new collaborations, shifting power internally and externally, and promoting self-managed abortion (SMA) with pills. These strategies, individually and collectively, provide concrete examples of how to fight for abortion access with an intersectional approach, without compromising the rights or the physical safety of the most vulnerable, and without treating issues as separate and isolated.

HOLISTIC ADVOCACY CONNECTS IDENTITIES AND ISSUES

As we have seen throughout this book, the reproductive justice lens emphasizes that our reproductive lives are structured by multiple and overlapping identities and systems of oppression. Reproductive justice leaders consistently call on us to keep our sights on the full RJ agenda, one that is composed of an integrated collectivity of issues that merge in daily life. As Marcela Howell, executive director of In Our Own Voice: National Black Women's Reproductive Justice Agenda, explained in her 2019 testimony to the U.S. House of Representative's House Committee on Oversight and Reform, "A Reproductive Justice framework acknowledges that a pregnant person cannot even get in the door of a health center to receive abortion care if they do not have the transportation, child care, necessary immigration documents and the time off from work needed to access services."[30]

The pieces in the second part of this chapter show how advocates bring this understanding to their advocacy for abortion access. When we invited leaders to contribute to the book, we specifically asked them to consider how the RJ vision impacts their work. Monica Simpson of SisterSong speaks directly to this in her piece, explaining, like Howell does above, the meanings and uses of holistic advocacy.

STORYTELLING

When in the late 1960s and early 1970s, during the struggle for legalization, people first talked publicly at rallies and other gatherings about their abortions, this was a new political tactic.[31] Today, personal abortion narratives are used all over the world, at in-person events; in print materials, films, dramatic readings and plays; and in social media.[32] These stories are included in legal briefs and are integral to other activist strategies focused on changing law and policy, expanding access, and fighting stigma. Historically, stories told by white, middle- and upper-class cisgender women received public attention, often through newspaper articles and other media coverage. Low-income people and people of color had few public spaces in which to tell their stories, which typically included information about how the impacts of multiple oppressions shaped their reproductive lives. And mainstream media rarely paid attention. Even in cases where abortion experiences then and now involve poverty, childcare, violence against women, unemployment, homelessness, and other issues, the media have tended to interpret the message more simplistically, conveying that abortion is *the* solution to all other problems.[33]

Storytelling is a central practice in the RJ movement because of the importance the movement places on making sure that political action and theory are tightly connected to the lived experiences of the people it wants to reach. Importantly, RJ organizations and campaigns feature stories previously unheard and storytellers previously unseen, stories that foreground structural inequalities of race, poverty, and citizenship status. These stories show how individuals must navigate a thicket of restrictions blocking their way to an abortion. RJ advocates believe that storytelling can potentially create new bases for political unity. Journalist and author Maya Dusenbery explains,

> "When storytellers share their whole story, then, they're able to tell us the role low wages, jobs without health insurance, racism, gender discrimination, and lack of access to food and child care may have played in their abortion experience." ... Actually hearing—and, just as importantly, responding to—the "whole story" often calls for empathy across not just one but many of the axes that divide us.[34]

Dusenbery adds a strategic caveat: Storytelling is also a "vehicle for social and political transformation ... but not in a chatty self-help style that ignores the structural, historical and political obstacles that women of color face."[35] She instructs us to honor the specifics of an individual's experiences while also acknowledging the larger context in which the experiences have occurred. Her point is also relevant to the value of RJ-ing storytelling for listeners. Being attentive to abortion stories has the potential to raise consciousness, generate empathy, create community, and counter the invisibility, stigma, and shame fostered by public silence surrounding abortion.

Abortion providers also benefit from telling their stories. Speaking out can break their isolation and disrupt stigma by providing a space for expressing pride in their work and gaining support.[36] For example, after abortion provider George Tiller was tragically murdered, an abortion clinic worker created the website "I Am Dr. Tiller" as a way to stave off what could have become "paralyzing fear." The storytelling website was a memorial to Dr. Tiller's lifework and a living testimony to the courageous lives of abortion providers.

While storytelling is a powerful weapon for fighting stigma, Anu Kumar, one of the first people to write about abortion stigma, issued this important note of caution: "I fear that it [storytelling] distracts from the structural inequalities of race, poverty, age, and education by placing too much emphasis on the individual. And I worry that it lets our politicians and policymakers off the hook."[37]

We think that reproductive justice storytelling addresses Kumar's concerns by keeping those "possibly forgotten" issues in the foreground. In contrast to a neoliberal account of abortion that focuses only on the rights and status of an individual, reproductive justice theory and practice emphasize that no individual can exist separate from their social and political structures, histories, or community.

FORGING NEW STRATEGIC ALLIANCES

By exposing the deep interconnections among systems of oppression, a reproductive justice analysis brings other social justice issues into reproductive politics, and vice versa.[38] With leadership and outreach from SisterSong, both RJ and choice-focused organizations are engaging in coalition work with Black Lives Matter, Black Mamas Matter, Moms Rising, Justice for Marissa Alexander, and the Ray for Hope Walk, among many other organizations and efforts. Since the reproductive justice framework is based in human rights, RJ naturally connects to struggles against Black maternal and infant mortality, mass incarceration, and ending state violence and police brutality. It is also in alignment with efforts to achieve birth justice, destigmatize and decriminalize sex work, campaigns for environmental justice in Black neighborhoods, and support for LGBTQIA+ rights, among other issues.[39]

These connections and alliances are based on a shared identification of the common enemy as white supremacy *and* all focus on people with often hidden vulnerabilities. All the issues are crucial points of connection for creating empathy, understanding, and resistance.

Not only do reproductive justice groups incorporate an array of social justice issues, but a large number of social justice organizations also integrate reproductive issues into their platforms. In 2016, speaking with leaders of SisterSong and Trust Black Women, Alicia Garza, one of the founders of BLM, put it this way:

> From our perspective, reproductive justice is very much situated within the Black Lives Matter movement.... [I]t's not just about the right for women to be able to determine when and how and where they want to start families, but it is also very much about our right to be able to raise families, to be able to raise children to become adults.[40]

Immigration rights advocates organized a national campaign after border officials denied Alejandra Pablos's request for an abortion while she was in detention.[41] Due to activist efforts she got her abortion, but advocates missed an important opportunity to fight simultaneously for abortion access and for adequate medical care for women in detention who want to carry their pregnancies to term. Due to poor care, an increasing number of pregnant people suffer miscarriages while they are incarcerated in detention facilities.[42]

ADOPTING BOLD STRATEGIES

Conceiving and pursuing the strategies mentioned here constitutes a radical RJ agenda. Advocates who are RJ-ing abortion in practice see these efforts as essential for doing bold work based on community needs. They are motivated by long-term comprehensive visions of justice and refuse to be encumbered by conventional wisdom defining what is politically "sensible." For example, the decades-long effort to overturn the Hyde Amendment draws on the idea of pursuing important goals even when they seem impossible to achieve and refusing to be exclusively tied to goals that seem reasonable and possible at a given time.

Rj-ing abortion activism pushes the boundaries of traditional tried and tired approaches to framing both the issues and the work of advocates. As one example, this boundary-pushing spirit is generating heightened interest in and acceptance of self-managed abortion (SMA) with pills, a solution that can be accomplished outside the formal medical system. In recent years, especially since *Dobbs*, we have seen a tremendous increase in online searches and internet orders for abortion pills and more activists involved in facilitating SMA. Still, RJ activists are well aware that self-managed abortion with pills, while the best course of action for many people, cannot suit the needs of everyone who needs an abortion. Since antiabortion activists are increasingly monitoring abortion seekers—taking pictures of their cars at clinics and following their internet use, for example—obtaining abortion pills may be a dangerous option for people who live in states that have criminalized abortion and in communities that are routinely overpoliced and surveilled. Pamela Merritt, executive director of Medical Students for Choice, a proponent of SMA, adds this important caveat: "So as a Black woman, I see very little comfort in people in the South, where the bulk of the Black population lives, having an option that basically requires breaking the law."[43] Risk-mitigation strategies and expanding legal options are, therefore, essential aspects for RJ-ing abortion.

With this important awareness, today's advocates for self-managed abortion with pills promote this method as both an immediate life- and health-saving strategy and as a possible path to empowerment for many pregnant people. Managing an abortion outside the formal medical system and putting knowledge and information about it into the public domain will eventually "flatten hierarchies of knowledge and subvert power dynamics of care."[44]

SHIFTING POWER INTERNALLY AND
EXTERNALLY

Earlier we saw that organizations and advocates engaged in RJ-ing abortion activism recognize that the laws governing abortion are part of an entire system of reproductive control erected by and necessary to maintaining white supremacy. RJ advocates call on us to dismantle that system and shift power and authority to disempowered communities. Reproductive justice activists reject any system of power that values some people more than others. They refuse to trade away the human rights of the most vulnerable. In order to move the RJ agenda forward, activists are building their own power bases that foster community power and lift up the leadership of people of color in movement organizations.

VOICES FROM THE FRONT LINES

To illustrate RJ-ing abortion in action, we invited thirteen movement leaders whose individual or organizational work foregrounds abortion access to consider the strategic value of RJ-ing abortion. We asked them to reflect on how reproductive justice shapes their clinical, spiritual, and legal activities, their research, and their advocacy. The leaders' responses share themes and concerns that incorporate the six principles we identified in the first chapter for RJ-ing abortion: bringing an intersectional approach to abortion access; understanding that abortion is deeply embedded in the social systems of oppression that constitute white supremacy; centering the lived experiences of the most vulnerable people and communities for whom the legal right to abortion does not provide access; connecting individual lived experience to the history and experiences of their communities; keeping oppression and agency in the same frame; and seeking community-based and -supported strategies to provide access to abortion and reproductive health care.

Those profiled here remind us to stay vigilant, even in cases where issues have supposedly been resolved by law and policy. We asked contributors to discuss the new challenges and losses following the *Dobbs* decision. They are emphatic that *Roe* was never adequate for their communities. They tell us that RJ-ing abortion advocacy is a dynamic process, and they urge us to find new avenues for securing reproductive justice. Their demands are strategic and concrete: Stop criminalizing and stigmatizing pregnant people; require that state and federal funding cover abortion and health care; and treat abortion seekers and all pregnant people with dignity and humanity. RJ activists are working to remove all barriers to obtaining a safe abortion while also making alternative abortion, birthing, and parenting options widely available.

These leaders pursue radical, bold, and courageous work that takes passion, dedication, and a belief in collective action to confront all the challenges to achieving reproductive justice. And their activist advice is always rooted in reproductive justice values: Center the people who bear the brunt of reproductive oppression; make bold demands; work across movements and create broad coalitions; dream, hope, inspire! It is an honor to continue the work of documenting this critical turn in reproductive politics. We include these voices to preserve their legacy and to inspire future advocacy. Together they show that there is a path to reproductive justice even during a time when threats to abortion rights and bodily autonomy are intensifying.

Dr. DeShawn Taylor

FOUNDER, DESERT STAR INSTITUTE

FAMILY PLANNING CLINIC

Abortion bans disproportionately affect marginalized and underrepresented communities. As a Black woman providing care in Arizona, these are my patients.[45]

When I decided to become an obstetrician/gynecologist, I knew I would be an abortion provider, but I didn't know that I would someday own an abortion clinic in a state where extreme antiabortion politicians passed nearly fifty restrictions on abortion over the past decade and a half.[46] I didn't know that I would experience the moral distress of having to turn people away for abortion care when I had skills and expertise to help them.

I moved to Arizona from California in 2009, the year the first sweeping restrictions on abortion were signed into law since abortion was legalized in Arizona. In 2013 I founded Desert Star Family Planning to bring services to ethnically diverse, medically underserved, and economically depressed communities in Arizona. I opened Desert Star, one of less than ten independent abortion clinics owned by an African American in the United States, during a time when abortion access in the state was shrinking rapidly, as law after law restricting abortion was passed year after year. Despite these laws, we had *Roe v. Wade* as the legal floor in the country, allowing us to fight to preserve access to abortion care in Arizona.

Under *Roe*, a nineteenth-century abortion ban in Arizona was deemed unenforceable but was never repealed. Even before *Dobbs*, a host of restrictive laws reduced the pool of abortion providers by prohibiting advanced practice clinicians from performing surgical and medication abortion, requiring physicians to have admitting privileges at a hospital within a certain mile radius of where abortion services were performed, banning telehealth for medication abortion, mandating in-person mifepristone administration by a physician, requiring notarized parental consent for minors, and imposing scripted information on abortion seekers with a twenty-four-hour forced delay of care after an ultrasound and the script. These laws diminished abortion access to the Phoenix metro area, with no access in northern Arizona and very little access in southern Arizona.

As in other states, the *Dobbs* decision, combined with the web of antiabortion laws already on the books and those newly passed, created chaos and confusion about whether abortion was legal in Arizona. The legality, and the perception of legality, of abortion changed daily. Arizona enforced the 1864 near total ban for a time, with one narrow exception—to save the life of the pregnant person. Abortion bans for the exception of "life" led to extreme morbidity and death, as we are now seeing across the country. Arizona settled on a fifteen-week ban to reconcile two abortion bans that went into effect simultaneously. I could not be prosecuted for providing abortion care in compliance with the fifteen-week ban while litigation on the 1864 ban continued. In the spring of 2024, the Arizona Supreme Court ruled that the 1864 ban could be enforced. This decision upended our status quo once again. Ultimately the Civil War–era ban was repealed, thankfully before it could ever be enforced again.

Abortion restrictions are also detrimental to the operations of independent clinics like mine. Year after year, these restrictions chipped away at our capacity to provide care. The legal upheaval and ever-changing landscape threaten Desert Star's sustainability. My patients, many of whom see me for care beyond abortion services—such as gender-affirming hormone therapy, well woman exams, and birth control—are at risk of losing access to the doctor they have come to know and trust as I struggle to keep the clinic open. Ultimately, the goal of these restrictions and bans is to close clinics and make abortion inaccessible.

Against the backdrop of a modern social justice movement, it is fitting that we move beyond "my body, my choice" to reproductive justice, which is about more than performing procedures and treating conditions.[47] It acknowledges the ways that the care people are seeking intersects with other parts of their lives. Looking at a patient's situation through this lens can be as simple as being compassionate around lateness to appointments due to unreliable transportation, unpredictable childcare, or lack of job flexibility. It might also involve acknowledging that strict fifteen-minutes-late-and-you're-out or no-children-in-the-waiting-room policies are often beyond an individual doctor's control.

They are part of a system-wide culture that fails to center the patients who are trying to receive care and harms the people who need care the most. "Minor" problems like these are examples of how social issues intersect with health care. Transportation, childcare, and access to resources are all problems that administering care through a reproductive justice framework helps to address.

On a deeper level, reproductive justice means that patients have a say in their care. Before learning about the reality of the repeated experiments performed on enslaved Black women without anesthesia by Marion J. Sims, the so-called father of gynecology, I was already reckoning with the loss of patient autonomy in the practice of obstetrics and the gatekeeping of options for womb-bearing people to control their fertility. Becoming aware of that legacy through my training set me on the path to decolonize my medical practice and fully ensconced me in the pursuit of reproductive justice.

People ask me what made me open an abortion clinic in a hostile state like Arizona. The answer is simple. My strong sense of social justice leads me to serve the underserved, and I do this by executing my vision of how the most marginalized people accessing abortion care deserve to feel and be treated. By centering my work around equitable access to health care for marginalized people, I understand that I am called to do more than "be a doctor." Desert Star was almost a casualty in the struggle for abortion access in Arizona and across the country. In the fall of 2024, the clinic was acquired by Desert Star Institute for Family Planning, the nonprofit reproductive justice organization I founded in 2017, keeping essential services in Arizona and enabling us to serve patients more holistically.

We don't live in a society in which every child born is loved and has the resources to grow and thrive. People aren't making the decision to have an abortion in a vacuum but within the context of their lives. We need to start seeing it that way, talking about it that way, and creating solutions that account for people's whole lives. Reproductive justice shows us the way.

Liza Fuentes

PUBLIC HEALTH RESEARCHER, GUTTMACHER
INSTITUTE, NATIONAL LATINA INSTITUTE FOR
REPRODUCTIVE JUSTICE, IBIS REPRODUCTIVE HEALTH

I do research to help make abortion more accessible for everyone. Technically, I'm trained in demography and epidemiology, but my motivation for studying abortion is rooted in reproductive justice. I helped cofound an abortion fund and then worked as an organizer, trainer, and researcher at the National Latina Institute for Reproductive Health. I like to say that I came up in the reproductive justice movement and then brought reproductive justice with me when my professional work moved into a space that traditionally did not incorporate it.

A reproductive justice approach to abortion research demands a complete accounting of people's needs and experiences regarding abortion. This means, for example, that the research must not only assess whether restrictive abortion laws impede people from obtaining them, but it should also document the additional burdens and costs people bear even when they do manage to obtain an abortion. This requires also asking how policies, programs, and practices seemingly unrelated to abortion—such as social welfare policies and immigration enforcement—may make abortion services more difficult or easier to obtain.

Texas provides a good example of putting these ideas into practice. In 2013 the Texas state legislature passed what was then one of the most restrictive abortion laws ever enforced, HB2. Among other medically unnecessary measures, it required that doctors who provide abortion services obtain hospital admitting privileges, and that all abortions, including those using pills, be performed in an ambulatory surgical center. At that time I was working on the Texas Policy Evaluation Team, and we studied how these restrictive laws affected access to abortion care. Until then, most of the research on abortion restrictions had focused on whether these laws stopped people from obtaining abortions: Did the abortion rate go down after the law?

In our research we looked beyond whether HB2 prevented some people from obtaining abortion services and investigated whether the law increased the time and money vulnerable people had to spend obtaining abortion care. We noted that after HB2 forced half the clinics to close, several Texas-Mexico border counties that are majority Latinx were left without abortion care. Getting to the nearest clinic, 150 miles away in San Antonio, required driving through an inland border security checkpoint. This checkpoint was not simply a barrier for undocumented people who may have needed an abortion. It also created a tremendous burden on anyone who wanted a parent, sibling, or other loved one who was undocumented or simply did not have government-issued identification to accompany them on the three-hundred-mile round-trip journey for an abortion. The RJ approach compels us to ask whether the barrier to abortion care here is restrictive immigration enforcement or restrictive abortion laws.

Texas has remained on the leading edge of restricting abortion, validating the RJ approach to research for understanding how burdens are differentially distributed by race and class. In 2021, Texas was the first state to pass so-called "vigilante" legislation, allowing anyone to bring a civil suit against a person who allegedly helped someone obtain an abortion. And in 2023, a person was forced to leave the state for an abortion after being denied care in Texas even though her fetus was diagnosed with a genetic abnormality that in almost all cases results in a miscarriage, stillbirth, or infant death.

People who do abortion rights work don't typically do immigrant rights work, and vice versa. The question arises, whose "job" is it to work on this problem? One of the brilliant ways in which reproductive justice has freed us to do our work is to make this question irrelevant because of the inherent intersectionality of the RJ framework. The need for and right to abortion must be understood within the context of real lives—and in real life, the denial of rights based on a person's immigration status and the system that denies their bodily autonomy are experienced simultaneously by immigrant women, and therefore affect them in ways that cannot be considered separately.

Simply measuring the travel distance to abortion care before and after the passage of HB2 would not adequately capture the effect of clinic closures on communities like the largely Latinx, mixed-immigration-status counties in Texas where immigration enforcement and abortion access are linked. A person cannot seek abortion care outside of their experience as an immigrant. Research exploring meaningful economic access to abortion must look beyond assessing the effects of health insurance bans on abortion coverage, since many immigrants are not eligible for health insurance at all. As an abortion researcher, it is imperative for me to integrate into my work the ways in which systems and structures that deny rights, resources, and dignity for women, immigrants, and people of color more broadly can also deny them access to abortion.

The reproductive justice approach also brings attention to how scientific research itself is an institution that can reproduce the white supremacy and sexism that ground efforts to deny people abortions. For example, a majority of the research regarding the health of Black, Latina, Asian, and Native American people and other people of color has been conducted by white people who work within white supremacist and patriarchal institutions. The uncritically examined social and political processes behind scientific research make white people and institutions "experts" on the health of people of color, often ignore the role of racism and sexism as causes of poor health, and pathologize the behaviors of people of color.

A reproductive justice approach looks to the research process itself to demonstrate, redistribute, and build power among those who are most affected by the efforts to deny abortion access. One small way I try to do this is to ensure that the young women and nonbinary people of color I work with engage with the research process beyond the tasks of their specific jobs. I consider all research team members emerging leaders in abortion research and try to provide mentoring and opportunities for them to develop and present their work. This enables all team members to meaningfully contribute to conversations about research questions, design, data collection, and interpretation regardless of their level of formal research training. Beyond that, RJ-ing abortion research means that it is led by the people who have historically been thought of as research subjects.

The reproductive justice framework provides purpose and direction to ensure that the needs and leadership of communities most affected are centered. It helps me do work that is intersectional and shifts power so that my work can contribute to ensure all people can obtain the abortion that is best for them.

Lynn Paltrow
LAWYER AND FOUNDER OF PREGNANCY
JUSTICE, FORMERLY NATIONAL ADVOCATES FOR
PREGNANT WOMEN

Pregnancy Justice (PJ), formerly National Advocates for Pregnant Women, is a nonprofit advocacy organization that seeks to ensure that no one loses their civil or human rights because of pregnancy. Our work focuses especially on those pregnant people most likely to be targeted for punitive state action, including low-income women, women of color, and women who use drugs. We provide pro bono (free) legal assistance to people directly or to their defense attorneys if the person is threatened or charged with a crime or child welfare action for having an abortion, giving birth, being pregnant, or experiencing a pregnancy loss. PJ also organizes with state-based activists and organizations as well as national coalitions and engages in public education on paper, online, and anywhere people might listen!

By choosing to focus on the full range of attacks on the rights of pregnant people—including efforts to establish separate legal rights for fertilized eggs, embryos, and fetuses under the law to hold women criminally liable for the outcome of their pregnancies, and to expand the drug war to women's wombs—PJ is making new allies and building new strength from a broad-based and integrated approach to reproductive and human rights.

What does abortion have to do with the criminal law system? For many people, abortion politics concern only the right to choose to end a pregnancy safely and effectively. However, antiabortion measures and the arguments for them are, in fact, key mechanisms for expanding that system. They give the government the power to lock up and control people with the capacity for pregnancy—especially Black and brown women and low-income white women. Before *Roe*, abortion was criminalized in nearly every state, and women who had abortions were far more likely to die as a result of unsafe abortions than they were to be arrested. However, some women were arrested and convicted of crimes such as manslaughter.

Following *Roe*, most states rewrote their abortion laws but kept them in the criminal code. The penalties under these laws were typically directed at those who perform abortions. However, since those who need and have abortions are pregnant people, such laws communicate directly and indirectly, explicitly and subtly, the idea that the people who have the capacity for pregnancy and who might someday have an abortion should be thought of as criminals; they are considered a class of persons who deserve to be arrested and locked up.

Antiabortion laws are drafted, promoted, and supported by activists who quite explicitly argue that abortion is the same or worse than murder,[48] and who often compare abortion to genocide.[49] They describe people who have abortions as the kind of people who commit murder and are carrying out a genocide worse than any in human history.[50]

Kansas's 2015 law outlawing a method of abortion known as dilation and evacuation illustrates subtler messaging.[51] The law's sponsors named it the Unborn Child Protection from Dismemberment Act.[52] It created civil and criminal penalties that apply only to physicians who perform such abortions, not to the women who have them. Nevertheless, the law unmistakably brands pregnant women as capable of monstrous criminal acts, that is to say, murdering and dismembering children.

This view is reinforced by the many feticide laws sponsored by antiabortion activists, typically proposed and passed in the wake of extreme violence against a pregnant woman. While they purport to protect pregnant women from violence and penalize only those who attack pregnant women, such laws equate pregnancy termination with murder and define fertilized eggs, embryos, and fetuses as separate persons who must be treated as independent crime victims. Even when abortion was protected as a constitutional right in the United States, pregnant women were being arrested for having or attempting to have an abortion. Among these are women PJ has helped to defend, including Jennie McCormack, Purvi Patel, Anna Yocca, and Kenlissia Jones. The charges in these cases included the crime of "self-abortion" as well as murder and feticide.

Even before *Dobbs*, criminal abortion and feticide laws were regularly cited as authority for arrests and other forms of control over pregnant women who were not trying to end a pregnancy. This often surprises people, but it should not. If fertilized eggs, embryos, and fetuses are viewed as potential crime victims, then it is, as some prosecutors and judges claim, illogical and unfair to exempt pregnant people from legal responsibility for doing or risking harm to them.

Between 1973, when *Roe* was decided, and 2022, when *Dobbs* overturned *Roe*, more than 1,800 pregnant women were arrested or in some other way deprived of their physical liberty by being arrested, detained in mental hospitals and involuntary treatment programs, and taken into custody so that they could be subjected to cesarean and other forced medical interventions.[53] Low-income women are the overwhelming majority of those subjected to all of these deprivations of liberty, and for the first thirty-one years after *Roe*, Black women were vastly overrepresented among those subjected to state control because of pregnancy.[54]

These cases, which PJ has documented and often successfully challenged, include pregnant women who fell down a flight of stairs, delayed having cesarean surgery, had a home birth, drank alcohol, didn't get to the hospital quickly enough on the day of delivery, attempted suicide, experienced a miscarriage or stillbirth, gave birth to a baby who did not survive, or used any amount of a controlled substance (including ones prescribed to them). In a majority of the cases, the woman gave birth to a healthy baby. Numerous crimes, such as "child endangerment," require a prosecutor only to show a risk of harm. Because pregnancy occurs inside the human body, everything a pregnant person does or does not do could potentially have an impact on her future child and thus provide a basis for arrest.

Our current criminal law system—radically expanded through the racist war on drugs—has resulted in mass criminalization implemented through an immense and increasingly privatized and profit-driven system of incarceration. According to the Prison Policy Initiative, U.S. prisons and jails now hold nearly two million people. Of these people, more than 170,000 are women and girls. In recent decades, women's incarceration has grown at twice the rate of men's incarceration, and women are disproportionately locked up in jails rather than prisons.[55] The majority are awaiting trial, not yet having been convicted of a crime. Another 3.7 million people are under some form of criminal justice supervision, such as probation and parole, and are often monitored by profit-making surveillance systems such as electronic shackles. More than 800,000 of the people being supervised and controlled in this manner are women. Black and American Indian / Alaska Native women are particularly overrepresented in prisons and jails.[56]

In a country where people with the capacity for pregnancy have been relentlessly stigmatized by antiabortion politics characterizing them as people capable of the most heinous crimes against children and humanity, and where laws categorize abortion as a crime and define the unborn as crime victims, every one of the more than 5.5 million women who become pregnant each year in the United States is a potential criminal.[57] (In the lead-up to *Dobbs* the National Association of Criminal Defense Lawyers published a report, "How Legislative Overreach Is Turning Reproductive Rights into Criminal Wrongs," documenting the extent to which antiabortion measures already on the books would open the door to mass criminalization on an unprecedented scale and without the need for new legislative action.)[58]

If we wish to ensure justice, including reproductive justice for all, efforts to protect the right to choose abortion must be linked to efforts to end mass incarceration and criminalization. Both movements must address not only the threat of abortion recriminalization, but also explicitly reject a politics that renders people with the capacity for pregnancy as villainous rather than as human beings entitled to full human and civil rights.

Monica Simpson

EXECUTIVE DIRECTOR, SISTERSONG WOMEN OF
COLOR REPRODUCTIVE JUSTICE COLLECTIVE

SisterSong Women of Color Reproductive Justice Collective is a Black women–led, national, multiethnic, and multicultural organization based in Atlanta. Formed in 1997, it has shaped the framework that sparked the reproductive justice (RJ) movement. Simpson has been the executive director since 2013.

SisterSong was created to be a powerful BIPOC collective, ready to organize and respond to moments such as this one [2023, post-*Dobbs*]. Our communities have always had to live in a world where we are constantly worried about our safety and ability to make decisions about our own lives. We stand on the shoulders of the queer Black women who created a feminism that was meant for us. And we stand on the shoulders of the Black women who created the reproductive justice movement in 1994, centering our experiences and our needs. They told us to fight for a holistic future in which we have the human rights to maintain personal bodily autonomy and have the children we want in the ways we want; that we should be able to end pregnancies without shame but with dignity; and that we should be able to parent our children in healthy and safe environments.[59]

This work is deeply rooted in bodily autonomy—to make decisions about our families, our bodies, and our futures. Our fight has always been urgent, but the *Dobbs* decision, along with increased police violence against our communities, anti-LGBTQIA+ legislation, and the dire maternal mortality crisis in our country, makes it even more immediately necessary.[60]

This political moment, although hard, is an opportunity to center the reproductive justice movement and framework—and that is just what we're doing. It has become evident that our work must be intersectional. Reproductive justice is connected to all facets of our lives, and SisterSong's work reflects that perspective.[61] The fall of *Roe* made it absolutely clear that our fight for reproductive justice is directly linked to racial justice, is directly linked to civil rights, is directly linked to economic justice, is directly linked to environmental justice, and so much more.

When the antiabortion movement created a billboard campaign that shamed Black women for having abortions, we responded with our own campaign, Trust Black Women, affirming Black women's lives and their right to self-determination.[62] Over the years we have expanded this campaign to include having a seat at the table for all Black women, whether or not they are fighting for abortion, and to emphasize having the right not to die in childbirth, to receive equal pay, and to be believed when speaking out about rape and assault.

Our intersectional understanding of reproductive justice means that we organize not just for abortion rights but around all aspects of racial oppression. That's why, for example, we work with Black Mamas Matter to raise awareness that Black women are dying at a rate that is so much higher than that of white women, and we advocate for lifesaving birthing policies.

Although SisterSong was not created to be a direct services organization, the current political climate has forced us to expand the ways we care for our communities because the needs of our people have really grown. We have increased the direct services we provide. Our Birth Justice Care Fund, which focuses on supporting pregnant people and their families, was our first program created to offer practical support to communities in need.[63] Whether it's baby supplies, doula care, or support for housing, we try to meet these needs.

The opposition intentionally spreads misinformation to divide us. SisterSong disrupts this through our culture-change work. We are focused on finding innovative ways to educate people about reproductive justice. Most people may not read the results of the most recent scientific study, but they are on social media, watching television shows, and buying their favorite brands. We understand that people will more likely stumble across a video from a content creator than they would something from the World Health Organization. Therefore, we work across industries and with influencers who have grabbed the public's attention and who have garnered trust in their messages and brands.

This is why our approach at SisterSong is really about deepening our culture-shift work. So much has been snatched away from us through the political system, and we have to think creatively about the new world that we need and how we get there. We are focused on finding innovative ways to reach new audiences and the next generation of leaders. In 2023 we brought together RJ leaders to cocreate a new vision for reproductive justice;[64] we presented the Trust Black Women Universe at the Essence Festival of Culture, the largest Black-led and Black-attended event in the country; and organized the reproductive justice bus tour, a series of educational gatherings across the rural South.[65]

Reproductive justice is focused on collective liberation. Every day, I believe we are getting closer to understanding how my liberation is tied to yours, and how your liberation is connected to the person beside you. If we lead with this, the power of the people will always prevail. The doors to the reproductive justice movement are open. Make your way in and find your way to do the work.

Oriaku Njoku

FORMER EXECUTIVE DIRECTOR, NATIONAL NETWORK
OF ABORTION FUNDS (NNAF)

Founded in 1993, NNAF is an organization of one hundred independent abortion funds and over nine thousand individual members who are dedicated to reducing economic and logistical barriers for people seek-ing abortions.

Abortion funds exist because *Roe v. Wade* left a tremendous gap between the legal right to abortion and the ability to get one. People who need abortions cannot wait for lengthy court battles or the legislative process to determine their fate. For thirty years NNAF and its member funds have filled that gap with care and support so that people without economic means can have their abortions with less hassle and hustle.

Abortion funds offer collective mutual aid, not individual charity.[66] NNAF supports member funds with grants, leadership training, infra-structure support, and technical assistance. In 2023, NNAF distributed almost half its budget to its member funds. Whether they are paying for procedures, abortion pills, transportation and lodging, childcare, doulas, or emotional support, our funds find innovative, nonjudgmental, and com-passionate ways to get as many people as possible the abortions they want and need. The network also advocates for a more permanent solution—government funding of abortion and removal of all access barriers.

I joined NNAF in July 2022, just twelve days after the *Dobbs* decision. I knew it would radically shift our work. I also knew that abortion funds would continue to be the heart of the abortion access movement, clear-ing a path for people who need abortions. I approached my job in a spirit of grounded optimism.

I was not in denial about the escalating crisis in abortion access, the attacks on gender-affirming care, and the full array of challenges to our health, lives, and dignity. But I believed that we could create a better and brighter future of abortion access by grounding ourselves in repro-ductive justice, our route toward collective liberation. Even during the global pandemic, NNAF piloted the Penny Portal, a case management system designed and built by NNAF in collaboration with member funds that allows payments and information to flow more seamlessly and securely between funds and clinics.

Immediately after *Dobbs*, abortion funds experienced tremendous spikes in donations and volunteers. This rapid response from people all across the country was exciting. At the same time, the changing legal landscape complicated the logistics of abortion access, stretching the capacity, knowledge, and infrastructure of the funds and NNAF. Clearly we had to scale up as best we could on the fly to meet new needs. For example, redistribution of wealth within our network became even more important: Several funds had to suspend operations to assess new legal risks, and more people had to travel for abortion care. The network helped funds create geographically larger networks of care to meet the needs of abortion seekers while continuing to organize and advocate at all levels of government for equitable policies that ensure abortion access, and more. And in the face of a continuing groundswell of need for rapid legal support, NNAF works closely with legal counsel to help funds make sense of service-delivery implications of the post-*Dobbs* legal landscape, assess risks, and offer guidance about managing increased surveillance.

For many people, the struggle to get an abortion is not isolated from other basic health needs, both medical and financial. Job loss, food insecurity, caring for sick loved ones, and a lack of childcare options are obstacles that can make it nearly impossible for vulnerable people to get an abortion. They are hit hardest by abortion restrictions and the deep inequities in our health care system. Racism and structural inequality also result in higher rates of maternal and infant death, especially in the Black community.

Fund members and providers have to learn the technical parts of the work and commit to centering the people who come to us for care, starting by acknowledging what it takes for a person just to get to a clinic. Our callers face daunting challenges—figuring out travel, lodging, and childcare, taking time off work, and paying for a procedure that may cost more than they make in a whole trimester. Sometimes people have experienced intentional deception and shaming from anti-abortion crisis pregnancy centers. And after the abortion, there is the toll from returning home to a state where abortion is actually or virtually banned, perhaps without the ability to follow up with a local provider because of the all too real fear of criminalization.

Even if a person walks through groups of protesters heaping threats and abuse from their "moral high ground," an abortion experience does not have to be clouded by fear, shame, stigma, criminalization, harm, or trauma. Having an abortion can be a transformative and liberatory moment. Our compassionate support in this challenging moment is just as crucial as meeting financial and logistical needs. Abortion fund members support each other and practice collective care and solidarity that is centered in reproductive and healing justice. From making the appointment, calling an abortion fund, and meeting frontline clinic workers to having the abortion, we all play a role. We strive to ensure that regardless of what it took to get there, each person will be treated with dignity and respect, and will be cared for by someone who believes they deserve care.

To do this in a post-*Dobbs* climate, abortion funds must continue tapping into the abundance of possibilities and not be demoralized by scarcity and fear. We are working toward a future that does not replicate the limitations of *Roe*. The choices we make now as a movement must ensure a future where abortions are available to all who need them—a future where we have all the funding, information, and resources required to adequately meet the needs of abortion funds and abortion seekers. We cannot continue to make compromises and create temporary fixes that focus only on protecting the legality of abortion. I am convinced that we have what we need to build power so long as we can find the space that allows us to dream, to love, and to move at the speed of trust.

Kinga Jelinska (Executive Director, Women Help Women),
Lucía Berro Pizzarossa (British Academy Fellow, Birmingham
Law School), and Natalia Broniarczyk (Abortion Dream Team)

WOMEN HELP WOMEN

Women Help Women (WHW) was founded in 2014 to decentralize and support feminist activism for self-managed abortion (SMA). The organization connects the personal experience of swallowing a pill to global political activism. We are an interactive telehealth (online) service that provides counseling and information about abortion pills in eight languages via email, available sixteen hours a day. People can request a package of mifepristone and misoprostol after an online consultation. Demand has grown significantly in recent years. In 2018 we received and responded to 106,042 emails, and in 2023 the number jumped to more than 145,000. More than 41,000 people asked for information; we sent abortion pills to 13,000 people from thirty-one countries.

WHW works with about a hundred national and local community organizations and groups to identify and develop locally appropriate strategies and create networks of activists to increase access to abortion. By fostering networks within and among country-based partners and working on the holistic security of activists, WHW has been able to expand access to information about safe medical abortion and services, and to make links to grassroots activism to change societal norms around abortion.

Putting pills and power in people's hands is an activist strategy that initially began at the margins of the medicolegal system as a self-defense strategy that has since developed fully demedicalized practices that have spread globally and radically transformed the abortion landscape.[67] It is also a subversive strategy that challenges the assumption that safe abortion can only be achieved through regulated legal, medical, and market control systems.[68] WHW rejects medicalized, stigmatized, and restrictive models of care in favor of a revolutionary process that creates alternative spaces and practices and reclaims abortion autonomy as a feminist political demand. We express our paradigm as the four D's: destigmatization, demystification, demedicalization, and decriminalization.

PRACTICING A MODEL OF ABORTION CARE   Studies that have documented the work and impact of Women Help Women and similar feminist networks and collectives have shown that most people who received pills and used them had successful abortions and highly favorable experiences. In WHW's 2016–17 study, almost all who responded said that they would recommend self-managed abortion to a friend. We take this as a clear signal that self-managed abortion with pills is not a last resort but a legitimate and appreciated care model that many people find works better for them.[69] In a qualitative study, researchers show that participants perceived the WHW service as good, trustworthy, fast, and affordable. They valued the confidentiality and privacy, the quantity and quality of information, having direct, personalized, and timely communication with service staff, being treated with respect, and feeling safe, cared for, and supported in their decisions.[70]

WEAVING CONNECTIONS AND CREATING SYNERGIES   WHW strongly emphasizes the collaborative dimension of SMA. Every self-managed abortion is built on the work of many people who are committed to diversifying and strengthening the options for abortion care, and who value locally led strategies. A self-managed abortion is shaped and influenced by several actors who function locally, nationally, and transnationally to enable and support that abortion.[71] Pushing back against the global backlash requires strong and organized solidarity among the advocates working to advance access to safe abortion in their respective countries. For example, Women Help Women cofounded the MAMA Network (Mobilizing Activists around Medical Abortion), a grassroots network comprising seventy-plus organizations across twenty-four African countries (as of August 2023). MAMA is led by its membership. Members share evidence-based and stigma-free information and strategies such as hotlines, community outreach, and technological innovations.

In Europe, WHW was a founding partner of Abortion Without Borders, an initiative of nine organizations in different countries working together to help people access abortions at home with pills or abroad in clinics. Catalyzed by the near-total ban on abortion imposed by Poland in 2020, the initiative now responds to the needs of people across Europe, including displaced people from Ukraine. In 2022 and 2023, Abortion Without Borders was the biggest provider of abortion care in Poland, helping more than one hundred thousand people and enabling as many abortions in a day as the state of Poland did in a whole year. In Poland its members are the leading voices for abortion access.

BUILDING THE MOVEMENT   Using the concept of reproductive justice, we understand that abortion is part of a larger political project.[72] Supporting self-managed abortion is fundamentally anti-oppression work: It decenters medical knowledge in favor of community-led, practical, and experiential ways of knowing; it places people and their communities, rather than law, at the center of abortion discourse; and it moves abortion access toward justice.

We are proud and vocal about fighting abortion stigma. We use our own bodies, stories, and experiences to spread and democratize the knowledge of how to do an abortion outside of oppressive systems.[73] We unapologetically celebrate abortion. Our goal is to demedicalize abortion, both inside and outside institutional medical systems. We call for increased collaboration between institutional medical systems and autonomous health movements and for recognition of the value of self-managed abortion as a model of care and a strategy for achieving reproductive justice.[74]

Susan Yanow

COFOUNDER, WOMEN HELP WOMEN (WHW), AND
DIRECTOR, SELF-MANAGED ABORTION; SAFE AND
SUPPORTED (SASS)

In late 2016, faced with the imminent inauguration of Donald Trump as president of the United States and the clear threat to abortion access, Women Help Women (WHW) launched SASS (Self-Managed Abortion; Safe & Supported in the United States).[75] SASS's mission remains the same: to increase knowledge about abortion pills, mitigate the legal risk of those who choose to use abortion pills without a clinician, and build acceptance and support for self-managed abortion across the reproductive rights and justice networks, including clinicians, lawyers, policymakers, and activists. SASS embraces the WHW's four D's model, advocating for the demystification, demedicalization, destigmatization, and decriminalization of abortion pills.

SASS builds on years of grassroots SMA work in the United States and is based on the practice that came from community groups using misoprostol in Latin America starting in the 1980s. The first article documenting misoprostol knowledge and use in the United States was published in 2000. In 2006, activists in the United States convened the Misoprostol Working Group. In 2012 and 2013, the Civil Liberties and Public Policy Program (CLPP, now Collective Power for Reproductive Justice) convened the first strategy meeting in Texas to discuss the actual and potential use of misoprostol for SMA after that state had passed the most restrictive abortion laws in the nation. At that time, SMA was controversial among abortion rights advocates. In order to foster movement-wide knowledge and discussion, in 2014, those of us who later founded SASS began offering values clarification exercises on SMA for reproductive rights and justice groups, beginning with Advocates for Youth and the National Latina Institute for Reproductive Health (now the National Latina Institute for Reproductive Justice).

In recent years a number of organizations have been created to support those who self-manage their abortions, including Plan C (referrals), If/When/How (legal information and support), Aid Access (sends pills from overseas), Red State Access (provides support and pills in states with abortion bans), and the M+A Hotline (Miscarriage and Abortion Hotline, staffed by clinicians). Since the *Dobbs* decision many small new grassroots collectives have mobilized across the United States to share information about abortion pills, identify reliable sources, and reach as many people as possible who need abortions and cannot or choose not to travel to another state for care. The groups provide doula support in their communities and pills, sometimes acquiring them from feminist groups in Mexico such as Las Libres and Marea Verde.

In the United States the greatest risk to people practicing SMA is legal, not medical. Those living in disempowered communities are the most vulnerable to criminal prosecution. According to a study by If/When/How, between 2000 and 2020 at least sixty-one people were arrested for using abortion pills outside of the medical system. It is important to note that many thousands of people have safely obtained pills from Aid Access and Las Libres, which are the only providers that share data on the number of users, so these arrests are only a tiny percentage of those choosing SMA. Nonetheless, it is critical to give users information about minimizing their risk. SASS provides information about how to determine when medical attention is needed and, in the rare cases when follow-up care is needed, what can and should be said to medical professionals as protection. People with questions contact SASS via a secure portal, which means that there is no electronic trail of communication, further protecting users of the SASS counseling service.

The reproductive justice lens highlights the ways in which SMA lies at the intersection of human rights, public health, empowerment, and access. The RJ tenet that every person should have the power and resources to determine their own reproductive futures, whether ending a pregnancy or having a child, is at the heart of SASS's work.

Supporting the use of pills on one's own and putting the tools for safe abortion directly in the hands of those who want and need them is an empowerment strategy. Abortion pills are safer than aspirin or Viagra, and it is not complicated to learn how to use them, what to expect, and how to deal with the rare cases where medical care may be needed. SMA breaks the various power structures and systems of control by state, medical practices, or social surveillance operating in our society. In this way, it is subversive and also deeply transformative. SMA challenges the prevailing narrative that frames abortion as safe only when supervised by a trained medical professional. It breaks the "safe and legal" versus "unsafe and illegal" dichotomy. By claiming this knowledge for ourselves, SMA is an expression of the fundamental feminist principle and basic human right to bodily autonomy, and the right to control our own health care.

Abortion pills have the potential to democratize access to safe abortion and flatten the inequities. Feminist collectives around the world have mobilized to spread information about self-management and access to it through hotlines, telehealth, and community distribution programs. In these strategies, self-managed abortion is seen as a health care practice that may be used out of necessity, convenience, or preference. SASS builds on this international history, recognizing the unique context of the United States, where surveillance is high and communities of color have a disproportionate risk of criminalization.

Self-managed abortion with medicines is much more than a solution to a single individual's problem of being pregnant when they determine the pregnancy is unsupportable at that time. At SASS we understand that SMA cannot mitigate all of the harm done by banning and criminalizing abortion. Nor does advocacy for SMA decrease the demand for the state to fulfill its obligation to provide health care, including abortion care. However, throughout history, when abortion has been criminalized or heavily restricted by law, policy, economics, or culture, activists have responded by creating safe alternatives outside the formal medical system. The SASS project builds on that history, informed by international networks with deep experience in supporting those who self-manage their abortion while embracing the reproductive justice principle of building power and knowledge in the communities most impacted by restrictive policies.

Farah Diaz-Tello

SENIOR COUNSEL AND LEGAL DIRECTOR, IF/WHEN/
HOW: LAWYERING FOR REPRODUCTIVE JUSTICE

If/When/How operates on the premise that excellent lawyering is necessary, but not sufficient, to achieve reproductive justice.[76] For more than twenty years, the organization—first as Law Students for Choice, then as Law Students for Reproductive Justice—has worked to change legal education and the legal profession in service of reproductive justice. The historic heart of this work is the law school chapters, which began as a means to demand coursework on reproductive rights on law school campuses, and today empowers students to learn, build power, and organize for reproductive and racial justice on their campus and beyond. In 2011, the organization created the Reproductive Justice Fellowship Program, which helps launch careers for law school graduates who want to change the face and practice of reproductive justice lawyering. This is the long-range work of culture change, giving future generations of lawyers, whatever their practice ends up looking like, reproductive justice as a lens through which to fight injustice. Over the course of the last five years, the organization's work has transformed to address the urgent needs of people facing state violence and coercion in their reproductive lives. Today, through direct legal services, strategic litigation, applied research, and policy advocacy, If/When/How is creating a future where every one of us has the power and support to make decisions about our bodies, families, and communities without barriers, coercion, or punishment, in safety and dignity. We now operate the Repro Legal Helpline, which provides free, confidential legal services for people's reproductive lives, including abortion, pregnancy loss, and birth, as well as the Repro Legal Defense Fund, which funds bail and strong defenses for people facing legal trouble for abortion, miscarriage, stillbirth, and other related needs.

The catalyst behind this evolution was the 2019 merger with a small repro-legal startup called the Self-Induced Abortion (SIA) Legal Team. The SIA Legal Team was formed with one simple fact in mind: Resourceful people will find ways to end untimely pregnancies, no matter what the law says. The group was, at its inception, a research consortium formed by several small reproductive rights and gender justice organizations concerned with the intensification of the criminalization of people who had self-managed their abortions. It set out with the mission of figuring out "what the law is" on self-managed abortion, only to realize that the chasm between what the law says and how people experience it requires action as much as it requires research. By 2017, led by the demands surfaced in a community-based participatory research project involving home abortion providers and people from communities most likely to experience criminalization of SMA, the core programs in litigation, policy advocacy, research, and direct legal services began.[77] Merging the SIA Legal Team with If/When/How brought together lawyering strategies for combating some of the most pernicious ways the state strips people of their dignity and self-determination in their reproductive lives, and a vast network of lawyers and lawyers-to-be were trained to care about these issues.

Of course, the world of repro lawyering was turned upside down with the *Dobbs* decision in 2022. But the forms of state violence If/When/How was working on existed even when *Roe* was in place; our work was laser focused on the communities that jurisprudence left behind and was developed and tested during the first Trump administration. Our helpline had been in place since 2018, and the legal defense fund had launched more than a year prior to *Dobbs*. As horrifying as the present reality is, it is no surprise to those of us who heeded reproductive justice leaders' warnings about white supremacy and how it undergirds authoritarianism, marginalization, and reproductive control.

The organization's work has continued to evolve since that time and now includes activities to improve young people's access to abortion care and eliminate forced parental involvement, ensure that birthing people can make decisions about their pregnancies and births with dignity and without coercion or violence, address economic injustice that robs people of their agency in reproductive decision-making, and dismantle the state's power to surveil, punish, and destroy families through the family regulation system. We recognize that the people least served by our medical systems—people of color, immigrants, people living in poverty, and trans and gender-expansive people—are the ones most likely to be ensnared by our punitive systems. Our calling is to right this balance and ensure that our systems resource and protect instead of marginalize and punish.

Most importantly, in all of our work we seek to challenge lawyerly habits that impede the path to justice. Lawyers are taught to advise clients to avoid risk. But just as we trust people to make the best decisions for themselves about a pregnancy, we also trust them to make their own decisions about how the law will influence their actions. As lawyers, it is not our task to decide the right way forward for someone making a decision about their reproductive life. Nor, in a context in which providing someone the means to end a pregnancy or helping a young person leave the state for an abortion is increasingly under fire, is it our place to tell people not to take on the risks of helping a loved one. The history of health care in the United States is filled with examples of principled resistance to the law that has led to lifesaving policy change. Instead, it is our task to give people the information they need to make decisions that are right for them, and to transform the legal landscape—dismantling barriers and shoring up protections—so that the path to reproductive justice is clear of the threat of punishment.

We have to do more than just defend lost ground. Now is the time for us to move in unison with the spirit of compassion to demand lasting changes to improve access to abortion, expand the social safety net, and ensure that we all have the freedom to decide if, when, and how to create, sustain, and defend our families.

Cherisse Scott

CEO AND FOUNDER, SISTERREACH

SisterReach is a Memphis, Tennessee–based grassroots nonprofit organization founded in 2011. We are one of very few reproductive justice organizations in the Southern United States. Using the RJ framework, we advocate for the reproductive and sexual health autonomy of Black women, women and teens of color, poor and rural women, queer and gender-expansive people, and their families.

Tennessee is among several Southern states where poverty rates are higher than the national average.[78] The impact of poverty is most severe among Black and Hispanic residents, youth, undocumented people of color, and the unhoused. The policy actions of our legislature, which is controlled by conservative evangelicals (a.k.a. Christian nationalists), compounds the harms. Using religious jargon and theological framing of biblical text in an effort to disguise its racist agenda, the legislature and its actions are not aligned with our understanding of Christianity and the teachings of Jesus Christ as compassionate, inclusive, teachable, visionary, and revolutionary. Instead, legislative policies undermine any attempt at self-determination or agency by rejecting intervention and prevention opportunities for young people's reproductive and sexual health, instead mandating abstinence-based sex education and refusing federal funding for vital medical and social support to people living with HIV/AIDS.

The state's refusal to comply with Title X guidelines specific to referrals for abortion care and gender-affirming care cost Tennesseans access to Title X funding. And the legislature still fails to expand Medicaid, criminalizes substance use disorder, and has eliminated state constitutional protections for abortion. Before *Dobbs* the state legislature passed a constitutional amendment empowering itself to enact, amend, or repeal state statutes regarding abortion, including in cases where the pregnancies result from rape or incest or when an abortion is necessary to protect the mother's life.

The Republican supermajority took away the right of low-income women to raise their children with a high quality of life by cutting social supports like Supplemental Nutrition Assistance Program (SNAP) benefits. They support antiabortion clinics and promote targeted and racist long-acting reversible contraception (LARC) enforcement among low-income and undocumented women and girls of color. And until the Anti-Sterilization Bill of 2018 passed, judges were permitted to offer LARCs to incarcerated women and girls in exchange for a reduced jail sentence.

For the last twelve years SisterReach has navigated this abusive terrain and shown up for the people we serve, often doing what our government should be doing, empowering Black women, women and youth of color, and pregnant-capable gender-expansive people, as well as meeting our base where they are, without judgment or shame. Reproductive justice guides us to mobilize our base to resist this entire agenda. Here we highlight a few of our major initiatives.

INTERFAITH-BASED ORGANIZING   Interfaith-based organizing has been a key strategy for us. We expanded our reach by including a faith-based curriculum for clergy, lay leadership, and advocates interested in organizing faith communities. It offers messaging and sermon-crafting tools on abortion, comprehensive sexuality education, LGBTQIA+ oppression, and self-help. Our Vacation Body School (VBS) program educates youth and adults in faith-based settings, and our Social Justice Preacher Series engages clergy, public health professionals, and laity. Lastly, the Interfaith Coalition for Human Rights is a way for us to work with clergy and laity, both religious and nonreligious, around issues that impact the most vulnerable. We offer training opportunities for participants so they can more actively and effectively mobilize their congregants and communities in support of reproductive and sexual justice and human rights.

COUNTERING THE ANTIABORTION MOVEMENT   In 2015, when Pro Life Across America (PLAA) erected fetal heartbeat billboards targeting Black fathers across Memphis, SisterReach countered with our own pro-woman billboard campaign. We brought local and national attention to the disingenuous nature of the PLAA campaign, which led to their billboards being taken down. Our campaign also demonstrated the power of national and local leadership and collaboration, and it became a model of Black women pushing back against the antiabortion movement. Cherisse Scott, our founder and CEO, was also a founding member of the national Trust Black Women (TBW) campaign organized by SisterSong Women of Color Reproductive Justice Collective. We adapted organizing strategies and messaging from the national campaign. Other reproductive justice organizations, like the Abortion

Rights Coalition (ARC Southeast) and the Afiya Center, have used the SisterReach billboard campaign strategy to push back against similar attacks in their local communities.

HARM REDUCTION OUTREACH AND ENGAGEMENT   After the *Dobbs* decision, we launched a project to teach people with the capacity for pregnancy to chart their menstrual cycles and control their fertility. At the height of the COVID-19 pandemic we offered gift cards, food, clothing, baby items, and other necessities to low-income people. In 2020, we moved $250,000 of our general support funding into gift cards and other supplemental supports. In partnership with local churches and aligned nonprofits, we served over five thousand Memphis residents.

Our syringe exchange and substance use intervention outreach supports community members who navigate substance use and deserve to navigate their health condition with safety, dignity, respect, and better access to substance use materials in nonclinic settings.

The goal of all our programming is to strengthen the reproductive and sexual justice movement's commitment to addressing the whole lives and human rights injustices experienced by women, youth, gender-expansive people, and all people of color who are victims of reproductive and sexual oppression.

Nourbese Flint
PRESIDENT, ALL* ABOVE ALL AND THE ALL* IN
ACTION FUND

This piece was originally written by Silvia Henriquez and Destiny Lopez, former copresidents of All* Above All and the All* Above All Action Fund, and was updated by Morgan Hopkins in 2023.

Women of color have led the effort to repeal the Hyde Amendment for decades, but the battle to exclude abortion coverage from the Affordable Care Act (ACA) in 2010 was a wake-up call for those of us who center women of color in our organizing and advocacy strategies.

The ACA promised to expand health insurance coverage to millions of previously uninsured people, the first opportunity in a generation to expand public insurance coverage of abortion. However, when faced with the prospect that this historic legislation championed by President Obama might fail, Democrats in Congress brokered a compromise on the backs of women of color that refused to treat abortion as basic health care and denied guaranteed coverage under the ACA. In response, leading reproductive justice organizations convened the first set of exploratory meetings with a broad cross section of national and state partners in the reproductive health, rights, and justice movement. This gathering ultimately led to the creation of the Coalition for Abortion Access and Reproductive Equity (CAARE) and, in 2013, its public-facing campaign, All* Above All.

More than ten years later, All* Above All affirms the positive and powerful belief that each of us, not just some of us, must be able to make the important decision of whether to end a pregnancy. Barriers to abortion care based on who we are, where we're from, or how much money we make should not be written into public policy. Our campaign activates the electorate of young people and people of color who are standing up to the continued avalanche of attempts to target them and their decision-making.

To counter the fragmentation and erasure that persists in the reproductive rights movement, at the outset All* Above All incorporated a reproductive justice lens centering the experiences of those most impacted by Hyde. The campaign made visible regular people's lives, the complex landscape of personal experiences, family legacies, historic injustices, and present-day inequalities. The intersections among reproductive rights, racial justice, LGBTQIA+ issues, and immigration rights became our road map and are central to All* Above All to this day.

Within this framework and burgeoning campaign, we established guiding principles to illustrate our values and to anchor our road map. We build the capacity of organizations that represent our priority constituencies and cultivate a new generation of leaders who represent them. We believe in the power of both people of color and those working to make ends meet to direct our movement's priorities and strategies, and to draw in new constituencies. Our coalition invests in advocacy efforts to alter the historically risk-averse pro-choice movement. Our strategies are proactive and champion our ultimate goals without privileging political expediency. We shift and share power to center communities of color in the movement.

Our campaign is charged with disrupting the centuries of cultural and institutional racism and power dynamics that brought about the Hyde Amendment in the first place. Overturning the Hyde Amendment, and more broadly supporting legal, affordable abortion, isn't an isolated idea. That's why, after seven years of game-changing work to lift abortion bans, we expanded our mission and scope to become a catalyst for abortion justice nationwide.

At its core, abortion justice is the understanding that our ability to make real decisions about pregnancy and parenting cannot be separated from systemic racism, economic insecurity, and immigrant injustices that multiply the barriers to care. We have always fought for the right to have children, not just to end pregnancies. We are *not* making a cost-based argument for abortion access; we *are* making a justice-based argument for freedom and autonomy and eliminating barriers to access based on who we are, where we're from, or how much money we have. Women of color know what it's like to fight against impossible odds. We've been gathering kindling for years, and now we're catalyzed to win!

Sung Yeon Choimorrow
EXECUTIVE DIRECTOR, NATIONAL ASIAN PACIFIC
AMERICAN WOMEN'S FORUM (NAPAWF)

NAPAWF is the only national, multi-issue Asian American and Pacific Islander (AAPI) women's organization in the country. Its mission is to build a movement to advance social justice and human rights for AAPI women and girls. NAPAWF played a leadership role in opposing anti-choice legislative bans on sex-selective abortion—abortions performed due to the sex of the fetus. These bans have gained sweeping popularity among antiabortion legislators in recent years. In 2013, sex-selective abortion bans were the second most proposed abortion restriction across the United States, and they continued to gain momentum in 2014 and 2015.[79] As of August 2023, eleven states have passed such legislation.[80] We are concerned that more Republican-controlled states will follow in the post-*Dobbs* climate.

Supporters of these bans rely heavily on xenophobic rhetoric suggesting that AAPI immigrants import "backwards" biases from Asian countries that favor the birth of sons, thus perpetuating anti-immigrant sentiment and negative stereotypes about AAPI women.[81] For example, records from Arizona's 2011 state legislative session reveal that a state senator said, "We know that [female infanticide] is pervasive in some areas [like China and India]. We know that people from those countries and from those cultures are moving and immigrating in some reasonable numbers to the United States and to Arizona."[82]

This statement is completely false: There is no evidence that Asian American women in the United States are seeking abortions due to a preference for sons. Asian women actually have higher birth rates for female babies than other races.[83]

Sex-selective abortion bans are premised on misinformation and stereotypes about Asian American women. In theory, the bans would punish doctors and health providers who perform or assist with so-called sex-selective abortions. In practice, however, sex-selective abortion bans target AAPI women and lead to discrimination against them. In many states, doctors and nurses who merely suspect a patient is seeking a sex-selective abortion are required to report them to authorities. Due to fear of criminal or civil penalties, doctors may scrutinize the decisions of women seeking an abortion—in this case, specifically AAPI women.

Not only can these racist stereotypes lead abortion providers to discriminate against AAPI women, but they may also lead medical providers and law enforcement to make dangerous assumptions about the pregnancy outcomes of AAPI women. In the early 2010s, two Asian women, Bei Bei Shuai and Purvi Patel, were both charged with feticide for their pregnancy outcomes when they sought out medical attention. It is no coincidence that these two cases happened in Indiana when future vice president Mike Pence was governor—and Indiana's sex-selective abortion ban was making its way through the state legislature.

Although Bei Bei Shuai and Purvi Patel were not seeking abortions, their experiences with medical care and criminal justice align with the underlying message of sex-selective abortion bans: Women of color, especially Asian immigrant women, cannot be trusted to make decisions for their own bodies and their own lives. Together with race-selective abortion bans, sex-selective abortion bans give doctors or politicians the power to prescribe what constitutes a "good reason" for a woman to seek an abortion, stripping away autonomy from women of color.

Legislators enjoy cloaking these abortion bans in the language of gender equality, yet the states that propose these bans are the very same ones that do not support pay equity, maternal health improvement, maternity leave, and other assistance central to providing women of color the tools that they need to make decisions about their bodies and their lives. These are also the states with the fastest-growing AAPI populations: Twelve of the fifteen states with the largest AAPI populations and ten of the fifteen states with highest AAPI growth rates have proposed this ban.[84] The large overlap illustrates how anti-immigrant sentiment and fear—not a desire to "save" Asian girls—are the driving forces behind these bans.

We do not view sex-selective abortion bans solely as an issue of abortion access; they must be regarded as an intersectional problem and one that enables racial prejudice and discrimination to restrict access to reproductive health for AAPI women. To address these abortion bans without centering the racial implications of these laws pushes AAPI women and the dangerous stereotypes they live with into the shadows, rendering them invisible in conversations about how to empower women of color to make decisions about their bodies and their lives.

Battles against sex-selective abortion bans in state legislatures and in Congress have effectively called out misinformation and the harmful, misguided stereotypes on which they are based, preventing passage of these bills in some states. However, reproductive rights groups must also apply an intersectional lens to their litigation efforts as these bans move their way up the court system. Currently, reproductive rights in the existing legal system and jurisprudence are divorced from the reality that these laws have disparate racial impacts and are fueled by racism. Without intersectional litigation, not only do the lived experiences of women of color remain invisible in the fights against these and all other bans, but the legal system will continue to fail in remedying injustices to women of color and women with intersecting identities.

Dusti Gurule

PRESIDENT AND CEO, COLORADO ORGANIZATION
FOR LATINA OPPORTUNITY AND REPRODUCTIVE
RIGHTS (COLOR)

COLOR works to enable Latinx people and their families to live safe, healthy, and self-determined lives. We are dedicated to intergenerational community-rooted advocacy and organizing efforts to advance RJ policy and youth leadership and to establish the narrative that embodies the honest lived experiences of the Latinx diaspora in Colorado.

For the past twenty-five years, COLOR's work to advance access to all forms of reproductive health care and to destigmatize abortion has always been tied to our right to parent or not, and the ability to plan, care for, and build our families as we see fit. We are all too familiar with what it looks like when the government tries to impose its will on our bodies and communities. From forcible sterilization and the coercion of

Latinas to use long-acting contraceptive methods, to the discriminatory Hyde Amendment, which pushes abortion care out of reach for
low-income people, to the very real maternal mortality crisis facing
women of color, we know who is harmed when political games are
being played on the backs of our communities. Abortion is health care,
and not being able to obtain and afford the health services we need contributes to health disparities.

Working in partnership with Cobalt Advocates (previously known
as NARAL Pro-Choice Colorado), and in collaboration with the
National Institute for Reproductive Health, we developed legislation
for the CARE Act in 2018, which would have expanded all reproductive
health services, including abortion, to immigrants regardless of citizenship status. Although this bill was never introduced due to the political climate in Colorado at the time, the effort that went into it laid the
groundwork for much of our work since, including the Reproductive
Health Care Program (SB21–009), the Reproductive Health Equity Act
(RHEA), and the Safe Access for Protected Health Care package.
These bills, and their success, represent what it means to create policy
solutions that are possible only when an intersectional reproductive
justice lens is utilized in decision-making.

Legality does not mean access; our communities know this all too
well. This is why it is critical to fight against attacks on abortion access
and acknowledge the reality that the rights to an abortion, contraceptive care, and family planning services are continuously being pushed
out of reach of our people even in states where abortion is "protected."
Our goal is to ensure that people can become parents when they are
ready to affirm that right. We also want to ensure that our legislation
enables people to prevent, terminate, or have a healthy pregnancy and
that care is not limited by income, insurance type, or immigration
status.

Insurance is not the only barrier to health and well-being for women
of color and our families. COLOR built a broad coalition of groups to
each speak out from different intersections. Faith leaders stood at the

podium talking about the importance of ensuring we can each follow our own beliefs when it comes to planning our families, and they affirmed the social justice commitment of churches to eliminating gaps in health care. Our reproductive rights partners stood next to our economic justice allies, who talked about how contraception is linked to financial stability and the fact that too many people in low-wage jobs still can't afford contraception or may feel like they can't have more children due to being trapped in the cycle of poverty.

After the overturning of *Roe*, we knew that women of color across the country would be disproportionately impacted. In fact, a study by the National Partnership for Women and Families and the National Latina Institute for Reproductive Justice found that Latinas are the largest group affected. Three-quarters of Latinas who live in states with abortion bans or restrictions are concentrated in Texas, Florida, and Arizona. This is why it was imperative for us as a Latina-led organization to ensure that Colorado is a safe haven for all those seeking care. Community care is reproductive justice.

We also know that protecting access to abortion and all other aspects of reproductive health care are major mobilizing issues for Latino voters in Colorado. Launched in 2021, the Colorado Latino Agenda (CLA) is a statewide public research initiative, co-led by our organization and Voces Unidas, that publishes relevant and timely in-depth reports about Latinas and Latinos in Colorado. The Colorado Latino Policy Agenda (CLPA) is our annual nonpartisan report designed to provide insights into the demographic makeup and views of Latino voters in Colorado on pressing policy, political, and social issues. In its latest release, we found that 52 percent of our respondents said that laws passed around the nation to limit or ban abortion makes them more likely to vote in 2023. When asked to evaluate a potential abortion-related ballot measure, a solid majority of those polled (62 percent) reported they are likely to support making abortion rights stronger in Colorado by allowing state-funded insurance programs to cover abortion costs.

None of this work would have been possible without our community coming together at the Capitol, at the polls, and in the streets. We told bolder justice-centered stories about what it means when someone can't get the contraception they need and how our fight for abortion access and health care was linked to our work to ensure equal pay and paid sick days. We challenged policymakers and activists to think about what it really looks like to develop innovative policies to make sure that every person can build the family they want, care for themselves and their families, and truly live with dignity.

That is what abortion access means to us—to be able to control our own bodies and futures—and that is what reproductive justice is—to have the right to determine who you are and what your life looks like and to be met with respect and honor. As we strive to reach our vision and advance our mission, we hope to get to a place where our community has the knowledge, freedom, and power to access a full range of opportunities for the health of our bodies, minds, and spirit.

Parker Dockray
EXECUTIVE DIRECTOR, ALL-OPTIONS

Since 2004, All-Options has been helping people find unbiased and judgment-free support for their decisions and experiences with pregnancy, parenting, abortion, adoption, infertility, and pregnancy loss. We use both direct service and social change strategies to meet people's immediate needs while also fighting for the more compassionate and just future we all deserve.

Abortion has always been a common part of reproductive decisions, on the same spectrum as experiences with parenting, pregnancy and infant loss, infertility, and adoption. Nearly two-thirds of people who have had abortions have already given birth to at least one child, and many will go on to parent in the future. In the reality of our everyday lives, these experiences are all woven together in our messy, complex experience of being human.

Politically, however, the opponents of abortion have successfully siloed abortion from pregnancy, parenting, and adoption—and the reproductive health and rights movement has historically bought into those divisions rather than seeking to bridge them. It is still incredibly difficult to find information, support, or resources for abortion, pregnancy loss, and parenting in the same space, or to find organizations working on these issues together. This disconnected landscape fuels the common perception that being "pro-choice" means being only for abortion, and being "pro-life" means being for parenting, adoption, and support for those facing infertility or pregnancy loss. Too many people have been alienated and turned off by this false dichotomy when they could be engaged as supporters. As advocates for reproductive justice, we have a responsibility and an opportunity to transform the abortion debate and mobilize people by demonstrating what a truly inclusive, just, and all-options future can look like.

All-Options is doing just that. We provide direct support and resources to thousands of people each year on our toll-free national Talkline, on our Faith Aloud clergy line, and at our Pregnancy Resource Center in Bloomington, Indiana. We engage community members and train them as advocates and activists for change. They go on to become ambassadors and leaders in our organization, in their professions, and in the movement. We also offer trainings and workshops so that more frontline providers are able to offer unbiased and nonjudgmental support to the people they work with.

On any given day our Talkline might hear from someone whose recent miscarriage is bringing up feelings about an abortion they had years ago but never told anyone about; a woman who terminated a pregnancy after a devastating fetal diagnosis but is not welcomed by her local pregnancy loss community; or someone for whom being adopted themselves adds layers of complexity to a decision about becoming a parent.

In 2015 we brought our decade of expertise and vision to open the nation's first All-Options Pregnancy Resource Center, where we offer free pregnancy tests, condoms, diapers and baby care supplies, and abortion funding and referrals, all under one roof. We are claiming and subverting the pregnancy-centered model in the spirit of truly judgment-free, all-options counseling and support. This approach reflects the reality of people's lived experiences; it is also strategic, demonstrating that antiabortion organizations do not have a monopoly on supporting parents and people who choose to continue their pregnancies.

Whether in person or on the phone, people often tell us that All-Options is the first place they have been able to talk about all of their reproductive concerns and experiences openly. Many people report having turned to loved ones or local providers for support, especially around abortion, only to find judgment and bias. In contrast, we increase the availability of support by sharing our approach with counselors, social workers, health educators, nurses, and advocates in all sectors through our Pregnancy Options workshops. These trainings give people a chance to explore their own biases and develop a more nuanced understanding of pregnancy options and experiences, as well as build the skills to provide judgment-free support and referrals. They bring this new knowledge and skill into all aspects of their lives, helping to transform the divisive political climate and create a more compassionate world— one where all reproductive experiences can be heard and supported. In the words of one of our volunteer advocates, "[All-Options helped me] become a better listener, more patient, more aware of my biases and less inclined to judge. I'm more confident holding space for people in my community, including myself, for the hard things life brings."

We believe that this radically compassionate, all-options approach can mobilize more people to advocate for reproductive justice by meeting their needs for support, providing meaningful skills and opportunities for action, and engaging them in a thriving activist community with a positive and inspiring vision for the future.

CHAPTER 5

Reproductive Justice Globally

In this chapter we look at the ways that people around the world are RJ-ing abortion. We will see that the struggles against reproductive oppression and for abortion rights and reproductive justice are being waged country by country in courts and legislatures, in the United Nations and other international bodies, and in the streets. The activists leading those struggles, especially in the Global South, have not separated feminism from the battles against colonialism and dictatorships and for human rights, social justice, and democracy. Because global feminism has been deeply embedded in all of these areas, the work for reproductive human rights has been intrinsically intersectional, holistic, and attuned to the impacts of law and policy on the lives of the most vulnerable people. In fact, the idea of joining the struggles for human rights and reproductive justice began in the international arena.

At the 1994 International Conference on Population and Development (ICPD) in Cairo, Loretta Ross, a U.S.-based activist who was one of the conceptualizers of the reproductive justice framework, first understood those synergies. Her grasp of each of these frameworks, both separately and the connections between them, was both theoretical and embodied, drawn from her own life history, which, like that of many women of color, was shaped by oppression and resistance. In Cairo, Ross witnessed a sea change in the approach to reproductive rights when conference participants explicitly renounced population control and affirmed the right to have children and families, a claim that became the core feature of reproductive justice. She recognized that reproductive justice, the concept she and others were birthing, and human rights are intersectional, and when these concepts are merged, they center the needs of the people most harmed by reproductive oppression. Over the course of the Cairo conference, Ross came to believe that human rights law could be a sturdier legal basis for reproductive health, rights, and justice than the U.S. constitutional system.

This women-led, rights-based internationalism drew on work that women from many countries had contributed to shaping the Universal Declaration of Human Rights (UDHR) in the years immediately after World War II. Many people are familiar with Eleanor Roosevelt's role: The former first lady of the United States chaired the committee that drafted the document. But women from Pakistan, the Dominican Republic, Latin America, India, Belarus, and other countries also played a critical role in constructing the 1948 document. These delegates demanded that women's specific needs and rights be explicitly written into the UDHR, arguing, for example, that the document recognize women's needs for equal rights in and outside of marriage and that it condemn child and forced marriage. Women delegates were also responsible for changing the language in the text from "All men" to "All human beings," for demanding equality between men and women, and for insisting that their countries affirm the document.[1]

While global feminists in Cairo and beyond have seen gender justice as a matter of human rights, they have had to fight for recognition of "women's issues" within the international human rights movement. Because that movement has historically been dominated by men, and has been heavily influenced by faith-based groups, abortion rights and gender equality have only relatively recently become a focus of human rights organizations, and these issues remain matters of conflict.[2] Additionally, many global feminists have been critical of the human rights movement for its reliance on Western and neoliberal understandings of rights. They argue that these understandings don't include the government's responsibilities to create the conditions that would facilitate people being able to exercise rights (the enabling conditions). Nonetheless, as we will explain, advocates found that human rights was a powerful intersectional frame for demanding bodily autonomy as a fundamental entitlement, and for facilitating solidarity with other movements.

Ross was inspired by ICPD to bring human rights into reproductive justice, although she did not expect this new framework to be adopted outside the United States. She doubted that activists from many different countries, each with its own distinctive history, mix of cultures, and politics, would be comfortable with any single approach—or any single vocabulary. Moreover, Ross and her U.S. colleagues considered that the fused RJ/human rights model might seem redundant in settings where human rights was already a well-established advocacy frame. Anthropologist Lynn Morgan affirmed the point when she recounted her experience of introducing reproductive justice to Argentinian feminists who insisted that the human rights framework was fully adequate for reproductive and sexual rights.[3]

Yet, as the reproductive justice movement grew in the United States, it gained traction internationally. Activists in other countries with histories of colonialism, white supremacy, capitalism, and other structures that had historically supported stratified reproduction began to adopt the language and framework of reproductive justice. In a number of countries, advocates accepted the holistic reproductive justice framework as a path toward building broad coalitions with other human rights and social justice organizations. Each country's specific context also determined the political space for advocacy.

Back in the United States after the Cairo conference, the RJ movement was bolstered by activism in other countries where feminists were developing strategies to build the power necessary to change local laws. Tactics of U.S. activists—both those who advocated for abortion rights and those who opposed abortion—also migrated across borders. Advocates in various countries imported and adapted strategies to suit their local situations. Activist/researcher Naomi Braine emphasizes that the heart of the international movement for self-managed abortion with pills is in community-based networks and activism in the Global South. For example, a group of young feminists in Ecuador in 2008 were trained in the basics of medication abortion by the Dutch NGO Women on Waves. They became Salud Mujeres and created the first abortion hotline in Latin America. That group inspired feminists in Concepción, Chile, and activists throughout the region to create hotlines.[4] "While I (and many others) cheered on 'the abortion boat' ... it is the grassroots work that began in South America and spread globally that has changed countless women's lives, redefined the possibilities for having a safe abortion, and transformed the conversation."[5]

Clearly, the strategies and tactics of activists around the world aligned closely with the work that women of color were carrying out in the United States: centering opposition to sterilization abuse and population control in general; framing resistance to reproductive oppression in human rights terms; insisting that advocacy campaigns be led by the people most harmed by reproductive oppression; organizing international solidarity to support individual cases; attacking abortion stigma through storytelling; and disseminating knowledge about and access to self-managed abortion (SMA) with pills.

In the next section we situate these developments in the history of abortion access globally.

ABORTION ACCESS GLOBALLY

By the end of the nineteenth century, almost every country in the world had enacted restrictive abortion laws.[6] But by the beginning of the 1970s, fifty countries had liberalized their laws, allowing for greater access.[7] Global feminists and the women's health movement, as well as a series of United Nations conferences, stimulated the change, beginning at the 1993 Conference on Human Rights in Vienna, where advocates spotlighted the failure of the international human rights system to protect women. They demanded that the conference's Programme of Action (PoA) explicitly define women's rights as human rights and affirm that violence against women is, therefore, a human rights violation.[8]

The following year, at the 1994 International Conference on Population and Development (ICPD) in Cairo, advocates for reproductive rights and health built on the momentum of Vienna. Although there were divisions among feminists over whether or not population growth itself should be seen as a major problem, there was no disagreement that unsafe, illegal abortion was a leading threat to women's health around the world. Feminists came together in Cairo to support a new global consensus that reproductive rights were human rights. Most significantly, the Cairo Programme of Action disassociated "family planning" from the "population control" paradigm. The PoA explicitly rejected the use of government-driven coercion in the form of offering targets and incentives to limit the childbearing of people in developing countries. In the recent past, women in some countries, such as Indonesia, had been forced at gunpoint to accept IUDs; elsewhere, others had faced equally egregious violence and threats.[9]

The Cairo PoA called on governments to stop constructing "population goals" and to instead meet the reproductive needs of their citizens.[10] This was first time an international policy had defined and prioritized reproductive health: "Reproductive health implies that people are able to have a satisfying and safe sex life and that they have the capability to reproduce and the freedom to decide if, when, and how often to do so."[11]

The Cairo conference was clearly important, but its accomplishments were limited in significant ways. Some feminist critics charged that Cairo had changed the rhetoric but did not alter conditions on the ground.[12] In order to achieve consensus, the PoA excluded abortion from the list of family planning strategies. The document names unsafe abortion several times as a cause of maternal mortality and morbidity, but it does not acknowledge the ravages of criminalization: "In cases where it is not against the law, abortion should be safe."[13] For many advocates, this sacrifice of health and rights was an unacceptable compromise and a terrible capitulation to the Vatican, a fierce opponent of legal abortion everywhere.[14]

For some feminists, the PoA was inadequate in other ways as well. In their ten-year assessment of Cairo, Sumati Nair and Preeti Kirbat of the Women's Global Network for Reproductive Rights (WGNRR) and

Sarah Sexton of The Corner House in London explained that the global neoliberal economic policies pursued by financial institutions—structural adjustment, deregulation of health services, and privatization of previously public institutions and services—harmed the most vulnerable people. When those institutions pressured countries to repay their debts before meeting domestic needs, many countries were forced to stop funding social services and investing in health care and education, which led to increased poverty and inequality and contributed to the large number of maternal and infant deaths worldwide.[15] The greatest problem was not a lack of contraceptive services. Rather, at the heart of these disastrous developments were poor nutrition, a persistent lack of food, infectious diseases, and other harmful consequences of poverty.

Still, it is undeniable that the Cairo agreement and other international treaties and rulings have proven to be invaluable tools for expanding reproductive rights, especially since there is no universally recognized right to abortion, nor any formal and independent enforcement system in international law.[16] Since the Cairo conference, several UN human rights bodies have reaffirmed that the denial of abortion is a violation of a woman's human rights, and have called for safe and legal abortion.[17]

The Fourth World Conference on Women in Beijing (1995) and subsequent international agreements, including the 2003 Maputo Protocol, went beyond Cairo and added momentum to the worldwide trend of liberalizing abortion laws.[18] Advocates relied on human rights instruments to pressure their governments for legal change and to galvanize public support for abortion rights. Since 2020, they have achieved dramatic changes in abortion laws. Thailand, South Korea, and New Zealand have eased their abortion restrictions. Argentina, the second largest country in Latin America, legalized abortion in 2021 as part of the "Green Wave" sweeping that continent, inspiring legal reforms in other countries.[19] That same year, the Supreme Court of Mexico decriminalized abortion in two states, establishing the precedent that it is unconstitutional to treat abortion as a crime. Colombia legalized abortion on demand up to twenty-four weeks of pregnancy in 2022, and Chile is moving in that direction. Given the power of the Catholic Church in Latin America, these developments are remarkable.

And in a dramatic development, in 2024 the French Parliament voted overwhelmingly to amend their constitution and enshrine the right to abortion, their action prompted by the *Dobbs* decision in the United States. Laura Slimani, from the Fondation des Femmes rights group, was clear: "This right (to abortion) has retreated in the United States. And so, nothing authorised us to think that France was exempt from this risk."[20] The French prime minister also pointed to the rollback of abortion rights in Hungary and Poland and dramatically underscored the importance of changing the constitution: "It [only] takes one generation, one year, one week for things to change drastically."[21]

Despite these gains, unsafe abortion remains one of the main causes of maternal mortality worldwide.[22] The World Health Organization (WHO) defines an unsafe abortion as "one performed by people lacking the necessary skills or using a hazardous technique, and/or in an environment that does not meet minimum medical standards."[23] Of the seventy-three million abortions worldwide annually, conservative estimates indicate that about 56 percent are unsafe; over half of these occur in Africa, and a third in Asia. Annual deaths worldwide from unsafe abortion are estimated at 22,500 to 44,000 women. The number varies from country to country, but the vast majority of deaths occur among poor people in developing countries.[24]

Some countries have total bans on abortion, with the most restrictive laws in Honduras, El Salvador, Dominican Republic, Nicaragua, Egypt, Jamaica, Madagascar, Senegal, and the Philippines.[25] Over 75 percent of the countries in the Global South impose legal penalties for abortion, including lengthy prison sentences and heavy fines for people having or assisting with the procedure.[26] Almost seven million women are treated annually in these regions for complications from unsafe abortion, and many more are untreated.

These statistics show that people who cannot manage a pregnancy, whatever their reasons, will pursue abortion regardless of stigma, health consequences, or the law. The statistics also make painfully obvious the outrageous truth that maternal mortality (actual deaths) and morbidity (harms to health) from unsafe abortion are not inevitable; they are not diseases for which there is no cure. Almost every death and complication would be prevented if abortion were legal and accessible everywhere.[27] Medical abortion with pills (using mifepristone and misoprostol or misoprostol alone) and manual vacuum aspiration are safe methods that have existed for decades. Activists have made both available by engaging in illegal grassroots direct action, often at great personal risk. Changing laws, national policies, and social attitudes would bring wider accessibility and a more profound transformation of women's lives.

Using the RJ lens, we pay particular attention to the distribution of harms where people lack access to safe methods of abortion and are denied lifesaving information and care. Inevitably, those with the fewest resources suffer the most. The most vulnerable pregnant people must risk their lives and health by self-inducing an abortion using unsafe methods, going to unskilled providers, or carrying to term pregnancies that they consider unsupportable. In countries with bans or severe restrictions, those who have abortions, along with providers and advocates, face serious legal consequences.[28] One in four of all women in prison in Rwanda, for example, are incarcerated for having an abortion. In El Salvador, where abortion is a crime with no exceptions—even in cases of rape, incest, severe fetal impairment, and life endangerment to the pregnant person—women charged with homicide after having stillbirths and miscarriages have received sentences of twenty-five to forty years in prison.[29] Those prosecuted are mostly young and poor women and girls who are criminalized when they go to a public hospital seeking treatment for complications after a miscarriage, stillbirth, or unsafe abortion. Sometimes people who are prosecuted have fought for justice through the human rights system, but this is a slow and uncertain process. For example, in March 2023 the Inter-American

Court of Human Rights finally considered the appeal of Beatriz, a woman incarcerated for abortion in El Salvador ten years earlier, in 2013.[30] Throughout the world, migrants, asylum seekers, and undocumented women face additional legal and social and economic barriers if they have to travel across borders to obtain an abortion.[31]

Opponents of abortion claim that legally restricting the procedure reduces the number of abortions and decreases maternal mortality yet repeated studies in all regions of the world prove that these claims are false. Research by the Guttmacher Institute and the World Health Organization demonstrates that where abortion is strictly controlled or criminalized, the number of abortions is larger, and abortions are more often performed under unsafe conditions than in countries where it is legal.[32]

Also well documented are facts about the health impacts of unsafe abortion showing that they are most severe for people who are poor and people of color.[33] Although legality and safety are not the same, the rates of maternal mortality from unsafe abortion are higher in countries with major legal restrictions than in those where abortion is generally available.[34] Where a person can obtain an abortion on request, there are few deaths from unsafe procedures.[35] These facts make the strongest possible case that decriminalizing abortion is necessary for health, justice, equity, and survival. Nonetheless, the antiabortion movement, the right/far right, the Catholic Church, Christian evangelical leaders, and conservative politicians throughout the world continue their efforts to limit rights and to decrease access. They use the most vulnerable people who do not have the resources to pay for healthcare as pawns to achieve their goals.

While the 1994 ICPD Programme of Action explicitly renounced population control targets and coercive family planning, these practices did not end. After Cairo, authorities in several countries promoted sterilization, making the argument that it increases women's choices and alleviates environmental degradation and poverty. Survivors of post-Cairo sterilizations tell a different story, one of reproductive oppression and human rights violations. For example, Rudecinda Quilla, an

Indigenous woman from Peru, testified in court that "she was forced onto a hospital bed, her hands and feet tied while she was injected with an anesthetic. When she woke up hours later, she had been sterilized and staff told her that she would 'never breed like an animal again.'"[36]

Unfortunately, Quilla's experience was not uncommon. In Peru, three hundred thousand women were sterilized between 1996 and 2001 under President Fujimori's family planning program. Indigenous women from poor rural areas were the primary targets.[37] Some estimates indicate that between eighteen and forty women died from the sterilizations, though the number is probably higher.[38] Publicly, Fujimori defended the program, promising women better life choices if they had fewer children. Government documents, however, revealed the regime's population control intention to stop "excessive births" among Indigenous women, not to empower the women.

The sterilizations in Peru were also driven by the international population control policies of the U.S. Agency for International Development (USAID), the World Bank, the Nippon Foundation (a Japanese nonprofit), and the UN Population Fund, which donated ten million dollars to the forced-sterilization campaign.[39] This group of institutions promoted aggressive family planning targets and programs, requiring proof of a country's population decline as a condition for receiving desperately needed loans and aid. The Peru example gives us insight into the lived experiences of reproductive degradation at the intersections of race, class, gender, and ethnicity.

In Peru, advocacy for justice has been primarily led by survivors of sterilization abuse, not by the country's mainstream feminist movement. Some feminists on the left did offer support and were critical of the larger movement, charging that its priorities represented only white middle-class women's rights and did not include the experiences of Indigenous women and others whose lives were shaped by severe structural violence and poverty. However, for the most part, neither the human rights movement nor a majority of feminists stepped up as allies. Some individuals and organizations simply dismissed the survivors' claims. Others did not believe the coercion was systemic; they thought that only a few bad doctors had abused their power, and that those actions should not overshadow the positive aspects of the program. Feminists were also divided over whether to work with the Fujimori dictatorship at all. Some groups were reluctant to oppose any form of contraception, even coerced sterilization, out of fear that any opposition could boost the power of the Catholic Church and undermine efforts to legalize abortion.[40]

The process of accepting government culpability for sterilization violations came slowly, even after the brutal totalitarian Fujimori regime ended in 2000. Feminist and human rights groups created a Peruvian Truth and Reconciliation Commission (PTRC) to address rape, sexual assault, and sexual slavery, but it did not include forced sterilization.[41] When Fujimori was indicted for crimes against humanity and sentenced to twenty-five years in prison, he was never charged in connection with forced sterilization. Undaunted, many women who were sterilized against their will continued to compile documentation over the years, as prosecutors continued to claim that they did not find evidence of coercion.[42] Finally, in 2021, Fujimori and three former health ministers were indicted in absentia on charges related to the forced sterilizations. The case is still pending, but the Peruvian congress passed a law requiring government compensation for the victims. As of June 2021, 6,103 people had registered claims, hoping for monetary awards if and when the court holds the perpetrators responsible.[43]

The Peru case is similar to programs in other countries where official ideas about overpopulation, poverty, and race drive government programs that determine who should have children and who should not. Privi Patel, a public health researcher, found documentation of targeted, coerced sterilization in Chile, the Czech Republic, the Dominican Republic, Hungary, India, Kenya, Mexico, Namibia, Slovakia, South Africa, Swaziland, Uzbekistan, and Venezuela.

From the 1930s to the 1980s, as in the United States, the governments in Japan, Canada, Sweden, Australia, Norway, Finland, Estonia,

Switzerland, and Iceland all enacted laws mandating sterilization of racial minorities, as well as people who were considered mentally disabled, alcoholics, and those who suffered from specific illnesses.[44] In 2015, Tami Kendall documented the sterilization of HIV-positive people in El Salvador, Honduras, Mexico, and Nicaragua. This research revealed that one-fourth of the 285 people in the study had encountered "pressure" from health care providers, who in some cases threatened denial of health care and economic support unless the person agreed to be sterilized. In other cases the sterilizations were performed during childbirth when the person was under anesthesia.[45] As of 2022, fourteen countries in the European Union still allow some form of forced sterilization, and only nine countries prohibit it.[46]

While official rationales may vary, the underlying eugenicist motivation fueling these programs remains the same across countries. Frequently, for example, some proponents of forced sterilization are adamant that overpopulation is the chief cause of environmental destruction and climate change, and they link fertility reduction to saving the planet. The Population Connection, the organization formerly known as Zero Population Growth (ZPG), issued an urgent call to its supporters in 2022 to participate in the organization's work: "Before COVID, there was Ebola ... Zika ... HIV and Sars. In fact, in recent decades, more than three hundred deadly infectious diseases have emerged. One of the major reasons is rapid population growth. We can—and must—stop it."[47] The organization appeals to the public to join Population Connection in the fight to empower people to exercise their reproductive rights, and to curb the reproductive excesses of poor women around the world whose babies are the cause of deadly viruses.

Racialized population policies have incited white nationalist extremists to violence throughout the world. Three recent mass murderers wrote manifestos foregrounding racialized "overpopulation," including the white person who murdered fifty-one people at two mosques in Christchurch, New Zealand, in 2019; the twenty-one-year-old white man in El Paso, Texas, who murdered twenty-three people, mostly

Latinas, at a Walmart; and the twenty-two-year-old white male who murdered ten Black people at a grocery store in Buffalo, New York, in 2022.[48]

Globally, people who are transgender have also been targeted for sterilization abuse. Many countries only allow a person to change their gender markers on official documents once they have undergone sterilization. As in other cases of forcible sterilizations, the message is clear: A transgender person is unfit for reproduction.[49] International human rights advocates have led the fight against these policies and the ideas behind them. A 2014 statement issued by several human rights bodies stated, "According to international and regional human rights bodies and some constitutional courts, and as reflected in recent legal changes in several countries, these sterilization requirements run counter to respect for bodily integrity, self-determination and human dignity, and can cause and perpetuate discrimination against transgender and intersex persons."[50] A 2022 report from the Council on Europe, a standing committee of heads of state and governments, reported substantial progress in legal gender recognition but characterized the progress as slow and uneven, and noted that there was some backtracking.[51]

INTERNATIONAL ANTIABORTION BACKLASH: GLOBAL GAG RULE AND BEYOND

In 1967 the National Right to Life Committee was founded in the United States (as the Right to Life League) under the auspices of the National Conference of Catholic Bishops, which was focused on blocking abortion through changes in law, government policy, and cultural values. The bishops' movement was exported internationally with funding from U.S. donors and through specific alliances between leaders of the New Right in the United States and those in other countries.[52] Today, many U.S.-based antiabortion organizations have established branches in other countries, which import tactics developed in the United States. One of the largest is the Texas-based organization

40 Days for Life, which has brought clinic protests to a thousand cities in sixty-five countries between 2008 and 2024.[53]

Antiabortion political leaders in the United States were also able to exert influence on abortion policy internationally by pressuring Congress to restrict foreign assistance. The U.S. Congress passed the Helms Amendment in 1973, which prohibited, with limited exceptions, the use of U.S. funding to provide safe abortion services. Building on the Helms prohibitions, President Reagan introduced the Global Gag Rule (GGR), also known as the Mexico City Policy (1984). The GGR went further, prohibiting international NGOs from using any of their funds to provide people seeking abortions with information or referrals. Any organization failing to meet these conditions would not be eligible to receive U.S. global family planning assistance.[54]

The Global Gag Rule became a political football, overturned by every Democratic president and reinstated by every Republican president since Reagan. In 2017, the Trump administration renamed the policy Protecting Life in Global Health Assistance and expanded it to cover virtually *all* forms of U.S. global health programs and research. For the first time, the GGR was applied to maternal and child health and included household-level water, sanitation, and hygiene, a collection of resources known as WASH; nutrition; HIV under the President's Emergency Plan for AIDS Relief (PEPFAR); tuberculosis; malaria and other typically neglected tropical diseases; and global health security.[55] The amount of foreign aid impacted increased from six hundred million to an estimated twelve billion dollars.[56] Again, the most vulnerable people bore the brunt of the policy.

Between 2016 and 2020, Trump administration officials repeatedly voiced their opposition to abortion in speeches at the UN, at other international gatherings, and in publications. In the 2018 government report on human rights, the Trump officials instructed the State Department to replace all references to sexual and "reproductive rights" with language defining women's access to contraception and abortion as "coercive population control."[57] In the 2020 preparation for the Cairo +25 conference and the World Health Assembly, Alex Azar, U.S. secretary of Health and Human Services, asserted the government's antiabortion stance in no uncertain terms:

> There is no international human right to abortion. On the other hand, there is an international human right to life. President Trump has been clear, at the U.N. and on the world stage: Health care exists to improve health and preserve human life.... If the other side's goal of making abortion an international human right becomes a reality, it will mean all countries with laws protecting the unborn will be in violation of international human rights laws, with all the consequences that could carry.[58]

The Trump doctrine was a response to pressure by the global antiabortion movement as well as pressure from his evangelical base in the United States.[59] Religious organizations have been key antiabortion players, exerting their power in individual countries by sharing strategies and resources across borders, strengthening their impact on constitutional and human rights litigation, and as representatives at the UN, the European Union, and other international bodies.[60]

The Global Gag Rule has had a chilling effect on providers who, out of confusion and fear of violating U.S. policy, sometimes refused to provide abortions that were, in fact, permissible. In Zambia, an organization removed information about emergency contraception from its brochure. Health provider organizations in Egypt stopped holding discussions of sepsis after unsafe abortions, even though it was a major public health concern. In some countries where providers have refused to deliver services, clinics have been forced to shut down, which has led to increases in unplanned, forced births.[61] As with all other restrictions, the gag rule disproportionately burdens those with the fewest resources. A health care worker in South Africa poignantly observed, "We have to act like we don't know about [abortion]. We have to act like we don't know about the girls dying because they go to a so-called doctor who tells them to drink bleach. These girls are overwhelmingly people already facing health and other life risks due to poverty."[62]

TRAP LAWS

In some countries where abortion laws had been liberalized, opponents advocated for new restrictions, adapting the Targeted Regulation of Abortion Providers (TRAP) laws pioneered in the United States.[63] For example, in Malaysia a doctor was prosecuted for offering medical abortion. He was also barred from using the manual vacuum aspiration method, which the authorities falsely claimed was a high-risk procedure and should only be performed in a hospital or similar setting.[64]

Even in European countries where the global trend liberalizing and legalizing abortion law began in the 1930s, opponents of abortion have been able to pass new restrictions, including bans, waiting periods, and mandatory counseling.[65] In Poland, for example, abortion was severely restricted in the 1990s, and in 2021 a constitutional tribunal banned virtually all abortions except when the woman's life or health is endangered by the continuation of the pregnancy and in cases where the pregnancy is the result of a criminal act.[66]

Abortion rights in Russia have been eroding since the 1990s, efforts that have accelerated under President Putin, who maintains close ties to the Russian Orthodox Church. Since his election in 2012, new legal restrictions require a person seeking an abortion to view an ultrasound, listen to the fetal heartbeat, and consult with a psychologist.[67] Additionally, there is a mandatory waiting period and a rule giving doctors the right to refuse to perform an abortion if the pregnancy does not directly threaten the life of the pregnant person.[68] In 2023 the health ministry restricted access to abortion pills and proposed a nationwide ban on abortion in private clinics. Clearly, these new restrictions are modeled on U.S. initiatives.[69]

RELIGIOUS REFUSALS (CONSCIENCE OBJECTIONS)

Laws allowing doctors to refuse to perform abortions are called "religious refusals" by supporters of abortion; opponents of abortion call them "conscience objections" (CO). In many countries, when abortion is decriminalized, the law includes a CO provision to accommodate providers with moral and religious objections to abortion. While conscience objections were originally intended to respect personal religious and ethical beliefs, in practice they often function in a different way. Sometimes opponents of abortion have turned these concessions into a political weapon, encouraging doctors to assert CO as a strategy to decrease the number of providers. Some studies show that CO claims may be due to a range of factors, including negative moral judgments about the sexual activity of abortion seekers, workload management, and fear of judgment by colleagues or retaliation from professional superiors.[70] For some physicians, claiming a CO can become an act of self-preservation. In Argentina a doctor who was labeled an abortionist was not able to find employment at any private clinic. Providers interviewed in a 2015 study described "experiences of 'loneliness,' 'finger pointing,' 'burnout,' and 'work overload.'" They expressed fears that performing abortions could lead to lower professional prestige and put them at risk for harassment.[71] Notably, those who claim a CO are not held accountable for denying care.[72]

In some countries, such as Italy, CO is a huge barrier to abortion access. When Italian lawmakers legalized abortion in 1978, the law limited abortion to public facilities but did not require staff at these hospitals and clinics to offer the procedure.[73] Since the Italian system is dominated by antiabortion Catholic administrators, the CO rate is so high that abortion is effectively unavailable in many parts of the country. According to a 2020 Italian Ministry of Health report, 64.6 percent of gynecologists refuse to do abortions; in Sicily it is 85 percent.[74] Support staff have also refused; 44.6 percent of anesthesiologists and 36.2 percent of nonmedical staff have opted out.[75] As a result, in roughly one in seven hospitals in Italy, 80 to 100 percent of the staff define themselves as objectors. Some researchers suggest that the prevalence of CO in Italy has more to do with doctors' fears about their careers than their religious or moral beliefs. In her study, public health researcher Caterina Muratori found that "non-objector gynecologists are often seen as the 'dirty' ones, [and] sometimes colleagues isolate them. [...] Moreover, they have more difficulties in advancing their career. The reason is simple: the majority of hospital directors are conscientious objectors, and they often come from religious schools. So in turn they tend to prefer doctors who are objectors."[76]

Whatever the reasons for a person making a CO claim, Italian abortion seekers, many of whom are themselves Catholics who have decided that an abortion is their best option, are harmed. Often they struggle to find information, have to wait a long time, or are forced to travel far from their homes to have the procedure since there are no abortions in private clinics.[77] In one reported case, a pregnant woman was rejected for an abortion by twenty-three different public hospitals on the basis of CO or administrative issues before she was eventually able to access abortion services.[78] In 2013 the European Committee for Social Rights condemned Italy for "shortcomings in the provision of abortion services."[79]

Similarly, in South Africa many people lack access to safe and legal procedures, stigma is high, and hostility to abortion persists, despite the fact that its abortion law, the Choice on Termination of Pregnancy Act (CTOP), is one of the most liberal in the world. The first study of CO in South Africa noted that the existence of a conscience claim had a large impact on abortion access in their context of inadequate and overburdened health services. CTOP did not include clear and consistent guidelines for what constitutes a legitimate objection to performing abortions, nor has there been a system for reporting cases of provider refusals.[80] CO has been a largely unregulated practice, and many people are denied services they are legally entitled to receive. In 2016, when a student in Johannesburg died from complications from an unsafe abortion, the South African representative to the UN identified the cause as the government's failure to adequately regulate conscience claims.[81]

Researchers point to cultural, religious, and political factors affecting the uses of CO in South Africa, particularly in rural areas, where some people associate abortion with the racist population policies of colonialism. Others who think of motherhood as women's natural state believe that women who don't want to be pregnant are revealing themselves as sexually promiscuous. In these cases, people believe that opposition to abortion is a defense of community values and traditions.[82]

Doctors for Life and the Christian Lawyers' Association have consistently challenged South Africa's abortion law. In 2010 these groups and their allies attempted to add more restrictive regulations, including early pregnancy ultrasounds, waiting periods, and mandatory counseling. These efforts, similar to those in other countries, relied on pseudoscientific claims that abortion caused breast cancer and "post-abortion trauma."[83]

We do not think the key questions about CO should be whether an individual's refusal to engage in abortion activities is sincere, or if they should be compelled to act against their own beliefs. Rather, in a democratic and pluralistic society the government is obligated to respect everyone's human rights. RJ-ing abortion reveals the disparate race and class impacts of a policy like CO. International organizations, including Amnesty International, the United Nations and various treaty bodies, the World Health Organization, and the International Federation of Gynecologists and Obstetricians have recognized that unregulated refusals of care have an impact on abortion access and cause particular harms to pregnant people who are poor, young, and displaced. Expanding CO reinforces barriers to care.[84] In various policy statements, these bodies have asserted that states and medical providers have an obligation to ensure that safe care is available and to urge careful monitoring.[85]

There are different paths to fulfilling that obligation. Sometimes institutions establish requirements for timely and accessible referrals in an effort to find a compromise that respects both an individual's sexual and reproductive rights and a provider's right of conscience. In a study of four countries taking this approach, researchers found that people on both sides of the issue objected both in principle and in practice.[86] Supporters of abortion argued that access would still be impeded, especially in places with few services and providers, and that CO is an intrusion by religion into a secular state. On the other side, abortion objectors claimed that referring someone for an abortion makes them complicit in a practice they consider immoral, and that the CO option is necessary to ensure their freedom of religion.[87]

As of 2023 four countries—Bulgaria, Ethiopia, Finland, and Sweden—do not allow CO in health care at all on the grounds that the practice allows an "unethical refusal of care" and an "abandonment of professional obligations."[88] In Sweden, for example, all hospital ob-gyn departments are required to perform abortions up to eighteen weeks. Medical authorities have taken the position that anyone who objects to performing an abortion or inserting an IUD cannot become a midwife or an ob-gyn.[89] As a practical matter, however, without enforcement mechanisms, if the law does not specifically prohibit or limit CO, it is the same as allowing it.

In a 2023 decision, Spain's Constitutional Court ruled that CO cannot be used to block the right to abortion. The case began in 2014, when doctors withheld from a pregnant woman, Antonia, the information that her fetus was nonviable, preventing her from being able to obtain an abortion in a "timely and dignified manner." When Antonia learned the truth and decided to have an abortion, no public hospital would comply. She was forced to travel 248 miles to a private clinic to have the procedure.[90] Irene Montero, Spain's equality minister, spoke out in 2021 about the need to restrict CO so as to guarantee that any woman can go "to a public hospital close to her home" to access an early abortion on request and be able to choose the abortion method herself. The minister was clear about whose rights must take precedence: "The right of doctors to conscientious objection cannot be above the right to decide of women."[91] In 2023 Montero was a driving force behind a law that enshrined in the Spanish constitution the right to have an abortion in a public hospital, as well as laws that strengthened transgender rights by guaranteeing any citizen over the age of sixteen the right to change their legal gender designation without medical supervision and that banned conversion therapy.[92]

In general, while international bodies have consistently taken the position that the right of the individual abortion seeker outweighs the rights of a fetus, in many countries the issue is not settled politically or legally. In fact, a new wave of antiabortion activism encourages and supports doctors who make CO claims despite dangerous and sometimes fatal consequences for abortion seekers.[93]

RJ-ING ABORTION RIGHTS RESISTANCE: ACTIVIST STRATEGIES OPPOSING POPULATION CONTROL

In the 1990s and beyond, the global women's health movement, especially in developing countries, led the resistance to population control internationally while simultaneously supporting abortion rights.[94] SAMA, a feminist group in India, Women Health and Likhaan Center for Women's Health in the Philippines, the Women's Global Network for Reproductive Rights (WGNRR), and the Asian Pacific Research and Resource Center for Women (ARROW) exposed and organized campaigns against coercive practices in their own countries and globally. These organizations highlighted the culpability of the U.S. government, their own governments, and nonprofit organizations that were involved in population control.[95]

In connecting sterilization abuse and other methods of coercive population control to the need for legal and safe abortion, the global feminist and women's health movement was ahead of the largest white-led abortion rights organizations in the United States. The international feminist movements' intersectional and human rights approach to reproductive and sexual rights explicitly identified colonialism, imperialism, and capitalism as impediments to human rights. In this way its politics were most closely allied with the more radical and expansive agenda of women-of-color-led organizations in the United States that prefigured reproductive justice. For example, the ideological platform of the Third World Women's Alliance asserted a basis for global solidarity: "As women, we recognize that our struggle is against an imperialistic sexist system that oppresses all minority peoples as well as exploits the majority."[96]

Some white feminist allies from the United States also played an important leadership and educational role globally. Early on, Betsy Hartmann, Bonnie Mass, and Pat Hines documented abuses and provided detailed critiques of the underlying assumptions of overpopulation ideology. They challenged the entire notion of overpopulation, arguing that it mistakenly blamed poor women of color for having too many children and prevented us from seeing and addressing the real causes of poverty and environmental destruction. In Hartmann's words, "Rapid population growth is not the cause of underdevelopment. It is a symptom of the slow pace of social reforms."[97]

ABORTION AND REPRODUCTIVE RIGHTS ARE HUMAN RIGHTS

Treaties and rulings by human rights bodies have strengthened abortion advocacy in Nicaragua, where abortion was prohibited in all circumstances. A coalition of feminist and human rights groups brought a challenge to that law. The collaboration submitted the case to various human rights bodies, and in 2009 the UN Committee against Torture ruled that the ban amounts to torture. Based on this finding, Amnesty International called on the Nicaraguan government to repeal the provisions of their penal code banning abortion.[98]

Human Rights Watch, an international NGO, interviewed people in Nicaragua who had direct knowledge about unwanted and crisis pregnancies and illegal abortions. The researchers spoke to women and girls, medical providers, lawyers, activists, and representatives of organizations that provided support and services to women and girls. Their report, "Over Their Dead Bodies: Denial of Access to Emergency Obstetric Care and Therapeutic Abortion in Nicaragua," outlined the devastating consequences of the law. The report found that the 2006 law punishing abortion—without any exceptions—has driven this medical procedure underground, creating a culture of fear and secrecy. The ban has not stopped abortion, but it has made it more unsafe.[99]

In May 2019, four organizations filed a suit with the United Nations Human Rights Committee on behalf of child rape survivors who were denied abortions, arguing that Nicaragua and four other countries "must bring their laws in step with international human rights standards that acknowledge the critical importance of allowing girls to lead lives they define for themselves."[100] In January 2025, the UN Committee ruled in three of the cases that the states should amend their laws to ensure access to abortion and to prevent girls from facing forced pregnancies and forced motherhood.[101]

SOUTH AFRICA EXPLICITLY ADOPTED THE REPRODUCTIVE JUSTICE FRAMEWORK

The first official adoption of reproductive justice outside the United States was in South Africa in 2014, a country where human rights claims have been at the heart of the struggle against racial apartheid. Anti-apartheid activists, both individuals and communities, demanded reparations for the decades of profound harms the system had caused. They argued that improving the health system to ensure access to safe abortion and to confront stigma was a relevant form of reparations.[102]

Bathabile Dlamini, the minister of social development in South Africa, announced that the ruling ANC party and the government would ground its positions on reproductive health in reproductive justice:

> We realize that [abortion] is but one of the reproductive experiences of women that needs to be enabled. We are also concerned about improving other elements of women's reproductive experiences, such as improving women's economic and educational statuses, we are concerned about whether women are in violent or abusive situations, whether their children have access to nutritious food, housing, clothing and other social protection services.[103]

This was the first time in any country that reproductive justice was taken as the foundation of government policy. Even after making this commitment, Dlamini acknowledged that barriers to safe abortion access in South Africa remained: "There are serious health systems challenges ... and issues of reproductive justice continue not to be central to programming and planning."[104]

In 2020 activists in South Africa founded the Sexual and Reproductive Justice Coalition (SRJC).[105] Marion Stevens, former president of the coalition, explained that a new organization was necessary because international sexual and reproductive health organizations operating in South Africa used reproductive justice language but did not practice it in their politics.[106] According to Stevens, South African NGOs, influenced by battles over abortion in the United States, depoliticized the reproductive justice framework. They ignored the radical input of their South African partners and settled for diluted abortion guidelines.[107] Stevens argued that these organizations have neither built a sustainable reproductive justice movement in South Africa nor held the government and the Department of Health accountable. In contrast, Stevens and her allies in the Sexual and Reproductive Justice Coalition continue to focus on the goal of achieving a broad and intersectional reproductive justice agenda that includes a direct challenge to existing power relations.[108]

SOUTH KOREA

South Korea furnishes us with an example of activists using a reproductive justice approach to expand abortion rights and access as part of a more inclusive agenda. Until January 2021 abortion was illegal in South Korea under the Mother and Child Health Act, and a person could face jail time or pay a fine for having or performing an abortion. The law created fear, stigma, and uncertainty, even though there were few prosecutions, and illegal abortion was often, though not always, available. During the years of criminalization, population and eugenic goals drove implementation of the law. During periods when the government wanted to change the size and improve the "quality" of the country's population, it forced abortion and sterilization on women who were poor, unmarried, or had disabilities, reinforcing their eugenics-based system of stratified reproduction.[109] But when the overall fertility rate in South Korea dropped in the 2000s, the government changed course in an effort to increase population by cutting the abortion rate among desirable reproducers. Any woman who was not poor, single, or disabled who sought an abortion could be subjected to government prosecution.

The organization Women with Disabilities Empathy played a leading role in the struggle for decriminalization. In 2015 the group embraced the reproductive justice framework and made opposition to eugenics and population control central in their agenda. However, when pro-choice "allies" approved a compromise position that allowed for abortion to be legal specifically for eugenic reasons, disability justice activists found this position unacceptable and vowed to continue their fight. They pointed out that eugenic abortion had violated human rights when it had been used to eliminate embryos that would develop into people with disabilities—people who absolutely had a right to be alive and to be full members of society.

In 2017 these members organized Joint Action for Reproductive Justice (Joint Action), a coalition of feminists, doctors, youth activists, religious organizations, and disability rights organizations that came together in a new attempt to change the law.[110] The coalition exposed the abortion ban as a government tool used to control women's sexuality and to place differential value on the people's lives and reproduction. In essence, they charged that the government's policies were really aimed at adjusting fertility rates and not about supporting women's choices or protecting human life. Joint Action was convinced that "choice" would never win when pitted against "life." With their rallying cry "If Abortion Is a Crime, the State Is the Criminal," the coalition promoted the ideal that government had the responsibility to protect *everyone's* reproductive rights and an obligation to rectify past injustices. Decriminalization of abortion was a justice issue.

RJ-ing abortion enabled the activists in Joint Action to build a diverse coalition that reflected breadth, intersectionality, and social justice and that included young girls, women living with HIV/AIDS, women with disabilities, queer and transgender women, and sex work-ers.[111] The demands put forth by the coalition expressed an intersec-tional analysis: (1) full legalization of abortion and the safe termination of pregnancy, (2) expansion of comprehensive sex education and access to contraceptives, (3) complete revision of the eugenic elements of the Mother and Child Health Act (the law criminalizing abortion), and (4) a guarantee of reproductive rights without stigma or discrimination.[112]

The coalition won an important victory in 2019 when the ban was overturned, but advocates continued to press for their goal of complete decriminalization. The effort finally succeeded on January 1, 2021, when the Korean Constitutional Court instructed the legislature to imple-ment policies that would reduce the need for abortion and guarantee a woman's right to self-determination. The court's decision affirmed the central pillars of reproductive justice: It renounced population control aims and emphasized that human beings should not be treated as a means for achieving other values, purposes, or legal interests.

Crucially, the court acknowledged that decisions about terminating a pregnancy had been deeply related to a person's socioeconomic cir-cumstances. But the status of abortion access in South Korea will not be fully settled until the national legislature passes a new bill to comply with the court's directives to take action to strengthen sex education, provide social welfare assistance for pregnant women and children, and provide medical insurance coverage.

BUILDING GLOBAL SOLIDARITY: THE INTERNATIONAL WOMEN AND HEALTH MEETING

As we have seen, regional and international gatherings fostered global feminist communication and bolstered campaigning for reproductive rights. The first International Women and Health Meeting (IWHM) in Rome, in 1977, brought together activists from Europe. In the late 1980s and 1990s, a series of UN conferences were opportunities for regional and transnational organizing, but some of the more radical participants at these meetings became convinced that the women's health movement needed a space independent of the UN to face the challenges posed by globalization and neo-capitalism. Navigating the inevitable tensions arising from vastly different political and economic contexts required a feminist movement not dominated by voices from the Global North. In this section we focus on the most effective activities organized by feminist networks and grassroots activists outside mainstream institutions.

Beginning in 1984, with a meeting entitled "No to Population Control: Women Decide!," and continuing until 2015, the IWHM was the largest and most sustained of these efforts. The Women's Global Network for Reproductive Rights (WGNRR) came out of the IWHM process and continues to organize global campaigns and provide space for information sharing and collaboration. Throughout its history, the organization has elevated and connected local and regional grassroots organizations and tried to bridge their political differences with more establishment organizations. WGNRR's website explains, "We are a Southern-based global, member-driven network that builds and strengthens movements for Sexual and Reproductive Health, Rights (SRHR) and justice. Access to justice is inextricably linked to SRHR, gender equality, and overall wellbeing of women and girls in all their diversity."[113]

IWHM meetings attracted individual advocates, academics, and networks involved in women's health and reproductive rights. Its origins in the global grassroots women's movement shaped its trajectory, especially the commitment to ensuring that representatives from the Global North should not control the meetings. To implement that goal, meeting organizers raised money to support significant representation from grassroots organizations and activists working in the Global South.

The IWHM functioned without ongoing commitments from foundations or other funders, a permanent leadership group, paid staff, or an office. At the end of each meeting several activists would volunteer to host the next one and to create a countrywide coalition to support the effort.[114] Initially, the local feminist coalition organizing the meeting set the agenda. In 2005, however, the Philippine Organizing Committee introduced an innovative process to ensure continuity and support local efforts, creating the International Advisory Committee, which was comprised of the major women's health networks, which would work with the local group but not supersede its authority.[115]

The organizers of the Manila meeting were committed to diverse representation among the attendees in terms of gender, race, class, caste, ethnicity, culture, disability, marital status, sexual orientation, and religious identity. To achieve that goal they instituted regional quotas for participants and dedicated subsidies to women from Africa, Asia, and poor communities in the Global North. According to Sylvia Estrada-Claudio, a member of the core organizing group and an internationally respected activist, this approach of bridging national boundaries and identities while at the same time honoring them was the reason the IWHM endured.[116]

> Indeed, the IWHM would never have survived if it did not understand that women are differentially positioned in interlocking systems of oppressions. Women's bodies are the quintessential focus of the international women's health movement.... The recognition that interlocking systems of oppression construct our bodies and identities is central to the conviction of many women and health activists that the struggle for reproductive and sexual rights and freedoms is fundamental to resisting neo-liberal capitalist hegemony.[117]

Without using the term "reproductive justice," Estrada-Claudio nevertheless invoked its core message regarding intersectional oppressions and identities. More recently, similar transnational gatherings have intentionally incorporated reproductive justice.

"ABORTION AND REPRODUCTIVE JUSTICE: THE UNFINISHED REVOLUTION"

Exposing the misinformation and mythology that abortion opponents present as facts is a core strategy for building support to change abortion law and policy. Between 2014 and 2018 three international conferences aimed to strengthen those efforts. The gatherings brought together researchers, academics, policy advocates, providers, and grass-roots activists dedicated to providing accurate, evidence-based information in order to raise awareness and catalyze activism.

The first of these conferences, "Abortion: The Unfinished Revolution," was held on Prince Edward Island (PEI), Canada, in 2014, a site selected because at that time it was the only province in Canada without abortion services. The organizers were making a political statement as part of their ongoing campaign to bring abortion services to PEI, which succeeded in 2017. The conference also inspired the participants from Northern Ireland to organize a second gathering in Belfast to bolster their efforts to legalize abortion. Convening "Abortion and Reproductive Justice: The Unfinished Revolution," a high-profile public conference, in Northern Ireland in 2016 was a pivotal part of the decades-long struggle to overturn the abortion ban.[118]

The third conference took place in Grahamstown, South Africa, in 2018. At the opening session Jacques van Zuydam, South Africa's chief director of population and development at the Department of Social Development, reiterated the government's commitment to reproductive justice. The conference raised awareness about the connection between abortion access and maternal mortality, and it stressed that African countries have the highest rates of maternal mortality from unsafe abortion in the world.

All three conferences shared the understanding that a lack of access to abortion is a symptom of underlying systems of oppression, and all three promoted abortion access as part of the larger agenda of achieving reproductive justice. Conference organizers understood that attacks on abortion are typically driven by an agenda to sustain the status quo and are opposed to expanded concepts of justice.

The conferences were urgent calls to action for building global solidarity, for expanding abortion access, for supporting efforts to achieve justice in all areas of life, and for combating abortion stigma. Sylvia

Estrada-Claudio movingly underscored these points in her closing keynote address in Belfast:

> I will take home what I have learned yet again in Belfast. That the dreams I have for the women and men of my country are dreams that actually know no national boundaries, dreams that do not recognize divisions of class or ethnicity or race or other markers of individual identity. That I will find in our struggles for reproductive justice passive and active, willful and unplanned support from various others who are also fighting for the same things, and that I must return that solidarity in equal measure.[119]

GLOBAL CAMPAIGNS FOR INDIVIDUAL CASES

Global campaigns publicizing examples of abortion denials with devastating consequences have built transnational solidarity across networks and organizations and have strengthened local activism. Paola Guzmán, a sixteen-year-old Ecuadorian girl, committed suicide in 2002 after becoming pregnant. She had been sexually abused by the vice principal of the school she attended and by the doctor who performed her abortion.[120] International activist organizations widely publicized her death and similar cases in El Salvador, Mexico, and Brazil, intensifying calls for the decriminalization of abortion. Those efforts were instrumental in securing the release of some of the women incarcerated in El Salvador for having had miscarriages or allegedly inducing their own abortions.

In 2012 Savita Halappanavar died in Northern Ireland from septicemia, an infection she contracted while having a miscarriage. The Catholic hospital where Savita was under care refused to perform an abortion or even to move her to another facility where she could have obtained one. International outrage over her case bolstered the advocacy efforts in Northern Ireland, and together these forces eventually brought about a change in the abortion law.

The Women's Global Network for Reproductive Rights has consistently called attention to those people who harass, threaten, and commit violence against individual advocates and providers, as well as the impacts of these acts. In September 2023 WGNRR issued a joint statement with the International Coalition on Women's Human Rights Defenders (ICWHRD). The statement called on all governments to:

> Stop the criminalisation and attacks on women human rights defenders, including abortion rights defenders and abortion providers!
>
> Work alongside abortion rights groups to support abortion seekers and ensure access to safe reproductive health care to all pregnant persons, including providing political and economic resources to reinforce and legitimise the work of abortion rights defenders.
>
> Recognise that the realisation of all human rights is intersectional and reparations for colonialism, racism, climate injustice and other forms of oppression also require reparations for sexual and reproductive injustices against pregnant persons, including neglect and denial of abortion care.[121]

ICWHRD advocated within the global human rights movement for recognition of sexual and reproductive rights as human rights and for providers to be seen as human rights defenders.

The importance of sharing activist strategies, victories, losses, and information in physical and virtual spaces and in global campaigns cannot be overstated. Throughout the world, the collective energy and passion of advocates is activist fuel. September 28, International Safe Abortion Day, began as a regional effort in Latin America and became an international campaign in 2018. It brings allies around the world closer together and offers inspiration and ideas that can be adapted to diverse settings. The International Campaign for Safe Abortion is a consistent and reliable source of news and activism, offering possibilities for global solidarity and connection. Its social media presence elevates and disseminates information about grassroots activities that would never be covered in mainstream media.[122]

Large international gatherings did not take place during the COVID pandemic, but reproductive justice activists, like those in other movements, continued global solidarity, support, and information sharing through the internet. And there are plans to resume in-person meetings.

Marevic Parcon, former executive director of WGNRR, says that the organization plans to hold a "Safe Abortion International Exchange." The Association of Women in Development (AWID) will also host its conference, and the Asia Safe Abortion Partnership is planning for "Abortion and Reproductive Justice: The Unfinished Revolution IV."

FIGHTING STIGMA / CHANGING CULTURE: SPEAKING OUT

Activists have stressed the role of abortion stigma as a global phenomenon contributing to the social, medical, and legal marginalization of abortion.[123] Stigma takes different forms depending on a country's law, culture, and religion, but casting abortion in negative terms can be a barrier to accessing safe abortion care regardless of its legal status.[124] The Guttmacher Institute found that stigma is one of the three most consequential barriers to reducing unsafe abortion.[125] Stigma can lead to an increase in abortion complications, injuries, and deaths. When antiabortion forces claim that women's sexuality, unwed pregnancy, and abortion are all immoral and should be legally restricted, they strengthen a culture of shame and silence. Where stigma and anti-choice propaganda prevail, individuals must struggle especially hard just to gather accurate information about services, and claims about the dangers and immorality of abortion often go unchallenged. Under these circumstances, people with unwanted pregnancies are more likely to delay care, use unsafe methods of self-abortion, and turn to untrained providers.[126] One-fifth of women in the world live in countries where abortion is criminalized, and evidence shows that stigma increases the likelihood that restrictive laws will be permanent.

Even in countries where laws have been liberalized, stigma, shame, and negative judgments remain obstacles to care. In various settings researchers found that women felt guilty after having a legal abortion and expressed negative attitudes toward other women who have abortions, especially those who have had more than one.[127] In all contexts, abortion stigma frequently leads people to keep silent about their abortions, reluctant to talk even with friends and colleagues out of fear they may be judged adversely.

A 2022 review of qualitative evidence demonstrated that stigma had an impact on providers, activists, and politicians.[128] The review cites many examples where stigma is a tool to keep people from pursuing abortion by generating real obstacles, obstructing access to abortion with arduous and unnecessary requirements, and perpetuating poor infrastructure, including a lack of designated locations for services. Stigma also underwrites systems of humiliating punishments and threats targeting people who seek and obtain abortions.[129] Some health care staff are affected by disparaging attitudes about abortion and end up treating their patients poorly.

The virulent and ongoing antiabortion backlash has intensified the urgency of work toward the social acceptability of abortion along with legal changes.[130] Stigma has tremendous power to silence everyone involved with abortion.[131] Patriarchy, gender discrimination, and organized religion are all forces underwriting abortion stigma and silence.[132] Resisting stigma is, therefore, a critical element to achieve legal and cultural change, and it is a critical part of supporting providers and people who have abortions. In the next section we will look at some of the most effective strategies activists are using transnationally.

BREAKING THE SILENCE

RJ-ing abortion shines a light on the abortion experiences that tend not to be told, those of ordinary women with the fewest resources. Putting their stories in the center of both the public debate and policymaking is a compelling way to normalize abortion and demonstrate that it is an ordinary part of reproductive life. When events are held in places where individuals tell their own abortion stories publicly, storytelling becomes a political tactic, pioneered by advocates in the United States before and after legalization. Today, people around the world use abortion storytelling to claim self-determination. Here are a few examples.

The X-ile Project in Ireland was named after the 1992 case of a person whose right to leave the country for an abortion was challenged by the Irish government. Photographer Katie O'Neill led the project, creating an online gallery of photos to personalize the women who were forced to go to Britain to have an abortion.[133] As she explained, "What we are trying to do with this project is to force the Irish public and the government to look at these women that they are exiling out of the country and to see that these women are their sisters, their mothers, their partners and people that they see every day in the street."[134] Storytelling was a key strategy in the 2018 Northern Ireland referendum campaign, which succeeded in repealing the abortion ban in that country. Exit polls revealed that the key factors influencing the vote were people's personal stories as covered in the media (43 percent) and experiences of people they knew (34 percent).[135]

Most interventions to reduce stigma have focused on the people having abortions, but it is also important to address the impact on providers. As we saw in Italy, the larger medical community has often shunned doctors who provide abortions and denied them the respect accorded to providers of other types of health care, which discourages physicians and other health care workers from delivering abortion services.

Researchers involved with the Don't Talk About It project documented the impact of stigma on providers and advocates in Prince Edward Island, many of whom reported frustration, anger, stress, burnout, hostility, and threats to their jobs.[136] Storytelling creates the space to tell the facts about your work from your own point of view, thus gaining new support.[137] Physicians who participated in the PEI research were able to connect with the larger feminist movement and a wider progressive community. They reported feeling that their participation in the project was itself a form of activism and emancipation.[138]

Training doctors to become vocal and visible advocates for abortion access is a relatively new and extremely effective strategy. Practitioners' voices are especially powerful in confronting colleagues who refuse to provide abortion and other reproductive health services based on claims of conscience. The organization Global Doctors calls on providers and professional medical/public health societies to find institutional responses to conscience-based refusals and to train these individuals and organizations to be effective advocates.[139]

In 2014–15, Planned Parenthood Global and Marie Stopes International initiated Provider Share Workshops in Latin America and sub-Saharan Africa. As of 2020, Provider Share, based on a U.S. model, was the only evidence-based intervention designed to reduce stigma suffered by providers.[140] The workshops encouraged people to talk about their experiences in a group in order to create a sense of community, combat internalized stigma, and offer an opportunity for participants to feel proud of their work.[141] The conversations brought other complexities to the surface, helping participants to understand the dynamics of stigma. For example, these encounters allowed some providers to see that experiencing stigma can trigger negative attitudes toward abortion seekers.[142]

SELF-MANAGED ABORTION WITH PILLS: RADICAL DIRECT ACTION, INSIDE AND OUTSIDE THE LAW

Self-inducing an abortion with misoprostol together with mifepristone or misoprostol alone is relatively easy and safe as long as a person has basic information about the correct protocol.[143] When a person needs medical attention after using the pills, the most likely complication is an incomplete abortion, and the person can repeat the procedure. Medical abortion with pills is relatively new in the United States, but misoprostol in the form of Cytotec has been widely used for abortion in Latin America since 1988.[144] Advocates attribute the decrease in maternal mortality in that region to increased access to the pills and to information about how to use misoprostol to have a safe self-managed abortion.[145]

Making abortion pills available and giving people the information and support needed to use them is a direct-action strategy that saves health and lives.[146] Growing numbers of people globally, likely in the millions each year, are taking abortion pills at home, outside the medical system.[147] Although we cannot know the exact number, we do know that it is happening in almost every country and not just where abortion access is a criminal offense or severely hindered. Many people prefer this option over going to a clinic or doctor.[148]

Unfortunately, law, medical practice, and research are out of step with reality. According to activist experts, "Abortion pills provide a perfect example of a technology that has outpaced the current legal restrictions which actually impede progress."[149] Of course, opponents of abortion are attempting to control and restrict access to the pills.[150] As we have seen, people have been prosecuted for using the pills themselves or helping others, even in countries where abortion is legal, including in various states in the United States, the United Kingdom, and Australia. In the United States the Supreme Court will issue its ruling in the case *Alliance for Hippocratic Medicine v. Food and Drug Administration (FDA)*. In the meantime, people involved in SMA, especially in U.S. states with abortion bans, take tremendous legal risks due to the single-minded dedication of the antiabortion movement to stop these efforts.[151]

But advocates for abortion access are also determined. Today, as in other eras, pregnant people and activists around the world are not waiting for politicians and policymakers to change law and policy. Regardless of the legal status of abortion, activist networks provide information and access to abortion pills and explain how to avoid legal risks. International organizations such as Women Help Women (WHW), Women on Web (WoW), Aid Access, and Safe2Choose are among the most active and well-known groups that give people looking for an abortion the information and the tools they need. WHW also trains local activists on medical abortion and brings advocates from different countries and regions together to share experiences, strategies, and resources.

Along with the internet, safe abortion hotlines have been the primary vehicle in the Global South for spreading the word about SMA with misoprostol. As of 2020, hotlines were operating in almost thirty countries.[152] Established by feminist collectives, not health institutions, the hotlines promote bodily autonomy and human rights for all people. In the tradition of self-help, historically embraced by the feminist health movement, the groups create their own resources in accessible language, train laypeople to provide support, and generally assist people who want to use this method. Hotlines/help lines provide person-centered care and community building.[153]

Proponents of SMA are emphatic that using abortion pills without consulting a doctor or other formally trained medical provider is not the same as trying to self-abort with a coat hanger or using other unsafe methods of self-abortion. SMA with pills is not a desperate last resort; it is a harm-reduction strategy that many people prefer, even when other clinical options are available. It is empowering for both those who share the knowledge and those who receive it. People of color and people who are transgender, have a disability, or are young might prefer this method because many feel they cannot trust a system that has ignored or mistreated their bodies in medical settings.

SMA advocates see this abortion option as the embodiment of a radical power-shifting theory of change. Sydney Calkin explains, "Instead of protesting unjust institutions, activists focus on enacting change immediately, building their own institutions and embodying the changes they want to see." Calkin quotes a Polish SMA activist: "We don't believe that law creates access—we believe that access creates law."[154] Leading champions of self-managed abortion Kinga Jelinska and Susan Yanow, from Women Help Women and Self-Managed Abortion; Safe & Supported (SASS), see SMA as radical in several ways: "SMA flattens hierarchies of knowledge and subverts power dynamics of care."[155] They explain, "Medical abortion is subversive because it challenges traditional assumptions about service delivery requirements, the definition of a provider, and the power dynamics related to providing abortion care."[156]

In Mexico, activists pioneered the strategy of "acompañamiento" (accompaniment).[157] Activists train volunteers to provide emotional and informational support to a person, staying in contact through their abortion, in person, by phone, or by text. Today, accompaniment networks in many parts of Latin America are expanding access to medication abortions. They provide misoprostol to pregnant people living in restrictive legal settings and offer safety guidelines and support.[158]

In Argentina, a group called the Socorristas also use this strategy during second-trimester medication abortions.[159] The Socorristas' dedication to feminist health care is grounded in a commitment to social justice and opposition to capitalism.[160] Self-managing an abortion radically redefines the concept of providers and experts: Since pills cause the abortion, the person taking them is the provider. Socorristas have altered the power position of medical professionals and the community providers who are now recognized as *the* medical experts on abortion.[161] SMA challenges what advocates see as the overmedicalization of abortion, even in countries where it is legal but still controlled by health systems that, intentionally or not, create barriers to access.

In Northern Ireland the abortion pill was an important part of the campaign to change the law. In 2012 two hundred activists signed a letter saying they had either taken the abortion pill or helped women to obtain it. This statement was an assertion of solidarity with a woman who was prosecuted for buying the pills on the internet for her daughter. Their actions and letter of resistance challenged Northern Ireland law and raised the visibility of medical abortion, which at that time was legal and available for all United Kingdom citizens *except* those living in Northern Ireland and on the Isle of Man.[162] In May 2016, three women from the Alliance for Choice in Derry, Ireland, turned themselves in to the police and admitted that they had helped many women access medical abortion pills. The next month, several groups joined together to bring abortion pills by drone into Northern Ireland. These actions, largely symbolic, highlighted the challenges faced by those seeking access to abortion and the steps people were willing to take to circumvent the restrictive law.

In their 2018 campaign in Seoul, South Korea, 125 activists publicly took a single pill—the exact number of people who have abortions in that country every hour.[163] At the time of their action, abortion was still illegal in most circumstances in South Korea, and the penalties for performing or inducing an abortion could be up to two years in prison or a fine.[164]

In Mexico, 172 people were imprisoned for the "crime" of illegal abortion between 2010 and 2020, when groups like Las Libres defied the law and distributed abortion pills. In 2021 the Mexican Supreme Court declared that abortion was not a crime. Supreme Court president Arturo Zaldívar acknowledged that the law had primarily affected poorer women. "Rich girls have always had abortions and never gone to prison."[165] The ruling also impacted activists who for many years operated in fear when they ignored the law and assisted people in having abortions. Las Libres has been engaged in direct action to increase abortion access since 2000. They provided accompaniment services for women who had illegal abortions. Even though no one from the group had been arrested, Veronica Cruz, cofounder of Las Libres, said, "Now I feel like it's safer for me to help other women."[166] After the *Dobbs* decision in 2022, Las Libres' activities have expanded tremendously within the United States. They are part of an international, community-based information and distribution network for illegal abortion with pills.[167] Most people who are part of the network are volunteers, and the pills are often supplied free of charge thanks to donations from individual and institutional donors.

In Poland, the 2023 prosecution and sentencing of Justyna Wydrzynska, a cofounder of the Abortion Dream Team, captured international attention and catalyzed widespread resistance to the Polish government.[168] And in 2023, Joanna Parniewska's psychiatrist reported her to the authorities for taking abortion pills. Officers strip-searched her, looking for names on her private phone. Parniewska explained, "I went public to protest against police impunity, against breach of medical confidentiality, and inhumane treatment."[169]

Globally, mobilizing SMA users is a key strategy. Women are directed to safe services, and organizers hope they will engage in activism. This form of direct action is a critical way to create social change, combat stigma, and support a culture of autonomy through self-help.

While the actual procedure of illegal self-induced abortion is relatively safe and easy, law and policy continue to make having an SMA abortion with pills risky. For this reason, many advocates of SMA argue that it is not a substitute for legal change.[170] The International Campaign for Safe Abortion calls on governments to decriminalize abortion and urges activists to continue to advocate for an end to the inequalities that shape the context within which people make reproductive decisions.[171] Marge Berer, longtime abortion rights advocate and organizer of the Campaign for Safe Abortion, tells us that "as long as abortion remains clandestine, it isn't as safe as it should be."[172] Berer promotes the ideal that self-managed abortion should be accepted and supported within health systems that would provide adequate follow-up care. "If only the law, the politicians, the health system and senior medical professionals in every county were willing to make it happen, it would be so simple."[173]

While the *Dobbs* decision catalyzed antiabortion actions globally, it has also inspired abortion rights activists around the world who find hope and inspiration in international victories and organizing such as the Green Wave in Latin America. Green scarves worn during demonstrations were originally the symbol of the fight for abortion rights in Argentina. This gesture honored an earlier struggle for human rights when the Mothers of Plaza de Mayo wore white headscarves as they confronted Argentina's vicious dictatorship, protesting the disappearance of their children and grandchildren.[174]

Today the green scarves have gone global and are worn in demonstrations around the world, from Buenos Aires and Poland to Texas. They are a signal that the contemporary abortion battle is also about human rights, democracy, and the defense against state terrorism. After years of resistance to military dictatorships, feminists in Latin America have developed a deep appreciation of the connections between democracy, gender rights, and other intersectional issues that drive their struggles for women's rights. The scarves are a visible sign of international solidarity and resistance.[175]

In this chapter we discussed the theory and practice of RJ-ing abortion internationally. We saw that the inspiration to incorporate human rights into the concept of reproductive justice emerged at an international gathering. At that time global feminists were leading struggles against reproductive oppression and for bodily autonomy in their respective countries and internationally. Since then, activist strategies for abortion access and reproductive justice have become increasingly globalized. This is not an entirely new phenomenon: Wherever and whenever law or practice has made abortion locally inaccessible, pregnant people have crossed borders when necessary, constrained as always by their race, class, and legal status.

What is new, however, is the scale of available support and the breadth of vision, advocacy, and solidarity. Worldwide feminist collaboration has made possible the increased ability to share strategies, tactics, victories, and defeats. It gives us models for immediate, large-scale direct action, informed by a radical vision of long-range systemic social change. Today's actions to expand abortion access and demand accountability and reparations for reproductive abuses are part of a transformative understanding of justice. They are the living link to a reproductive justice future.

Conclusion

When Donald Trump was elected to a second presidential term, the road to reproductive justice got longer. Even as activists celebrate abortion rights victories in several states, new restrictions are certain. While "abortion" appears only once in the official Republican Party platform, it takes up much more space in the Heritage Foundation's Project 2025. Considered by many to be the real party platform, this nine-hundred-page detailed plan is designed to permanently embed political conservatism in every American institution and community.[1] Although Trump claimed not to know much about it, CNN exposed that at least 140 people who worked in his former administration were involved in writing it.[2]

Project 2025 includes several proposals that directly threaten reproductive autonomy. It would eliminate medication abortion (currently used in 63 percent of abortions in the United States) by revoking FDA approval of mifepristone, one of two medicines that are part of the process; allow hospitals to deny emergency lifesaving abortion care to pregnant patients in crisis; bypass the FDA and instead enforce the 1873 Comstock law that prohibits mailing anything intended to produce an abortion; prosecute people for shipping and transporting abortion pills and supplies, effectively banning medication abortion; allow the harassment of abortion clinic staff and patients; and establish an abortion surveillance system that would force states to report the intimate personal details of all patients receiving abortion care.[3] And the plan calls for continued efforts that would make it difficult or impossible to obtain birth control, emergency contraception, IVF, and other reproductive services. Its goal is also to promote restrictive policies that would undermine reproductive rights across the globe.[4]

Confronting Project 2025 will require sustained vigilance, enduring hope, and collective action, as activists tie together the threads of oppression highlighted in this book. Legislators dedicated to maintaining white supremacy are hyper-focused on censoring public school curricula and libraries. They aim to rewrite American history by erasing oppression. For example, teaching about genocide against Native Americans, enslavement, sexism, and heterosexism is forbidden, and books about them are removed from libraries.

Also taboo are the voices for civil rights, women's and LGBTQIA+ liberation, and other social movements dedicated to human rights for all. To ensure that the forces and voices of oppression do not eclipse those of survival, we were determined to expose the harms and legacies of racism, colonization, and reproductive oppression, and to keep the resisters in the foreground.

This book calls readers to join in, and to continue to develop the theory and the practice of reproductive justice. As one example, Loretta Ross and others are articulating a new critical lens, reproductive justice futurism (RJF), to ensure that emerging technological solutions to global problems do not replicate systems of injustice and oppression. The individuals and organizations profiled in chapter 4 show that the activist arena is bursting with energy, ideas, and the determination to build a radical reproductive justice future outside mainstream power structures. Abortion funds model community care and support. Networks for self-managed abortion reclaim feminist histories and practices, and they put abortion care directly into the hands of pregnant people. Advocates for birthing justice create pregnancy and birth support teams of doulas and midwives.

The 2024 conference organized by Collective Power for Reproductive Justice affirmed the power of reproductive justice to inspire bold, radical, creative, intersectional thought and action. The gathering centered community care and do-it-yourself (DIY) practices to resist domination, overcome stigma, and combat authoritarianism around the globe. Dozens of speakers reminded us that dreaming expansively is essential to hope, and that hope is essential to activism. Performances by Indigenous drag performers Lady Shug and Papi Churro (in a show called the "LaLa Land Back Tour") made the audience confront racism, genocide, and homophobia and brought us to our feet in celebration of their bravery.[5]

The pillars of reproductive justice—the right to have children, the right not to have children, the right to raise children in safe and healthy communities, and the right to sexual freedom and expression—contain all the threads of bodily autonomy and sovereignty. By making the connections, we think that reproductive justice is a bridge to other movements, and the path to collective freedom and liberation.

NOTES

PREFACE

1. Hannah Silver and Cloee Cooper, "101 Abortion Abolitionists," Political Research Associates, October 2023.

2. Guttmacher Institute, "State Bans on Abortion throughout Pregnancy," October 7, 2024. See also Allison McCann and Amy Schoenfeld Walker, "Tracking Abortion Bans across the Country," *New York Times*, November 6, 2024.

3. "Human Rights Crisis: Abortion in the United States after Dobbs," Human Rights Watch, April 18, 2023.

4. Leslie Reagan, *When Abortion Was a Crime: Women, Medicine and the Law in the United States, 1867–1973* (University of California Press, 2022). Reagan frames the debate as an ideological struggle over the position of women. How free should they be to have sexual experiences, in or out of marriage, without paying the price of pregnancy, childbirth, and motherhood? How many rights should they have to achieve their own needs, interests, and well-being with respect to childbearing or anything else? How subordinate should they be to men, how deeply embedded in the family, and how firmly controlled by national or racial objectives?

5. Anne M. Valk, *Radical Sisters: Second-Wave Feminism and Black Liberation in Washington, DC* (University of Illinois Press, 2008), 11.

6. According to research by Black Women's Blueprint, 60 percent of Black girls experience sexual assault by the time they reach eighteen. They are most at risk for the subsequent consequences, such as pregnancy or STDs, over which they may have even less control.

CHAPTER ONE

1. Loretta Ross and Rickie Solinger, *Reproductive Justice: An Introduction* (University of California Press, 2017), provides an excellent account of its history and current application. Although reproductive justice was created by Black feminists, it is not an identity-based human rights framework. Anyone can adapt and use RJ, as we will continuously clarify in this book.

2. In some states trigger bans have been on the books for years.

3. The exact number is a moving target since new legislation is regularly introduced.

4. Constitutional lawyer Rhonda Copelon argues that the notion of privacy could have been more liberatory and expansive, but the Supreme Court's language in the *Roe* decision limited the meaning of that term. Rhonda Copelon, "From Privacy to Autonomy: The Condition for Sexual and Reproductive Freedom," in *From Abortion to Reproductive Freedom: Transforming a Movement*, ed. Marlene Fried (South End Press, 1990), 27–43.

5. Medicaid is a federal government-funded program providing medical coverage for people who meet the poverty-line criteria. Some states also have their own programs. Initially, life threat to the pregnant person was the only exception included in Hyde legislation. Before Hyde, the government paid for one-third of all abortions, about 333,000 per year. After Hyde, only about 200 a year were covered. In 1993, the Coalition for Abortion Access and Reproductive Equity (CAARE) campaign, a coalition of diverse groups led by the National Black Women's Health Project, successfully pressured Congress to add exceptions for rape and incest. But the Hyde Amendment had a disparate and devastating impact by race and class, effectively denying abortion rights to low-income women, who are disproportionately women of color.

6. For more about Hyde, see Guttmacher Institute, "State Funding of Abortion under Medicaid, as of August 31, 2023"; ACLU, "Access Denied: Origins of the Hyde Amendment and Other Restrictions on Public Funding for Abortion," December 1994; Heather D. Boonstra, "Abortion in the Lives of Women Struggling Financially: Why Insurance Coverage Matters," *Guttmacher Policy Review*, July 14, 2016.

7. Katy Backes Kozhimannil, Asha Hassan, and Rachel R. Hardeman, "Abortion Access as a Racial Justice Issue," *New England Journal of Medicine* 387, no. 17 (2022): 1537–39.

8. Nambi Ndugga, Drishti Pallai, and Samantha Artiga, "Disparities in Health and Health Care: 5 Key Questions and Answers," Kaiser Family Foundation, August 14, 2024.

9. Diana Greene Foster, *The Turnaway Study: Ten Years, a Thousand Women, and the Consequences of Having—or Being Denied—an Abortion*, Advancing New Standards in Reproductive Health (ANSIRH), June 2020. The study followed one thousand women over the course of ten years.

10. Nicole Chavez, "Texas Woman Died after an Unsafe Abortion Years Ago. Her Daughter Fears Same Thing May Happen Again," CNN, October 11, 2021.

11. Chavez, "Texas Woman Died."

12. Elizabeth Harned and Liza Fuentes, "Abortion Out of Reach: The Exacerbation of Wealth Disparities after Dobbs v. Jackson Women's Health Organization," *Guttmacher Policy Analysis*, January 2023.

13. Harned and Fuentes, "Abortion Out of Reach."

14. Erica White, "Racial Disparities in Women's Health," *Network for Public Health Law*, August 1, 2022.

15. Liza Fuentes, "Inequity in US Abortion Rights and Access: The End of Roe Is Deepening Existing Divides," *Guttmacher Policy Analysis*, January 2023.

16. Matt Gonzales, "Race and Roe: Black Women Talk Effects of Court Decision," *SHRM*, July 11, 2022. Also see Amanda Jean Stevenson, "The Pregnancy-Related Mortality Impact of a Total Abortion Ban in the United States: A Research Note on Increased Deaths Due to Remaining Pregnant," *Demography* 58, no. 6 (2021).

17. Marian F. MacDorman, Marie Thoma, Eugene Declercq, and Elizabeth A. Howell, "Racial and Ethnic Disparities in Maternal Mortality in the United States Using Enhanced Vital Records, 2016–2017," *American Journal of Public Health* 111, no. 9 (September 1, 2021): 1673–81.

18. Lynn M. Paltrow and Jeanne Flavin, "Arrests of and Forced Interventions on Pregnant Women in the United States (1973–2005): The Implications for Women's Legal Status and Public Health," *Journal of Health Politics, Policy and Law* 38, no. 2 (2013): 299–343. Also see Amnesty International, "Criminalizing Pregnancy: Policing Pregnant Women Who Use Drugs in the U.S.," 2017.

19. Arline Geronimus, *Weathering: The Extraordinary Stress of Ordinary Life in an Unjust Society* (Little Brown Spark, 2023). Also see Alisha Haridasani Gupta, "How 'Weathering' Contributes to Racial Health Disparities," *New York Times*, April 14, 2023.

20. Gupta, "How 'Weathering' Contributes."

21. The twelve founders were Toni M. Bond Leonard, Reverend Alma Crawford, Evelyn S. Field, Terri James, Bisola Marignay, Cassandra

McConnell, Cynthia Newbille, Loretta Ross, Elizabeth Terry, "Able" Mable Thomas, Winnette P. Willis, and Kim Youngblood.

22. Ross and Solinger, *Reproductive Justice*, 64.

23. For a more detailed account, see chapter 4 of this volume. Also see Jael Silliman et al., *Undivided Rights: Women of Color Organize for Reproductive Justice*, 2nd ed. (Haymarket Press, 2016); Jennifer Nelson, *Women of Color and the Reproductive Rights Movement* (New York University Press, 2003); Patricia Romney, *We Were There: The Third World Women's Alliance* (The Feminist Press, 2021).

24. For a full account of the RJ birth story, see Ross and Solinger, *Reproductive Justice*, 63–73.

25. Beverly Yuen Thompson, "Centering Reproductive Justice: Transitioning from Abortion Rights to Social Justice," in *Radical Reproductive Justice*, ed. Loretta J. Ross, Lynn Roberts, Erika Derkas, Whitney Peoples, and Pamela Bridgewater Toure (Feminist Press, 2017), 252–71.

26. Alexis Pauline Gumbs, China Martens, and Mai'a Williams, eds., *Revolutionary Mothering: Love on the Front Lines* (PM Press, 2016), preface.

27. Asian Communities for Reproductive Justice (ACRJ), "A New Vision for Advancing Our Movement," 2005.

28. Ross and Solinger, *Reproductive Justice*, 71.

29. All* Above All coined the term *abortion justice* to highlight the fact that racism, economic insecurity, and immigration status multiply the massive barriers to abortion care. As a result, solutions must include racial, economic, and immigrant justice.

30. Additional resources on Black feminism are Keeanga-Yamahtta Taylor, "Until Black Women Are Free, None of Us Will Be Free: Barbara Smith and the Black Feminist Visionaries of the Combahee River Collective," *New Yorker*, July 20, 2020; Ula Taylor, "The Historical Evolution of Black Feminist Theory and Praxis," *Journal of Black Studies* 29, no. 2 (1998): 234–53; bell hooks, *Ain't I a Woman* (South End Press, 1999); Angela Davis, *Women, Race, and Class* (Vintage, 1981).

31. Legal scholar and activist Dorothy Roberts named such policies repro ductive oppression, arguing that this was the central narrative describing the reproductive lives of women of color. See her *Killing the Black Body: Race, Reproduction, and the Meaning of Liberty* (Vintage Books, 1997, 2017).

32. Roberts's pathbreaking analysis was especially influential.

33. The following stories are used with permission from We Testify, originally a project of the National Network of Abortion Funds (NNAF), now an independent entity committed to lifting the voices of those whose abortion experiences have not been visible in mainstream abortion advocacy.

34. Jack is also featured on the *Black Lash* podcast: https://translash.org /category/trans-bodies-trans-choices/.

35. According to the Guttmacher Institute, 90 percent of fourteen-year-olds surveyed said they involved at least one parent or guardian in their abortion decision. In 2016, 193 minors navigated the same complicated bypass process in order to access abortion.

36. *Anchor babies* is the term that mistakenly, but intentionally, suggests that undocumented people come to the United States to have their babies in order for them to become U.S. citizens.

37. Ross and Solinger, *Reproductive Justice*, 71.

38. Kimberlé Crenshaw coined the term *intersectionality* in 1989 in order to advocate for an African American female who was refused a job because of both her identities. At that time there was no way to make a legal claim of discrimination based on being Black and female. The law only recognized two separate identities.

39. Kimala Price, "What Is Reproductive Justice?" *Meridians* 10, no. 2 (2010): 42–65. Price and others note that *reproductive justice* was not intended to be a substitute term for abortion rights, family planning, etc. It is instead a different way of conceptualizing reproductive freedom that is broader in scope than its predecessors. Price analyzes the important role of such narratives in creating the reproductive justice movement.

40. Restrictions include providing state funding only in cases of life endangerment, rape, or incest, requiring youth to have parental consent before they can have an abortion, and a requirement that anyone having an abortion must have and look at a transvaginal ultrasound.

41. Ross and Solinger, *Reproductive Justice*, 117.

42. Anita Valerio, "The Weeping Was All Our Pain—A Collective Wound—It Is Larger Than Each Individual … Our Past as Native People before Being Colonized and Culturally Liquidated," in *This Bridge Called My Back: Writings by Radical Women of Color*, ed. Cherríe Moraga and Gloria E. Anzaldúa (Persephone Press, 1981), 43.

43. Patricia Donovan, "Judging Teenagers: How Minors Fare When They Seek Court-Authorized Abortions," *Family Planning Perspectives* 15, no. 6 (November–December 1983): 259–62, 264–67.

44. Ross and Solinger, *Reproductive Justice*, 12. See also Gila Stopler, "Biopolitics and Reproductive Justice: Fertility Policies between Women's Rights and State and Community Interests," *University of Pennsylvania Journal of Law and Social Change* 18, no. 2 (2015).

45. Elizabeth "Betita" Martinez, "What Is White Supremacy?," *Catalyst Project*, 2017.

46. Charles Mills, *The Racial Contract* (Cornell University Press, 1997), 20.

47. *Ableism* refers to the systemic favoring, intentional and unintentional, of people without disabilities. People with disabilities are considered defective and are discriminated against. This term was introduced by disability rights activists during the civil rights movement of the 1960s and adopted more widely by U.S. feminists in the 1980s. Talila A. Lewis gives the following working definition of ableism: a "system that places value on people's bodies and minds based on societally constructed ideas of normalcy, intelligence and excellence" ("Ableism 2020: An Updated Definition," January 25, 2020).

48. White power elites have historically made significant distinctions among people who all "look white," classifying some as white and others not. These distinctions are tools of racial power because "whiteness," somewhat mediated by gender and class, confers citizenship, allocates benefits, and determines privileges. The perpetuation of anti-Semitism, for example, constructs being Jewish as a racial identity.

49. Walter Rhein, "All Bigotry Is Ignorance, But Not All Ignorance Is Bigotry," *Medium*, November 2, 2023.

50. Brittany Cooper, *Eloquent Rage: A Black Feminist Discovers Her Superpower* (St. Martin's Press, 2018), 4.

51. Shirley Chisholm, the first Black congresswoman, who also ran for president in 1972, captured the absurdity of failing to recognize multiple identities when she said that she could never remember whether she had been born Black or female first. See Shirley Chisholm, *Unbought and Unbossed* (Hodge Taylor Associates, 1970), 113–22.

52. Kimberlé Crenshaw, "Mapping the Margins: Intersectionality, Identity Politics, and Violence against Women of Color," *Stanford Law Review* 43, no. 6 (1991). While this was a pivotal point in terms of the academic acceptance of the term, the concept was widely understood within social movements, although it was expressed differently.

53. When we look at the various arenas of power in the United States—economic, social, political, legal, religious, and more—the vast majority of those with wealth and power are white males. They get to make the rules and continue to legitimize the racial order through a belief system that attributes any socioeconomic inequalities that exist among individuals to their own efforts and abilities. A key assumption of patriarchy, like white supremacy, is the idea that the uneven distribution of wealth and power in the United States

by race and gender is because people are not born with equal capacities and talents. The inequalities are inevitable and accepted, so long as it seems that people get what they deserve.

54. Calling it "hetero-patriarchy" brings attention to this assumption, and President Trump is attempting to institutionalize it. On the first day of his second term in office he signed an executive order that states, "It is the policy of the United States to recognize two sexes, male and female. These sexes are not changeable and are grounded in fundamental and incontrovertible reality."

55. For more on eugenics, see Roberts, *Killing the Black Body;* Betsy Hartmann, *The America Syndrome: Apocalypse, War, and Our Call to Greatness* (Seven Stories Press, 2017), 188.

56. COLOR, "Urging a Human Rights and Justice-Based Approach to Environmental Protection," *DifferenTakes* 93 (Fall 2018).

57. Anne Hendrixson, in collaboration with Ellen E. Foley, Rajani Bhatia, Daniel Bendix, Susanne Schultz, Kalpana Wilson, and Wangui Kimari, "A Renewed Call for Feminist Resistance to Population Control," University at Albany, State University of New York Scholars Archive, Fall 2019.

58. We take up this issue in chapter 4.

59. Rosie Jiménez was the first woman known to die after the Hyde Amendment banned federal Medicaid funding for abortion.

60. For a feminist critique of human rights, see chapter 5.

61. Earlier documents asserted individual rights: The Magna Carta (1215), the English Bill of Rights (1689), the French Declaration of the Rights of Man and Citizen (1789), and the U.S. Constitution and Bill of Rights (1791) are the written precursors to many of today's human rights documents. While those documents expressed the notion of human rights, often, when operationalized, they excluded specific groups based on their race and gender.

62. "Universal Declaration of Human Rights," General Assembly Resolution, 217A, United Nations General Assembly, December 10, 1948.

63. Structural Adjustment Policies (SAPs) are economic reforms that a country must adhere to in order to secure a loan from the International Monetary Fund and/or the World Bank. SAPs often include reducing government spending, opening to free trade, and emphasizing production of goods that benefit the Global North, at the expense of local investments in public welfare services, education, health care, and infrastructure. These restrictions were sharply criticized by women from the Global South, who argued that providing family planning to countries that lacked basic health care infrastructure

was a Western-imposed form of population control, not a people-centered strategy for human development that also protected human rights.

64. According to Ross, at that time the human rights grounding was controversial among reproductive justice activists in the United States, who were concerned that it did not resonate in this country. However, Ross observed that increasingly, as women led human rights organizations, RJ activists dropped their opposition.

65. Ari L. Goldman, "Catholic Bishops Hire Firms to Market Fight on Abortion," *New York Times*, April 6, 1990.

66. Towey Shawn, "Abortion Funding: A Matter of Justice," National Network of Abortion Funds, 2005.

67. Population Reference Bureau, "Abortion Facts and Figures, 2021."

68. Personal anecdote from Marlene Fried.

69. Pew Research Center, "America's Abortion Quandary," May 6, 2022.

70. Ross and Solinger, *Reproductive Justice*, 124–25.

71. World Health Organization, "Abortion: Key Facts," May 17, 2024.

72. Silliman et al., *Undivided Rights*.

CHAPTER TWO

1. Martha Hodes, *White Women, Black Men: Illicit Sex in the Nineteenth-Century South* (Yale University Press, 1997), 1.

2. Ned Blackhawk, *The Rediscovery of America: Native Peoples and the Unmaking of U.S. History* (Yale University Press, 2023).

3. For the origin of white supremacist/Christian nationalist ideology, see Ronald Sanders, *Lost Tribes and Promised Lands* (Echo Point Books, 2015). Sanders explains that white supremacy as an economic system originated in medieval Europe. It was based on anti-Semitism that transformed religious prejudice against Jews into racial prejudice and demonization, and on the piracy of North and West Africa that transformed historical intercontinental trading between kingdoms as equals into plunder and enslavement.

4. See chapter 1, note 47 for a working definition of ableism.

5. Gary Okihiro, *American History Unbound: Asians and Pacific Islanders* (University of California Press, 2015), 1, 2. Okihiro aptly captures this aspect of the history: "The British and Europeans, through the artifices of whiteness and birth, installed themselves as the nation's people, its citizens. Their efforts to keep the U.S. nation-state white and to maintain white supremacy as globally

triumphant constituted the color line and the systems of oppression against which peoples of color have struggled to achieve self-determination" (p. 29).

6. Joseph P. Gone, "Indigenous Historical Trauma: Alter-Native Explanations for Mental Health Inequities," *Daedalus* 152, no. 4 (2023): 130–50.

7. Joseph P. Gone, "Indigenous Historical Trauma: Alter-Native Explanations for Mental Health Inequities," *Daedalus* 152, no. 4 (2023): 130–50. Maria Yellow Horse Brave Heart, an expert in historical trauma suffered by Lakota and other peoples worldwide, is credited with introducing the concept of "historical trauma" into mental health literature and applying it to the experiences of American Indians in the United States. She explains that disenfranchised grief remains consequential for Indigenous communities owing to long-standing disruptions of Indigenous ceremonial practices and to broad societal denial of its genocidal policies.

8. For a full account of Native American genocide, see David Stannard, *American Holocaust: The Conquest of the New World* (Oxford University Press, 1992); Andrea Smith, *Conquest* (South End Press, 2005; Duke University Press, 2015); Barbara Gurr, *Reproductive Justice: The Politics of Health Care for Native American Women* (Rutgers University Press, 2015), 125–28.

9. Gurr, *Reproductive Justice*, 28–31. Also see Betsy Hartmann, *The American Syndrome: Apocalypse, War, and Our Call to Greatness* (Seven Stories Press, 2017).

10. Stannard, *American Holocaust*, 119.

11. The schools were declared illegal when Congress passed the Indian Child Welfare Act (ICWA) in 1978, which has survived numerous challenges since that time. The Supreme Court decided in *Haaland v. Brackeen* (2023) that ICWA was constitutional. The vote was 7 to 2, with only Justices Alito and Thomas dissenting. This case was brought by the state of Texas, which challenged its constitutionality. For a summary of other challenges, see Scott Trowbridge, "Legal Challenges to ICWA: An Analysis of Current Case Law," *ABA*, January–February 2017.

12. Brianna Theobald, *Reproduction on the Reservation: Pregnancy, Childbirth, and Colonialism in the Long Twentieth Century* (University of North Carolina Press, 2019), 22–25.

13. Enslavers used eugenicist ideas to guide their choices for sexual pairings in order to yield the next generation of fit field workers. See the definition of eugenics in chapter 1 of this volume.

14. Gregory Smithers, *Slave Breeding: Sex, Violence, and Memory in African American History* (University Press of Florida, 2012), 3.

15. John H. Morgan, "An Essay on the Causes of the Production of Abortion among Our Negro Population," *Nashville Journal of Medicine and Surgery* 19, no. 117 (1860). Also see Angela Davis, *Women, Race, and Class* (Vintage, 1981), 6–7.

16. Fletcher M. Green, "Documenting the American South," in *Ferry Hill Plantation Journal, January 4, 1838–January 15, 1839* (University of North Carolina Press, 1998), 25–26.

17. Owens Dierdre Cooper and Sharla M. Fett, "Black Maternal and Infant Health: Historical Legacies of Slavery," *American Journal of Public Health* 109, no. 10 (October 2019): 1342–45.

18. Cheryl Harris, "Whiteness as Property," *Harvard Law Review* 106, no. 8 (1993): 1707–91.

19. Kathy Roberts Forde and Byron Bowman, "Exploiting Black Labor after Slavery," *The Conversation*, February 6, 2017.

20. A further complication was the fact that Congress refused to naturalize Chinese laborers, effectively barring them from becoming American citizens.

21. Catherine Lee, "Where the Danger Lies: Race, Gender, and Chinese and Japanese Exclusion in the United States, 1870–1924," *Sociological Forum*, May 2010, 248.

22. *Loving v. Virginia*, 388 U.S. 1 (1967).

23. Chinese family formation and settlement in the West specifically threatened the association of the West with white national identity.

24. Loretta Ross and Rickie Solinger, *Reproductive Justice: An Introduction* (University of California Press, 2017), 31. In 1911 the Dillingham Commission Report (https://immigrationhistory.org/item/dillingham-commission-reports/) condemned the "quality" of eastern and southern European immigrants and recommended quotas.

25. Khiara Bridges, "Race, Pregnancy, and the Opioid Epidemic: White Privilege and the Criminalization of Opioid Use During Pregnancy," *Harvard Law Review* 133, no. 3 (January 2020).

26. When immigration to the United States changed from Europeans to people from Latin America, Mexico, and Africa, immigration laws were tightened.

27. Sociologist Edward A. Ross coined the phrase "race suicide" in 1900. See Laura L. Lovet, "The Political Economy of Sex: Edward A. Ross and Race Suicide," in *Conceiving the Future: Pronatalism, Reproduction, and the Family in the United States, 1890–1938* (University of North Carolina Press, 2009), 77–108.

28. James C. Mohr, *Abortion in America: The Origins and Evolution of National Policy* (Oxford University Press, 1978), 43.

29. Alys Eve Weinbaum, *Wayward Reproduction: Genealogies of Race and Nation in Transatlantic Modern Thought* (Duke University Press, 2004), 20. Also see Charles Mills, *The Racial Contract* (Cornell University Press, 1997); Linda Martín Alcoff, *The Future of Whiteness* (Polity Press, 2015).

30. Rickie Solinger, *Pregnancy and Power: A Short History of Reproductive Politics in America* (New York University Press, 2005), 22. We use Solinger's definition of *racializing* as the process carried out by elites that divided the people of the nation into racial groups and subjected each to laws and rules depending on race. The overall goal was maintaining white supremacy.

31. Ross and Solinger, *Reproductive Justice*, 23.

32. Ross and Solinger, *Reproductive Justice*, 22–23. The authors cite numerous sources (271, note 18).

33. Mohr, *Abortion in America*, 49.

34. Mohr, *Abortion in America*, chapter 3.

35. Linda Gordon, *The Moral Property of Women: A History of Birth Control Politics in America* (University of Illinois Press, 2002), 25.

36. Mohr, *Abortion in America*, 9.

37. Mohr, *Abortion in America*, 75–76.

38. Mohr, *Abortion in America*, 100.

39. Mohr, *Abortion in America*, 90, note 13.

40. Mohr, *Abortion in America*, 106.

41. Theobald, *Reproduction on the Reservation*, 33.

42. Angela Taylor, Tonantzin Juarez, and Brandon Azevedo, "Continuing the Legacy of Granny Midwives," *Weitzman Institute Blog*, February 7, 2023.

43. See Jennifer Wright, *Madame Restell: The Life, Death, and Resurrection of Old New York's Most Fabulous, Fearless, and Infamous Abortionist* (Hachette Books, 2023).

44. Gordon, *Moral Property*, 25.

45. Until the end of the 1930s, the United States had one of the highest rates of maternal mortality in the world. It declined through 1987, when it began to rise again. Today the United States has the highest maternal mortality rate of high-income countries. Disparities by race have been persistent. See Regine A. Douthard, Iman K. Martin, Theresa Chapple-McGruder, Ana Langer, and Soju Chang, "U.S. Maternal Mortality within a Global Context: Historical Trends, Current State, and Future Directions," *Journal of Women's Health* 30, no. 2 (2021): 168–77.

46. Owens and Fett, "Black Maternal and Infant Health."

47. Leslie J. Reagan, *When Abortion Was a Crime: Women, Medicine, and Law in the United States* (University of California Press, 1997, 2022), 42.

48. Judith Walzer Leavitt, "Under the Shadow of Maternity: American Women's Responses to Death and Debility Fears in Nineteenth-Century Childbirth," *Feminist Studies* 12, no. 1 (Spring 1986), cited in J. Shoshanna Ehrlich and Alesha E. Doan, *Abortion Regret: The New Attack on Reproductive Freedom* (Praeger, 2019), 22.

49. Ehrlich and Doan, *Abortion Regret*, 22.

50. Ehrlich and Doan, *Abortion Regret*, 22.

51. Helen L. Horowitz, *Rereading Sex: Battles over Sexual Knowledge and Suppression in Nineteenth-Century America* (Knopf, 2002).

52. Anthony argued that abortion presented a very specific social danger to women: If women could prevent pregnancy and childbearing, men would be freer to have sexual intercourse inside and outside of marriage without consequences. Some white feminists disagreed. Like many contemporary feminists, they made a case for legalizing contraception and abortion, claiming that abortion and contraception would free women from that "death sentence."

53. For a full account of how doctors used abortion to implement their own goals, see Kristen Luker, *Abortion and the Politics of Motherhood* (University of California Press, 1984), chapter 2.

54. Reagan, *When Abortion Was a Crime*.

55. Michele Goodwin, "The Racist History of Abortion and Midwifery Bans," *ACLU News & Commentary*, 2020.

56. Lauren Fung and Leana Lacy, "A Look at the Past, Present, and Future of Black Midwifery in the United States," *Urban Wire*, May 18, 2023. Also see Dominique Tobbell, "Black Midwifery's Complex History," *UVA School of Nursing*, February 12, 2021.

57. Goodwin, "Midwifery Bans."

58. Goodwin, "Midwifery Bans."

59. Sims's racism has been exposed. In 2018 his statue was removed from Central Park. Deirdre Cooper Owens, *Medical Bondage: Race, Gender, and the Origins of American Gynecology* (University of Georgia Press, 2017). For more on scientific racism and the ideologies that made it possible, see Dána-Ain Davis, *Reproductive Injustice: Racism, Pregnancy, and Premature Birth* (New York University Press, 2019).

60. "Call and Response: A Narrative of Reverence to Our Foremothers in Gynecology," Dell Marie Hamilton and the *Resilient Sisterhood Project*, curators (2023). This exhibit is a moving and excellent portrayal of this monstrous history.

61. Simone M. Caron, "Abortion and Contraception in the Nineteenth Century," in *"Who Chooses?" American Reproductive History since 1830*, online edition, Florida Scholarship Online, September 14, 2011.

62. Ehrlich and Doan, *Abortion Regret*, chapter 1. Also see Mohr, *Abortion in America*, 184.

63. Mohr, *Abortion in America*.

64. Reagan, *When Abortion Was a Crime*, 11.

65. For a full account of how doctors leading the campaign used abortion to implement their own goals, see Luker, *Abortion and the Politics of Motherhood*, chapter 2. It is also important to note that many doctors continued to provide abortions after criminalization. They saw a conflict between their leaders' expressed antiabortion views and their economic self-interest. If the doctors refused to perform abortions, they would lose clients to midwives and other nonphysician abortionists. At the same time, the physicians were aligned with the anti-immigrant reproductive politics of their profession.

66. Francis Galton defined eugenics in 1883.

67. As we will see in chapter 3, eugenics lacked any scientific basis. Melissa Murray, "Abortion, Sterilization, and the Universe of Reproductive Rights," *William and Mary Law Review* 63 (2021–22). Also see David Kevles, *In the Name of Eugenics: Genetics and the Uses of Human Heredity* (Harvard University Press, 1995).

68. Eugenics was taught at over three hundred colleges and universities, including Harvard and Stanford. Adam Cohen, *Imbeciles: The Supreme Court, American Eugenics, and the Sterilization of Carrie Buck* (Penguin, 2016).

69. Theobald, *Reproduction on the Reservation*, 29–31.

70. The state laws criminalizing abortion in the nineteenth century banned abortions in all states, with the only exception for "therapeutic reasons." Reagan, *When Abortion Was a Crime*, chapter 2. Edward Veitch and R. R. S. Tracey note that almost every state abortion law had a therapeutic exception. "Abortion in the Common Law World," *American Journal of Comparative Law* 22, no. 4 (1974): 652–96.

71. Carole Joffe and Jody Steinauer, "Even Texas Allows Abortion to Protect a Woman's Life. Or Does It?," *New York Times*, September 21, 2021. The authors fear that if disagreements among doctors increase, the arbitrariness of the old therapeutic abortion committees will be replicated.

72. Rickie Solinger, "'A Complete Disaster': Abortion and the Politics of Hospital Abortion Committees, 1950–1970," *Feminist Studies* 19, no. 2 (Summer 1993): 241–68.

73. Reagan, *When Abortion Was a Crime*, 328, note 51.

74. Reagan, *When Abortion Was a Crime*, 205–7. Reagan cautions that it is important not to overstate the availability of therapeutic abortions to women with racial and economic privilege. Most abortions were still illegal.

75. Cynthia Greenlee, "Race, Rubella, and the Long Road to Abortion Reform," *Scalawag Magazine*, February 18, 2016. Doctors had established the connection between the disease and severe birth anomalies.

76. Leslie Reagan, *Dangerous Pregnancies: Mothers, Disabilities, and Abortion in Modern America, 1867–1973* (University of California Press, 2012).

77. At that time Grady Hospital still had segregated wings. See Greenlee, "Race, Rubella."

78. Rachel Benson Gold and Megan K. Donovan, "Lessons from before Abortion Was Legal," *Scientific American* 317, no. 3 (September 1, 2017).

79. Frances Beal, "Double Jeopardy: To Be Black and Female," *Meridians: Feminism, Race, Transnationalism* 8, no. 2 (2008): 173.

80. Solinger, *The Abortionist* (University of California Press, 1994). Solinger notes that there were very few prosecutions of abortion providers from Black and Puerto Rican neighborhoods.

81. Solinger, *The Abortionist*, 210–11.

82. For more on the history of how welfare policy has been used to manipulate childbearing by women of color, see Dorothy Roberts, *Killing the Black Body: Race, Reproduction, and the Meaning of Liberty* (Vintage Books, 1997, 2017); Solinger, *Beggars and Choosers: How the Politics of Choice Shapes Adoption, Abortion, and Welfare in the United States* (Hill and Wang, 2002).

83. Johnnie Tillmon, "Welfare Is a Women's Issue," *Ms.* 1 (Spring 1972).

84. Best estimates suggest that the membership of the movement was roughly 85 percent African American, 10 percent white, and 5 percent Latina, with a small number of Native American participants as well. Premilla Nadasen, "Expanding the Boundaries of the Women's Movement: Black Feminism and the Struggle for Welfare Rights," *Feminist Studies* 28, no. 2 (Summer 2002).

85. Gold and Donovan, "Lessons from before Abortion Was Legal."

86. Andy Sullivan, "Explainer: How Abortion Became a Divisive Issue in U.S. Politics," Reuters, June 24, 2022.

87. Sullivan, "Explainer," 224. We note that a large part of the Democratic base in 1972 was comprised of Catholics.

88. Reagan, *When Abortion Was a Crime*, 222.

89. Linda Greenhouse and Reva B. Siegel, "Before Roe v. Wade: Voices That Shaped the Abortion Debate before the Supreme Court's Ruling (2012)," Yale Law School, Public Law Working Paper no. 257.

90. Greenhouse and Siegel, "Before Roe v. Wade," 24. Twelve states adopted the ALI recommendation: Arkansas, California, Colorado, Delaware, Georgia, Kansas, Maryland, Mississippi, New Mexico, North Carolina, South Carolina, and Virginia.

91. The physicians' campaigns popularized the notion that they alone could provide safe abortions. In the political battles before and after *Roe*, abortion rights advocates used the trope of the "back-alley butcher" in order to bolster their arguments for making and keeping abortion legal. Carole Joffe, Rickie Solinger, and others have pointed out that this was not an accurate picture. There were many safe abortions performed during the illegal era.

92. Carole Joffe, *Doctors of Conscience: The Struggle to Provide Abortion before and after Roe v. Wade* (Beacon Press, 1995). Joffe documents the range of activities besides performing abortions that "conscience doctors" engaged in, including providing consultations, backup medical services, and referrals, as well as working within the medical community for legalization.

93. Solinger, *The Abortionist.*

94. Greenhouse and Siegel, "Before Roe v. Wade," 26.

95. Some scholars use the term *population control* to refer to all efforts to manage the size and composition of populations in every era. We are, however, using it here to refer to the specific policies of the 1950s and '60s.

96. For a comprehensive history and analysis of population control, see Betsy Hartmann, *Reproductive Rights and Wrongs: The Global Politics of Population Control*, 3rd ed. (Haymarket Books, 2016).

97. Greenhouse and Siegel, "Before Roe v. Wade," 55.

98. Emily Klancher Merchant, "How Foundations Got the U.S. Government Invested in International Population Control," *HistPhil*, June 24, 2016. Also see Caitlin Fendley, "Eugenics Is Trending. That's a Problem," *Washington Post*, February 17, 2020.

99. Rickie Solinger, *Wake Up Little Susie: Single Pregnancy and Race before Roe v. Wade* (Routledge, 1992).

100. Solinger, *Wake Up Little Susie*, 209.

101. Reagan, *When Abortion Was a Crime*, 231.

102. Elena Gutiérrez, *Fertile Matters: The Politics of Mexican-Origin Women's Reproduction* (University of Texas Press, 2008), 17. Gutiérrez sees the creation of the commission as evidence of growing concerns in Congress about population and reproduction. Also see Rosalind Pollack Petchesky, *Abortion and Women's Choice: The State, Sexuality, and Reproductive Freedom* (Northeastern University Press, 1984; Verso, 2024), 122.

103. We include women's liberation, civil rights, Black and Puerto Rican nationalism, the New Left, the anti–Vietnam War movement, the American Indian Movement, the movement for LGBTQIA+ rights, welfare rights, and a youth movement as those that fostered a general disdain for entrenched power.

104. Jael Silliman et al., *Undivided Rights: Women of Color Organize for Reproductive Justice*, 2nd ed. (Haymarket Press, 2016); Jennifer Nelson, *Women of Color and the Reproductive Rights Movement* (New York University Press, 2003); Patricia Romney, *We Were There: The Third World Women's Alliance and the Second Wave* (The Feminist Press, 2021).

105. Frances Beal, quoted in Greenhouse and Siegel, "Before Roe v. Wade," 52. Also see Romney, *We Were There.*

106. Romney, *We Were There.*

107. Romney, *We Were There,* 219.

108. NBFO statement, 1973.

109. Keeanga Yamahtta Taylor, ed., *How We Get Free: Black Feminism and the Combahee River Collective* (Haymarket Books, 2017). This collection commemorates the fortieth anniversary of the Combahee River Collective statement.

110. Jennifer A. Nelson, "Abortions under Community Control: Feminism, Nationalism, and the Politics of Reproduction among New York City's Young Lords [Part 1 of 5]," *Journal of Women's History* 13, no. 1 (Spring 2001).

111. Pat Parker, "Revolution: It's Not Neat, Pretty, or Quick," in *This Bridge Called My Back: Writings by Black Radical Women,* 4th ed., ed. Cherríe Moraga and Gloria Anzaldúa (SUNY Press, 2015), 242. Black Power groups inspired others, including Chicanos and Native Americans, to form organizations based on their racial and cultural identities.

112. Nelson, "Abortions under Community Control." The Young Lords encompassed both feminism and nationalism in a way that other groups saw as incompatible. Nationalism focused on poor people's right to control their own institutions, opposed genocide, and worked to end poverty. Feminism made a woman's control of her reproduction central.

113. Felicia Kornbluh, *A Woman's Life Is a Human Life: My Mother, Our Neighbor, and the Journey from Reproductive Rights to Reproductive Justice* (Grove Press, 2023).

114. See Silliman et al., *Undivided Rights;* Sandra Morgan, *Into Our Own Hands: The Women's Health Movement in the United States, 1969–1990* (Rutgers University Press, 2002). Also see Marlene Fried, "Reproductive Rights Activism in the Post-Roe Era," *American Journal of Public Health* 103, no. 1 (January 2013).

115. Silliman et al., *Undivided Rights.* Other groups include the National Latina Health Organization, Asian Pacific Islanders for Choice, African

American Women Evolving, the Native American Women's Health Education Resource Center, and the Colorado Organization for Latina Opportunity and Reproductive Rights.

116. Boston Women's Health Book Collective, *Our Bodies, Ourselves* (Simon and Schuster, 1984, 1992, 1998, 2005, 2011), inspired grassroots women's health activists around the world.

117. "Our Bodies Ourselves Today," October 2023 newsletter, https://ourbodiesourselves.org/.

118. The only book about Jane is Laura Kaplan, *The Story of Jane: The Legendary Underground Feminist Abortion Service* (University of Chicago Press, 2019). There are also several movies about Jane, including a 2021 HBO documentary, *The Janes.*

119. Committee for Abortion Rights and Against Sterilization Abuse (CARASA), "Women under Attack: Abortion, Sterilization Abuse, and Reproductive Freedom," 1979, 52.

120. Reproductive Rights National Network Records, Sophia Smith Collection, Smith College, Northampton, MA.

121. Petchesky, *Abortion and Women's Choice*, 165.

122. Sue Hyde, ed., *Women under Attack: Victories, Backlash and the Fight for Reproductive Freedom* (South End Press, 1988).

123. Solinger, *Pregnancy and Power*, 212.

124. Silliman et al., *Undivided Rights*, 18–19.

125. Lucinda Cisler, "Unfinished Business: Birth Control and Women's Liberation," in *Sisterhood Is Powerful: An Anthology of Writings from the Women's Liberation Movement*, ed. Robyn Morgan (Vintage Books, 1970). This issue split the movement along racial lines and provided fuel for the suspicions and critique of contraception by the mostly male leadership in the Black Liberation movement, and support for their pronatalist position.

126. Gutiérrez, *Fertile Matters*, 104–5.

127. Silliman et al., *Undivided Rights*, 11.

128. Luker, *Abortion and the Politics of Motherhood*, 241.

129. Nellie Gilles, Sarah Kramer, and Joe Richman, "Before Roe, the Women of Jane Provided Abortions for the Women of Chicago," *NPR Radio Diaries*, January 19, 2018.

130. Racist opposition to the Civil Rights Act of 1964 and the Voting Rights Act also fueled the backlash. Sociologist Susan Staggenborg argues that the pro-choice movement did not disappear, although there was a difference between the large national groups that institutionalized themselves in this

period and the weakening of the grassroots activism that had been at the heart of the protest movement before legalization. This nuance is important because it laid the groundwork for subsequent abortion rights activism. Susan Staggenborg, *The Pro-Choice Movement: Organization and Activism in the Abortion Conflict* (Oxford University Press, 1991), introduction.

131. Statement of Rep. Henry Hyde, 123 CONG. REC. 19,700 (1977).

132. Mark Pitcavage, *Surveying the Landscape of the American Far Right*, Program on Extremism, George Washington University, August 2019.

133. Gillian Frank and Neil J. Young, "What Everyone Gets Wrong about Evangelicals and Abortion," *Washington Post*, May 16, 2022. Also see Thomas B. Edsall, "Abortion Has Never Been Just about Abortion," *New York Times*, September 15, 2021.

134. Frank and Young, "What Everyone Gets Wrong."

135. Frank and Young, "What Everyone Gets Wrong."

136. Initially abortion opponents were focused primarily on the federal level, aiming to amend the Constitution and looking to the Supreme Court. These efforts failed, signaling that such changes were part of a longer-term strategy. The SCOTUS decision in *Planned Parenthood of Southeastern Pennsylvania v. Casey* (1992) opened the floodgates to state-level restrictions, and the fight moved to the states.

137. Loretta J. Ross and Heidi Dorow, "Women's Watch Report," Center for Democratic Renewal, mentioned in Loretta Ross, "Hunting Hate," in *Southern Exposure* 22, no. 4 (December 1, 1994). Also see Jean Hardisty, *Mobilizing Resentment: Conservative Resurgence from the John Birch Society to the Promise Keepers* (Beacon Press, 1999); Carol Mason, *Killing for Life: The Apocalyptic Narrative of Pro-Life Politics* (Cornell University Press, 2002).

138. Hardisty, *Mobilizing Resentment*, 10–11.

139. Carol Mason and Alex Dibranco, "The Long History of the Anti-Abortion Movement's Links to White Supremacists," *The Nation*, February 2020.

140. "Anti-Abortionists and White Supremacists Make Common Cause," *The Progressive, Inc.*, The Free Library, October 1, 1994.

141. T. Dugdale-Pointon, "The Army of God," *History of War*, August 17, 2007.

142. Moira Donegan, "White Nationalists Are Flocking to the U.S. Antiabortion Movement," *The Guardian*, January 24, 2022.

143. Mason, "Killing for Life."

144. Those murdered include four doctors, two clinic employees, a security guard, a police officer, two patients, and a clinic escort. The National

Abortion Federation and the Feminist Majority Foundation websites both have detailed information about antiabortion violence.

March 10, 1993: Dr. David Gunn of Pensacola, Florida, was fatally shot during a protest.

July 29, 1994: Dr. John Britton, a physician, and James Barrett, a clinic escort, were both shot to death outside the Ladies Center in Pensacola.

December 30, 1994: Two receptionists, Shannon Lowney and Leanne Nichols, were killed in two clinic attacks in Brookline, Massachusetts.

January 29, 1998: Robert Sanderson, an off-duty police officer who worked as a security guard at an abortion clinic in Birmingham, Alabama, was killed when his workplace was bombed.

October 23, 1998: Dr. Barnett Slepian was shot to death with a high-powered rifle at his home in Amherst, New York.

May 31, 2009: Dr. George Tiller was shot and killed by Scott Roeder as Tiller served as an usher at a church in Wichita, Kansas.

November 29, 2015: Three people were murdered at a Planned Parenthood clinic in Colorado Springs, including officer Garrett Swasey, Ke'Arre M. Stewart (twenty-nine), and Jennifer Markovsky (thirty-five), who was accompanying a friend to the clinic. Nine others—five police officers and four civilians—were wounded and admitted to local hospitals.

145. Vera Bergengruen, "Armed Demonstrators and Far-Right Groups Are Escalating Tensions at Abortion Protests," *Time*, July 8, 2022.

146. The movement's first political targets were school integration and interracial dating or marriage. There was a lawsuit against Bob Jones University, which did not admit Black students until the 1970s and prohibited interracial dating until 2000.

147. Alfred Lubrano, "Rate of Births to White Single Moms Accelerates," *Philadelphia Inquirer*, November 12, 2018.

148. Walter Einenkel, "Right-wing Iowa School Board Candidate Abruptly Withdraws. Guess Why," *Daily Kos*, September 23, 2021.

149. Cassie Miller, "Male Supremacy Is at the Core of the Hard Right's Agenda," Southern Poverty Law Center, April 18, 2023.

150. Commonwealth Fund, "The U.S. Maternal Health Divide: The Limited Maternal Health Services and Worse Outcomes of States Proposing New Abortion Restrictions," *Commonwealth Fund, Issue Briefs*, December 14, 2022.

151. Heather D. Boonstra, "Abortion in the Lives of Women Struggling Financially: Why Insurance Coverage Matters," *Guttmacher Policy Review*, July 14, 2016.

152. Abigail R.A. Aiken, Elisa S. Wells, Rebecca Gomperts, et al., "Provision of Medications for Self-Managed Abortion before and after the Dobbs v Jackson Women's Health Organization Decision," *JAMA* 331, no. 18 (2024): 1558–65.

153. The case *Alliance for Hippocratic Medicine v. US Food and Drug Administration* (2024), www.supremecourt.gov/opinions/23pdf/23-235_n7ip.pdf, threatens access nationwide. Also see the statement by the Guttmacher acting co-CEO, Destiny Lopez, "Guttmacher Leadership Speaks Out against Attacks on Medication Abortion," March 26, 2024.

154. Dorothy Roberts, "The State We Are In: Building an Intersectional Movement for Reproductive Justice," Egbal Ahmed Lecture, Hampshire College, October 13, 2022.

155. Silliman et al., *Undivided Rights.* See also Beverly Yuen Thompson, "Centering Reproductive Justice: Transitioning from Abortion Rights to Social Justice," in *Radical Reproductive Justice*, ed. Loretta J. Ross, Lynn Roberts, Erika Derkas, Whitney Peoples, and Pamela Bridgewater Toure (Feminist Press, 2017); Jennifer Nelson, *More Than Medicine* (New York University Press, 2015); Joyce Follet, *Roots of Reproductive Justice: 500 Years of Movement Stories*, https://rootsofrj.org.

CHAPTER THREE

1. Meena Venkataramanan, "She Survived a Forced Sterilization. She Fears More Could Occur Post-Roe," *Washington Post*, July 24, 2022. Also see Melissa Murray, "Abortion, Sterilization, and the Universe of Reproductive Rights," *William and Mary Law Review* 63 (2021–22): 1599.

2. Contemporary examples to achieve these goals include establishing sperm banks where eugenically desirable traits, such as intelligence, are either criteria for donors or listed as present in the donor for users to consider in their choices. See R. Wilson, "Eugenics: Positive vs Negative," *Eugenics Archive*, December 31, 2019; Alexandra Minna Stern, *Eugenic Nation: Faults and Frontiers of Better Breeding in Modern America*, 2nd ed. (University of California Press, 2015).

3. Stern, *Eugenic Nation.*

4. *Indiana Eugenics: History and Legacy, 1907–2007.* That law was eventually found unconstitutional, but a revised law, passed in 1927, made mandatory sterilization permissible under *Buck v. Bell.*

5. Daniel Kevles, *In the Name of Eugenics: Genetics and the Uses of Human Heredity* (Harvard University Press, 1995), 78. Goddard was director of the labora-

tory for the study of mental deficiency at the Training School for Feeble-minded Girls and Boys.

6. Virginia Board of Charities and Corrections, "Mental Defectives in Virginia" (1995), Internet Archive, September 2011. The report defined a feebleminded person as someone who is "permanently, expensively, and often-dangerously anti-social."

7. Natalie Lira, *Laboratories of Deficiency: Sterilization and Confinement in California, 1900–1950s* (University of California Press, 2022).

8. Brendon Wolfe, "*Buck v. Bell*," *Virginia Humanities, Encyclopedia Virginia.*

9. Lira, *Laboratories of Deficiency*; Stern, *Eugenic Nation*; Adam Cohen, *Imbeciles: The Supreme Court, American Eugenics, and the Sterilization of Carrie Buck* (Penguin, 2016).

10. Hansen and King, *Sterilized by the State*, 110–15.

11. Kevles, *In the Name of Eugenics*, 112, note 48. The IQ tests that were used to diagnose Carrie Buck have since been discredited for use as measures of general intelligence. Buck's daughter died as a child, but her teachers considered her very bright.

12. *Buck v. Bell*, 274 U.S. 200 (1927).

13. Eugenic sterilization was also popular in Britain, Scandinavia, Canada, Latin America, and elsewhere.

14. Rebecca M. Kluchin, *Fit to Be Tied: Sterilization and Reproductive Rights in America, 1950–1980* (Rutgers University Press, 2009).

15. Mark A. Largent, *Breeding Contempt: The History of Coerced Sterilization in the United States* (Rutgers University Press, 2008). While Largent acknowledges that some support for eugenics was motivated by a genuine desire to prevent suffering from genetic diseases for which no cures or palliatives existed at the time, he also notes that it went further. He sees it as a story of good intentions and professional authority leading to horrible results. Also see Randall Hansen and Desmond King, *Sterilized by the State: Eugenics, Race, and the Population Scare in Twentieth-Century North America* (Cambridge University Press, 2013), 181.

16. Cohen, *Imbeciles*.

17. Stephen J. Taylor, "*The Black Stork*: Eugenics Goes to the Movies," *Hoosier State Chronicles*, Indiana's Digital Historic Newspaper Program, February 4, 2016. The film was also known as *Are You Fit to Marry?* See also "The Black Stork: Movie Ads," program 4, "Beyond Affliction: The Disability History Project" documentary series, Tomorrow's Children, Evidence Highlights Index, 1870–1930.

18. Daniel Kevles, "Eugenics and Human Rights," *British Medical Journal* 319, no. 7207 (1999): 435–38. Also see Daniel Kevles, *In the Name of Eugenics*; Hansen and

King, *Sterilized by the State*, 157; James Q. Whitman, *Hitler's American Model: The United States and the Making of Nazi Race Law* (Princeton University Press, 2017).

19. Jasmine Harris, "Why *Buck v. Bell* Still Matters," *Bill of Health*, October 14, 2020.

20. Garland Allen, "Eugenics and Modern Biology: Critiques of Eugenics, 1920–1945," *Wiley Online Library*, April 13, 2011. Biologists demonstrated that the understanding of Mendelian genetics, the basis of eugenics theory, was incorrect. Social scientists argued that the claim that abstract human qualities (e.g., intelligence and social behaviors) were inherited, and that complex diseases and disorders were solely the outcome of genetic inheritance, was simplistic and lacked any foundation.

21. *Skinner v. Oklahoma*, 316 U.S. 535 (1942); Victoria F. Nourse, *In Reckless Hands: Skinner v. Oklahoma and the Near Triumph of American Eugenics* (W. W. Norton, 2008).

22. "Eugenics and Scientific Racism."

23. For example, Oregon continued to sterilize people under its eugenics law until 1981. The governor apologized in 2002. Also see Deborah Josefson, "Oregon's Governor Apologises for Forced Sterilisations," *British Medical Journal* 325, no. 7377 (December 2002).

24. Audrey Farley, "How Dismantling Welfare Continues the Legacy of Eugenics," *Washington Post*, September 17, 2019.

25. Center for Genetics and Society, "Social Justice and Human Rights Principles for Global Deliberations on Heritable Human Genome Editing," press statement, February 14, 2024.

26. Betsy Hartmann, *Reproductive Rights and Wrongs: The Global Politics of Population Control*, 3rd ed. (Haymarket Books, 2016), 21. Hartmann provides detailed critiques of the underlying assumptions of overpopulation ideology. She argues that because it is the wrong diagnosis of the problem it gives the wrong solution, and it diverts us from seeing and addressing the real causes of poverty and environmental destruction. "Rapid population growth is not the cause of underdevelopment; it is a symptom of the slow pace of social reforms" (37). She and others offer convincing alternative accounts that center human rights and social justice.

27. Hartmann, *Reproductive Rights and Wrongs*, 27–29. "Paul Ehrlich has probably done more than any other single scientist to legitimize and popularize the belief that overpopulation is the main cause of the environmental crisis, from global warming to the depletion of the ozone layer."

28. Hartmann, *Reproductive Rights and Wrongs*, 21.

29. For excellent critiques of population control and overpopulation thinking, see Hartmann, *Reproductive Rights and Wrongs;* Betsy Hartmann, Banu Subramaniam, Charles Zerner, Alan Goodman, and Jeanne Guillemin, *Making Threats: Biofears and Environmental Anxieties* (Rowman & Littlefield, 2005).

30. Mieke C.W. Eeckhaut and Yuko Hara, "Reproductive Oppression Enters the Twenty-First Century: Pressure to Use Long-Acting Reversible Contraception (LARC) in the Context of 'LARC First,'" *Socius: Sociological Research for a Dynamic World* 9 (June 22, 2023), doi.org/10.1177/23780231231180378.

31. Elena Gutiérrez, *Fertile Matters: The Politics of Mexican-Origin Women's Reproduction* (University of Texas Press, 2008), chapter 6.

32. Dorothy Roberts, *Killing the Black Body: Race, Reproduction, and the Meaning of Liberty* (Vintage Books, 1997, 2017), chapter 2. Also see Jael Silliman et al., *Undivided Rights: Women of Color Organize for Reproductive Justice,* 2nd ed. (Haymarket Press, 2016); Brianna Theobald, *Reproduction on the Reservation: Pregnancy, Childbirth, and Colonialism in the Long Twentieth Century* (University of North Carolina Press, 2019).

33. Laura Briggs, *How All Politics Became Reproductive Politics: From Welfare Reform to Foreclosure to Trump* (University of California Press, 2017). See also Alexandra Minna Stern, "Forced Sterilization Policies in the US Targeted Minorities and Those with Disabilities—and Lasted into the 21st Century," *The Conversation,* August 26, 2020; and Kluchin, *Fit to Be Tied,* 3, 20.

34. Martha J. Bailey, "Fifty Years of Family Planning: New Evidence on the Long-Run Effects of Increasing Access to Contraception," National Bureau of Economic Research, October 2013.

35. Roberts, *Killing the Black Body,* 89–98.

36. Roberts, *Killing the Black Body,* 90.

37. Nancy Ordover, *American Eugenics: Race, Queer Anatomy, and the Science of Nationalism* (University of Minnesota Press, 2003), 167–68.

38. Angela Davis, *Women, Race and Class* (Vintage, 1981), 125.

39. Davis, *Women, Race, and Class,* 125.

40. Michael Murphy, "The Troubling Past of Forced Sterilization of Black Women and Girls in Mississippi and the South," *Mississippi Free Press,* June 4, 2021. Also see Julius Paul, "The Return of Punitive Sterilization Proposals: Current Attacks on Illegitimacy and the AFDC Program," *Law & Society Review* 3, no. 1 (August 1968): 77–106. Paul documents an interest in punitive sterilization in several states, including California, Delaware, Georgia, Illinois, Iowa, Louisiana, Maryland, Mississippi, North Carolina, Pennsylvania, Virginia, and Wisconsin. Proposals included loss of welfare benefits, imprisonment, fining the mother, and loss of child custody.

41. "Three Carolina Doctors Are Under Inquiry in Sterilization of Welfare Mothers," *New York Times*, July 22, 1973. Also see Ordover, *American Eugenics*, 166.

42. Rebekah Sager, "How Anti-Abortion Laws Disproportionately Impact Indigenous People," *American Journal News*, April 10, 2023.

43. The U.S. government had a long history of population control in Puerto Rico, including writing it into Puerto Rican law in 1937. This was the basis for the program that sterilized one-third of all women of childbearing age in the 1950s and '60s. As in Mississippi, the procedure was so routinely performed it was known as "la operación" (the operation).

44. Felicia Kornbluh, *A Woman's Life Is a Human Life: My Mother, Our Neighbor, and the Journey from Reproductive Rights to Reproductive Justice* (Grove Press, 2023), 17–20.

45. The conference was organized by COFO. Established in 1961, COFO was an umbrella organization that brought together activists in various statewide and national groups, including the SNCC, the Congress of Racial Equality (CORE), and the National Association for the Advancement of Colored People (NAACP).

46. Keisha N. Blain, *Until I Am Free: Fannie Lou Hamer's Enduring Message to America* (Beacon Press, 2022).

47. Jazmine Walker, "The 50th Anniversary of Mississippi's Freedom Summer: Remembering What Fannie Lou Hamer Taught Us," *Rewire News*, June 2, 2014.

48. "Genocide in Mississippi," created by the Student Nonviolent Coordinating Committee (SNCC), in the Digital Collections at the University of Southern Mississippi. The title was meant to publicize the Mississippi Democratic Party's opposition to the United Nations Convention on the Prevention and Punishment of the Crime of Genocide.

49. Murphy, "The Troubling Past of Forced Sterilization of Black Women."

50. Silliman et al., *Undivided Rights*, 118. Also see Sally J. Torpy, "Native American Women and Coerced Sterilization: On the Trail of Tears in the 1970s," *American Indian Culture and Research Journal* 24, no. 2 (2000): 1–22. Torpy argues that the sterilizations were hidden behind "an additional curtain of bureaucratic secrecy" because the federal government insisted that trial proceedings remain secret and refused to release documents related to sterilization, even though they were requested through the Freedom of Information Act.

51. Silliman et al., *Undivided Rights*, 118. This was particularly egregious given the long-standing policy of federal and state governments removing

Native children from their homes and tribes. That history is still being uncovered and reparations sought. The film *Dawnland* (2018) documents child welfare practices in Maine aimed at breaking up Wabanaki families. For more information, see https://upstanderproject.org/individual.

52. Torpy, "Native American Women," 6.

53. Silliman et al., *Undivided Rights*, 118.

54. The suit was brought by the National Welfare Rights Organization and the Southern Poverty Law Center. A nurse in a federally funded agency had been giving the girls Depo-Provera shots, at that time an experimental contraceptive. See Kornbluh, *A Woman's Life Is a Human Life*, 232.

55. Kornbluh, *A Woman's Life Is a Human Life*, 234.

56. Kornbluh, *A Woman's Life Is a Human Life*, 234.

57. Ordover, *American Eugenics*, 171.

58. HEW (the U.S. Department of Health, Education, and Welfare, now the Department of Health and Human Services) withdrew the regulations that enabled forced sterilizations, which caused many parts of the case to be moot. A suit for damages was dismissed on a technicality.

59. Linda Villarosa, *Under the Skin: The Hidden Toll of Racism on American Lives and the Health of Our Nation* (Doubleday, 2022), 85.

60. The information in this section comes from Gutiérrez, *Fertile Matters*, chapters 3 and 6. The book also provides a comprehensive account of the organizing efforts against sterilization abuse. The PBS documentary film *No Más Bebés* is a moving account of the lawsuit. Released in 2015, it is currently available at www.nomasbebesmovie.com/.

61. Gutiérrez, *Fertile Matters*, 1, 2.

62. Gutiérrez, *Fertile Matters*, chapters 1 and 2 and pp. 45–47.

63. Gutiérrez, *Fertile Matters*, chapters 1 and 2 and pp. 45–47.

64. A 1972 study in *Family Planning Digest* showed that 94 percent of ob-gyns "favored compulsory sterilization or withholding of welfare support for unwed mothers who already had three children." Doctors at the medical center in Los Angeles added deportation to the list of appropriate responses to irresponsible reproduction. Also see Rickie Solinger, *Pregnancy and Power: A Short History of Reproductive Politics in America* (New York University Press, 2005), 196. These attitudes continue. See Corey G. Johnson, "Female Inmates Sterilized in California Prisons without Approval," *Center for Investigative Reporting*, July 7, 2013.

65. Gutiérrez, *Fertile Matters*, 46–47.

66. Rodney Coates, "What Is the Great Replacement Theory? A Scholar of Race Relations Explains," *The Conversation*, March 15, 2024. In the United

States, white supremacists and anti-immigration activists and terrorists accuse liberal elites of conspiring to replace declining white populations with non-white people. This "Great Replacement theory" charges that mass immigration of non-white peoples, the legalization of abortion, and same-sex relationships are all part of a liberal conspiracy to lower white birth rates. Popularized by media and cultural influencers such as Tucker Carlson of Fox News, these ideas prey on white people's anxieties about demographic changes in "their" country and intensify hostility to immigrants, especially Black and brown people.

67. Gutiérrez, *Fertile Matters*, 108.

68. Some activists use identity-first language (such as "disabled person"), while others use people-first language (such as "person living with a disability"). See Susan Baglieri and Arthur Shapiro, "Perspectives on Disability," in *Disability Studies and the Inclusive Classroom*, 2nd ed., ed. Susan Baglieri and Arthur Shapiro (Routledge, 2017), 17–32.

69. See the Sins Invalid website at www.sinsinvalid.org/.

70. The measles vaccine was not developed until 1969.

71. Mary Ziegler, "The Disability Politics of Abortion," *Utah Law Review* 3 (2017).

72. It was presumed that if tests showed fetal anomaly, the person would have an abortion. See Barbara Katz Rothman, *The Tentative Pregnancy: How Amniocentesis Changes the Experience of Motherhood* (W. W. Norton, 1986).

73. Mary Ziegler, "The Disability Politics of Abortion," 599–600.

74. The 1984 antiabortion film *The Silent Scream* is a good example. In the United States it was sent to every Supreme Court justice and every person in Congress, and it was also regularly shown in Catholic high schools.

75. Sujatha Jesudason and Julia Epstein, "The Paradox of Disability in Abortion Debates: Bringing the Pro-Choice and Disability Rights Communities Together," *Contraception* 84, no. 6 (2011): 541–43.

76. Richard Dawkins, "Abortion & Down Syndrome: An Apology for Letting Slip the Dogs of Twitterwar," Richard Dawkins Foundation for Reason and Science, August 21, 2014. Also see Erin Matson, "Reproductive Justice Activists Must Combat Anti-Choicers' False Push for Disability Rights," *Rewire News*, September 14, 2014.

77. Barbarin quoted in Char Adams, "Disability Rights Groups Are Fighting for Abortion Access and against Ableism," *NBC News*, July 21, 2022. Also see Imani [Barbarin], #MyDisabilityIsWorthy, *Crutches & Spice*, January 26, 2022. The blog post was a response to Rochelle Walensky's assertions on the part of

the CDC that COVID was only a danger to people who had additional underlying conditions.

78. Jesudason and Epstein, "Paradox of Disability."

79. Robyn Powell, "Including Disabled People in the Battle to Protect Abortion Rights: A Call-to-Action," *UCLA Law Review* 70 (2023): 774. Also see Liz Bowen, "The End of Roe Will Be a Nightmare for Disabled Americans," *Hastings Center Forum*, June 24, 2022.

80. National Women's Law Center (NWLC), with help from the Autistic Women and Non Binary Network, "Forced Sterilization of People with Disabilities," *NWLC Sterilization Report*, January 2021.

81. National Women's Law Center (NWLC), "Forced Sterilization," 10. The Ashley Treatment is named for a woman who was sterilized by hysterectomy at the age of six. Her parents wanted her to stay small so she would not get her period and be at risk for pregnancy.

82. Jasmine Harris urges us to pay attention to "the interdependence of race and disability in maintaining institutional subordination. Harris, "Why *Buck v. Bell* Still Matters."

83. National Women's Law Center (NWLC), "Forced Sterilization," 8.

84. Ayanna Pressley and Rebecca Cokley, "There Is No Justice That Neglects Disability," *Stanford Social Innovation Review* 20, no. 1 (Winter 2022).

85. National Women's Law Center (NWLC), "Forced Sterilization."

86. Hannah Getahun, "'I Would Die': People with Disabilities Say Abortion Bans Could Have Fatal Consequences," *Business Insider*, July 31, 2022; Meena Venkataramanan, "Their Medications Cause Pregnancy Issues. Post-Roe, That Could Be a Problem," *Washington Post*, July 25, 2022.

87. Association of Maternal and Child Health Programs, "The Forced Sterilization of Disabled People in the United States: An Interview with Ma'ayan Anafi, Senior Counsel for Health Equity and Justice at the National Women's Law Center," March 2022. Also see Bryan Barks, "When Medications Risk Birth Defects, Abortion Bans Force Women into an Agonizing Dilemma," *Slate*, August 31, 2022. I added this to the bibliography.

88. Alison Kafer, "Using Disability and Access Statements to Get Resources for Students with Disabilities," in *Fighting Mad: Resisting the End of Roe v. Wade*, ed. Krystale E. Littlejohn and Rickie Solinger (University of California Press, 2024).

89. Ericka Ayodele Dixon, "Disability, Dobbs and a Black Perspective," in *Fighting Mad: Resisting the End of Roe v. Wade*, ed. Krystale E. Littlejohn and Rickie Solinger (University of California Press, 2024).

90. Laura Ungar and Amanda Seitz, "Post–Roe v. Wade, More Patients Rely on Early Prenatal Testing as States Toughen Abortion Laws," *Greenfield Commonwealth*, February 12, 2024.

91. Robyn Powell, "Disability Reproductive Justice," *University of Pennsylvania Law Review* 170, no. 7/4 (2022).

92. See the website of the Lesbian, Gay, Bisexual & Transgender Community Center, https://gaycenter.org/.

93. Cullen Peele, "Roundup of Anti-LGBTQ+ Legislation Advancing across the Country," Human Rights Campaign press release, May 23, 2023.

94. Peele, "Roundup."

95. Amy Littlefield and Heron Greenesmith, "Fresh Off Victory against Roe, the Religious Right Is Pushing a Record Number of Anti-Trans Bills," *The Nation*, January 31, 2023.

96. Alex Nguyen, "'I Want to Fight': LGBTQ Texans Ready for Legislative Session as GOP Lawmakers Target Them in Dozens of Bills," *Texas Tribune*, January 9, 2023.

97. Steve Contorno, "DeSantis Signs into Law Restrictions on Trans Floridians' Access to Treatments and Bathrooms," CNN, May 17, 2023.

98. Littlefield and Greenesmith, "Fresh Off Victory." Carlson was fired from Fox in April 2023.

99. Media Matters, "Doctors Who Provide Gender-Affirming Care Should Be Executed," *Media Matters Daily Wire*, February 22, 2023.

100. Littlefield and Greenesmith, "Fresh Off Victory."

101. Southern Poverty Law Center, "The Intelligence Report," 1998 Summer Issue (September 1988). The names were compiled by the Feminist Majority Foundation.

102. "Bill O'Reilly in Hot Seat after Kan. Murder," *Hollywood Reporter*, June 2, 2009.

103. The antiabortion group Operation Rescue had on its website a "Tiller Watch" page, which publicized the names and addresses of Dr. Tiller and the other clinic employees and family members. The rhetoric was intended to incite vigilante action and murderous violence. Dr. Tiller's murderer was an unapologetic zealot.

104. Shoshanna Goldberg, "Report Says at Least 32 Transgender People Were Killed in the U.S. in 2022," *PBS News Hour*, November 16, 2022.

105. Positive Women's Network, "Trans-Centered Reproductive Justice: Family Formation and Sustainable Living," October 23, 2019.

106. KC Clements, "6 Tips for Making Your Conversations about Reproductive Rights More Inclusive," *Everyday Feminism*, October 29, 2018.

107. In a ruling on February 3, 2025, Judge Tanya M. Jones Bosier of the Superior Court of the District of Columbia issued a ruling that effectively means that Proud Boys chapters across the country can no longer legally use their own name or the group's traditional symbols without the permission of a church that they attacked, the Metropolitan African Methodist Episcopal Church. Alan Feuer, "Proud Boys Lose Control of Their Name to a Black Church They Vandalized," *New York Times*, February 3, 2025.

108. Dennis Romero, "Drag Queen Story Hour Disrupted by Men Shouting Slurs, Authorities Say," *NBC News*, June 12, 2022.

109. Elly Belle, "Don't Say Gay Protests: How Florida Students Like Jack Petocz Are Fighting against Hatred," *Teen Vogue*, June 13, 2022.

110. Christy Mallory and Elana Redfield, "The Impact of 2023 Legislation on Transgender Youth," UCLA School of Law, Williams Institute, October 2023.

111. Andrew Demillo, "Judge Rules Arkansas Ban on Gender-Affirming Care for Transgender Minors Violates the U.S. Constitution," AP News, June 20, 2023.

112. For more information, see the website of CHOICES, Center for Reproductive Health, https://yourchoices.org/.

113. Julian Cyr and Rebecca Hart Holder, "Simultaneous Attacks on Abortion and LGBTQ Rights Are Not Coincidental," *Cognoscenti*, April 26, 2022.

114. Grace Panetta and Orion Rummler, "Lawmakers in Blue States Are Linking Protections for Abortion and Gender-Affirming Care," *The 19th*, June 9, 2023.

115. Judith A. M. Scully, "Cracking Open CRACK: Unethical Sterilization Movement Gains Momentum," *DifferenTakes* 2 (Spring 2000).

116. Scully's interview with Barbara Harris, originally quoted in 1998 in *Marie Claire*, British edition. Cecilia Vega, "Sterilization Offer to Addicts Reopens Ethics Issues," *New York Times*, January 6, 2003. The birth rate of poor women at that time was 1.5—hardly litters.

117. Schlessinger was extremely popular in the 2000s. At its peak, her show had nine million listeners a week, second only to Rush Limbaugh.

118. Barry Yeoman, "Surgical Strike," *Mother Jones*, November 1, 2001. Pittsburgh billionaire Richard Mellon Scaife, sometimes called the Funding Father of the New Right, is another supporter named in the article.

119. Jed Bickman, "Should Addicts Be Sterilized?," *Salon*, May 2, 2012.

120. Vega, "Sterilization Offer."

121. Helen Ubiñas, "Prevention through Bribery," *Hartford Courant*, November 16, 2006.

122. Jacquelyn Monroe and Rudolph Alexander Jr., "C.R.A.C.K: A Progeny of Eugenics and a Forlorn Representation for African Americans," *Journal of African American Studies* 9, no. 1 (2005): 19–31. The researchers argue that there is a stark contrast between an individual deciding to use birth control and the Project Prevention agenda: "The former is a personal decision while the latter is eugenics."

123. Scully, "Cracking Open."

124. Bickman, "Should Addicts Be Sterilized?"

125. Theryn Kigvamasud'vashti, "Fact Sheet on Positive Prevention/CRACK (Children Requiring a Caring Kommunity)." The kit and other materials are in the Sophia Smith Collection (SSC) at Smith College, https://libraries.smith.edu/special-collections/about/sophia-smith-collection-womens-history.

126. "Join Us in Opposing CRACK," CWPE Action Alert, SSC, July 9, 2000; Kylee Sunderlin and Laura Huss, "The Mythology of 'Addicted Babies': Challenging Media Distortions, Laws, and Policies That Fracture Communities," *DifferenTakes* 86 (Fall 2015).

127. Paltrow compared the group's cash-for-birth-control concept to "Hitleresque eugenics." Daniel Costello, "Is CRACK Wack?," *Salon*, April 8, 2003.

128. Pregnancy Justice is one of the organizations profiled in chapter 4.

129. Lynn M. Paltrow, "Why Caring Communities Must Oppose C.R.A.C.K. / Project Prevention: How C.R.A.C.K. Promotes Dangerous Propaganda and Undermines the Health and Well Being of Children and Families," *Journal of Law and Society* 5, no. 11 (2003): 83.

130. American Public Health Association (APHA), "Opposition to the CRACK Campaign," *American Journal of Public Health Association News* 9, no. 3 (March 2001): 516–17.

131. American Public Health Association (APHA), "Opposition to the CRACK Campaign," 517.

132. David D. Lewis, "Stop Perpetuating the 'Crack Baby' Myth," Brown University News Service, March 29, 2004.

133. Lynn Paltrow and Kathryn Jack, "Pregnant Women, Junk Science, and Zealous Defense," National Association of Criminal Defense Lawyers, Inc., May 2010. Also see Editorial Board of the *New York Times*, "Slandering the Unborn," *New York Times*, December 28, 2018.

134. National Perinatal Association, "Perinatal Substance Abuse: A Position Statement," 2017.

135. American Medical Association (AMA), "Treatment versus Criminalization: Physician Role in Drug Addiction during Pregnancy, H420–970," *AMA Policy Finder*. See also Paltrow, "Why Caring Communities Must Oppose C.R.A.C.K."

136. Savannah Levins and Meilin Tompkins, "Report: Controversial Push to Keep Drug Addicts from Having Children," WCNC, Charlotte, May 30, 2019.

137. Katelyn Newman, "Harm Prevention of Population Control: Amid Efforts to Curb the U.S. Opioid Crisis, a North Carolina Nonprofit Is Offering Money to Drug Users Who Go on Long-Term Birth Control," *US News and World Report*, April 11, 2019.

138. The argument in this section is from Khiara Bridges, "Race, Pregnancy, and the Opioid Epidemic: White Privilege and the Criminalization of Opioid Use During Pregnancy," *Harvard Law Review* 133, no. 3 (January 2020): 793–94.

139. Bridges, "Race, Pregnancy, and the Opioid Epidemic," 805, 820, 827.

140. Susan Okie, "The Epidemic That Wasn't," *New York Times*, January 26, 2009.

141. The term was introduced by the prison abolitionist organization Critical Resistance, which defined it as embodying "the overlapping interests of government and industry that use surveillance, policing, and imprisonment as solutions to economic, social and political problems." Prison abolition is both the group's long-term goal and an organizing tool.

142. Over twenty thousand people, disproportionately Black and Latino people, were sterilized under California's eugenic sterilization law, which was repealed in 1979.

143. Sarah Mizes-Tan, "For Decades, California Forcibly Sterilized Women under Eugenics Law. Now, the State Will Pay Survivors," *CapRadio*, July 20, 2021.

144. Corey G. Johnson, "California Bans Coerced Sterilization of Female Inmates," *Reveal*, September 26, 2014. In addition, an unknown number of cis women and trans people were sterilized during other abdominal procedures, as in Dillon's case.

145. Joseph Hayes, Justin Goss, Heather Harris, and Alexandria Gumbs, "California's Prison Population," UC Riverside Presley Center of Crime and Justice Studies fact sheet, July 2019. Of the state's 5,849 female prisoners, 25.9 percent are African American, compared to only 5.7 percent of the state's adult

female residents. African American women are imprisoned at a rate of 171 per 100,000—more than five times the imprisonment rate of white women, which is 30 per 100,000. Imprisonment rates for Latino women and women of other races are 38 and 14 per 100,000, respectively.

146. Corey G. Johnson, "California Prison Doctor Linked to Sterilizations No Stranger to Controversy," *Reveal*, February 13, 2014.

147. Johnson, "Female Prison Inmates Sterilized Illegally, California Audit Confirms," *Reveal*, July 7, 2013.

148. "Information Collection Request on Consent for Sterilization Form (937 0166)."

149. "Information Collection Request on Consent for Sterilization Form (937 0166)."

150. Rachel Roth and Sarah L. Ainsworth, "If They Hand You a Paper, You Sign It," *Hastings Women's Law Journal* 26, no. 1 (Winter 2015).

151. Bill Chappell, "California's Prison Sterilizations Reportedly Echo," *The Two Way*, July 9, 2013.

152. President Biden issued an executive order to phase out private prisons, citing their underperformance and not prioritizing rehabilitation and redemption. See the Executive Order on Reforming Our Incarceration System to Eliminate the Use of Privately Operated Criminal Detention Facilities, 2021.

153. The new law covers all surgeries on prison inmates that destroy reproductive capacity, including tubal ligations and hysterectomies. In life-threatening situations, it mandates that inmates first receive extensive counseling from independent physicians. The law adds a layer of public accountability in those cases: "Local jails and state prisons are required to track and report the surgeries online." Johnson, "California Bans Coerced Sterilization of Female Inmates."

154. Emily Galpern, "Social Justice Coalition Key to Success in California's New Sterilization Compensation Program: From Budget Allocation to Rollout," Center for Genetics and Society, January 26, 2022.

155. Lawmakers in blue states are linking protections for abortion and gender-affirming care. See Cayla Mihalovich, "Survivors from California's Period of Forced Sterilization Denied Reparations," KQED, November 21, 2023.

156. Sarah Mizes-Tan, "For Decades, California Forcibly Sterilized Women."

157. Diane Herbst, "'Like an Experimental Concentration Camp': Women at Detention Center Report High Numbers of Hysterectomies," *People*, September 15, 2020.

158. Herbst, "Like an Experimental Concentration Camp."

159. Karina Cisneros Preciado, Opening Statement, U.S. Senate Permanent Committee on Investigations, Committee on Homeland Security and Governmental Affairs, November 15, 2022.

160. Preciado, Opening Statement.

161. Daniella Silva, "Migrant Women File Class-Action Lawsuit for Alleged Abuse at ICE Detention Center," *NBC News*, December 22, 2020.

162. Public health researchers Elizabeth C. Ghandakly and Rachel Fabi saw this as a call to action for the Biden administration, and for all people in public health, to oppose oppression in the public health system. "Sterilization in US Immigration and Customs Enforcement's (ICE's) Detention: Ethical Failures and Systemic Injustice," *American Journal of Public Health* 111, no. 5 (May 2021): 832–34.

163. Ordover, *American Eugenics*, 160–61. Also see Emily Medosch, "Not Just ICE: Forced Sterilization in the United States," *Immigration and Human Rights Law Review*, May 28, 2021.

164. Silva, "Migrant Women File Class-Action Lawsuit."

165. "ICE, a Whistleblower and Forced Sterilization," *1A*, September 22, 2020.

166. Brigitte Amiri, "Reproductive Abuse Is Rampant in the Immigrant Detention System," *ACLU News & Commentary,* September 23, 2020.

167. Scott Bixby, "The Number of Miscarriages in ICE Detention Have Nearly Doubled under Trump," *Daily Beast*, March 2, 2019.

168. "The Shut Down Irwin Campaign," Anti-Eugenics Project: Legacies/ Reckonings, Futures.

169. Project South website.

170. Project South website.

171. Elizabeth Hargrett. "Eugenics in Georgia," *New Georgia Encyclopedia*.

172. Wendy Dowe, "The Traumas of Irwin Continue to Haunt Me: Non-Consensual Surgery Survivor Seeks Restitution, Calls to Shut Down Detention Centers," *Ms.*, December 9, 2021.

173. Congresswoman Pramila Jayapal, "House Passes Jayapal Resolution Condemning Unwanted, Unnecessary Medical Procedures Performed on Immigrant Women without Their Consent at the Irwin County Detention Center," October 2, 2020.

174. Jayapal, "House Passes Jayapal Resolution."

175. Jayapal, "House Passes Jayapal Resolution."

176. Sarah Paoletti and Azadeh Shahshahan, "Where Is the Accountability? Alleged Abuses Persist in ICE Detention," *The Hill*, November 18, 2022.

Homeland Security secretary Mayorkas finally directed ICE to end its relationship with ICDC, but soon after ICE expanded its arrangements to house female immigrants at the formerly male-only Stewart Detention Center in Lumpkin, Georgia.

177. "Re: Sexual Assault of Detained Immigrants by a Nurse at Steward Detention Center, a U.S. Department of Homeland Security Immigration Detention Facility Operated by CoreCivic," July 12, 2022.

178. José Olivares and John Washington, "The Worst Day of My Life," *The Intercept*, July 13, 2022.

179. The complaint demands an end to immigrant detention and a shift to more humane community-based models.

180. Andrews et al., "Health, Healing Justice & Liberation Statement."

181. Daniel Bendix, Ellen E. Foley, Anne Hendrixson, and Susanne Schultz, "Targets and Technologies: Sayana Press and Jadelle in Contemporary Population Policies," *Gender, Place and Culture* 27, no. 3 (2020).

182. Largent, *Breeding Contempt*, 146, note 36.

183. In the first two examples in this section, the lines between private and public institutions are blurred, and ultimately are irrelevant.

CHAPTER FOUR

1. While in practice there are generally agreed upon criteria, there is no accepted authority that decides whether a person or organization is appropriately claiming reproductive justice. For example, within the reproductive justice movement there is still disagreement over whether a group needs to be led by people of color in order to claim the name.

2. Zakiya Luna, *Reproductive Rights as Human Rights: Women of Color and the Fight for Reproductive Justice* (New York University Press, 2020). Luna explains that mainstream organizing focuses on gender as the only or primary site of women's oppression, as opposed to considering multiple sites of oppression simultaneously.

3. For more about the history of the march, see Luna, *Reproductive Rights as Human Rights*.

4. Luna, *Reproductive Rights as Human Rights*, 121.

5. Loretta Ross, Lynn Roberts, Erika Derkas, Whitney Peoples, and Pamela Bridgewater Toure, eds., *Radical Reproductive Justice* (Feminist Press, 2017), 22. Ross articulated reproductive justice's wide appeal: "It is important to reiterate that although reproductive justice was created by African American

women and popularized by women of color, it does not apply only to women of color.... It is not a matter of difference versus commonality, but difference as the pathway to fairer outcomes based on justice and equity."

6. Luna, *Reproductive Rights as Human Rights*, 119. According to Luna, this was the first public document from NOW that used the term *reproductive justice*.

7. Silvia Henriquez, who was the executive director of the National Latina Institute for Reproductive Health, played a key role in persuading SisterSong to support the march when she spoke in a plenary session at the 2003 conference.

8. Luna, *Reproductive Rights As Human Rights*, 122–24.

9. Luna, *Reproductive Rights As Human Rights*, 127.

10. Monica Simpson, "Reproductive Justice and 'Choice': An Open Letter to Planned Parenthood," *Rewire News*, August 5, 2014.

11. Abigail Abrams, "'We Are Grabbing Our Own Microphones': How Advocates of Reproductive Justice Stepped into the Spotlight," *Time*, November 21, 2019.

12. On her website at www.jofreeman.com/, historian Jo Freeman observes, "Although the name was the same, and abortion was still the primary issue, the number of sponsors and the number of themes was vastly expanded over previous years."

13. The Opportunity Agenda, "Reproductive Justice: A Communications Overview," 2008, 1–5. In 2008 the Ford Foundation commissioned messaging research to inform the promise and the challenges of the framework for political campaigns. The project, overseen by an advisory group composed of reproductive justice leaders from around the country, consisted of three distinct activities: (1) a survey of the reproductive justice movement's communications goals, activities, and capacity; (2) case studies of best communications practices; and (3) a media scan and analysis. The goal was to develop a shared understanding of the framing and media environment in order to lay the groundwork for a collaborative strategy.

14. Loretta Ross and Rickie Solinger, *Reproductive Justice: An Introduction* (University of California Press, 2017), 71.

15. Ross and Solinger, *Reproductive Justice*, chapter 2, section 9.

16. Zakiya Luna and Kristin Luker, "Reproductive Justice," *Annual Review of Law and Social Science* 9 (2013): 327–52, 336–37.

17. Luna and Luker, "Reproductive Justice."

18. Luna and Luker, "Reproductive Justice."

19. The communications study found possibilities for expanding support for reproductive justice among younger activists and through disrupting the standard narratives.

20. Jon O'Brien, "Why We Are and Must Remain 'Pro-Choice,'" *Rewire News*, April 25, 2013.

21. Furedi and O'Brien led the effort to produce the "London Declaration of Pro Choice Principles," a manifesto that was developed in 2012 by an international group of abortion providers, advocates, and academics in order to "foster reflection, conversation and our understanding of what it means to support choice."

22. Ann Furedi, *The Moral Case for Abortion* (Palgrave Macmillan, 2016).

23. Marlene Fried, Loretta Ross, and Rickie Solinger, "Understanding Reproductive Justice: A Response to O'Brien," *Rewire News*, May 8, 2013.

24. Loretta Ross, "Race, Class, and Rights in Mississippi: How Reproductive Justice Can Save the Pill and Save the Vote," *Rewire News*, October 29, 2011.

25. Nina Henry, "Suffrage and the Fight for Reproductive Justice," *Jewish Women's Archive*, June 9, 2020.

26. Imani Gandy, "The Forgotten Story of How Voting Rights Drive Abortion Access," *Rewire News*, September 20, 2021.

27. Carrie Baker, "Linking Voter Suppression and Abortion Restrictions: If We Lose Voting Rights, We Lose Women's Rights," *Ms.*, May 7, 2021.

28. The groups' cofounder, art activist Margaret Kargbo, was killed in a traffic accident in 2015.

29. Avow, "Texas Abortion Rights Organization 'NARAL Pro-Choice Texas' Relaunches as 'Avow,'" January 25, 2021.

30. Howell's full testimony is at www.congress.gov/116/meeting/house /110211/witnesses/HHRG-116-GO00-Wstate-HowellM-20191114.pdf.

31. In 1969, when New York State was considering a bill to reform its abortion laws, a panel of twelve men and a nun comprised the expert panel. Feminists, outraged by the blatant misogyny and disregard for women's needs and experiences, disrupted the hearing and demanded that the committee take testimony from the "real experts," those who had had abortions. When the committee refused, the activists organized the first documented public Speakout, in a church in New York City. Many women spoke publicly for the first time about their abortion experiences.

32. Examples of the Speakout strategy in action include the "1 in 3 Campaign" Advocates for Youth; *The Abortion Diaries*, a 2005 film, https://vimeo .com/3195236; I'mnotsorry.net, a site for sharing positive stories about abortion;

and websites such as https://womenonweb.org and https://exhaleprovoice .org/pro-voice. The Speakout strategy has been adapted internationally as well. In Ireland the first booklet of women's stories was published in 2000. In Manila, the theatrical presentation "Breaking the Silence: The Truth about Abortion" was performed at a private invitation-only event in January 2014.

33. Rose Soma, ed. and comp., *Women Speak Out about Abortion: By Women, for Women in Their Own Words* (N.p., 1978). The testimonies were written anonymously by women ages fourteen to forty-four in response to a nationwide questionnaire. More than four thousand questionnaires were distributed through feminist organizations and publications.

34. Maya Dusenbery, "Can Storytelling Help Destroy Abortion Stigma?," *Pacific Standard*, June 14, 2017.

35. Dusenbery, "Can Storytelling Help."

36. Planned Parenthood Global implemented Provider Share Workshops in Latin America to help reduce their internalized stigma. Their research consisted of interviews with clients and providers. In a debriefing session, the providers expressed their excitement about being involved in the research. They reported that their clients were happy to help the people who had helped them, and they were grateful for the chance to present their stories as testimony. See chapter 5 of this volume.

37. Anu Kumar, "Combating Abortion Stigma Requires More Than Just Storytelling," *Rewire News*, January 14, 2015.

38. Sometimes the values and practices of funders are barriers to alliance building. For example, the Catholic Church is heavily invested in supporting immigration rights and opposition to domestic violence, but it is utterly opposed to abortion and contraception. Fears about losing Catholic financial support prevent some groups from entering into coalitions that would strengthen the advocacy on all sides.

39. National Advocates for Pregnant Women (NAPW), now Pregnancy Justice, was the leader in incorporating the increasing criminalization and policing of pregnant people, the war on drugs, and birth justice into abortion politics. Although there are unresolved tensions between those focused on birthing and the abortion advocacy community, NAPW showed that they are inevitably interconnected. See also Moira Tan, "Decarceration and Abolition as a Reproductive Justice Framework," *Reproductive Justice Briefing Book*, vol. 2 (Sistersong and Civil Liberties and Public Policy Program, 2020), 20.

40. Kenrya Rankin, "Black Lives Matter Partners with Reproductive Justice Groups to Fight for Black Women," *Colorlines*, February 9, 2016.

41. Pablos's experience is one of the three accounts from We Testify that we include in chapter 1. The Trump administration adopted the practice of selecting opponents of abortion for political appointments as a way of reinforcing Trump's antiabortion commitments to his voting base, and of ensuring that antiabortion policies would be widespread throughout government agencies.

42. Negar Esfandiari and Maddy McKeague, "Crossing the Intersection of Immigration and Reproductive Justice," *National Women's Health Network*, May 3, 2018. The authors noted that immigrant women confront attacks on their reproductive health, their documentation status, and often their racial identity. Many women must deal with other forms of oppression such as disability or socioeconomic class. Health care access is under attack for all women, but drastically more so for women who live at these intersections. For example, immigrant Latina women are four times less likely to have health insurance than white women, and undocumented immigrants and individuals with DACA status were not covered by the Affordable Care Act until a new law was passed in 2024.

43. Sarah Leonard, "While Pro-Choice Politics Collapsed, Organizers Took a Different Approach," *Lux Magazine, 5*.

44. Joanna N. Erdman, Kinga Jelinska, and Susan Yanow, "Understandings of Self-Managed Abortion as Health Inequity, Harm Reduction and Social Change," *Reproductive Health Matters* 26, no. 54 (2018): 13–19.

45. Dr. Taylor is the author of *Undue Burden* (Advantage Books, 2023).

46. Guttmacher Institute, "Interactive Map: US Abortion Policies after Roe, as of October 1, 2024."

47. Renee Bracey Sherman, "Black and Brown Critique Is a Gift. Will White Abortion Advocates Listen?," *Rewire News*, July 2, 2020.

48. For example, Marco Rubio remarked, "I think future generations will look back at this history of our country and call us barbarians for murdering millions of babies who we never gave them a chance to live." Marco Rubio, "Future Generations Will Call Us Barbarians for Murdering Millions of Babies," *CNSNews*, August 7, 2015.

49. See, e.g., Will Wrigley, "Dick Black, Virginia GOP Lawmaker, Compares Abortion to Holocaust," *Huffington Post*, January 23, 2013; Luke Brinker, "Mike Huckabee: Abortion Worse Than Holocaust, U.S. Will 'Pay the Consequences' of Gay Marriage," *Salon*, November 25, 2014; Eric W. Dolan, "Mike Huckabee: Abortion an 'Incredible Holocaust of Our Own,'" *Raw Story*, February 23, 2013.

50. See Brian Fisher, "Abortion: The Most Devastating Genocide in History," *Human Coalition*, 2018.

51. Erik Eckholm and Frances Robles, "Kansas Limits Abortion Method, Opening a New Line of Attack," *New York Times*, April 7, 2015.

52. Kansas Senate Bill 95 (2015).

53. Purvaja S. Kavattu, Somjen Frazer, Abby El-Shafei, Kayt Tiskus, Laura Laderman, Lindsey Hull, Fikayo Walter-Johnson, Dana Sussman, and Lynn M. Paltrow, "The Rise of Pregnancy Criminalization: A Pregnancy Justice Report," Pregnancy Justice, September 2023.

54. Lynn M. Paltrow and Jeanne Flavin, "Arrests of and Forced Interventions on Pregnant Women in the United States (1973–2005): The Implications for Women's Legal Status and Public Health," *Journal of Health Politics, Policy and Law* 38, no. 2 (2013).

55. Wendy Sawyer, "The Gender Divide: Tracking Women's State Prison Growth," Prison Policy Initiative, January 9, 2018.

56. Aleks Kajstura and Wendy Sawyer, "Women's Mass Incarceration: The Whole Pie 2024," Prison Policy Initiative, March 5, 2024.

57. Brian Tsai, "US Pregnancy Rate Drop during the Last Decade," *NCHS*, April 2023.

58. National Association of Criminal Defense Lawyers (NACDL), "Abortion in America: How Legislative Overreach Is Turning Reproductive Rights into Criminal Wrongs," August 2021.

59. View Monica Simpson's remarks at the sixtieth anniversary of the March on Washington at www.c-span.org/video/?c5082534/user-clip-monica-simpsons-sistersong-speech.

60. Kathy Katella, "Maternal Mortality Is on the Rise: 8 Things to Know," *Yale Medicine*, May 22, 2023.

61. Tamar Sarai, "There's No Reproductive Justice without an End to Police Violence," *Prism*, May 21, 2021.

62. See SisterSong, "Birth Justice Care Fund," www.sistersong.net/bjcf-english.

63. SisterSong, "Birth Justice Care Fund."

64. SisterSong, "Visioning New Futures for Reproductive Justice Declaration 2023."

65. Alexa Spencer, "This Organization Is Bringing Reproductive Justice to Southern Cities," *Word in Black*, June 29, 2023.

66. The website for the Access Reproductive Care (ARC) Southeast explains mutual aid: "They [abortion funds] plant seeds of collective care and

responsibility, by pooling community resources to help members access essential healthcare. This mutual aid practice reflects the feminist ethic 'the personal is political,' private troubles stem from and reveal public, systemic injustices caused by the capitalist state. Abortion funds put solidarity into action, asserting that we *can* and *must* take care of each other even when the state refuses." Abortion Funds, Aid and Solidarity, ARC Southeast, September 2023.

67. Naomi Braine, "Autonomous Health Movements: Criminalization, De-Medicalization, and Community-Based Direct Action," *Health and Human Rights Journal* 22, no. 2 (December 2020): 85–97.

68. Erdman, Jelinska, and Yanow, "Understandings of Self-Managed Abortion," 13–19.

69. Tara Shochet, Lucía Berio Pizzarossa, Sara Larrea, et al., "Self-Managed Abortion via the Internet: Analysis of One Year of Service Delivery Data from Women Help Women," *Gates Open Research* 7 (2023).

70. Sara Larrea, Camila Hidalgo, Constanza Jacques-Aviñó, Carme Borrell, and Laia Palència, "'*No One Should Be Alone in Living This Process*': Trajectories, Experiences and User's Perceptions about Quality of Abortion Care in a Telehealth Service in Chile," *Sexual and Reproductive Health Matters* 29, no. 3 (2021).

71. Lucía Berro Pizzarossa and Rishita Nandagiri, "Self-Managed Abortion: A Constellation of Actors, a Cacophony of Laws?," *Sexual and Reproductive Health Matters* 29, no. 1 (2021): 23–30.

72. Ross and Solinger, *Reproductive Justice*.

73. "The Abortion Dream Team (ADT)," 2017–24.

74. Susan Yanow, Lucía Berro Pizzarossa, and Kinga Jelinska, "Self-Managed Abortion: Exploring Synergies between Institutional Medical Systems and Autonomous Health Movements," *Contraception* 104, no. 3 (2021): 219–21.

75. The website of Women Help Women is www.womenhelp.org. SASS is at www.abortionpillinfo.org.

76. Farah Diaz-Tello is deeply grateful for the contributions to an earlier version of this essay by Jill E. Adams, who guided Law Students for Choice to its evolution to Law Students for Reproductive Justice during her six-year tenure as executive director, founded the SIA Legal Team in 2015, and helmed it until returning to serve as If/When/How's executive director from 2019 to 2023. Diaz-Tello is also ever in appreciation for Adams's friendship and unwavering belief over nearly a decade and a half of co-conspiratorship.

77. "SIA in Our Communities: A Conversation," SIA Legal Team, November 2017.

78. In 2021 the Sycamore Institute reported that the official poverty rates held relatively steady at 13.6 percent—compared to 13.9 percent in 2019—and child poverty fell 1.6 points to 18.1 percent.

79. Jaeah Lee and Molly Redde, "Meet 330 Lawmakers Who Made 2013 'A Terrible Year for Women's Health,'" *Mother Jones*, last modified January 27, 2014.

80. Guttmacher Institute, "Abortion Bans in Cases of Sex or Race Selection or Genetic Anomaly."

81. Sital Kalantry, *Women's Human Rights and Migration: Sex-Selective Abortion Laws in the United States and India* (University of Pennsylvania Press, 2017).

82. Miriam Wasser, "ACLU Challenges 'Racist and Sexist' Arizona Abortion Law," *Phoenix New Times*, December 10, 2015.

83. The University of Chicago Law School—International Human Rights Clinic, National Asian Pacific American Women's Forum, and Advancing New Standards in Reproductive Health, "Replacing Myths with Facts: Sex-Selective Abortion Laws in the United States," *Global Human Rights Clinic*, June 2014.

84. California (AB 2336 [2014]), New York (A07610 [2011–12], S05033 [2011–12], A02553 [2013–14], S02286 [2013–14]), Texas (HB 309 [2012–13]), New Jersey (AB 3951 [2009], AB 2157 [2012–13]), Illinois (Illinois Abortion Law of 1975, 720 ILCS 510/6[8]), Florida (HB 1327 [2012], SB 1702 [2012], HB 845 [2013], SB 1072 [2013]), Virginia (HB 1316 [2013], HB 98 [2014]), Pennsylvania (Pennsylvania Abortion Control Act. 18 Pa.C.S.A. § 3204 [1982]), Massachusetts (H 484 [2011–12], HB 1567 [2013–14]), Georgia (SB 529 [2010], HB 1155 [2010]), North Carolina (H716 [2013]), Michigan (HB 5125 [2009], SB 799 [2009], HB 5731 [2012]); US Census Bureau, American Community Survey 5-Year Estimates, https://factfinder.census.gov/faces/nav/jsf/pages/index.xhtml; Arizona (HB 2784 [2010], H.C.R. 2049 [2010], HB 2443 [2011]), North Carolina (H716 [2013]), North Dakota (HB 1305, § 14–02.1 [2013]), Georgia (SB 529 [2010], HB 1155 [2010]), Indiana (HB 1430 [2013], SB 0183 [2013]), Texas (HB 309 [2012–13]), Florida (HB 1327 [2012], SB 1702 [2012], HB 845 [2013], SB 1072 [2013]), Virginia (HB 1316 [2013], HB98 [2014]), South Dakota (HB 1162 [2014]), Idaho (HB 693 [2010]); US Census Bureau, American Community Survey 5-Year Estimates, https://factfinder.census.gov/faces/nav/jsf/pages/index.xhtml.

CHAPTER FIVE

1. "How Women Shaped the Universal Declaration of Human Rights," Robert F. Kennedy Human Rights, March 2, 2023.

2. "How Women Shaped," 103.

3. Lynn Morgan, "Reproductive Rights or Reproductive Justice? Lessons from Argentina," *Health and Human Rights Journal* 17, no. 1 (2015).

4. Naomi Braine, *Abortion beyond the Law: Building a Global Feminist Movement for Self-Managed Abortion* (Verso Books, 2023), 4.

5. Braine, *Abortion beyond the Law*, 2.

6. Barbara B. Crane and Emily A. Maistrellis, "The Role of Abortion in Population Policies," in *International Handbook of Population Policies*, ed. J.F. May, John F. Goldstone, and Jack A. Goldstone (Springer, 2022). In many developing countries, restricting abortion was a legacy of their former status as European colonies. Crane and Maistrellis note that abortion policies are also in constitutions, criminal and civil codes, family laws, court decisions, medical ethics codes, health provider laws, and clinical guidelines. In Latin America, Asia, and Africa, restrictive abortion laws are legacies of the civil, criminal, and common law codes of former colonial governments.

7. Center for Reproductive Rights, "Accelerating Progress: Liberalization of Abortion Laws since ICPD," 2019.

8. Fleur van Leeuwen, *Women's Rights Are Human Rights: The Practice of the United Nations Human Rights Committee and the Committee on Economic, Social and Cultural Rights*, School of Human Rights Research Series 8, vol. 36 (2009), 2.

9. Padmini Murthy and Clyde Smith, eds., *Women's Global Health and Human Rights* (Jones & Bartlett International, 2010), 78.

10. Lara Knudson, *Reproductive Rights in a Global Context* (Vanderbilt University Press, 2006), 6.

11. Cairo Programme of Action (PoA), 1994, paragraph 7.2.

12. Critics point out that while Cairo added reproductive rights, it did not reject neo-Malthusian imperatives to reduce the global population. See Rosalind Pollack Petchesky, "From Population Control to Reproductive Rights: Feminist Fault Line," *Reproductive Health Matters* 3, no. 6 (1995): 152–61.

13. Cairo Programme of Action (PoA), article 8.25.

14. Marge Berer, "The Cairo 'Compromise' on Abortion and Its Consequences for Making Abortion Safe and Legal," in *Reproductive Health and Human Rights: The Way Forward*, ed. Laura Reichenbach and Mindy Jane Roseman (University of Pennsylvania Press, 2009), 152–64.

15. Sumati Nair, Sarah Sexton, and Preeti Kirbat, "A Decade after Cairo: Women's Health in a Free Market Economy," *Indian Journal of Gender Studies* 13, no. 2 (2006): 171–93.

16. Aisling McMahon and Bríd Ní Ghráinne, "After the 8th: Ireland, Abortion, and International Law," *Medico-Legal Journal of Ireland* (2019). Six treaties

set out rights that are relevant in the abortion context. The content and substance of international treaty obligations are elaborated in detail by their respective treaty monitoring bodies (TMBs) and in the European Convention on Human Rights, originally issued in 1950 by the Council on Europe, and now implemented by the European Court of Human Rights (ECHR).

17. In 2007 Amnesty International called for the decriminalization of abortion and access to it in a limited set of cases, "when women's health or human rights are in danger." Amnesty expanded its position in 2018, calling on states not just to decriminalize abortion, but to guarantee access to safe and legal abortion in a way that fully respects the rights of all women, girls, and people who can get pregnant. In the long battle to decriminalize abortion in the Republic of Ireland (1992–2018), the European Court of Human Rights ruled several times that the Irish law violates human rights. While human rights bodies do not have enforcement powers, they do have a significant symbolic impact.

18. The Maputo Protocol to the African Charter on Human and People's Rights on the Rights of Women in Africa was the first treaty to recognize abortion, under certain conditions, as a woman's human right. The protocol is the main legal instrument for the protection of the rights of women and girls in Africa. It calls on states "to take all appropriate measures to protect the reproductive rights of women by authorizing medical abortion in cases of sexual assault, rape, incest, and where the continued pregnancy endangers the mental and physical health of the mother or the life of the mother or the foetus." See General Comment No. 2 on Article 14.1 (a), (b), (c), and (f) and Article 14.2 (a) and (c) of the Maputo Protocol to the African Charter on Human and Peoples' Rights on the Rights of Women in Africa. Despite this progressive language, many countries that formally agreed to the protocol have not implemented it. For more information, see Marge Berer, Christina Boateng, and Pauline Diaz, "Conference Report, Decriminalisation of Abortion, Medical Abortion and Advocacy for Change: Three Discussion Workshops," July 2018.

19. Brazil is the largest.

20. George Wright, "France Makes Abortion a Constitutional Right," *BBC News*, March 4, 2024.

21. Wright, "France Makes Abortion."

22. World Health Organization, "Abortion: Key Facts," May 17, 2024.

23. See also "Unsafe Abortion: A Forgotten Emergency," Médecins sans Frontières / Doctors without Borders, March 7, 2019.

24. Gilda Sedgh et al., "Abortion Incidence between 1990 and 2014: Global, Regional, and Subregional Levels and Trends," *The Lancet* 388, no. 10041 (2016).

25. Madeline Fitzgerald, "Countries with the Most Restrictive Abortion Bans," *US News and World Report*, July 13, 2022.

26. World Health Organization, "Abortion," August 19, 2024.

27. MSI [previously Marie Stopes International], "Unsafe Abortion: Consequences, Facts & Statistics," October 2022.

28. According to the World Population Review, as of 2025, countries which completely prohibit abortion include: Andorra, Aruba, Democratic Republic of the Congo, Dominican Republic, El Salvador, Haiti, Honduras, Iraq, Jamaica, Palestine, Madagascar, Malta, Mauritania, Nicaragua, Palau, Suriname, Philippines, San Marino, Senegal, Sierra Leone, and Tonga.

29. Human Rights Watch, "Amicus Curiae in Case Beatriz and Others v. El Salvador," April 7, 2023.

30. Human Rights Watch, "Amicus Curiae."

31. See Colleen MacQuarrie, "Feminist Liberation Psychology: Animating Systemic Change on Abortion Access in PEI," in *Crossing Troubled Waters: Abortion in Ireland and Prince Edward Island*, ed. Colleen MacQuarrie, Claire Pierson, Shannon Stettner, and Fiona Bloomer (Island Studies Press, 2018).

32. Nina Brooks et al., "USA Aid Policy and Induced Abortion in Sub-Saharan Africa: An Analysis of the Mexico City Policy," *Lancet Global Health* 7, no. 8 (2019): e1046–53.

33. Legal restrictions that limit the grounds on which a woman may terminate a pregnancy increase the percentage of unlawful and unsafe procedures.

34. Louise Finer and Johanna B. Fine, "Abortion Laws around the World: Progress and Pushback," *American Journal of Public Health* 103, no. 4 (April 2013): 585–89.

35. Marge Berer, "Abortion Law and Policy around the World: In Search of Decriminalization," *Health and Human Rights* 19, no. 1 (June 2017): 13–27.

36. "Peru Forced Sterilizations Case Reaches Key Stage," BBC, March 1, 2021.

37. "Peru Forced Sterilizations." Estimated sterilizations range from 200,000 to 350,000. Anastasia Moloney, "Haunted by Forced Sterilizations, Peruvian Women Pin Hopes on Court Hearing," Reuters, January 8, 2021.

38. "Peru Forced Sterilizations."

39. Moloney, "Haunted by Forced Sterilizations."

40. For more details about the divisions in the movement, see Lucía Stavig, "Feminist Assemblages: Peruvian Feminisms, Forced Sterilization, and the Paradox of Rights in Fujimori's Peru," MA thesis, School of Graduate Studies, University of Lethbridge, 2017, 87–101.

41. Stavig, "Feminist Assemblages." The PTRC was modeled on processes used in Rwanda and the former Yugoslavia in the wake of national traumatic violence and as part of creating a new regime.

42. Indigenous women created an archive of testimonies and pressured the government to hold hearings and make reparations available.

43. Moloney, "Haunted by Forced Sterilizations."

44. Privi Patel, "Forced Sterilization of Women as Discrimination," *Public Health Review* 38, no. 15 (2017). Also see Open Society Foundations, "Against Her Will: Forced and Coerced Sterilization of Women Worldwide," 2011.

45. Tami Kendall and Claire Albert, "Experiences of Coercion to Sterilize and Forced Sterilization among Women Living with HIV in Latin America," *Journal of the International AIDS Society* 18, no. 1 (March 2015): 19462. Also see Karen Feldscher, "Under Pressure: Latin American Women Faced Forced Sterilization," interview with Tami Kendall, Harvard Chan School of Public Health, July 23, 2014.

46. European Disability Forum, "Forced Sterilization of People with Disabilities in the European Union," *European Disability Forum Report*, 2022.

47. John Seager, "Conference Call with Population Connection Members to Discuss Population Growth and Pandemics," *Population Connection*, May 4, 2020.

48. See Alistair Walsh, "Eco-Fascism: The Greenwashing of the Far Right," *Deutsche Welle (DW)*, May 19, 2022.

49. In 2017 the European Court of Human Rights found that the sterilization requirement for the legal recognition of gender violates human rights. This landmark decision meant that the remaining twenty European countries using the infertility requirement needed to change their laws, and countries planning to introduce new gender-recognition laws would not include an infertility requirement. Many transgender people in several U.S. states must undergo sterilizing medical procedures in order to obtain birth certificates and driver's licenses that reflect their gender.

50. World Health Organization, "Eliminating Forced, Coercive and Otherwise Involuntary Sterilization: An Interagency Statement," 2014.

51. Emma Kenny and Emily Bloom, "Explainer: The Crucial Fight for Legal Gender Recognition," *International IDEA*, April 3, 2023.

52. L. Murray, "'Missing the Point: A Conversation with Sonia Corrêa about the Emergence and Complexities of Anti-Gender Politics at the Intersections of Human Rights and Health," *Global Public Health* 17, no. 11 (2022): 3243–53. Corrêa explained that Paul Weyrich, founder of the Heritage

Foundation and the Conservative Political Action Caucus (CPAC), an early leader of the New Right in the United States, had a strong relationship with Brazilian conservative Plinio Corrêa de Oliveira.

53. Jessica Bateman, "US Anti-Abortion Activists Are Spreading Clinic Protests around the World," *New Republic*, January 9, 2023.

54. Tiaji Salaam-Blyther, "U.S. Global Health Assistance," *Congressional Research Service*, July 9, 2018.

55. Kaiser Family Foundation (KFF), "The Mexico City Policy: An Explainer," January 28, 2021.

56. Kaiser Family Foundation (KFF), "The Mexico City Policy." The Trump administration extended the policy to the vast majority of U.S. bilateral global health assistance, including funding for HIV under the U.S. President's Emergency Plan for AIDS Relief (PEPFAR), maternal and child health, malaria, nutrition, and other programs. This was a significant expansion of its scope, potentially encompassing $7.4 billion in fiscal year 2018, to the extent that such funding is ultimately provided to foreign NGOs, directly or indirectly. (Family planning assistance accounts for approximately six hundred million dollars of that total.)

57. Carol Morello, "State Department Strikes Reproductive Rights, 'Occupied Territories' from Human Rights Report," *Washington Post*, April 20, 2018.

58. Avery Anapol, "Trump Official Claimed the US Is a 'Pro-Life' Nation in UN Meeting Report," *The Hill*, April 17, 2018.

59. Violence and harassment meant to intimidate and frighten providers and people seeking abortion were tactics pioneered in the United States and have spread to other countries. In Colombia, the offices of Women's Link Worldwide, the legal advocacy group that brought the case successfully legalizing abortion in Colombia, was a target for gunshots, as were providers in Canada and New Zealand.

60. Antiabortion arguments have evolved from a focus on the need to protect fetuses to claims about protecting women and society. Susanna Mancini and Kristina Stoeckl, "Transatlantic Conversations: The Emergence of Society-Protective Antiabortion Arguments in the United States, Europe, and Russia," in *The Conscience Wars: Rethinking the Balance between Religion and Equality*, ed. S. Mancini and M. Rosenfeld (Cambridge University Press, 2018).

61. Zara Ahmed, "The Unprecedented Expansion of the Global Gag Rule: Trampling Rights, Health, and Free Speech," *Guttmacher Institute Policy Review*, August 28, 2020.

62. Pontsho Pilane, "Trump's Gag Rule Causes Global Damage," *Health-E News*, January 28, 2019.

63. As described in chapter 2, these laws threaten the medical practices of those providing abortions.

64. Marlene Fried, "Safe Abortion Action Fund (SAAF) Evaluation," internal document prepared for WGNRR, 2013.

65. Center for Reproductive Rights, "European Abortion Laws: A Comparative Overview," 2020. In Malta in 2023, the abortion ban was amended, with exceptions added if the life or health of the pregnant person is threatened.

66. Letta Tayler, "Two Years On, Poland's Abortion Crackdowns and the Rule of Law," *Open Democracy*, October 22, 2022.

67. Mancini and Stoeckl, "Transatlantic Conversations," 232, 246.

68. Mancini and Stoeckl, "Transatlantic Conversations," 244–47. The law is called On the Fundamental Health Care Principles in the Russian Federation.

69. For more on abortion in the Soviet Union, see Mie Nakchi, *Replacing the Dead: The Politics of Abortion in the Postwar Soviet Union* (Oxford University Press, 2021).

70. Fiona de Londras, "Corrigendum to 'The Impact of "Conscientious Objection" on Abortion-Related Outcomes: A Synthesis of Legal and Health Evidence,'" *Health Policy*, March 2023.

71. De Londras, "Conscientious Objection."

72. De Londras, "Conscientious Objection."

73. Christian Fiala and Joyce H. Arthur, "Refusal to Treat Patients Does Not Work in Any Country—Even If Misleadingly Labeled 'Conscientious Objection,'" letter to the editor, *Health and Human Rights Journal* 19, no. 2 (2017).

74. Hannah Roberts, "Italy Slowly Erodes Abortion Access, Riding US Wave," *Politico*, May 13, 2022.

75. Annalisa Camilli, "How Italy's 'Conscientious Objector' Doctors—De Facto—Limit Abortion Rights," *Worldcrunch*, February 24, 2023.

76. Caterina Muratori, "Does Physician Conscience-Based Refusal to Perform Abortions Increase Self-Induced Abortion? Evidence from Italian Provinces," Center for Health Economics and Policy Studies, Working Papers Series, San Diego State University, April 3, 2023, 8.

77. Slattery, Elise, "The Hidden Consequences of Forcing Women to Travel for Abortions," *Open Society Foundations*, July 7, 2016.

78. Elena Caruso, "Abortion in Italy: Forty Years On," *Feminist Legal Studies* 28, no. 1 (April 2020).

79. Mancini and Stoeckl, "Transatlantic Conversations," 250.

80. Jane Harries, Diane Copper, Anna Strebel, and Christopher J. Colvin, "Conscientious Objection and Its Impact on Abortion Service Provision in South Africa: A Qualitative Study," *Reproductive Health* 11, article no. 16 (2014).

81. Jane Harries, "Briefing: Barriers to Safe and Legal Abortion," *Amnesty International Publications*, 2017.

82. Harries, "Briefing," 67–68.

83. Karen A. Trueman and Makgoale Magwentshu, "Abortion in a Progressive Legal Environment: The Need for Vigilance in Protecting and Promoting Access to Safe Abortion Services in South Africa," *American Journal of Public Health* 103 (March 2013).

84. Agustina Ramón Michel, Stephanie Kung, Alyse López-Salm, and Sonia Ariza Navarrete, "Regulating Conscientious Objection to Legal Abortion in Argentina: Taking into Consideration Its Uses and Consequences," *Health and Human Rights Journal* 22, no. 2 (December 2020): 271–83.

85. See "Amnesty International's Policy on Abortion: Explanatory Note," September 28, 2020.

86. Wendy Chavkin, Laurel Swerdlow, and Jocelyn Fifield, "Regulation of Conscientious Objection to Abortion," *Journal of Health and Human Rights* 19, no. 1 (June 2017).

87. Some critics of CO raise an in-principle objection that accommodating religious refusals obliterates the line between church and state. Zoe Tongue argues for programs that address abortion stigma and gender inequality in her "On Conscientious Objection to Abortion: Questioning Mandatory Referral as a Compromise in the International Human Rights Framework," *Medical Law International* 22, no. 4 (2022).

88. Christian Fiala, Kristina Gemzell Danielsson, Oskari Heikinheimo, Jens A. Gudmundsson, and Joyce Arthur, "Yes We Can! Successful Examples of Disallowing 'Conscientious Objection' in Reproductive Health Care," *European Journal of Contraception and Reproductive Healthcare* 21, no. 3 (2016).

89. Christian Fiala and Joyce Arthur, "There Is No Defence for 'Conscientious Objection' in Reproductive Health Care," *European Journal of Obstetrics and Gynecology and Reproductive Biology* 216 (September 2017).

90. Women's Link Worldwide, "Spain's Constitutional Court Acknowledges That the Fundamental Rights of Antonia, Who Faced Multiple Barriers to Access to Abortion, Were Violated," July 3, 2023.

91. International Campaign for Women's Right to Safe Abortion, "Spain—Minister for Equality Plans to Remove Abortion Barriers," July 20, 2021.

92. Fernando Heller, "Spanish Lawmakers Approve Abortion, Transgender Rights Reforms," *Euractiv*, February 17, 2023.

93. Caruso, "Abortion in Italy."

94. Etobssie Wako and Anne Hendrixson call for rejecting "overly simplistic and often damaging" ideas about the relationship between environments, economies and population. See their "Reproductive Justice beyond Population Control: An Invitation to Funders," *Nonprofit Quarterly*, October 25, 2022.

95. Deepa Dhanraj's 1991 film *Something Like a War* exposed the coercion and deception involved in India's family planning program. Similarly, Ana Maria Garcia's film *La Operación* is a formidable critique of Puerto Rico's family planning program. Both films highlight the perspectives of the women who were the victims/survivors of the policies. For more on global feminist resistance to population control, see Ruth Dixon-Mueller and Adrienne Germain, "Population Policy and Feminist Political Action in Three Developing Countries," *Population and Development Review* 20 (1994): 197–219; Meredith Turshen, *Women's Health Movements: A Global Force for Change* (Palgrave MacMillan, 2006).

96. Patricia Romney, *We Were There: The Third World Women's Alliance and the Second Wave* (The Feminist Press, 2021), 258.

97. Betsy Hartmann, "Population Control: Birth of an Ideology," *International Journal of Health Services* 27, no. 3 (1997): 523–40.

98. Amnesty International, "The Total Abortion Ban in Nicaragua: Women's Lives and Health Endangered, Medical Professionals Criminalized," Amnesty International, 2009.

99. Human Rights Watch, "Letter from Human Rights Watch to the Government of Nicaragua: Re Women's and Girls' Health in Nicaragua," June 30, 2017.

100. Center for Reproductive Rights, "'They Are Girls, Not Mothers' (Norma v. Ecuador, Lucía v. Nicaragua, Susanna v. Nicaragua, Fatima v. Guatamala)," May 29, 2019.

101. Center for Reproductive Rights, "Victory at the UN in the 'They Are Girls, Not Mothers' Cases," January 22, 2025, https://reproductiverights.org/victory-un-girls-not-mothers/.

102. Fiona Bloomer, Claire Pierson, and Sylvia Estrada-Claudio, *Reimagining Global Abortion Politics* (Policy Press, 2019), 119–20.

103. Bloomer, Pierson, and Estrada-Claudio, *Reimagining*, 119.

104. Marion Stevens, "South Africa: Need for National Traction on Reproductive Justice in South Africa Following Elections," International Campaign for Women's Right to Safe Abortions, July 17, 2019.

105. Stevens, "South Africa."

106. Email communication from Stevens to Fried, February 12, 2020.

107. Marion Stevens, "From North to South: The Evolution of Reproductive Justice in South Africa," in *Reproductive Justice and the Afterlife of Colonial Reproductive Violence*, ed. Susanne M. Klausen (University of California Press, forthcoming).

108. Stevens, "From North to South."

109. Lina Yoon, "South Korea's Constitutional Right to Abortion: Activists Fought Hard for Change," Human Rights Watch, June 9, 2022.

110. The South Korean story retold here comes from Sunhye Kim, Na Young, and Yurim Lee, "The Role of Reproductive Justice Movements in Challenging South Korea's Abortion Ban," *Health and Human Rights Journal* 21, no. 2 (December 2019): 97–105.

111. Kim, Young, and Lee, "The Role of Reproductive Justice Movements."

112. Kim, Young, and Lee, "The Role of Reproductive Justice Movements."

113. Reproductive justice was explicitly named in WGNRR's 2014–18 strategic plans.

114. There were ten meetings between 1977 and 2015.

115. The original WGNRR group included the Argentine Commission of the 5th Feminist Encuentro of Latin America and the Caribbean, Catholics for a Free Choice, Feminist International Network for Resistance Against Reproductive and Genetic Engineering (FINNRAGE), International Women's Health Coalition (IWHC), ISIS-International-Latin America and the Caribbean Women's Health Network, and First African Regional Meeting on Women and Health Organizing Committee.

116. Sylvia Estrada-Claudio, "The International Women and Health Meetings: Catalyst and End Product of the Global Feminist Health Movement," workshop talk at the International Women and Health Meeting, "Transnationalization of Solidarities and Women's Movements," Université de Montréal, April 27–28, 2006.

117. Estrada-Claudio, "The International Women and Health Meetings," 7–8.

118. The call for each conference asked participants to focus on abortion in this wider reproductive justice framework: "The conference aims to contribute to the vision of universal access to reproductive justice."

119. Read the full speech at www.safeabortionwomensright.org/what-binds-us-read-the-speech-by-sylvia-estrada-claudio/.

120. The vice principal of the school, who was fifty years older than Paola at the time, offered to help her with her schoolwork on the condition that she would have sex with him. He raped Paola repeatedly, and when he learned of her pregnancy, he asked her to get an abortion and sent her to the school doctor to perform the procedure. The school doctor agreed under one condition: that Paola also have sex with him. Paola attempted to take her own life. The school failed to get her proper medical attention in time, and she died.

121. Joint Statement between the WGNRR and the ICWHRD, issued in 2023.

122. The campaign held its first conference in 2019 and identified as its three advocacy priorities to drive change: (1) medical abortion, (2) decriminalization, and (3) lessons learned from advocacy and campaigning.

123. Leila Hessini, "A Learning Agenda for Abortion Stigma: Recommendations from the Bellagio Expert Group Meeting," September 25, 2014.

124. Bloomer, Pierson, and Estrada-Claudio, *Reimagining*, 67. Also see Annik Mahalia Sorhaindo and Antonella Francheska Lavelanet, "Why Does Abortion Stigma Matter? A Scoping Review and Hybrid Analysis of Qualitative Evidence Illustrating the Role of Stigma in the Quality of Abortion Care," *Social Science and Medicine* 311 (October 2022).

125. Sneha Barot, "The Roadmap to Safe Abortion Worldwide: Lessons from New Global Trends on Incidence, Legality and Safety," *Guttmacher Institute Policy Report* 21 (March 2018).

126. Hessini, "A Learning Agenda." Given the way that the evidence was gathered, there is no way to know how many abortion seekers are impacted altogether.

127. Hessini, "A Learning Agenda." They termed this "internalized stigma."

128. Sorhaindo and Lavelanet, "Why Does Abortion Stigma Matter?"

129. Sorhaindo and Lavelanet, "Why Does Abortion Stigma Matter?"

130. Shelly Makleff, Ana Labandera, Fernanda Chirbao, Jennifer Friedman, Roosbelinda Cardenas, Eleuthera Sa, and Sarah E. Baum, "Experience Obtaining Legal Abortion in Uruguay: Knowledge, Attitudes, and Stigma among Abortion Clients," *BMC Women's Health*, 2019, 6.

131. Leslie J. Reagan, *When Abortion Was a Crime: Women, Medicine, and Law in the United States* (University of California Press, 1997, 2022), 20. Reagan suggested that when abortion was still criminalized, secrecy was a more apt term than silence as a way of describing the reality. She argued that while the metaphor of the silenced woman draws attention to the dominance of male voices, it portrays women "as more isolated, helpless and victimized than they felt."

132. In Ireland, Catholicism's stern teaching has prevailed, fostering a climate of guilt about having sex outside of marriage and preventing any discussion of sexuality and a general ignorance about bodies and pregnancy. In Prince Edward Island, conservative Christianity is the driving force behind the antiabortion climate.

133. For more information, see www.katie-oneill.com/The-X-ile-Project.

134. Henry McDonald, "Pro-Choice Irish Women Go Public on Being 'Exiled' by Need for an Abortion," *The Guardian*, December 10, 2015.

135. In the key weeks leading up to the referendum, the "cervical check" scandal was publicized. This involved the misdiagnosis of women's cervical smear results as normal, which delayed early intervention and treatment in the cases of 209 women. Some women were not diagnosed until they were terminally ill, and the mistakes were subsequently concealed within the healthcare system.

136. MacQuarrie, Bloomer, Pierson, and Stettner, eds., *Crossing Troubled Water.*

137. MacQuarrie, "Feminist Liberation Psychology."

138. Angele DesRoches, "Conceivable Possibilities: Space, Stigma and Subjectivity," in *Crossing Troubled Waters: Abortion in Ireland and Prince Edward Island,* ed. Colleen MacQuarrie, Claire Pierson, Shannon Stettner, and Fiona Bloomer (Island Studies Press, 2018).

139. Wendy Chavkin, Liddy Leitman, and Kate Polin for Global Doctors for Choice, "Conscientious Objection and Refusal to Provide Reproductive Healthcare: A White Paper Examining Prevalence, Health Consequences, and Policy Responses," *International Journal of Gynecology and Obstetrics* 123 (December 10, 2013).

140. Elizabeth A. Mosley, Lisa Martin, Meghan Seewald, Jane Hassinger, Kelly Blanchard, Sarah E. Baum, Diana Santana, Lina Echeverri, Jenna Garrett, Jesse Njunguru, and Lisa H. Harris, "Addressing Abortion Provider Stigma: A Pilot Implementation of the Providers Share Workshop in Sub Saharan Africa and Latin America," *International Perspectives on Sexual and Reproductive Health* 46 (2020): 35–50.

141. Lisa Martin et al., "Abortion Providers, Stigma and Professional Quality of Life," *Contraception* 90, no. 6 (December 2014): 581–87.

142. Mosley et al., "Addressing Abortion Provider Stigma."

143. Two books published in 2023 provide excellent overviews of SMA: Braine, *Abortion beyond the Law,* and Sydney Calkin, *Abortion Pills Go Global: Reproductive Freedom across Borders* (University of California Press, 2023). In 1988

advocates in Brazil discovered that misoprostol was an abortifacient. Berer, "Reconceptualizing Safe Abortion and Abortion Services in the Age of Abortion Pills: A Discussion Paper," in Best Practice & Research Clinical Obstetrics and Gynecology, 63 (February 2020), note 3. Current research by Ibis Reproductive Health and others highlights the safety of self-induction when supported by well-trained advocates at the community level. See Angel Foster, "Medication Abortion: A Guide For Health Professionals," IBIS Reproductive Health.

144. Bela Ganatra, Phillip Guest, and Marge Berer, "Expanding Access to Medical Abortion: Challenges and Opportunities," *Reproductive Health Matters* 22, sup. 44 (2014).

145. Raquel Irene Drovetta, "Safe Abortion Information Hotlines: An Effective Strategy for Increasing Women's Access to Safe Abortions in Latin America," *Reproductive Health Matters* 23, no. 45 (2015): 47–57.

146. See the sections "Susan Yanow" and "Kinga Jelinksa, Lucía Berro Pizzarossa, and Natalia Broniarczyk" in chapter 4 of this volume.

147. Opponents of abortion recognize the tremendous potential of the pills to increase abortion access and have resisted the manufacture and distribution of abortion pills from their inception. In 1988 in France, where the pills were developed, threats from antiabortion forces pressured the pharmaceutical company that manufactured RU-486 to take it off the market. They only resumed distribution after being ordered to do so by the French health minister, who proclaimed that the drug was the "moral property of women." It took another twelve years of persistent advocacy, led by the Feminist Majority Foundation, to have it approved in the United States for use in medical settings, but the resistance and efforts to constrain its use continue here and around the world.

148. Berer, "Accepting the Global Reality of 'Self-Help' Abortions," *The Berer Blog*, July 20, 2015.

149. Patty Skusker, Kinga Jelinska, and Susan Yanow, "Self-Managed Abortion Highlights Need to Decriminalize Abortion Worldwide," *Rewire News*, November 12, 2018.

150. Kaiser Family Foundation (KFF), "The Availability and Use of Medication Abortion," March 20, 2024 (updated October 7, 2024).

151. Amy Howe, "Justices Will Review Lower-Court Ruling on Access to Abortion Pill," *Scotus Blog*, December 13, 2023. The Supreme Court granted a full stay, which means that access continues until the appeal is decided. SCOTUS heard the appeal in March 2024.

152. Drovetta, "Safe Abortion Information Hotlines."

153. Sarah E. Baum, "'It's Not a Seven-Headed Beast': Abortion Experience among Women That Received Support from Helplines for Medication Abortion in Restrictive Settings," *Health Care for Women International* 41 (November 6, 2020). Women's descriptions of the support they received were strikingly more positive that those of the experiences they had under the formal healthcare system, which were characterized by stigma, negative judgments, and denial of services.

154. Calkin, *Abortion Pills Go Global*, 8.

155. Joanna N. Erdman, Kinga Jelinska, and Susan Yanow, "Understandings of Self-Managed Abortion as Health Inequity, Harm Reduction and Social Change," *Reproductive Health Matters* 26, no. 54 (2018): 13–19.

156. Kinga Jelinska and Susan Yanow, "Putting Abortion Pills into Women's Hands: Realizing the Full Potential of Medical Abortion," *Contraception* 89 (2018): 86–89.

157. Braine, *Abortion beyond the Law*, 76.

158. Cassia Roth, "Abortion Access in the Americas: A Hemispheric and Historical Approach," *Frontiers in Public Health* 11 (2023).

159. Ruth Zurbriggen, Brianna Keefe-Oates, and Caitlin Gerdt, "Accompaniment of Second-Trimester Abortions: The Model of the Feminist Socorristas Network of Argentina," *Contraception* 97 (2018): 108–15.

160. Zurbriggen, Keefe-Oates, and Gerdt, "Accompaniment."

161. Zurbriggen, Keefe-Oates, and Gerdt, "Accompaniment."

162. Zurbriggen, Keefe-Oates, and Gerdt, "Accompaniment."

163. "Abortion Pill Protest in Seoul, South Korea: Abortion Declaration by 125 Women." Women on Waves, August 26, 2018.

164. The fact-checking website Snopes reported that the invitation for the event informed participants that while one activist would truly be taking the abortion drug mifepristone, all 125 volunteers would be given a vitamin pill and only one person actually used the abortion pill. Dan Evon, "Did 125 Women Terminate Their Pregnancies during a Protest in South Korea?," September 15, 2018.

165. Laura Gottesdiener, "'Feeling Free': Women Criminalized by Mexico's Abortion Bans Celebrate Ruling," September 9, 2021.

166. Gottesdiener, "Feeling Free."

167. Caroline Kitchener, "Covert Network Provides Pills for Thousands of Abortions in U.S. Post Roe," *Washington Post*, October 18, 2022.

168. Anna Louise Sussman, "What the U.S. Could Learn from Abortion Without Borders," *New Yorker*, May 17, 2022.

169. Eglė Krištopaitytė, "Strip-Search of Polish Woman Who Had Abortion Sparks Outcry," *Health News*, July 26, 2023.

170. Sally Sheldon, "Empowerment and Privacy? Home Use of Abortion Pills in the Republic of Ireland," *Signs*, Summer 2018, 844.

171. "The Campaign is a membership-based network, initiated in 2012, to serve as an umbrella for those working for the right to safe abortion internationally.... Our remit is to create a shared platform for advocacy, debate and dialogue; foster solidarity; promote coalition building; share information and experience to inform policy and programmes; and hold relevant stakeholders to account for the right of girls and women to make decisions about their own bodies and lives." See Berer, Boateng, and Diaz, "Conference Report."

172. Berer, "Reconceptualizing," 52.

173. Berer, "Reconceptualizing," 54.

174. Even though some of the early leaders of the movement were themselves "disappeared," beginning in 1977, every Thursday they marched around the plaza in the center of Buenos Aires. Nayla Luz Vacarezza, "The Green Scarf for Abortion Rights: Affective Contagion and Artistic Reinventions of Movement Symbols," in *Affect, Gender and Sexuality in Latin America*, ed. Cecilia Macón, Mariela Solana, and Nayla Luz Vacarezza (Palgrave Macmillan, 2021).

175. Barbara Sutton and Nayla Luz Vacarezza, eds., *Abortion and Democracy: Contentious Body Politics in Argentina, Chile, and Uruguay* (Routledge, 2021).

CONCLUSION

1. The Heritage Foundation, "Project 2025: Commentary by Spencer Chretien." Also see Guttmacher Institute, "How Project 2025 Seeks to Obliterate Sexual and Reproductive Health and Rights," fact sheet, October 2024.

2. Steve Contorno, "Trump Claims Not to Know Who Is behind Project 2025. A CNN Review Found at Least 140 People Who Worked for Him Are Involved," CNN, July 11, 2024.

3. Center for Reproductive Rights, "The Top 5 Ways Project 2025 Would Destroy Abortion Access," September 18, 2024.

4. Hannah Silver and Cloee Cooper, "101 Abortion Abolitionists," Political Research Associates, October 2023.

5. Landback (https://landback.org) is a movement to return Indigenous lands to Indigenous people. It is a campaign and a framework for narrative and political organizing.

BIBLIOGRAPHY

"The Abortion Dream Team (ADT)." 2017–24. https://aborcyjnydreamteam
.pl/en/i-am-justyna/.

"Abortion Pill Protest in Seoul, South Korea: Abortion Declaration by 125
Women." Women on Waves, August 26, 2018. www.womenonwaves.org/en
/page/7462/abortion-pill-protest-in-seoul--south-korea-2018.

Abrams, Abigail. "'We Are Grabbing Our Own Microphones': How Advocates
of Reproductive Justice Stepped into the Spotlight." *Time*, November 21,
2019. https://time.com/5735432/reproductive-justice-groups/.

ACLU. "Access Denied: Origins of the Hyde Amendment and Other Restrictions on Public Funding for Abortion." December 1994. www.aclu.org
/documents/access-denied-origins-hyde-amendment-and-other-restrictions-
public-funding-abortion.

Adams, Char. "Disability Rights Groups Are Fighting for Abortion Access
and against Ableism." *NBC News*, July 21, 2022. www.nbcnews.com/news
/us-news/disability-rights-groups-are-fighting-abortion-access-ableism-
rcna38703.

Ahmed, Zara. "The Unprecedented Expansion of the Global Gag Rule:
Trampling Rights, Health, and Free Speech." *Guttmacher Institute Policy
Review*, August 28, 2020. www.guttmacher.org/gpr/2020/04/unprecedented-
expansion-global-gag-rule-trampling-rights-health-and-free-speech.

Aiken, Abigail R. A., Elisa S. Wells, Rebecca Gomperts, et al. "Provision of
Medications for Self-Managed Abortion before and after the Dobbs v

Jackson Women's Health Organization Decision." *JAMA* 331, no. 18 (2024): 1558–65. https://doi.org/10.1001/jama.2024.4266.

Alcoff, Linda Martin. *The Future of Whiteness*. Polity Press, 2015.

Allen, Garland. "Eugenics and Modern Biology: Critiques of Eugenics, 1920–1945." *Wiley Online Library*, April 13, 2011. https://doi.org/10.1111/j.1469-1809.2011.00649.x.

American Medical Association (AMA). "Treatment versus Criminalization: Physician Role in Drug Addiction During Pregnancy, H420–970." *AMA Policy Finder*, last modified 2020. https://policysearch.ama-assn.org/policyfinder/detail/addiction%20pregnancy.

American Public Health Association (APHA). "Opposition to the CRACK Campaign." *American Journal of Public Health Association News* 9, no. 3 (March 2001): 516–17. www.ncbi.nlm.nih.gov/pmc/articles/PMC1446614/pdf/11236456.pdf.

Amiri, Brigitte. "Reproductive Abuse Is Rampant in the Immigrant Detention System." *ACLU News & Commentary*, September 23, 2020.

Amnesty International. "Criminalizing Pregnancy: Policing Pregnant Women Who Use Drugs in the U.S." 2017. www.amnesty.org/en/documents/amr51/6203/2017/en/.

———. "The Total Abortion Ban in Nicaragua: Women's Lives and Health Endangered, Medical Professionals Criminalized." Amnesty International, 2009. www.amnesty.org/es/wp-content/uploads/2021/06/amr430012009en.pdf.

Anapol, Avery. "Trump Official Claimed the US Is a 'Pro-Life' Nation in UN Meeting Report." *The Hill*, April 17, 2018. https://thehill.com/policy/healthcare/383579-trump-officials-claimed-us-is-a-pro-life-nation-pushed-for-abstinence-based/.

Andrews, Courtni, Tanvi Avasthi, benita sokari brown, Tamika Middleton, Cara Page, and Rita Valenti. "Health, Healing Justice & Liberation Statement." Project South. https://projectsouth.org/healing-justice-statement/?eType=EmailBlastContent&eId=f2e6eeb8-ce6e-4c82-af06-88d4ba69b39a.

"Anti-Abortionists and White Supremacists Make Common Cause." *The Progressive, Inc.*, The Free Library, October 1, 1994. www.thefreelibrary.com/Antiabortionists+and+white+supremacists+make+common+cause.-a015783407.

Asian Communities for Reproductive Justice (ACRJ). "A New Vision for Advancing Our Movement for Reproductive Health, Reproductive Rights, and Reproductive Justice." 2005. https://forwardtogether.org/wp-content/uploads/2017/12/ACRJ-A-New-Vision.pdf.

Association of Maternal and Child Health Programs. "The Forced Sterilization of Disabled People in the United States: An Interview with Ma'ayan
Anafi, Senior Counsel for Health Equity and Justice at the National
Women's Law Center." March 2022. https://amchp.org/2022/03/17/the-
forced-sterilization-of-disabled-people-in-the-united-states-an-interview-
with-maayan-anafi-senior-counsel-for-health-equity-and-justice-at-the-
national-womens-law-center/.

Avow. "Texas Abortion Rights Organization 'NARAL Pro-Choice Texas'
Relaunches as 'Avow.'" January 25, 2021. https://avowtexas.org/2021/01/25
/for-immediate-release-texas-abortion-rights-organization-naral-pro-choice-
texas-relaunches-as-avow/.

Baglieri, Susan, and Arthur Shapiro. "Perspectives on Disability." In *Disability
Studies and the Inclusive Classroom*, 2nd ed., edited by Susan Baglieri and
Arthur Shapiro. Routledge, 2017.

Bailey, Martha J. "Fifty Years of Family Planning: New Evidence on the Long-
Run Effects of Increasing Access to Contraception." National Bureau of
Economic Research, October 2013. https://doi.org/10.3386/w19493.

Baker, Carrie. "Linking Voter Suppression and Abortion Restrictions: If We
Lose Voting Rights, We Lose Women's Rights." *Ms.*, May 7, 2021. https://
msmagazine.com/2021/05/07/voter-suppression-abortion-restrictions-
womens-rights/.

Barks, Bryan. "When Medications Risk Birth Defects, Abortion Bans Force
Women into an Agonizing Dilemma." *Slate*, August 31, 2022.

Barot, Sneha. "The Roadmap to Safe Abortion Worldwide: Lessons from New
Global Trends on Incidence, Legality and Safety." *Guttmacher Institute Policy
Report* 21 (March 2018). www.guttmacher.org/sites/default/files/article_
files/gpr2101718.pdf.

Bateman, Jessica. "US Anti-Abortion Activists Are Spreading Clinic Protests
around the World." *New Republic*, January 9, 2023. https://newrepublic.com
/article/169587/us-anti-abortion-activists-spreading-clinic-protests-around-
world.

Baum, Sarah E. "'It's Not a Seven-Headed Beast': Abortion Experience among
Women That Received Support from Helplines for Medication Abortion
in Restrictive Settings." *Health Care for Women International* 41 (November 6,
2020). https:/doi.org/10.1080/07399332.2020.1823981.

Beal, Frances. "Double Jeopardy: To Be Black and Female." *Meridians:
Feminism, Race, Transnationalism* 8, no. 2 (2008): 166–76. www.jstor.org/stable
/40338758.

Belle, Elly. "Don't Say Gay Protests: How Florida Students Like Jack Petocz Are Fighting against Hatred." *Teen Vogue*, June 13, 2022. www.teenvogue .com/story/jack-petocz-dont-say-gay-florida.

Bendix, Daniel, Ellen E. Foley, Anne Hendrixson, and Susanne Schultz. "Targets and Technologies: Sayana Press and Jadelle in Contemporary Population Policies." *Gender, Place and Culture* 27, no. 3 (2020). https://doi.org/10.1080 /0966369X.2018.1555145.

Berer, Marge. "Abortion Law and Policy around the World: In Search of Decriminalization." *Health and Human Rights Journal* 19, no. 1 (June 2017): 13–27.

———. "Accepting the Global Reality of 'Self-Help' Abortions." *The Berer Blog*, July 20, 2015. https://bererblog.wordpress.com/2015/07/20/accepting-the-global-reality-of-self-help-abortions/.

———. "The Cairo 'Compromise' on Abortion and Its Consequences for Making Abortion Safe and Legal." In *Reproductive Health and Human Rights: The Way Forward*, edited by Laura Reichenbach and Mindy Jane Roseman. University of Pennsylvania Press, 2009. www.ncbi.nlm.nih.gov/pmc /articles/PMC5473035/.

———. "Reconceptualizing Safe Abortion and Abortion Services in the Age of Abortion Pills: A Discussion Paper." In *Best Practice & Research Clinical Obstetrics and Gynecology* 63 (February 2020): 45–55. https://doi.org/10.1016 /j.bpobgyn.2019.07.012.

Berer, Marge, Christina Boateng, and Pauline Diaz. "Conference Report, Decriminalisation of Abortion, Medical Abortion and Advocacy for Change: Three Discussion Workshops." July 2018. www.safeabortion womensright.org/wp-content/uploads/2020/09/Report-of-an-International-Campaign-Workshop-Abortion-Reproductive-Justice-Conference-South-Africa-9-12-July-2018.pdf.

Bergengruen, Vera. "Armed Demonstrators and Far-Right Groups Are Escalating Tensions at Abortion Protests." *Time*, July 8, 2022.

Bickman, Jed. "Should Addicts Be Sterilized?" *Salon*, May 2, 2012. www.salon .com/2012/05/02/should_addicts_be_sterilized_salpart.

"Bill O'Reilly in Hot Seat after Kan. Murder." *Hollywood Reporter*, June 2, 2009. www.hollywoodreporter.com/business/business-news/bill-oreilly-hot-seat-kan-84866/.

Bixby, Scott. "The Number of Miscarriages in ICE Detention Have Nearly Doubled under Trump." *Daily Beast*, March 2, 2019. www.thedailybeast .com/immigrant-miscarriages-in-ice-detention-have-nearly-doubled-under-trump.

Blackhawk, Ned. *The Rediscovery of America: Native Peoples and the Unmaking of U.S. History.* Yale University Press, 2023.

Blain, Keisha N. *Until I Am Free: Fannie Lou Hamer's Enduring Message to America.* Beacon Press, 2022.

Bloomer, Fiona, Claire Pierson, and Sylvia Estrada-Claudio. *Reimagining Global Abortion Politics.* Policy Press, 2019.

Boonstra, Heather D. "Abortion in the Lives of Women Struggling Financially: Why Insurance Coverage Matters." *Guttmacher Policy Review,* July 14, 2016. www.guttmacher.org/gpr/2016/07/abortion-lives-women-struggling-financially-why-insurance-coverage-matters.

Boston Women's Health Book Collective. *Our Bodies, Ourselves.* Simon and Schuster, 1984, 1992, 1998, 2005, 2011. https://ourbodiesourselves.org/the-nine-us-editions.

Bowen, Liz. "The End of Roe Will Be a Nightmare for Disabled Americans." *Hastings Center Forum,* June 24, 2022. www.thehastingscenter.org/the-end-of-roe-v-wade-will-be-a-nightmare-for-disabled-americans/.

Braine, Naomi. *Abortion beyond the Law: Building a Global Feminist Movement for Self-Managed Abortion.* Verso Books, 2023.

———. "Autonomous Health Movements: Criminalization, De-Medicalization, and Community-Based Direct Action." *Health and Human Rights Journal* 22, no. 2 (December 2020): 85–97.

Bridges, Khiara. "Race, Pregnancy, and the Opioid Epidemic: White Privilege and the Criminalization of Opioid Use During Pregnancy." *Harvard Law Review* 133, no. 3 (January 2020). https://harvardlawreview.org/print/vol-133/race-pregnancy-and-the-opioid-epidemic-white-privilege-and-the-criminalization-of-opioid-use-during-pregnancy/.

Briggs, Laura. *How All Politics Became Reproductive Politics: From Welfare Reform to Foreclosure to Trump.* University of California Press, 2017.

Brinker, Luke. "Mike Huckabee: Abortion Worse Than Holocaust, U.S. Will 'Pay the Consequences' of Gay Marriage." *Salon,* November 25, 2014. www.salon.com/2014/11/25/mike_huckabee_abortion_worse_than_holocaust_u_s_will_pay_the_consequences_of_gay_marriage/.

Brooks, Nina, et al. "USA Aid Policy and Induced Abortion in Sub-Saharan Africa: An Analysis of the Mexico City Policy." *Lancet Global Health* 7, no. 8 (2019): e1046–53. https://doi.org/10.1016/s2214-109x(19)30267-0.

Calkin, Sydney. *Abortion Pills Go Global: Reproductive Freedom across Borders.* University of California Press, 2023.

"Call and Response: A Narrative of Reverence to Our Foremothers in Gynecology." 2023. Dell Marie Hamilton, curator. Featuring the art of Jules Arthur, Michelle Browder, Michelle Hartney, Jeremy Daniel, Vinnie Bagwell, King Cobra, Anyika McMillan-Herod, Malcolm Herod, Charly Evon Simpson, Tsedaye Makonnen, Sarah Krulwich, Howard Simmons, and Spencer Platt. https://hutchinscenter.fas.harvard.edu/call-and-response.

Camilli, Annalisa. "How Italy's 'Conscientious Objector' Doctors—De Facto—Limit Abortion Rights." *Worldcrunch*, February 24, 2023. https://worldcrunch.com/women-worldwide/abortion-italy-doctors-conscientious-objection.

Caron, Simone M. "Abortion and Contraception in the Nineteenth Century." In *"Who Chooses?" American Reproductive History since 1830*, online edition. Florida Scholarship Online, September 14, 2011. https://doi.org/10.5744/florida/9780813031996.003.0002.

Caruso, Elena. "Abortion in Italy: Forty Years On." *Feminist Legal Studies* 28, no. 1 (April 2020). https://doi.org/10.1007/s10691-019-09419-w.

Castronuovo, Celine. "Migrant Women File Class-Action Lawsuit for Alleged Medical Abuse at ICE Detention Center." *The Hill*, December 23, 2020.

Center for Genetics and Society. "Social Justice and Human Rights Principles for Global Deliberations on Heritable Human Genome Editing." Press statement, February 14, 2024. www.geneticsandsociety.org/internal-content/principles-heritable-genome-editing.

Center for Reproductive Rights. "Accelerating Progress: Liberalization of Abortion Laws since ICPD." 2019. https://reproductiverights.org/sites/default/files/documents/World-Abortion-Map-AcceleratingProgress.pdf.

———. "Accelerating Progress: Liberalization of Abortion Laws since ICPD." Fact sheet, 2021. https://reproductiverights.org/wp-content/uploads/2020/12/World-Abortion-Map-AcceleratingProgress.pdf.

———. "European Abortion Laws: A Comparative Overview." 2020. https://reproductiverights.org/wp-content/uploads/2020/12/European-abortion-law-a-comparative-review.pdf.

———. "'They Are Girls, Not Mothers' (UN Human Rights Committee) (Norma v. Ecuador, Lucía v. Nicaragua, Susanna v. Nicaragua, Fatima v. Guatamala)." May 29, 2019. https://reproductiverights.org/case/girls-not-mothers-forced-childbirth-un-human-rights-committee/.

———. "The Top 5 Ways Project 2025 Would Destroy Abortion Access." September 18, 2024. https://reproductiverights.org/project-2025-abortion-access/.

————. "Victory at the UN in the 'They Are Girls, Not Mothers' Cases." January 22, 2025. https://reproductiverights.org/victory-un-girls-not-mothers/.

Chappell, Bill. "California's Prison Sterilizations Reportedly Echo Eugenics Era." *The Two Way*, July 9, 2013. www.npr.org/sections/thetwo-way/2013/07/09/200444613/californias-prison-sterilizations-reportedly-echoes-eugenics-era.

Chavez, Nicole. "Texas Woman Died after an Unsafe Abortion Years Ago. Her Daughter Fears Same Thing May Happen Again." CNN, October 11, 2021. https://ktvz.com/news/2021/10/11/texas-woman-died-after-an-unsafe-abortion-years-ago-her-daughter-fears-same-thing-may-happen-again/.

Chavkin, Wendy, Liddy Leitman, and Kate Polin for Global Doctors for Choice. "Conscientious Objection and Refusal to Provide Reproductive Healthcare: A White Paper Examining Prevalence, Health Consequences, and Policy Responses." *International Journal of Gynecology and Obstetrics* 123 (December 10, 2013). https://doi.org/10.1016/S0020-7292(13)60002-8.

Chavkin, Wendy, Laurel Swerdlow, and Jocelyn Fifield. "Regulation of Conscientious Objection to Abortion." *Journal of Health and Human Rights* 19, no. 1 (June 2017): 55–68.

Chisholm, Shirley. *Unbought and Unbossed*. Hodge Taylor Associates, 1970.

Chretian, Spencer. *Project 2025*. The Heritage Foundation, January 31, 2023.

Cisler, Lucinda. "Unfinished Business: Birth Control and Women's Liberation." In *Sisterhood Is Powerful: An Anthology of Writings from the Women's Liberation Movement*, edited by Robyn Morgan. Vintage Books, 1970.

Clements, KC. "6 Tips for Making Your Conversations about Reproductive Rights More Inclusive." *Everyday Feminism*, October 29, 2018. https://everydayfeminism.com/2018/10/6-tips-for-making-your-conversations-about-reproductive-rights-more-trans-inclusive/.

Coates, Rodney. "What Is the Great Replacement Theory? A Scholar of Race Relations Explains." *The Conversation*, March 15, 2024.

Cohen, Adam. *Imbeciles: The Supreme Court, American Eugenics, and the Sterilization of Carrie Buck*. Penguin, 2016.

COLOR. "Urging a Human Rights and Justice-Based Approach to Environmental Protection." *DifferenTakes* 93 (Fall 2018).

Committee for Abortion Rights and Against Sterilization Abuse (CARASA), "Women Under Attack: Abortion, Sterilization Abuse, and Reproductive Freedom," 1979, 52.

Commonwealth Fund. "The U.S. Maternal Health Divide: The Limited Maternal Health Services and Worse Outcomes of States Proposing New

Abortion Restrictions." *Commonwealth Fund, Issue Briefs*, December 14, 2022. www.commonwealthfund.org/publications/issue-briefs/2022/dec/us-maternal-health-divide-limited-services-worse-outcomes.

Contorno, Steve. "DeSantis Signs into Law Restrictions on Trans Floridians' Access to Treatments and Bathrooms." CNN, May 17, 2023.

———. "Trump Claims Not to Know Who Is behind Project 2025. A CNN Review Found at Least 140 People Who Worked for Him Are Involved." CNN, July 11, 2024.

Cooper, Brittany. *Eloquent Rage: A Black Feminist Discovers Her Superpower.* St. Martin's Press, 2018.

Copelon, Rhonda. "From Privacy to Autonomy: The Condition for Sexual and Reproductive Freedom." In *From Abortion to Reproductive Freedom: Transforming a Movement*, edited by Marlene Fried. South End Press, 1990.

Costello, Daniel. "Is CRACK Wack?" *Salon*, April 8, 2003. www.salon.com/2003/04/08/crack_4/.

Crane, Barbara B., and Emily A. Maistrellis. "The Role of Abortion in Population Policies." In *International Handbook of Population Policies*, edited by J. F. May, John F. Goldstone, and Jack A. Goldstone. Springer, 2022.

Crenshaw, Kimberlé. "Mapping the Margins: Intersectionality, Identity Politics, and Violence against Women of Color." *Stanford Law Review* 43, no. 6 (1991): 1241–99. https://doi.org/10.2307/1229039.

Cyr, Julian, and Rebecca Hart Holder. "Simultaneous Attacks on Abortion and LGBTQ Rights Are Not Coincidental." *Cognoscenti*, April 26, 2022. www.wbur.org/cognoscenti/2022/04/26/abortion-rights-lgbtq-rights-roe-vs-wade-julian-cyr-rebecca-hart-holder.

Davis, Angela. *Women, Race, and Class.* Vintage, 1981.

Davis, Dána-Ain. *Reproductive Injustice: Racism, Pregnancy, and Premature Birth.* New York University Press, 2019.

Davis, Susan E. *Women under Attack: Victories, Backlash and the Fight for Reproductive Freedom.* South End Press, 1999.

Dawkins, Richard. "Abortion & Down Syndrome: An Apology for Letting Slip the Dogs of Twitterwar." Richard Dawkins Foundation for Reason and Science, August 21, 2014.

"Dawnland." PBS documentary, 2018. https://upstanderproject.org/individual.

de Londras, Fiona. "Corrigendum to 'The Impact of "Conscientious Objection" on Abortion-Related Outcomes: A Synthesis of Legal and Health Evidence.'" *Health Policy*, March 2023. https://doi.org/10.1016/j.healthpol.2023.104757.

Demillo, Andrew. "Judge Rules Arkansas Ban on Gender-Affirming Care for Transgender Minors Violates the U.S. Constitution." AP News, June 20, 2023.

DesRoches, Angele. "Conceivable Possibilities: Space, Stigma and Subjectivity." In *Crossing Troubled Waters: Abortion in Ireland and Prince Edward Island*, edited by Colleen MacQuarrie, Claire Pierson, Shannon Stettner, and Fiona Bloomer. Island Studies Press, 2018.

Dhanraj, Deepa, dir. "Something Like a War." Documentary film, 1991. www.wmm.com/catalog/film/something-like-a-war/.

Dixon, Ericka Ayodele. "Disability, Dobbs and a Black Perspective." In *Fighting Mad: Resisting the End of Roe v. Wade*, edited by Krystale E. Littlejohn and Rickie Solinger. University of California Press, 2024.

Dixon-Mueller, Ruth, and Adrienne Germain. "Population Policy and Feminist Political Action in Three Developing Countries." *Population and Development Review* 20 (1994): 197–219. https://doi.org/10.2307/2807947.

Dolan, Eric W. "Mike Huckabee: Abortion an 'Incredible Holocaust of Our Own.'" *Raw Story*, February 23, 2013. www.rawstory.com/2013/02/huckabee-abortion-an-incredible-holocaust-of-our-own/.

Donegan, Moira. "White Nationalists Are Flocking to the U.S. Anti-abortion Movement." *The Guardian*, January 24, 2022.

Donovan, Patricia. "Judging Teenagers: How Minors Fare When They Seek Court-Authorized Abortions." *Family Planning Perspectives* 15, no. 6 (November–December 1983): 259–67. https://doi.org/10.2307/2135291.

Douthard, Regine A., Iman K. Martin, Theresa Chapple-McGruder, Ana Langer, and Soju Chang. "U.S. Maternal Mortality within a Global Context: Historical Trends, Current State, and Future Directions." *Journal of Women's Health* 30, no. 2 (2021): 168–77.

Dowe, Wendy. "The Traumas of Irwin Continue to Haunt Me: Non-Consensual Surgery Survivor Seeks Restitution, Calls to Shut Down Detention Centers." *Ms.*, December 9, 2021. https://msmagazine.com/2021/12/09/immigrants-ice-detention-center-georgia-irwin-women-reparations-sexual-violence/.

Drovetta, Raquel Irene. "Safe Abortion Information Hotlines: An Effective Strategy for Increasing Women's Access to Safe Abortions in Latin America." *Reproductive Health Matters* 23, no. 45 (2015). https://doi.org/10.1016/j.rhm.2015.06.004.

Dugdale-Pointon, T. "The Army of God." *History of War*, August 17, 2007. www.historyofwar.org/articles/weapons_army_of_god.html.

Dusenbery, Maya. "Can Storytelling Help Destroy Abortion Stigma?" *Pacific Standard*, June 14, 2017. https://psmag.com/social-justice/abortion-storytelling-may-reduce-stigma.

Eckholm, Erik, and Frances Robles. "Kansas Limits Abortion Method, Opening a New Line of Attack." *New York Times*, April 7, 2015. www.nytimes.com/2015/04/08/us/kansas-bans-common-second-trimester-abortion-procedure.html.

Editorial Board of the *New York Times*. "Slandering the Unborn." *New York Times*, December 28, 2018.

Edsall, Thomas B. "Abortion Has Never Been Just about Abortion." *New York Times*, September 15, 2021. www.nytimes.com/2021/09/15/opinion/abortion-evangelicals-conservatives.html.

Eeckhaut, Mieke C. W., and Yuko Hara. "Reproductive Oppression Enters the Twenty-First Century: Pressure to Use Long-Acting Reversible Contraception (LARC) in the Context of 'LARC First.'" *Socius: Sociological Research for a Dynamic World* 9 (June 22, 2023). doi.org/10.1177/23780231231180378.

Ehrlich, J. Shoshanna, and Alesha E. Doan. *Abortion Regret: The New Attack on Reproductive Freedom*. Praeger, 2019.

Einenkel, Walter. "Right-wing Iowa School Board Candidate Abruptly Withdraws. Guess Why." *Daily Kos*, September 23, 2021. www.dailykos.com/stories/2021/9/23/2054061/-Right-wing-Iowa-schoemailol-board-candidate-abruptly-withdraws-Guess-why.

Erdman, Joanna N., Kinga Jelinska, and Susan Yanow. "Understandings of Self-Managed Abortion as Health Inequity, Harm Reduction and Social Change." *Reproductive Health Matters* 26, no. 54 (2018): 13–19. https://doi.org/10.1080/09688080.2018.1511769.

Esfandiari, Negar, and Maddy McKeague. "Crossing the Intersection of Immigration and Reproductive Justice." *National Women's Health Network*, May 3, 2018. https://beyondthevessel.com/resources.

Estrada-Claudio, Sylvia. "The International Women and Health Meetings: Catalyst and End Product of the Global Feminist Health Movement." Workshop talk at the International Women and Health Meeting, "Transnationalization of Solidarities and Women's Movements," Université de Montréal, April 27–28, 2006. http://cccg.umontreal.ca/pdf/Sylvia%20Estrada-Claudio_en.pdf.

——— "What Binds Us?" Keynote speech at the "Abortion and Reproductive Justice: The Unfinished Revolution International Conference," Ulster University, June 2016. www.safeabortionwomensright.org/what-binds-us-read-the-speech-by-sylvia-estrada-claudio/.

"Eugenics and Scientific Racism." www.genome.gov/about-genomics/fact-sheets /Eugenics-and-Scientific-Racism.

European Disability Forum. "Forced Sterilization of People with Disabilities in the European Union." *European Disability Forum Report,* 2022. www .edf-feph.org/content/uploads/2022/09/Final-Forced-Sterilisarion-Report-2022-European-Union-copia_compressed.pdf.

Evon, Dan. "Did 125 Women Terminate Their Pregnancies during a Protest in South Korea?" September 15, 2018. www.snopes.com/fact-check/pregnancies-protest-south-korea/.

Farley, Audrey. "How Dismantling Welfare Continues the Legacy of Eugenics." *Washington Post,* September 17, 2019. www.washingtonpost.com/outlook /2019/09/17/how-dismantling-welfare-continues-legacy-eugenics/.

Feldscher, Karen. "Under Pressure: Latin American Women Faced Forced Sterilization." Interview with Tami Kendall, Harvard Chan School of Public Health, July 23, 2014. www.hsph.harvard.edu/news/features/latin-american-women-face-forced-sterilization/.

Fendley, Caitlin. "Eugenics Is Trending. That's a Problem." *Washington Post,* February 17, 2020. www.washingtonpost.com/outlook/2020/02/17/eugenics-is-trending-thats-problem/.

Feuer, Alan. "Proud Boys Lose Control of Their Name to a Black Church They Vandalized." *New York Times,* February 3, 2025.

Fiala, Christian, and Joyce H. Arthur. "Refusal to Treat Patients Does Not Work in Any Country—Even If Misleadingly Labeled 'Conscientious Objection.'" Letter to the editor, *Health and Human Rights Journal* 19, no. 2 (2017): 299–302. www.researchgate.net/publication/322114794.

———. "There Is No Defence for 'Conscientious Objection' in Reproductive Health Care." *European Journal of Obstetrics and Gynecology and Reproductive Biology* 216 (September 2017): 254–58. https://doi.org/10.1016/j.ejogrb.2017 .07.023.

Fiala, Christian, Kristina Gemzell Danielsson, Oskari Heikinheimo, Jens A. Gudmundsson, and Joyce Arthur. "Yes We Can! Successful Examples of Disallowing 'Conscientious Objection' in Reproductive Health Care." *European Journal of Contraception and Reproductive Health Care* 21, no. 3 (2016): 201–6. https://doi.org/10.3109/13625187.2016.1138458.

Figueroa, Ariana. "Migrant Women Endured Medical Mistreatment at Georgia ICE Facility, U.S. Senate Report Finds." *Iowa Capital Dispatch,* November 15, 2022.

Finer, Louise, and Johanna B. Fine. "Abortion Laws around the World: Progress and Pushback." *American Journal of Public Health* 103, no. 4 (April 2013): 585–89. https://doi.org/10.2105/AJPH.2012.301197.

Fisher, Brian. "Abortion: The Most Devastating Genocide in History." *Human Coalition*, 2018. www.humancoalition.org/2018/02/26/abortion-devastating-genocide-history/.

Fitzgerald, Madeline. "Countries with the Most Restrictive Abortion Bans." *US News and World Report*, July 13, 2022. www.usnews.com/news/best-countries/slideshows/countries-with-the-most-restrictive-abortion-laws.

Follet, Joyce. *Roots of Reproductive Justice: 500 Years of Movement Stories*. https://rootsofrj.org.

Forde, Kathy Roberts, and Byron Bowman. "Exploiting Black Labor after Slavery." *The Conversation*, February 6, 2017. https://theconversation.com/exploiting-black-labor-after-the-abolition-of-slavery-72482.

Foster, Angel. "Medication Abortion: A Guide For Health Professionals." IBIS Reproductive Health. www.ibisreproductivehealth.org/sites/default/files/files/publications/Med_ab_A_guide_for_health_professionals_English.pdf.

Foster, Diana Greene. *The Turnaway Study: Ten Years, a Thousand Women, and the Consequences of Having—or Being Denied—an Abortion*. Advancing New Standards in Reproductive Health (ANSIRH), June 2020.

Frank, Gillian, and Neil J. Young. "What Everyone Gets Wrong about Evangelicals and Abortion." *Washington Post*, May 16, 2022. www.washingtonpost.com/outlook/2022/05/16/what-everyone-gets-wrong-about-evangelicals-abortion/.

Fried, Marlene. "Reproductive Rights Activism in the Post-Roe Era." *American Journal of Public Health* 103, no. 1 (January 2013). https://doi.org/10.2105/AJPH.2012.301125.

Fried, Marlene, Loretta Ross, and Rickie Solinger. "Understanding Reproductive Justice: A Response to O'Brien." *Rewire News*, May 8, 2013. https://rewire.news/article/2013/05/08/understanding-reproductive-justice-a-response-to-obrien/.

Fuentes, Liza. "Inequity in US Abortion Rights and Access: The End of Roe Is Deepening Existing Divides." *Guttmacher Policy Analysis*, January 2023. www.guttmacher.org/2023/01/inequity-us-abortion-rights-and-access-end-roe-deepening-existing-divides.

Fung, Lauren, and Leana Lacy. "A Look at the Past, Present, and Future of Black Midwifery in the United States." *Urban Wire*, May 18, 2023. www

.urban.org/urban-wire/look-past-present-and-future-black-midwifery-united-states.

Furedi, Ann. *The Moral Case for Abortion.* Palgrave Macmillan, 2016.

Galpern, Emily. "Social Justice Coalition Key to Success in California's New Sterilization Compensation Program: From Budget Allocation to Rollout." Center for Genetics and Society, January 26, 2022. www.geneticsandsociety .org/biopolitical-times/social-justice-coalition-key-success-californias-new-sterilization-compensation.

Ganatra, Bela, Phillip Guest, and Marge Berer. "Expanding Access to Medical Abortion: Challenges and Opportunities." *Reproductive Health Matters* 22, sup. 44 (2014): 1–3. https://doi.org/10.1016/S0968-8080(14)43793-5.

Gandy, Imani. "The Forgotten Story of How Voting Rights Drive Abortion Access." *Rewire News*, September 20, 2021. https://rewirenewsgroup .com/2021/09/20/the-forgotten-story-of-how-voting-rights-drive-abortion -access/.

"Genocide in Mississippi." Created by the Student Nonviolent Coordinating Committee (SNCC), in the Digital Collections at the University of Southern Mississippi. https://usm.access.preservica.com/uncategorized /IO_fb32ec67-517f-46df-819b-8704c87cb0dc.

Geronimus, Arline. *Weathering: The Extraordinary Stress of Ordinary Life in an Unjust Society.* Little Brown Spark, 2023.

Getahun, Hannah. "'I Would Die': People with Disabilities Say Abortion Bans Could Have Fatal Consequences." *Business Insider,* July 31, 2022.

Ghandakly, Elizabeth C., and Rachel Fabi. "Sterilization in US Immigration and Customs Enforcement's (ICE's) Detention: Ethical Failures and Systemic Injustice." *American Journal of Public Health* 111, no. 5 (May 2021): 832–34. https://doi.org/10.2105/AJPH.2021.306186.

Gilles, Nellie, Sarah Kramer, and Joe Richman. "Before Roe, the Women of Jane Provided Abortions for the Women of Chicago." *NPR Radio Diaries*, January 19, 2018. www.npr.org/2018/01/19/578620266/before-roe-v-wade-the-women-of-jane-provided-abortions-for-the-women-of-chicago.

Gold, Rachel Benson, and Megan K. Donovan. "Lessons from before Abortion Was Legal." *Scientific American* 317, no. 3 (September 1, 2017): 58. www.scientificamerican.com/article/lessons-from-before-abortion-was-legal/.

Goldman, Ari L. "Catholic Bishops Hire Firms to Market Fight on Abortion." *New York Times*, April 6, 1990. www.nytimes.com/1990/04/06/us/catholic -bishops-hire-firms-to-market-fight-on-abortion.html.

Gone, Joseph P. "Indigenous Historical Trauma: Alter-Native Explanations for Mental Health Inequities." *Daedalus* 152, no. 4 (2023): 130–50. https://doi.org/10.1162/daed_a_02035.

Gonzales, Matt. "Race and Roe: Black Women Talk Effects of Court Decision." *SHRM*, July 11, 2022. www.shrm.org/topics-tools/news/inclusion-diversity/race-roe-black-women-talk-effects-court-decision.

Goodwin, Michele. "The Racist History of Abortion and Midwifery Bans." *ACLU News & Commentary*, 2020. www.aclu.org/news/racial-justice/the-racist-history-of-abortion-and-midwifery-bans.

Gordon, Linda. *The Moral Property of Women: A History of Birth Control Politics in America*. University of Illinois Press, 2002.

Gottesdiener, Laura. "'Feeling Free': Women Criminalized by Mexico's Abortion Bans Celebrate Ruling." Reuters, September 9, 2021. www.reuters.com/world/americas/feeling-free-women-criminalized-by-mexicos-abortion-bans-celebrate-ruling-2021-09-09/.

Green, Fletcher M. "Documenting the American South." In *Ferry Hill Plantation Journal, January 4, 1838–January 15, 1839*, 25–26. University of North Carolina Press, 1998. Originally published in 1961.

Greenhouse, Linda, and Reva B. Siegel. "Before Roe v. Wade: Voices That Shaped the Abortion Debate before the Supreme Court's Ruling (2012)." Yale Law School, Public Law Working Paper no. 257. https://ssrn.com/abstract=2131505, http://dx.doi.org/10.2139/ssrn.2131505.

Greenlee, Cynthia. "Race, Rubella, and the Long Road to Abortion Reform." *Scalawag Magazine*, February 18, 2016. www.scalawagmagazine.org/2016/02/race-rubella-abortion.

Gumbs, Alexis Pauline, China Martens, and Mai'a Williams, eds. *Revolutionary Mothering: Love on the Front Lines*. PM Press, 2016.

Gupta, Alisha Haridasani. "How 'Weathering' Contributes to Racial Health Disparities." *New York Times*, April 14, 2023. www.nytimes.com/2023/04/12/well/live/weathering-health-racism discrimination.html.

Gurr, Barbara. *Reproductive Justice: The Politics of Health Care for Native American Women*. Rutgers University Press, 2015.

Gutiérrez, Elena. *Fertile Matters: The Politics of Mexican-Origin Women's Reproduction*. University of Texas Press, 2008.

Guttmacher Institute. "Abortion Bans in Cases of Sex or Race Selection or Genetic Anomaly." Last modified August 2023. www.guttmacher.org/state-policy/explore/abortion-bans-cases-sex-or-race-selection-or-genetic-anomaly.

————. "How Project 2025 Seeks to Obliterate Sexual and Reproductive Health and Rights." Fact sheet, October 2024. www.guttmacher.org/fact-sheet/how-project-2025-seeks-obliterate-srhr.

————. "Interactive Map: US Abortion Policies after Roe, as of October 1, 2024." https://states.guttmacher.org/policies/arizona/abortion-policies.

————. "State Bans on Abortion throughout Pregnancy." October 7, 2024. www.guttmacher.org/state-policy/explore/state-policies-later-abortions.

————. "State Funding of Abortion under Medicaid, as of August 31, 2023." www.guttmacher.org/state-policy/explore/state-funding-abortion-under-medicaid.

Hansen, Randall, and Desmond King. *Sterilized by the State: Eugenics, Race, and the Population Scare in Twentieth-Century North America.* Cambridge University Press, 2013.

Hardisty, Jean. *Mobilizing Resentment: Conservative Resurgence from the John Birch Society to the Promise Keepers.* Beacon Press, 1999.

Hargrett, Elizabeth. "Eugenics in Georgia." *New Georgia Encyclopedia.* www.georgiaencyclopedia.org/articles/government-politics/eugenics-in-georgia/. Last modified August 21, 2019.

Harned, Elizabeth, and Liza Fuentes. "Abortion Out of Reach: The Exacerbation of Wealth Disparities after Dobbs v. Jackson Women's Health Organization." *Guttmacher Policy Analysis*, January 2023. www.guttmacher.org/article/2023/01/abortion-out-reach-exacerbation-wealth-disparities-after-dobbs-v-jackson-womens. First published in American Bar Association's *Human Rights Magazine*, January 25, 2023.

Harries, Jane. "Briefing: Barriers to Safe and Legal Abortion in South Africa." *Amnesty International Publications*, 2017. https://amnesty.org.za/wp-content/uploads/2018/06/Womens-rights-Briefing-Barriers-to-Safe-and-Legal-Abortion-in-South-Africa-2017_Web.pdf.

Harries, Jane, Diane Copper, Anna Strebel, and Christopher J. Colvin. "Conscientious Objection and Its Impact on Abortion Service Provision in South Africa: A Qualitative Study." *Reproductive Health* 11, no. 16 (2014). https://doi.org/10.1186/1742-4755-11-16.

Harris, Cheryl I. "Whiteness as Property." *Harvard Law Review* 106, no. 8 (1993): 1707–91. https://doi.org/10.2307/1341787.

Harris, Jasmine. "Why *Buck v. Bell* Still Matters." *Bill of Health*, October 14, 2020. https://blog.petrieflom.law.harvard.edu/2020/10/14/why-buck-v-bell-still-matters/.

Hartmann, Betsy. *The America Syndrome: Apocalypse, War, and Our Call to Greatness*. Seven Stories Press, 2017.

———. "Population Control: Birth of an Ideology." *International Journal of Health Services* 27, no. 3 (1997): 523–40. www.jstor.org/stable/45130847.

———. *Reproductive Rights and Wrongs: The Global Politics of Population Control*, 3rd ed. Haymarket Books, 2016.

Hartmann, Betsy, Banu Subramaniam, Charles Zerner, Alan Goodman, and Jeanne Guillemin. *Making Threats: Biofears and Environmental Anxieties*. Rowman & Littlefield, 2005.

Hayes, Joseph, Justin Goss, Heather Harris, and Alexandria Gumbs. "California's Prison Population." UC Riverside Presley Center of Crime and Justice Studies fact sheet, July 2019. https://presleycenter.ucr.edu/article-compendium/2019/07/01/californias-prison-population-2019.

Heller, Fernando. "Spanish Lawmakers Approve Abortion, Transgender Rights Reforms." *Euractiv*, February 17, 2023. www.euractiv.com/section/politics/news/spanish-lawmakers-approve-abortion-transgender-rights-reforms/.

Hendrixson, Anne, in collaboration with Ellen E. Foley, Rajani Bhatia, Daniel Bendix, Susanne Schultz, Kalpana Wilson, and Wangui Kimari. "A Renewed Call for Feminist Resistance to Population Control." University at Albany, State University of New York Scholars Archive, Fall 2019.

Henry, Nina. "Suffrage and the Fight for Reproductive Justice." *Jewish Women's Archive*, June 9, 2020. https://jwa.org/blog/suffrage/suffrage-and-fight-reproductive-justice.

Herbst, Diane. "'Like an Experimental Concentration Camp': Women at Detention Center Report High Numbers of Hysterectomies." *People*, September 15, 2020.

The Heritage Foundation. "Project 2025: Commentary by Spencer Chretien." www.heritage.org/conservatism/commentary/project-2025.

Hessini, Leila. "A Learning Agenda for Abortion Stigma: Recommendations from the Bellagio Expert Group Meeting." September 25, 2014. https://doi.org/10.1080/03630242.2014.919987.

Hodes, Martha. *White Women, Black Men: Illicit Sex in the Nineteenth-Century South*. Yale University Press, 1997.

hooks, bell. *Ain't I a Woman*. South End Press, 1999.

Horowitz. Helen L. *Rereading Sex: Battles over Sexual Knowledge and Suppression in Nineteenth-Century America*. Knopf, 2002.

"How Women Shaped the Universal Declaration of Human Rights." Robert F. Kennedy Human Rights, March 2, 2023. https://rfkhumanrights.org

/voices-articles/how-women-shaped-the-universal-declaration-of-human-rights.

Howe, Amy. "Justices Will Review Lower-Court Ruling on Access to Abortion Pill." *Scotus Blog*, December 13, 2023. www.scotusblog.com/2023/12/justices-will-review-lower-court-ruling-on-access-to-abortion-pill/.

"Human Rights Crisis: Abortion in the United States after Dobbs." Human Rights Watch, April 18, 2023. www.hrw.org/news/2023/04/18/human-rights-crisis-abortion-united-states-after-dobbs.

Human Rights Watch. "Amicus Curiae in Case Beatriz and Others v. El Salvador." April 7, 2023. www.hrw.org/news/2024/06/17/human-rights-watch-amicus-curiae-case-beatriz-and-others-v-el-salvador.

———. "Letter from Human Rights Watch to the Government of Nicaragua: re Women's and Girls' Health in Nicaragua." June 30, 2017. www.hrw.org/news/2017/07/31/letter-human-rights-watch-government-nicaragua.

———. "World Report 2022." www.hrw.org/previous-world-reports.

Hyde, Sue, ed. *Women under Attack: Victories, Backlash and the Fight for Reproductive Freedom*. South End Press, 1988.

"ICE, a Whistleblower and Forced Sterilization." *1A*, September 22, 2020. www.npr.org/2020/09/18/914465793/ice-a-whistleblower-and-forced-sterilization.

Imani [Barbarin]. "#MyDisabilityIsWorthy." *Crutches & Spice*, January 26, 2022. https://crutchesandspice.com/2022/01/26/%EF%BF%BCi-started-mydisabledlifeisworthy-heres-why-the-response-from-nondisabled-people-and-medical-professionals-should-alarm-you/.

Indiana Eugenics: History and Legacy, 1907–2007. Indiana University, Scholar Works. Website archived at https://hdl.handle.net/1805/384.

"Information Collection Request on Consent for Sterilization Form (937 0166)." Archived April 18, 2022, at www.hivlawandpolicy.org/sites/default/files/Comments%20on%20Sterilization%20Consent%20Form%2C%20NHeLP%202022.pdf.

International Campaign for Women's Right to Safe Abortion. "Spain—Minister for Equality Plans to Remove Abortion Barriers." July 20, 2021. www.safeabortionwomensright.org/news/spain-minister-for-equality-plans-to-remove-abortion-barriers/.

Jayapal, Pramila. "House Passes Jayapal Resolution Condemning Unwanted, Unnecessary Medical Procedures Performed on Immigrant Women without Their Consent at the Irwin County Detention Center." October 2, 2020. https://jayapal.house.gov/2020/10/02/house-condemns-forced-medical-procedures/.

Jelinska, Kinga, and Susan Yanow. "Putting Abortion Pills into Women's Hands: Realizing the Full Potential of Medical Abortion." *Contraception* 89 (2018): 86–89. https://doi.org/10.1016/j.contraception.2017.05.019.

Jesudason, Sujatha, and Julia Epstein. "The Paradox of Disability in Abortion Debates: Bringing the Pro-Choice and Disability Rights Communities Together." *Contraception* 84, no. 6 (2011): 541–43. www.contraceptionjournal.org/article/S0010-7824(11)00519-1/abstract.

Joffe, Carole. *Doctors of Conscience: The Struggle to Provide Abortion before and after Roe v. Wade.* Beacon Press, 1995.

Joffe, Carole, and Jody Steinauer. "Even Texas Allows Abortion to Protect a Woman's Life. Or Does It?" *New York Times*, September 21, 2021. www.nytimes.com/2021/09/12/opinion/abortion-texas-roe.html/.

Johnson, Corey G. "California Bans Coerced Sterilization of Female Inmates." *Reveal*, September 26, 2014. https://revealnews.org/article-legacy/california-bans-coerced-sterilization-of-female-inmates/.

———. "California Prison Doctor Linked to Sterilizations No Stranger to Controversy." *Reveal*, February 13, 2014. https://revealnews.org/article/calif-prison-doctor-linked-to-sterilizations-no-stranger-to-controversy-2/.

———. "Female Inmates Sterilized in California Prisons without Approval." Center for Investigative Reporting, July 7, 2013. https://revealnews.org/article/female-inmates-sterilized-in-california-prisons-without-approval/.

———. "Female Prison Inmates Sterilized Illegally, California Audit Confirms." *Reveal*, July 7, 2013. https://revealnews.org/article/female-prison-inmates-sterilized-illegally-california-audit-confirms/.

Josefson Deborah. "Oregon's Governor Apologises for Forced Sterilisations." *British Medical Journal* 325, no. 7377 (December 2002). https://doi.org/10.1136/bmj.325.7377.1380/b.

Jurasz, Olga, and Fleur van Leeuwen. "Women's Rights Are Human Rights: The Practice of the United Nations Human Rights Committee and the Committee on Economic, Social and Cultural Rights." *Human Rights Law Review* 11, no. 2 (June 2011): 414–17. https://doi.org/10.1093/hrlr/ngr007.

Kafer, Alison. "Using Disability and Access Statements to Get Resources for Students with Disabilities." In *Fighting Mad: Resisting the End of Roe v. Wade*, edited by Krystale E. Littlejohn and Rickie Solinger. University of California Press, 2024.

Kaiser Family Foundation (KFF). "The Availability and Use of Medication Abortion." March 20, 2024 (updated October 7, 2024). www.kff.org

/womens-health-policy/fact-sheet/the-availability-and-use-of-medication-abortion/.

———. "The Mexico City Policy: An Explainer." January 28, 2021. www.kff .org/global-health-policy/fact-sheet/mexico-city-policy-explainer/.

Kajstura, Aleks, and Wendy Sawyer. "Women's Mass Incarceration: The Whole Pie 2024." Prison Policy Initiative, March 5, 2024. www.prisonpolicy .org/reports/pie2024women.html.

Kalantry, Sital. *Women's Human Rights and Migration: Sex-Selective Abortion Laws in the United States and India.* University of Pennsylvania Press, 2017.

Kaplan, Laura. *The Story of Jane: The Legendary Underground Feminist Abortion Service.* University of Chicago Press, 2019.

Katella, Kathy. "Maternal Mortality Is on the Rise: 8 Things to Know." *Yale Medicine,* May 22, 2023. www.yalemedicine.org/news/maternal-mortality-on-the-rise.

Kavattu, Purvaja S., Somjen Frazer, Abby El-Shafei, Kayt Tiskus, Laura Laderman, Lindsey Hull, Fikayo Walter-Johnson, Dana Sussman, and Lynn M. Paltrow. "The Rise of Pregnancy Criminalization: A Pregnancy Justice Report." Pregnancy Justice, September 2023.

Kendall, Tami, and Claire Albert. "Experiences of Coercion to Sterilize and Forced Sterilization among Women Living with HIV in Latin America." *Journal of the International AIDS Society* 18, no. 1 (March 2015): 19462. https:// doi.org/10.7448/IAS.18.1.19462.

Kenny, Emma, and Emily Bloom. "Explainer: The Crucial Fight for Legal Gender Recognition." *International IDEA,* April 3, 2023. www.idea.int/blog /explainer-crucial-fight-legal-gender-recognition.

Kevles, Daniel. "Eugenics and Human Rights." *British Medical Journal* 319, no. 7207 (1999): 435–38. https://doi:10.1136/bmj.319.7207.435.

———. *In the Name of Eugenics: Genetics and the Uses of Human Heredity.* Harvard University Press, 1995.

Kigvamasud'vashti, Theryn. "Fact Sheet on Positive Prevention / CRACK (Children Requiring a Caring Kommunity)." https://libraries.smith.edu /special-collections/about/sophia-smith-collection-womens-history. Last updated February 12, 2002.

Kim, Sunhye, Na Young, and Yurim Lee. "The Role of Reproductive Justice Movements in Challenging South Korea's Abortion Ban." *Health and Human Rights Journal* 21, no. 2 (December 2019): 97–105. www.ncbi.nlm.nih.gov /pmc/articles/PMC6927381/pdf/hhr-21-02-097.pdf.

Kitchener, Caroline. "Covert Network Provides Pills for Thousands of Abortions in U.S. Post Roe." *Washington Post*, October 18, 2022. www.washington post.com/politics/2022/10/18/illegal-abortion-pill-network/.

Kluchin, Rebecca M. *Fit to Be Tied: Sterilization and Reproductive Rights in America, 1950–1980*. Rutgers University Press, 2009.

Knudson, Lara. *Reproductive Rights in a Global Context*. Vanderbilt University Press, 2006.

Kornbluh, Felicia. *A Woman's Life Is a Human Life: My Mother, Our Neighbor, and the Journey from Reproductive Rights to Reproductive Justice*. Grove Press, 2023.

Kozhimannil, Katy Backes, Asha Hassan, and Rachel R. Hardeman. "Abortion Access as a Racial Justice Issue." *New England Journal of Medicine* 387, no. 17 (2022). https://doi.org/10.1056/NEJMp2209737.

Krishnan, Shweta. "The London Declaration of Prochoice Principles." Asia Safe Abortion Partnership, January 3, 2013. https://asap-asia.org/blog /london-declaration-of-prochoice-principles/.

Krištopaitytė, Eglė. "Strip-Search of Polish Woman Who Had Abortion Sparks Outcry." *Health News*, July 26, 2023. www.safeabortionwomensright .org/news/poland-polish-court-rejects-womans-claim-against-police-who-made-her-strip-after-taking-abortion-pills/.

Kumar, Anu. "Combating Abortion Stigma Requires More Than Just Storytelling." *Rewire News*, January 14, 2015. https://rewirenewsgroup.com/2015 /01/14/combating-abortion-stigma-requires-more-than-just-storytelling/.

Largent, Mark A. *Breeding Contempt: The History of Coerced Sterilization in the United States*. Rutgers University Press, 2008.

Larrea, Sara, Camila Hidalgo, Constanza Jacques-Aviñó, Carme Borrell, and Laia Palència. "'No One Should Be Alone in Living This Process': Trajectories, Experiences and User's Perceptions about Quality of Abortion Care in a Telehealth Service in Chile." *Sexual and Reproductive Health Matters* 29, no. 3 (2021). https://doi.org/10.1080/26410397.2021.1948953.

Leavitt, Judith Walzer. "Under the Shadow of Maternity: American Women's Responses to Death and Debility Fears in Nineteenth-Century Childbirth." *Feminist Studies* 12, no. 1 (Spring 1986).

Lee, Catherine. "Where the Danger Lies: Race, Gender, and Chinese and Japanese Exclusion in the United States, 1870–1924." *Sociological Forum*, May 2010. https://doi.org/10.1111/j.1573-7861.2010.01175.x.

Lee, Jaeah, and Molly Redde. "Meet 330 Lawmakers Who Made 2013 'A Terrible Year for Women's Health.'" *Mother Jones*, January 27, 2014. www

.motherjones.com/politics/2014/01/state-legislators-sponsored-abortion-restriction-2014/.

Leonard, Sarah. "While Pro-Choice Politics Collapsed, Organizers Took a Different Approach." *Lux Magazine, 5.* https://lux-magazine.com/article/the-next-abortion-strategy/.

Levins, Savannah, and Meilin Tompkins. "Report: Controversial Push to Keep Drug Addicts from Having Children." WCNC, Charlotte, May 30, 2019. www.wcnc.com/article/news/report-controversial-push-to-keep-drug-addicts-from-having-children/275-b828db54–3d47–49d5-bad1–1fa270c300e0.

Lewis, David D. "Stop Perpetuating the 'Crack Baby' Myth." Brown University News Service, March 29, 2004. www.brown.edu/Administration/News_Bureau/2003-04/03-099.html.

Lewis, Talila A. "Ableism 2020: An Updated Definition." January 25, 2020. www.talilalewis.com/blog/ableism-2020-an-updated-definition.

Lira, Natalie Lira. *Laboratories of Deficiency: Sterilization and Confinement in California, 1900–1950.* University of California Press, 2022.

Littlefield, Amy, and Heron Greenesmith. "Fresh Off Victory against Roe, the Religious Right Is Pushing a Record Number of Anti-Trans Bills." *The Nation,* January 31, 2023. www.thenation.com/article/society/transgender-abortion-rights-attacks/.

Lopez, Destiny. "Guttmacher Leadership Speaks Out against Attacks on Medication Abortion." March 26, 2024. www.guttmacher.org/2024/03/guttmacher-leadership-speaks-out-against-attacks-medication-abortion.

Lovet, Laura L. *Conceiving the Future: Pronatalism, Reproduction, and the Family in the United States, 1890–1938.* University of North Carolina Press, 2009.

Lubrano, Alfred. "Rate of Births to White Single Moms Accelerates." *Philadelphia Inquirer,* November 12, 2018. www.inquirer.com/philly/news/unwed-white-mothers-babies-marriage-philadelphia-poverty-women-20181112.html.

Luker, Kristen. *Abortion and the Politics of Motherhood.* University of California Press, 1984.

Luna, Zakiya. *Reproductive Rights as Human Rights: Women of Color and the Fight for Reproductive Justice.* New York University Press, 2020.

Luna, Zakiya, and Kristin Luker. "Reproductive Justice." *Annual Review of Law and Social Science* 9 (2013): 327–52. https://ssrn.com/abstract=2350738, http://dx.doi.org/10.1146/annurev-lawsocsci-102612-134037.

MacDorman, Marian F., Marie Thoma, Eugene Declercq, and Elizabeth A. Howell. "Racial and Ethnic Disparities in Maternal Mortality in the United States Using Enhanced Vital Records, 2016–2017." *American Journal of Public Health* III, no. 9 (September 1, 2021): 1673–81. https://doi.org/10.2105/AJPH.2021.306375.

MacQuarrie, Colleen. "Feminist Liberation Psychology: Animating Systemic Change on Abortion Access in PEI." In *Crossing Troubled Waters: Abortion in Ireland and Prince Edward Island*, edited by Colleen MacQuarrie, Claire Pierson, Shannon Stettner, and Fiona Bloomer. Island Studies Press, 2018.

Makleff, Shelly, Ana Labandera, Fernanda Chirbao, Jennifer Friedman, Roosbelinda Cardenas, Eleuthera Sa, and Sarah E. Baum. "Experience Obtaining Legal Abortion in Uruguay: Knowledge, Attitudes, and Stigma among Abortion Clients." *BMC Women's Health*, 2019. https://doi.org/10.1186/s12905-019-0855-6.

Mallory, Christy, and Elana Redfield. "The Impact of 2023 Legislation on Transgender Youth." UCLA School of Law, Williams Institute, October 2023. https://williamsinstitute.law.ucla.edu/wp-content/uploads/Trans-Legislation-Summary-Oct-2023.pdf.

Mancini, Susanna, and Kristina Stoeckl. "Transatlantic Conversations: The Emergence of Society-Protective Antiabortion Arguments in the United States, Europe, and Russia." In *The Conscience Wars: Rethinking the Balance between Religion, Identity, and Equality*, edited by S. Mancini and M. Rosenfeld. Cambridge University Press, 2018. https://doi.org/10.1017/9781316780053.

Manion, Maya. "Immigration Detention and Coerced Sterilization: History Tragically Repeats Itself." *ACLU News & Commentary*, September 29, 2020. www.aclu.org/news/immigrants-rights/immigration-detention-and-coerced-sterilization-history tragically-repeats-itself.

Martin, Lisa A., Michelle Debbink, Jane Hassinger, Emily Youatt, and Lisa H. Harris. "Abortion Providers, Stigma and Professional Quality of Life." *Contraception* 90, no. 6 (December 2014): 581–87. https://doi.org/10.1016/j.contraception.2014.07.011.

Martinez, Elizabeth "Betita." "What Is White Supremacy?" *Catalyst Project*, 2017.

Mason, Carol. *Killing for Life: The Apocalyptic Narrative of Pro-Life Politics*. Cornell University Press, 2002.

Mason, Carol, and Alex Dibranco. "The Long History of the Anti-Abortion Movement's Links to White Supremacists." *The Nation*, February 2020. www.thenation.com/article/politics/anti-abortion-white-supremacy/.

Matson, Erin. "Reproductive Justice Activists Must Combat Anti-Choicers' False Push for Disability Rights." *Rewire News*, September 14, 2014. https://rewirenewsgroup.com/2014/09/24/reproductive-justice-activists-must-combat-anti-choicers-false-push-disability-rights/.

McCann, Allison, and Amy Schoenfeld Walker. "Tracking Abortion Bans across the Country." *New York Times*, November 6, 2024. www.nytimes.com/interactive/2024/us/abortion-laws-roe-v-wade.html.

McDonald, Henry. "Pro-Choice Irish Women Go Public on Being 'Exiled' by Need for an Abortion." *The Guardian*, December 10, 2015. www.theguardian.com/world/2015/dec/10/pro-choice-irish-women-go-public-exiled-need-for-abortion.

McMahon, Aisling, and Bríd Ní Ghráinne. "After the 8th: Ireland, Abortion, and International Law." *Medico-Legal Journal of Ireland*, 2019. www.academia.edu/37625326/After_the_8th_Ireland_Abortion_and_International_Law.

Media Matters. "Doctors Who Provide Gender-Affirming Care Should Be Executed." *Media Matters Daily Wire*, February 22, 2023. www.mediamatters.org/matt-walsh/daily-wire-host-doctors-who-provide-gender-affirming-care-should-be-executed.

Medosch, Emily. "Not Just ICE: Forced Sterilization in the United States." *Immigration and Human Rights Law Review*, May 28, 2021. https://lawblogs.uc.edu/ihrlr/2021/05/28/not-just-ice-forced-sterilization-in-the-united-states/.

Merchant, Emily Klancher. "How Foundations Got the U.S. Government Invested in International Population Control." *Journal of the History of Philosophy*, June 24, 2016. https://histphil.org/2016/06/24/how-foundations-got-the-u-s-government-invested-in-international-population-control/.

Mihalovich, Cayla. "Survivors from California's Period of Forced Sterilization Denied Reparations." KQED, November 1, 2023. www.kqed.org/news/11965926/survivors-of-californias-forced-sterilization-denied-reparations.

Miller, Cassie. "Male Supremacy Is at the Core of the Hard Right's Agenda." Southern Poverty Law Center, April 18, 2023. www.splcenter.org/hatewatch/2023/04/18/male-supremacy-core-hard-rights-agenda.

Mills, Charles. *The Racial Contract.* Cornell University Press, 1997.

Mizes-Tan, Sarah. "For Decades, California Forcibly Sterilized Women under Eugenics Law. Now, the State Will Pay Survivors." *CapRadio*, July 20, 2021. www.capradio.org/articles/2021/07/20/for-decades-california-forcibly-sterilized-women-under-eugenics-law-now-the-state-will-pay-survivors/.

Mohr, James C. *Abortion in America: The Origins and Evolution of National Policy.* Oxford University Press, 1978.

Moloney, Anastasia. "Haunted by Forced Sterilizations, Peruvian Women Pin Hopes on Court Hearing." Reuters, January 8, 2021. www.reuters.com /article/business/healthcare-pharmaceuticals/haunted-by-forced-sterilizations-peruvian-women-pin-hopes-on-court-hearing-idUSL8N2JH4WB/.

Monroe, Jacquelyn, and Rudolph Alexander Jr. "C.R.A.C.K.: A Progeny of Eugenics and a Forlorn Representation for African Americans." *Journal of African American Studies* 9, no. 1 (2005): 19–31. www.jstor.org/stable/41819075.

Morello, Carol. "State Department Strikes Reproductive Rights, 'Occupied Territories' from Human Rights Report." *Washington Post*, April 20, 2018. www.washingtonpost.com/world/national-security/state-department-strikes-reproductive-rights-occupied-territories-from-annual-report/2018/04/20 /46ef0874-44a6-11e8-ad8f-27a8c409298b_story.html.

Morgan, John H. "An Essay on the Causes of the Production of Abortion among Our Negro Population." *Nashville Journal of Medicine and Surgery* 19, no. 17 (August 1860).

Morgan, Lynn. "Reproductive Rights or Reproductive Justice? Lessons from Argentina." *Health and Human Rights Journal* 17, no. 1 (2015). www.hhrjournal .org/2015/04/16/reproductive-rights-or-reproductive-justice-lessons-from-argentina/.

Morgan, Sandra. *Into Our Own Hands: The Women's Health Movement in the United States, 1969–1990.* Rutgers University Press, 2002.

Mosley, Elizabeth A., Lisa Martin, Meghan Seewald, Jane Hassinger, Kelly Blanchard, Sarah E. Baum, Diana Santana, Lina Echeverri, Jenna Garrett, Jesse Njunguru, and Lisa H. Harris. "Addressing Abortion Provider Stigma: A Pilot Implementation of the Providers Share Workshop in Sub-Saharan Africa and Latin America." *International Perspectives on Sexual and Reproductive Health* 46 (2020): 35–50. https://doi.org/10.1363/46e8720.

MSI [previously Marie Stopes International] "Unsafe Abortion: Conse-quences, Facts & Statistics." October 2022. www.msichoices.org/latest /unsafe-abortion-consequences-facts-statistics/.

Muratori, Caterina. "Does Physician Conscience-Based Refusal to Perform Abortions Increase Self-Induced Abortion? Evidence from Italian Prov-inces." Center for Health Economics and Policy Studies, Working Papers Series, San Diego State University (April 3, 2023): 8. https://cheps.sdsu .edu/_resources/docs/working-papers/cheps-working-paper-2023402.pdf.

Murphy, Michael. "The Troubling Past of Forced Sterilization of Black Women and Girls in Mississippi and the South." *Mississippi Free Press,* June 4, 2021. www.mississippifreepress.org/the-troubling-past-of-forced-sterilization-of-black-women-and-girls-in-mississippi-and-the-south/.

Murray, L. "Missing the Point: A Conversation with Sonia Corrêa about the Emergence and Complexities of Anti-Gender Politics at the Intersections of Human Rights and Health." *Global Public Health* 17, no. 11 (2022): 3243–53. https://doi.org/10.1080/17441692.2022.2135751.

Murray, Melissa. "Abortion, Sterilization, and the Universe of Reproductive Rights." *William and Mary Law Review* 63 (2021–22): 1599. https://scholarship.law.wm.edu/wmlr/vol63/iss5/4.

Murthy, Padmini, and Clyde Smith, eds. *Women's Global Health and Human Rights.* Jones & Bartlett International, 2010.

Nadasen, Premilla. "Expanding the Boundaries of the Women's Movement: Black Feminism and the Struggle for Welfare Rights." *Feminist Studies* 28, no. 2 (Summer 2002).

Nair, Sumati, Sarah Sexton, and Preeti Kirbat. "A Decade after Cairo: Women's Health in a Free Market Economy." *Indian Journal of Gender Studies* 13, no. 2 (2006): 171–93. https://doi.org/10.1177/097152150601300203.

Nakchi, Mie. *Replacing the Dead: The Politics of Abortion in the Postwar Soviet Union.* Oxford University Press, 2021.

National Association of Criminal Defense Lawyers (NACDL). "Abortion in America: How Legislative Overreach Is Turning Reproductive Rights into Criminal Wrongs." August 2021. www.nacdl.org/Document/AbortioninAmericaLegOverreachCriminalizReproRights.

National Perinatal Association. "Perinatal Substance Abuse: A Position Statement." 2017. www.nationalperinatal.org/substance-use.

National Women's Law Center (NWLC), with help from the Autistic Women and Non Binary Network. "Forced Sterilization of Disabled People in the United States." 2022. https://nwlc.org/wp-content/uploads/2022/01/%C6%92.NWLC_SterilizationReport_2021.pdf.

Ndugga, Nambi, Drishti Pallai, and Samantha Artiga. "Disparities in Health and Health Care: 5 Key Questions and Answers." Kaiser Family Foundation, August 14, 2024. www.kff.org/racial-equity-and-health-policy/issue-brief/disparities-in-health-and-health-care-5-key-question-and-answers/.

Nelson, Jennifer. "Abortions under Community Control: Feminism, Nationalism, and the Politics of Reproduction among New York City's Young

Lords [Part 1 of 5]." *Journal of Women's History* 13, no. 1 (Spring 2001). http://palante.org/Women&Health.htm.

———. *More Than Medicine.* New York University Press, 2015.

———. *Women of Color and the Reproductive Rights Movement.* New York University Press, 2003.

Newman, Katelyn. "Harm Prevention of Population Control: Amid Efforts to Curb the U.S. Opioid Crisis, a North Carolina Nonprofit Is Offering Money to Drug Users Who Go on Long-Term Birth Control." *US News and World Report*, April 11, 2019. www.usnews.com/news/healthiest-communities/articles/2019–04–11/drug-addicts-offered-money-to-start-long-term-birth-control.

Nguyen, Alex. "'I Want to Fight': LGBTQ Texans Ready for Legislative Session as GOP Lawmakers Target Them in Dozens of Bills." *Texas Tribune*, January 9, 2023. www.texastribune.org/2023/01/09/transgender-laws-gender-care-texas-legislature/.

No Más Bebés. PBS documentary, 2015. www.nomasbebesmovie.com/.

Nourse, Victoria F. *In Reckless Hands: Skinner v. Oklahoma and the Near Triumph of American Eugenics.* W. W. Norton, 2008.

O'Brien, Jon. "Why We Are and Must Remain 'Pro-Choice.'" *Rewire News*, April 25, 2013. https://rewirenewsgroup.com/2013/04/25/why-we-are-and-must-remain-for-choice/.

Okie, Susan. "The Epidemic That Wasn't." *New York Times*, January 26, 2009. www.nytimes.com/2009/01/27/health/27coca.html.

Okihiro, Gary. *American History Unbound: Asians and Pacific Islanders.* University of California Press, 2015.

Olivares, José, and John Washington. "The Worst Day of My Life." *The Intercept*, July 13, 2022. https://theintercept.com/2022/07/13/ice-stewart-detention-sexual-misconduct/.

Open Society Foundations. "Against Her Will: Forced and Coerced Sterilization of Women Worldwide." 2011. www.opensocietyfoundations.org/publications/against-her-will-forced-and-coerced-sterilization-women-worldwide.

The Opportunity Agenda. "Reproductive Justice: A Communications Overview." 2008. https://wearefre.org/docman/rj-toolkit-documents-1/10-reproductive-justice-a-communications-overview/file.

Ordover, Nancy. *American Eugenics: Race, Queer Anatomy, and the Science of Nationalism.* University of Minnesota Press, 2003.

Owens, Deirdre Cooper. *Medical Bondage: Race, Gender, and the Origins of American Gynecology.* University of Georgia Press, 2017.

Owens, Deirdre Cooper, and Sharla M. Fett. "Black Maternal and Infant Health: Historical Legacies of Slavery." *American Journal of Public Health* 109, no. 10 (October 2019). https://doi.org/10.2105%2FAJPH.2019.305243.

Paltrow, Lynn M. "Why Caring Communities Must Oppose C.R.A.C.K./ Project Prevention: How C.R.A.C.K. Promotes Dangerous Propaganda and Undermines the Health and Well Being of Children and Families." *Journal of Law and Society* 5, no. 11 (2003): 83. www.fwhc.org/pdfs/caring_communities_oppose_crack.pdf.

Paltrow, Lynn M., and Jeanne Flavin. "Arrests of and Forced Interventions on Pregnant Women in the United States (1973–2005): The Implications for Women's Legal Status and Public Health." *Journal of Health Politics, Policy and Law* 38, no. 2 (2013): 299–343. https://doi.org/10.1215/03616878-1966324.

Paltrow, Lynn, and Kathryn Jack. "Pregnant Women, Junk Science, and Zealous Defense." National Association of Criminal Defense Lawyers, Inc., May 2010.

Panetta, Grace, and Orion Rummler. "Lawmakers in Blue States Are Linking Protections for Abortion and Gender-Affirming Care." *The 19th*, June 9, 2023. https://19thnews.org/2023/06/abortion-trans-health-care-shield-laws/.

Paoletti, Sarah, and Azadeh Shahshahan. "Where Is the Accountability? Alleged Abuses Persist in ICE Detention." *The Hill*, November 18, 2022. https://thehill.com/opinion/immigration/3739781-where-is-the-accountability-alleged-abuses-persist-in-ice-detention/.

Parker, Pat. "Revolution: It's Not Neat, Pretty, or Quick." In *This Bridge Called My Back: Writings by Black Radical Women*, 4th ed., edited by Cherríe Moraga and Gloria Anzaldúa. SUNY Press, 2015.

Patel, Priti. "Forced Sterilization of Women as Discrimination." *Public Health Review* 38, no. 15 (2017). https://doi.org/10.1186/s40985-017-0060-9.

Paul, Julius. "The Return of Punitive Sterilization Proposals: Current Attacks on Illegitimacy and the AFDC Program." *Law & Society Review* 3, no. 1 (August 1968): 77–106.

Peele, Cullen. "Roundup of Anti-LGBTQ+ Legislation Advancing across the Country." Human Rights Campaign press release, May 23, 2023. www.hrc.org/press-releases/roundup-of-anti-lgbtq-legislation-advancing-in-states-across-the-country.

"Peru Forced Sterilizations Case Reaches Key Stage." BBC, March 1, 2021. www.bbc.com/news/world-latin-america-56201575.

Petchesky, Rosalind Pollack. *Abortion and Women's Choice: The State, Sexuality, and Reproductive Freedom.* Northeastern University Press, 1984; Verso, 2024.

———. "From Population Control to Reproductive Rights: Feminist Fault Line." *Reproductive Health Matters* 3, no. 6 (1995): 152–61. https://doi .org/10.1016/0968-8080(95)90172-8.

Pew Research Center. "America's Abortion Quandary." May 6, 2022. www .pewresearch.org/religion/2022/05/06/americas-abortion-quandary/.

Pilane, Pontsho. "Trump's Gag Rule Causes Global Damage." *Health-E News,* January 28, 2019. https://health-e.org.za/2019/01/28/trumps-gag-rule-causes-global-damage/.

Pitcavage, Mark. *Surveying the Landscape of the American Far Right.* Program on Extremism, George Washington University, August 2019. https:// extremism.gwu.edu/sites/g/files/zaxdzs5746/files/Surveying%20The%20 Landscape%20of%20the%20American%20Far%20Right_0.pdf.

Pizzarossa, Lucía Berro, and Rishita Nandagiri. "Self-Managed Abortion: A Constellation of Actors, a Cacophony of Laws?" *Sexual and Reproductive Health Matters* 29, no. 1 (2021): 23–30. https://doi.org/10.1080/26410397.2021.1899764.

Population Reference Bureau. "Abortion Facts and Figures, 2021." www.prb .org/wp-content/uploads/2021/03/2021-safe-engage-abortion-facts-and-figures-media-guide.pdf.

Positive Women's Network. "Trans-Centered Reproductive Justice: Family Formation and Sustainable Living." October 23, 2019. www.pwn-usa.org /issues/policy-agenda/trans-rights-safety-justice/trans-centered-rj/.

Powell, Robyn. "Disability Reproductive Justice." *University of Pennsylvania Law Review* 170, no. 7/4 (2022).

———. "Including Disabled People in the Battle to Protect Abortion Rights: A Call-to-Action." *UCLA Law Review* 70 (2023): 774. https://doi.org/10.2139 /ssrn.4090764.

Preciado, Karina Cisneros. "Opening Statement, U.S. Senate Permanent Committee on Investigations, Committee on Homeland Security and Governmental Affairs." November 15, 2022.

Pressley, Ayanna, and Rebecca Cokley. "There Is No Justice That Neglects Disability." *Stanford Social Innovation Review* 20, no. 1 (Winter 2022). www .nytimes.com/interactive/2024/us/abortion-laws-roe-v-wade.html.

Ramón Michel, Agustina, Stephanie Kung, Alyse López-Salm, and Sonia Ariza Navarrete. "Regulating Conscientious Objection to Legal Abortion in Argentina: Taking into Consideration Its Uses and Consequences." *Health and Human Rights Journal* 22, no. 2 (December 2020): 271–83.

Rankin, Kenrya. "Black Lives Matter Partners with Reproductive Justice Groups to Fight for Black Women." *Colorlines*, February 9, 2016. www .colorlines.com/articles/black-lives-matter-partners-reproductive-justice-groups-fight-black-women.

Reagan, Leslie J. *Dangerous Pregnancies: Mothers, Disabilities, and Abortion in Modern America*. University of California Press, 2012.

———. *When Abortion Was a Crime: Women, Medicine, and Law in the United States, 1867–1973*. University of California Press, 1997, 2022.

"Re: Sexual Assault of Detained Immigrants by a Nurse at Steward Detention Center, a U.S. Department of Homeland Security Immigration Detention Facility Operated by CoreCivic." July 12, 2022. www.splcenter.org/sites /default/files/stewart-detention-center-nurse-complaint-07-12-2022.pdf.

Rhein, Walter. "All Bigotry Is Ignorance, But Not All Ignorance Is Bigotry." *Medium*, November 2, 2023. https://medium.com/our-human-family/all-bigotry-is-ignorance-but-not-all-ignorance-is-bigotry-efoa181f112d.

Roberts, Dorothy. *Killing the Black Body: Race, Reproduction, and the Meaning of Liberty*. Vintage Books, 1997, 2017.

———. "The State We Are In: Building an Intersectional Movement for Reproductive Justice." Egbal Ahmed Lecture, Hampshire College, October 13, 2022. www.hampshire.edu/news/23rd-annual-eqbal-ahmad-lecture-tackles-reproductive-justice-issues-black-feminist-scholar.

Roberts, Hannah. "Italy Slowly Erodes Abortion Access, Riding US Wave." *Politico*, May 13, 2022. www.politico.eu/article/italy-abortion-access-erodes-riding-united-states-wave/.

Romero, Dennis. "Drag Queen Story Hour Disrupted by Men Shouting Slurs, Authorities Say." *NBC News*, June 12, 2022. www.nbcnews.com/news /us-news/drag-queen-story-hour-disrupted-men-shouting-slurs-authorities-say-rcna33184.

Romney, Patricia. *We Were There: The Third World Women's Alliance and the Second Wave*. The Feminist Press, 2021.

Ross, Loretta. "Race, Class, and Rights in Mississippi: How Reproductive Justice Can Save the Pill and Save the Vote." *Rewire News*, October 29, 2011. https://rewirenewsgroup.com/2011/10/29/race-class-and-rights-in-mississippi-how-a-reproductive-justice-campaign-can-save-the-pill-and-save-the-vote/.

Ross, Loretta J., and Heidi Dorow. "Women's Watch Report." Center for Democratic Renewal, 1992.

Ross, Loretta, Lynn Roberts, Erika Derkas, Whitney Peoples, and Pamela Bridgewater Toure, eds. *Radical Reproductive Justice*. Feminist Press, 2017.

Ross, Loretta, and Rickie Solinger. *Reproductive Justice: An Introduction.* University of California Press, 2017.

Roth, Cassia. "Abortion Access in the Americas: A Hemispheric and Historical Approach." *Frontiers in Public Health* 11 (2023). https://doi.org/10.3389/fpubh.2023.1284737.

Roth, Rachel, and Sarah L. Ainsworth. "If They Hand You a Paper, You Sign It." *Hastings Women's Law Journal* 26, no. 1 (Winter 2015). www.prisonpolicy.org/scans/Roth_If_They_Hand_You_1_15_2015.pdf.

Rothman, Barbara Katz. *The Tentative Pregnancy: How Amniocentesis Changes the Experience of Motherhood.* W. W. Norton, 1986.

Rubio, Marco. "Future Generations Will Call Us Barbarians for Murdering Millions of Babies." *CNSNews*, August 7, 2015. www.cnsnews.com/news/article/cnsnewscom-staff/marco-rubio-future-generations-will-call-us-barbarians-murdering.

Sager, Rebekah. "How Anti-Abortion Laws Disproportionately Impact Indigenous People." *American Journal News*, April 10, 2023. https://americanjournalnews.com/abortion-indigenous-native-americans-alaska-hyde-amendment-colonization/.

Salaam-Blyther, Tiaji. "U.S. Global Health Assistance." *Congressional Research Service*, July 9, 2018. https://digital.library.unt.edu/ark:/67531/metadc227874/.

Sanders, Ronald. *Lost Tribes and Promised Lands.* Echo Point Books, 2015.

Sarai, Tamar. "There's No Reproductive Justice without an End to Police Violence." *Prism*, May 21, 2021. https://prismreports.org/2021/05/21/ending-police-violence-is-integral-to-achieving-reproductive-justice/.

Sawyer, Wendy. "The Gender Divide: Tracking Women's State Prison Growth." Prison Policy Initiative, January 9, 2018. www.prisonpolicy.org/reports/women_overtime.html.

Schoenbaum, Hannah. "Report Says at Least 32 Transgender People Were Killed in the U.S. in 2022." *PBS News Hour*, November 16, 2022. www.pbs.org/newshour/nation/report-says-at-least-32-transgender-people-were-killed-in-the-u-s-in-2022.

Scully, Judith A. M. "Cracking Open CRACK: Unethical Sterilization Movement Gains Momentum." *DifferenTakes* 2 (Spring 2000). https://papers.ssrn.com/sol3/papers.cfm?abstract_id=1646144.

Seager, John. "Conference Call with Population Connection Members to Discuss Population Growth and Pandemics." *Population Connection*, May 4, 2020. https://populationconnection.org/blog/john-seager-presentation-covid-19/.

Sedgh, Gilda, et al. "Abortion Incidence between 1990 and 2014: Global, Regional, and Subregional Levels and Trends." *The Lancet* 388, no. 10041 (2016). https://doi.org/10.1016/S0140-6736(16)30380-4.

Sheldon, Sally. "Empowerment and Privacy? Home Use of Abortion Pills in the Republic of Ireland." *Signs*, Summer 2018, 844. www.journals.uchicago.edu/doi/pdfplus/10.1086/696625.

Sherman, Renee Bracey. "Black and Brown Critique Is a Gift. Will White Abortion Advocates Listen?" *Rewire News*, July 2, 2020. https://rewirenewsgroup.com/2020/07/02/black-and-brown-critique-is-a-gift-will-white-abortion-advocates-listen/.

Shochet, Tara, Lucía Berio Pizzarossa, Sara Larrea, et al. "Self-Managed Abortion via the Internet: Analysis of One Year of Service Delivery Data from Women Help Women." *Gates Open Research* 7 (2023). https://doi.org/10.12688%2Fgatesopenres.14369.1.

Shoichet, Catherine E. "In a Horrifying History of Forced Sterilizations, Some Fear the US Is Beginning a New Chapter." CNN, September 16, 2020. www.cnn.com/2020/09/16/us/ice-hysterectomy-forced-sterilization-history/index.html.

"The Shut Down Irwin Campaign." Anti-Eugenics Project: Legacies/Reckonings, Futures. https://antieugenicsproject.org/video-archive/the-shut-down-irwin-campaign/.

"SIA in Our Communities: A Conversation." SIA Legal Team, November 2017. www.youtube.com/watch?v=CdYos-ZGYHU.

Silliman, Jael, et al. *Undivided Rights: Women of Color Organize for Reproductive Justice*, 2nd ed. Haymarket Press, 2016.

Silva, Daniella. "Migrant Women File Class-Action Lawsuit for Alleged Abuse at ICE Detention Center." *NBC News*, December 22, 2020.

Silver, Hannah, and Cloee Cooper. "101 Abortion Abolitionists." Political Research Associates, October 2023.

Simpson, Monica. "Reproductive Justice and 'Choice': An Open Letter to Planned Parenthood." *Rewire News*, August 5, 2014. https://rewirenewsgroup.com/2014/08/05/reproductive-justice-choice-open-letter-planned-parenthood/.

———. "User Clip: Monica Simpson's SisterSong Speech." www.c-span.org/video/?c5082534/user-clip-monica-simpsons-sistersong-speech.

SisterSong. "Birth Justice Care Fund." www.sistersong.net/bjcf-english.

———. "Visioning New Futures for Reproductive Justice Declaration 2023." www.sistersong.net/visioningnewfuturesforrj.

Skusker, Patty, Kinga Jelinska, and Susan Yanow. "Self-Managed Abortion Highlights Need to Decriminalize Abortion Worldwide." *Rewire News*, November 12, 2018. https://rewirenewsgroup.com/2018/11/12/self-managed-abortion-decriminalize/.

Slattery, Elisa. "The Hidden Consequences of Forcing Women to Travel for Abortions." *Open Society Foundations*, July 7, 2016. www.opensociety foundations.org/voices/hidden-consequences-forcing-women-travel-abortions.

Smith, Andrea. *Conquest*. South End Press, 2005; Duke University Press, 2015.

Smithers, Gregory. *Slave Breeding: Sex, Violence, and Memory in African American History*. University Press of Florida, 2012.

Solinger, Rickie. *The Abortionist*. University of California Press, 1994.

———. *Beggars and Choosers: How the Politics of Choice Shapes Adoption, Abortion, and Welfare in the United States*. Hill and Wang, 2002.

———. "'A Complete Disaster': Abortion and the Politics of Hospital Abortion Committees, 1950–1970." *Feminist Studies* 19, no. 2 (Summer 1993): 241–68.

———. *Pregnancy and Power: A Short History of Reproductive Politics in America*. New York University Press, 2005.

———. *Wake Up Little Susie: Single Pregnancy and Race before Roe v. Wade*, Routledge, 1992.

Soma, Rose, ed. and comp. *Women Speak Out about Abortion: By Women, for Women in Their Own Words*. N.p., 1978.

Sorhaindo, Annik Mahalia, and Antonella Francheska Lavelanet. "Why Does Abortion Stigma Matter? A Scoping Review and Hybrid Analysis of Qualitative Evidence Illustrating the Role of Stigma in the Quality of Abortion Care." *Social Science and Medicine* 311 (October 2022). https://doi.org/10.1016/j.socscimed.2022.115271.

Southern Poverty Law Center. "The Intelligence Report." 1998 Summer Issue (September 1988).

Spencer, Alexa. "This Organization Is Bringing Reproductive Justice to Southern Cities." *Word in Black*, June 29, 2023. https://wordinblack.com/2023/06/sistersong-bus-tour-bringing-reproductive-justice-to-southern-cities/.

Staggenborg, Susan. *The Pro-Choice Movement: Organization and Activism in the Abortion Conflict*. Oxford University Press, 1991.

Stannard, David. *American Holocaust: The Conquest of the New World*. Oxford University Press, 1992.

Stavig, Lucía. "Feminist Assemblages: Peruvian Feminisms, Forced Sterilization, and the Paradox of Rights in Fujimori's Peru." MA thesis, School of Graduate Studies, University of Lethbridge, 2017. https://hdl.handle.net/10133/4850.

Stern, Alexandra Minna. *Eugenic Nation: Faults and Frontiers of Better Breeding in Modern America*, 2nd ed. University of California Press, 2015.

———. "Forced Sterilization Policies in the US Targeted Minorities and Those with Disabilities—and Lasted into the 21st Century." *The Conversation*, August 26, 2020. https://theconversation.com/forced-sterilization-policies-in-the-us-targeted-minorities-and-those-with-disabilities-and-lasted-into-the-21st-century-143144.

Stevens, Marion. "From North to South: The Evolution of Reproductive Justice in South Africa." In *Reproductive Justice and the Afterlife of Colonial Reproductive Violence*, ed. Susanne M. Klausen. University of California Press, forthcoming.

———. "South Africa: Need for National Traction on Reproductive Justice in South Africa Following Elections." International Campaign for Women's Right to Safe Abortions, July 17, 2019. www.safeabortionwomensright.org/south-africa-need-for-national-traction-on-reproductive-justice-in-south-africa-following-elections/.

Stevenson, Amanda Jean. "The Pregnancy-Related Mortality Impact of a Total Abortion Ban in the United States: A Research Note on Increased Deaths Due to Remaining Pregnant." *Demography* 58, no. 6 (2021). https://doi.org/10.1215/00703370-9585908.

Stopler, Gila. "Biopolitics and Reproductive Justice: Fertility Policies between Women's Rights and State and Community Interests." *University of Pennsylvania Journal of Law and Social Change* 18, no. 2 (2015). https://scholarship.law.upenn.edu/jlasc/vol18/iss2/3.

Sullivan, Andy. "Explainer: How Abortion Became a Divisive Issue in U.S. Politics." Reuters, June 24, 2022. www.reuters.com/world/us/how-abortion-became-divisive-issue-us-politics-2022-06-24/.

Sunderlin, Kylee, and Laura Huss. "The Mythology of 'Addicted Babies': Challenging Media Distortions, Laws, and Policies That Fracture Communities." *DifferenTakes* 86 (Fall 2015).

Sussman, Anna Louise. "What the U.S. Could Learn from Abortion Without Borders." *New Yorker*, May 17, 2022. www.newyorker.com/news/news-desk/what-the-us-could-learn-from-abortion-without-borders.

Sutton, Barbara, and Nayla Luz Vacarezza, eds. *Abortion and Democracy: Contentious Body Politics in Argentina, Chile, and Uruguay.* Routledge, 2021.

Tan, Moira. "Decarceration and Abolition as a Reproductive Justice Framework." *Reproductive Justice Briefing Book*, vol. 2. Sistersong and Civil Liberties and Public Policy Program, 2020.

Tayler, Letta. "Two Years On, Poland's Abortion Crackdowns and the Rule of Law." *Open Democracy*, October 22, 2022. www.hrw.org/news/2022/10/22/two-years-polands-abortion-crackdowns-and-rule-law.

Taylor, Angela, Tonantzin Juarez, and Brandon Azevedo. "Continuing the Legacy of Granny Midwives." *Weitzman Institute Blog*, February 7, 2023. www.weitzmaninstitute.org/blog-continuing-the-legacy-of-granny-midwives/.

Taylor, Keeanga Yamahtta, ed. *How We Get Free: Black Feminism and the Combahee River Collective.* Haymarket Books, 2017.

Taylor, Keeanga-Yamahtta. "Until Black Women Are Free, None of Us Will Be Free: Barbara Smith and the Black Feminist Visionaries of the Combahee River Collective." *New Yorker*, July 20, 2020. www.newyorker.com/news/our-columnists/until-black-women-are-free-none-of-us-will-be-free.

Taylor, Stephen J. "*The Black Stork:* Eugenics Goes to the Movies." *Hoosier State Chronicles,* Indiana's Digital Historic Newspaper Program, February 4, 2016. https://blog.newspapers.library.in.gov/the-black-stork-eugenics-goes-to-the-movies/.

Taylor, Ula. "The Historical Evolution of Black Feminist Theory and Praxis." *Journal of Black Studies* 29, no. 2 (1998): 234–53. www.jstor.org/stable/2668091.

Theobald, Brianna. *Reproduction on the Reservation: Pregnancy, Childbirth, and Colonialism in the Long Twentieth Century.* University of North Carolina Press, 2019.

Thompson, Beverly Yuen. "Centering Reproductive Justice: Transitioning from Abortion Rights to Social Justice." In *Radical Reproductive Justice*, edited by Loretta J. Ross, Lynn Roberts, Erika Derkas, Whitney Peoples, and Pamela Bridgewater Toure. Feminist Press, 2017.

"Three Carolina Doctors Are Under Inquiry in Sterilization of Welfare Mothers." *New York Times*, July 22, 1973. www.nytimes.com/1973/07/22/archives/3-carolina-doctors-are-under-inquiry-in-sterilization-of-welfare.html.

Tillmon, Johnnie. "Welfare Is a Women's Issue." *Ms.* 1 (Spring 1972). https://msmagazine.com/2021/03/25/welfare-is-a-womens-issue-ms-magazine-spring-1972/.

Tobbell, Dominique. "Black Midwifery's Complex History." *UVA School of Nursing*, February 12, 2021.

Tongue, Zoe. "On Conscientious Objection to Abortion: Questioning Mandatory Referral as a Compromise in the International Human Rights Framework." *Medical Law International* 22, no. 4 (2022). https://doi.org/10.1177/09685332221119503.

Torpy, Sally J. "Native American Women and Coerced Sterilization: On the Trail of Tears in the 1970s." *American Indian Culture and Research Journal* 24, no. 2 (2000): 1–22. https://escholarship.org/uc/item/2254n09g.

Towey, Shawn. "Abortion Funding: A Matter of Justice." National Network of Abortion Funds, 2005. https://books.google.com/books/about/Abortion_Funding.html?id=NgH_tgAACAAJ.

Trowbridge, Scott. "Legal Challenges to ICWA: An Analysis of Current Case Law." ABA, January–February 2017. www.americanbar.org/groups/public_interest/child_law/resources/child_law_practiceonline/child_law_practice/vol-36/january-2017/legal-challenges-to-icwa-an-analysis-of-current-case-law/.

Trueman, Karen A., and Makgoale Magwentshu. "Abortion in a Progressive Legal Environment: The Need for Vigilance in Protecting and Promoting Access to Safe Abortion Services in South Africa." *American Journal of Public Health* 103 (March 2013). https://doi.org/10.2105/AJPH.2012.301194.

Tsai, Brian. "US Pregnancy Rate Drop during the Last Decade." *NCHS*, April 2023. https://blogs.cdc.gov/nchs/2023/04/12/7328/.

Turshen, Meredith. *Women's Health Movements: A Global Force for Change.* Palgrave MacMillan, 2006.

Ubiñas, Helen. "Prevention through Bribery." *Hartford Courant*, November 16, 2006. www.courant.com/2006/11/16/prevention-through-bribery/.

Ungar, Laura, and Amanda Seitz. "Post–Roe v. Wade, More Patients Rely on Early Prenatal Testing as States Toughen Abortion Laws." AP News, February 12, 2024. https://apnews.com/article/abortion-genetic-testing-ultrasound-amniocentesis-01e4c591617773efb91d9583be6244c4.

United Nations, Department of Economic and Social Affairs. "Population and Development: Programme of Action at the International Conference on Population and Development, Cairo, 5–13 September 1994." Paragraph 7.2. www.un.org/development/desa/pd/sites/www.un.org.development.desa.pd/files/files/documents/2020/Jan/un_1995_programme_of_action_adopted_at_the_international_conference_on_population_and_development_cairo_5-13_sept._1994.pdf.

"Universal Declaration of Human Rights." General Assembly Resolution 217A, United Nations General Assembly, December 10, 1948. www.ohchr .org/en/resources/educators/human-rights-education-training/universal-declaration-human-rights-1948.

University of Chicago Law School—Global Human Rights Clinic, National Asian Pacific American Women's Forum, and Advancing New Standards in Reproductive Health. "Replacing Myths with Facts: Sex-Selective Abortion Laws in the United States." *Global Human Rights Clinic*, June 2014. https://chicagounbound.uchicago.edu/cgi/viewcontent.cgi?article= 1004&context=ihrc.

"Unsafe Abortion: A Forgotten Emergency." Médecins sans Frontières / Doctors without Borders, March 7, 2019. www.msf.org/unsafe-abortion-forgotten-emergency-womens-health.

Vacarezza, Nayla Luz. "The Green Scarf for Abortion Rights: Affective Contagion and Artistic Reinventions of Movement Symbols." In *Affect, Gender and Sexuality in Latin America*, edited by Cecilia Macón, Mariela Solana, and Nayla Luz Vacarezza. Palgrave Macmillan, 2021.

Valerio, Anita. "The Weeping Was All Our Pain—A Collective Wound—It Is Larger Than Each Individual … Our Past as Native People before Being Colonized and Culturally Liquidated." In *This Bridge Called My Back: Writings by Radical Women of Color*, edited by Cherríe Moraga and Gloria E. Anzaldúa. Persephone Press, 1981.

Valk, Anne M. *Radical Sisters: Second-Wave Feminism and Black Liberation in Washington, DC.* University of Illinois Press, 2008.

van Leeuwen, Fleur. *Women's Rights Are Human Rights: The Practice of the United Nations Human Rights Committee and the Committee on Economic, Social and Cultural Rights.* School of Human Rights Research Series 8, vol. 36 (2009).

Vega, Cecilia. "Sterilization Offer to Addicts Reopens Ethics Issue." *New York Times*, January 6, 2003. www.nytimes.com/2003/01/06/nyregion/sterilization-offer-to-addicts-reopens-ethics-issue.html.

Veitch, Edward, and R.R.S. Tracey. "Abortion in the Common Law World." *American Journal of Comparative Law* 22, no. 4 (1974). https://doi.org/10.2307 /839442.

Venkataramanan, Meena. "She Survived a Forced Sterilization. She Fears More Could Occur Post-Roe." *Washington Post*, July 24, 2022.

———. "Their Medications Cause Pregnancy Issues. Post-Roe, That Could Be a Problem." *Washington Post*, July 25, 2022. www.washingtonpost.com /health/2022/07/25/disabled-people-abortion-restrictions/.

Villarosa, Linda. *Under the Skin: The Hidden Toll of Racism on American Lives and the Health of Our Nation.* Doubleday, 2022.

Virginia Board of Charities and Corrections. "Mental Defectives in Virginia: A Special Report of the State Board of Charities and Corrections to the General Assembly of Nineteen Sixteen on Weak-Mindedness in the State of Virginia, Together with a Plan for the Training, Segregation and Prevention of the Procreation of the Feeble-Minded." 1915. www.archive.org /details/mentaldefectives00virg.

Wako, Etobssie, and Anne Hendrixson. "Reproductive Justice beyond Population Control: An Invitation to Funders." *Nonprofit Quarterly*, October 25, 2022.https://nonprofitquarterly.org/reproductive-justice-beyond-population-control-an-invitation-to-funders/.

Walker, Jazmine. "The 50th Anniversary of Mississippi's Freedom Summer: Remembering What Fannie Lou Hamer Taught Us." *Rewire News*, June 2, 2014.

Walsh, Alistair. "Eco-Fascism: The Greenwashing of the Far Right." Deutsche Welle, May 19, 2022. www.dw.com/en/what-is-eco-fascism-the-greenwashing-of-the-far-right-terrorism-climate-change-buffalo-shooter /a-61867605.

Wasser, Miriam. "ACLU Challenges 'Racist and Sexist' Arizona Abortion Law." *Phoenix New Times*, December 10, 2015. www.phoenixnewtimes.com /news/aclu-challenges-racist-and-sexist-arizona-abortion-law-7885179.

Weinbaum, Alys Eve. *Wayward Reproduction: Genealogies of Race and Nation in Transatlantic Modern Thought.* Duke University Press, 2004.

White, Erica. "Racial Disparities in Women's Health." *Network for Public Health Law*, August 1, 2022. www.networkforphl.org/news-insights/racial-disparities-in-womens-health/.

Whitman, James Q. *Hitler's American Model: The United States and the Making of Nazi Race Law.* Princeton University Press, 2017.

Wilson, R. "Eugenics: Positive vs Negative." *Eugenics Archive*, December 31, 2019.

Wolfe, Brendon. "*Buck v. Bell.*" *Virginia Humanities, Encyclopedia Virginia.* https:// encyclopediavirginia.org/entries/buck-v-bell-1927/.

Women's Link Worldwide. "Spain's Constitutional Court Acknowledges That the Fundamental Rights of Antonia, Who Faced Multiple Barriers to Access to Abortion, Were Violated." July 3, 2023. https://womenslinkworldwide .org/en/spains-constitutional-court-acknowledges-that-the-fundamental-rights-of-antonia-who-faced-multiple-barriers-to-access-to-abortion-were-violated/.

World Health Organization. "Abortion: Key Facts." May 17, 2024. www.who .int/news-room/fact-sheets/detail/abortion.

———. "Eliminating Forced, Coercive and Otherwise Involuntary Sterilization: An Interagency Statement." 2014. www.who.int/publications/i/item /9789241507325.

———. "Preventing Unsafe Abortion." September 2020 (updated August 19, 2024). https://iris.who.int/bitstream/handle/10665/329887/WHO-RHR-19.21-eng.pdf.

Wright, George. "France Makes Abortion a Constitutional Right." *BBC News*, March 4, 2024. www.bbc.com/news/world-europe-68471568.

Wright, Jennifer. *Madame Restell: The Life, Death, and Resurrection of Old New York's Most Fabulous, Fearless, and Infamous Abortionist*. Hachette Books, 2023.

Wrigley, Will. "Dick Black, Virginia GOP Lawmaker, Compares Abortion to Holocaust." *Huffington Post*, January 23, 2013. www.huffingtonpost.com /2013/01/23/dick-black-virginia_n_2535167.html.

Yanow, Susan, Lucía Berro Pizzarossa, and Kinga Jelinska. "Self-Managed Abortion: Exploring Synergies between Institutional Medical Systems and Autonomous Health Movements." *Contraception* 104, no. 3 (2021): 219–21. https://doi.org/10.1016/j.contraception.2021.06.006.

Yeoman, Barry. "Surgical Strike." *Mother Jones*, November 1, 2001. www .motherjones.com/politics/2001/11/surgical-strike/.

Yoon, Lina. "South Korea's Constitutional Right to Abortion: Activists Fought Hard for Change." Human Rights Watch, June 9, 2022. www.hrw.org/news /2022/06/09/south-koreas-constitutional-right-abortion.

Ziegler, Mary. "The Disability Politics of Abortion." *Utah Law Review* 3 (2017). https://dc.law.utah.edu/ulr/vol2017/iss3/4/.

Zurbriggen, Ruth, Brianna Keefe-Oates, and Caitlin Gerdt. "Accompaniment of Second-Trimester Abortions: The Model of the Feminist Socorristas Network of Argentina." *Contraception* 97, no. 2 (2018): 108–15. www.researchgate .net/publication/318993888_Accompaniment_of_second-trimester_abortions _The_model_of_the_feminist_Socorrista_network_of_Argentina.

INDEX

As indicated at the end of Chapter 1 (pages 33–34), we recognize that language describing gender identities (e.g. female, male, women, men, cis, trans, etc.) and ethnicity identities (e.g. Black, African American, Latinx, Hispanic, Native, Indigenous, American Indian, etc.) remains unsettled and is used in different ways in the various sources and contributions contained within this volume. To direct readers to related topics, we have made extensive use of *See also* references in this index. The abbreviation "RJ" is frequently used for "reproductive justice." Page numbers followed by "n" or "nn" indicate endnote numbers.

crediting of RJ movement, 146–47; "pro-choice" chosen as expression, 29; as pro-choice vs. pro-life divide, 11, 28–29, 30; the right to have children as ignored in, 31, 65; sterilization waiting period requirement opposed by mainstream choice activists, 81–82. *See also* mainstream choice movement for abortion advocacy

CHOICES (clinic in Memphis, TN), 123

Choimorrow, Sung Yeon, 191–94

Christian Broadcasting Network, 86

Christian evangelicals, joining Republican Party (1980), 84–86, 88–89

Christian Lawyers' Association, 221

Christian nationalism: "made natural" by white supremacy, 19, 88–89; Tennessee supermajority in legislature, 186–87

Christian right/religious right, 88–89, 187

citizenship (U.S.): birthright, and immigration policy, 48–49; Black people granted (1868), 44; the Fourteenth Amendment and birthright citizenship, 42, 44, 48; of groups denied whiteness, 42, 49; Native Americans granted (1924), 42; naturalized, Chinese immigrants denied, 258n20; whiteness monitored by, 42, 256–57n5

Civil Liberties and Public Policy Program (CLPP, now Collective Power for Reproductive Justice), 181

Civil Rights Act (1964), 265–66n130

civil rights movement: disability rights activism in, 254n47; mainstream choice advocates coming from, 79; population controllers viewing "overpopulation" as cause of, 68; sterilization abuse activism in,

106–7; white allies of RJ coming from, 78

class: and the AMA's attacks on midwives, 57–58; Hyde Amendment and disparate impacts of, 5–6, 250n5; and "welfare-reform" policies tailored to curtail reproduction, 101, 187. *See also* abortion access barriers; eugenics; low-income and poor women; mainstream choice movement for abortion advocacy—ignoring disparate impacts of race and class on women's lives; population control; poverty; sterilization abuse; white women—middle- and upper-class cisgender women

Clements, KC, 121–22

Clinton, Bill, health care reform plan, 10

Coalition for Abortion Access and Reproductive Equity (CAARE), 190, 250n5

Coalition to Fight Infant Mortality, 72

Cobalt Advocates (formerly NARAL Pro-Choice Colorado), 195

coerced/forced abortion: vs. chosen, 96; criminal courts punitively imposing, 83; global women's health movement and rejection of, 104; as population control policy, 95, 103, 104; post-*Dobbs* period and likelihood of, 101

coerced sterilization. *See* sterilization abuse

COFO (1961), 272n45

Cole, Sheryl, 7

collective action: confronting Project 2025 requires, 246; "doing collectively what we cannot do individually" as mantra of SisterSong, 146; the March for Women's Lives as demonstration of, 146; RJ leaders address mainstream fears that RJ would

Depo-Provera shots, 135, 273n54
DeSantis, Ron, 120, 122
Desert Star Institute for Family Planning, 161–64
Dhanraj, Deepa, *Something Like a War* (1991 film), 297n95
Diaz-Tello, Farah, 183–86, 288n76
Dillingham Commission Report, 258n24
Dillon, Kelli, 131–32, 279n144
disabilities, people with: abortion bans foreclosing options for, 117; as acutely aware *Roe* did not make abortion accessible or available to everyone, 5; the Ashley Treatment, 275n81; Black girls with, as disproportionately criminalized in US schools, 116; disability-selective abortion bans, as access barrier for, 115; with intellectual and developmental disabilities, sterilization of, 116; Nazi eugenics and annihilation of, 23; percentage of people murdered by police with (50%), 115; sterilization abuse of, 97, 112, 115–17, 275nn81–82
disability justice movement: overview of move to justice and human rights perspective, 112; alliances between RJ movement and, as challenging due to eugenicist arguments used in legalization and defense of abortion, 112–15, 274n72; alliances between RJ movement and, conditions for, 115, 117–18; bodily autonomy as central concern of, as shared with RJ movement, 116–18, 153; in the civil rights movement, 254n47; intersectional framework for understanding accessibility, 117; "nothing about us without us" as motto of, 112; post-*Dobbs* abortion bans as foreclosing options for disabled women, 117; RJ agenda, call for, 118; sterilization abuse activism

as commitment of, 112, 115–18, 275nn81–82; terminology used in, 274n68
Disability Rights Education and Defense Fund, 134
discrimination: employment, and coining of intersectionality as term, 21, 253n38; sterilization requirements for trans and intersex people as perpetuating, 215. *See also* health care discrimination; racism; racist stereotypes and myths
Dixon, Ericka Ayodele, 117–18
DIY. *See* menstrual extraction; self-managed abortion with pills
Dlamini, Bathabile, 225–26
Dobbs v. Jackson Women's Health Organization (2022): denial of bodily autonomy in, as similar to coerced sterilization, 95–96; Elena Kagan's dissenting opinion citing disparate impacts on women living in poverty, 7; overturning *Roe* and its concept of the right to privacy, 4; states' individual right to make abortion laws reestablished by, 4. *See also* post-*Dobbs* period
Dockray, Parker, 197–99
Doctors for Life, 221
doctors. *See* AMA (American Medical Association); providers of abortion; sterilization abuse
domestic violence: Catholic Church funding prevention of, 285n38; and judicial bypass of parental notification law, 15. *See also* sexual abuse and violence
Dominican Republic, 204, 209
Down syndrome, 113, 114
drag and drag events: performers, 122, 247; state laws banning, 119, 120; Story Hour events, and violent disruption of, 122

experiences alone, 82; the Hyde Amendment denying funds for abortions of indigent women, no objection to, 82–83; the legal right is inadequate to ensure everyone can access that right, 10, 16, 24–25, 82–83; and misappropriation and co-optation of RJ language, 147–48; the needs of working-class women and women of color as invisible to, 81; sterilization abuse ignored by global feminists, 212–13; sterilization guidelines to protect against abuse not supported by, 71, 79, 81–82
—MISSED OPPORTUNITIES FOR BUILDING ALLIANCES: failure to stand with women of color for voting rights, 152; failure to stand with women of color in fight against sterilization abuse, 82, 128, 265n125
—AND THE RJ FRAMEWORK: belief RJ undermines bodily autonomy, 150, 151; belief RJ would mean the end of focused advocacy, 150–51; "choice" removed from PPFA website, and eventual crediting of RJ movement (2014), 146–47; communication study (2008) as fueling reluctance to embrace RJ, 149–50; disagreement between RJ and choice activists in strategy to defeat "fetal rights" bill on same ballot as voter suppression bill (2011), 151–52; hostility toward RJ, 150; internal conflicts about choice vs. RJ framings, 150–51; SisterSong credited for success of March for Women's Lives, 146
mainstream news media: eugenics articles published in, 99; mainstream choice organizations given biggest megaphone by, 147; personal abortion narrative coverage by, 155–56

Maistrellis, Emily A., 290n6
Malta, 295n65
Malthus, Thomas, 103. *See also* population control (limiting reproduction within targeted communities)
MAMA Network (Mobilizing Activists around Medical Abortion), 179
Maputo Protocol (2003), 208, 291n18
March for Women's Lives (2004, Washington, DC): allocation of funds to allow underresourced communities to attend, 144, 145; attendance as wildly successful, 145–46; choice framing rejected by RJ organizations (original name was March for Choice), 144–45, 147; diversification of leadership and broadened agenda, 144, 145–46, 283n12; inequalities of organizational resources as obstacle, 145, 283n7; mainstream choice organizations putting out call for (1995), 144; mainstream choice organizations reverting to choice paradigm following, 147; NOW statement announcing expanded scope and reach of event, 145, 283n6; Loretta Ross as codirector, 145; SisterSong credited by mainstream choice organizations for crucial role in success of, 146; "Women of Color for Reproductive Justice" contingent, 146
March of Dimes, 129
Marea Verde (Mexico), SMA support, 181
Marie Stopes International, Provider Share Workshops, 237
Marignay, Bisola, 251–52n21
Markovsky, Jennifer, murder of, 266–67n144

higher than national average, 186–87, 289n78. *See also* abortion access barriers; eugenics (pseudoscientific theory of white supremacist biological determinism); low-income and poor women; mainstream choice movement for abortion advocacy—ignoring disparate impacts of race and class on women's lives

Powell, Robyn, 115, 118

Praise the Lord Club, 86

Preciado, Karina Cisneros, 135

pregnancy, "quickening" of, 51

pregnancy, forced: as denial of bodily autonomy, 95–96; in the wake of *Dobbs*, x, 9, 10

Pregnancy Justice (legal services): antiabortion laws establishing separate legal rights for embryos and fetuses result in criminalization of pregnant people, 168–72, 285n39; legal services provided, 168; name change from National Advocates for Pregnant Women, 148. *See also* Paltrow, Lynn

pregnancy loss (miscarriage and stillbirth): arrest and convictions of women for, 168, 170–71, 192–93, 210–11; and community, need for, xii; enslaved women and, 46; of immigrant women in detention centers, 136–37, 158; and reproductive justice, xii. *See also* deaths of pregnant persons due to abortion or denial of

pregnant people, criminalization of. *See* criminalization of pregnant people post-*Roe*

prenatal genetic testing: abortion as assumed outcome of, 101, 113, 114, 274n72; antiabortion forces exploiting controversy of, 113–14, 115; post-*Dobbs* denial of care for severe abnormalities revealed in,

166; prejudices involved in deciding characteristics to be eliminated, 101; too-early testing in post-*Dobbs* period, 118. *See also* fetal anomalies

Presley, Ayanna, 116

Price, Kimala, 253n39

Prince Edward Island (PEI), Canada: Don't Talk About It project, 236; international conference, "Abortion: The Unfinished Revolution" (2014), 231, 298n118; stigma of abortion and, 236, 300n132

Princeton University, critics of eugenics, 100

Prison Policy Initiative, 171

prisons and jails: global population of women incarcerated for pregnancy loss or abortion, 210–11; majority incarcerated are awaiting trial, 171; mass incarceration driven by war on drugs and welfare reform, 129, 130, 171; population incarcerated in the U.S., 171; population of women, as disproportionately women of color, 170, 171, 279–80n145; population of women, total number of, 171; population under post-incarceration supervision, and monitoring with electronic shackles, 171; as prison industrial complex, 131, 171, 279n141; privatization and lack of accountability, 133–34, 171; privatized, President Biden's executive order to phase out (2021), 280n152; RJ abolition movement needed, 172; sterilization abuse of women in the South, as racially disproportionate, 104–5. *See also* California—women's prison system and sterilizations; criminalization of pregnant people post-*Roe*

privacy rights: contraception as, 3; *Dobbs* as cancelling *Roe* and its concept of the right to privacy, 4;

Rakow, Dr. Raymond, 75
Ray for Hope Walk, 157
Reagan, Leslie J., 249n4, 261n70, 262n74, 299n131
Reagan, Ronald: Global Gag Rule (1984, Mexico City Policy), 216; Human Life Amendment as campaign promise of (1980), 85, 266n136
Redmond, Malika, 152
Red State Access (SMA support and pills), 181
Relf, Mary Alice and Minnie Lee (sisters), 109, 273n54
Relf v. Weinberger, 108–9, 273nn54,58
religion: advertising in publications for abortion services (19th century), 52; Christian nationalist legislatives policies cloaked in, 187; of Indigenous peoples, forbidden, 44; patriarchy relying on, despite Constitutional separation of church and state, 21; stigma of abortion perpetuated by, 235. *See also* Catholic Church; interfaith-based organizing; New Right
reprocide (eugenics achieved through reproductive policy). *See* coerced/ forced abortion; eugenics; population control (limiting reproduction within targeted communities); sterilization abuse; sterilization abuse resistance (feminists of color led)
Reproductive Equity Now (formerly NARAL Pro Choice Massachusetts), 124
reproductive health defined and prioritized (1994), 207
Reproductive Justice: An Introduction (Loretta Ross and Rickie Solinger), as resource, 12, 16, 250n1
reproductive justice (RJ): appropriate claims to RJ, 143, 147–48, 282n1; Black feminist founders coining the

term and developing (1994), 3, 10–13, 26, 143, 203, 251–52n21; communications study to inform messaging strategy (2008), 147, 149–50, 283n13, 284n19; definition of, 3, 12; identity is not the basis of, 250n1; and linking of justice movements, 12; name changes by organizations, 148, 154; as open source code used to pursue fresh critical thinking, 12, 148; power and resources as central to (Asian Communities for Reproductive Justice), 11; widespread appeal of, 143–45, 153, 205, 282n5. *See also* alliances between RJ and other social justice movements; Black feminism; bodily autonomy; global RJ solidarity; reproductive rights movement (Black and women-of-color feminist led); RJ-ing abortion (looking at abortion through the RJ lens); SisterSong Women of Color Reproductive Justice Collective; trans-centered reproductive justice
—CORE TENETS OF: (1) the human right not to have a child, 12; (2) the human right to have a child, 12; (3) the human right to parent children in safe and healthy environments, 12; (4) the human right to bodily autonomy and sexual and gender freedom, 12. *See also* abortion; bodily autonomy; childbearing rights as core tenet of reproductive justice; parenting children in safe and healthy environments as human right
—HUMAN RIGHTS AS BASIS OF: airline travel as example of positive rights obligations of government, compared to the exceptional treatment of abortion, 27–28; coalition building aided by, 205; distinguished from legal rights, 26,

Women on Waves (Dutch NGO), 205
Women on Web (WoW), 238
Women's Global Network for
Reproductive Rights (WGNRR):
calling attention to violence against
individual abortion advocates and
providers, 232–33; critique of
neoliberal economic policies,
207–8; founding of (1984), 229;
original members of coalition,
298n115; RJ explicitly named in
2014–18 strategic plans, 298n113;
"Safe Abortion International
Exchange" (planning), 234
women's health movement: overview,
75–76, 90–91; abortion services pre-
and post-*Roe*, 76, 77; Boston Women's
Health Book Collective (*Our Bodies,
Ourselves*), 76, 265n116; developed as
alternative institutions to the
medical establishment, 75–76;
empowerment of women-centered
care, 76; Federation of Feminist
Women's Health Centers, 76, 77;
Jane Collective (Chicago), 77, 83,
265n118; National Women's Health
Network, 77; policy successes, 76;
women of color forming organizations for, 76–77, 264n115. *See also*
global women's health movement;
National Black Women's Health
Project; self-managed abortion with
pills (SMA)
women's liberation movement. *See*
feminism
Women's Link Worldwide, 294n59
Women with Disabilities Empathy
(South Korea), 227
Woodhill, Jim, 125
Wooten, Dawn, 135
work, time off as abortion access issue,
155, 163–64, 176
World Bank: stringent population
control policies demanded by, 212;

structural adjustment policies, 26,
208, 255–56n63
World Health Organization (WHO):
CO as reinforcing barriers to care,
221; research showing where
abortion is strictly controlled, the
number of abortions is larger, 211;
unsafe abortion, definition of, 209
World War II: forced sterilization of
Japanese women interned during,
136; Nazi eugenics and forcible
sterilization and annihilation of
"inferiors," 23, 99–100, 101
Wydrzynska, Justyna, 241

Yanow, Susan, 180–83, 239
Yellow Horse Brave Heart, Maria,
257n7
Yeoman, Barry, 125–26
Yocca, Anna, 170
Youngblood, Kim, 251–52n21
Young Lords Party (YLP), 74–75,
264n112
Young, Neil, 85
young people: as acutely aware *Roe* did
not make abortion accessible or
available to everyone, 5; All* Above
All activating electorate of, 190;
conservative evangelical policies
structured to undermine agency
and autonomy of, 187; percentage
involving at least one parent or
guardian in their abortion decision
(90%), 253n35. *See also* parental
notification laws
youth movement, as social justice
movement, 264n103

Zaldívar, Arturo, 241
Zambia, 217
Zero Population Growth (later
Population Connection), 68, 81,
214
Zuydam, Jacques van, 231